PERSONS & POLEMICS

Persons
&
Polemics

E P THOMPSON

MERLIN PRESS
LONDON

First published 1994 by Merlin Press Ltd
10 Malden Road, London NW5 3HR

94 96 98 97 95
1 3 5 7 6 4 2

British Library Cataloguing in Publication Data
A catalogue record for this book is available from
the British Library

Designed, typeset and produced for Merlin Press by
Chase Production Services, Chipping Norton, OX7 5QR
Printed in Finland by WSOY

Contents

Preface

Collected here will be found historical essays from the past thirty years. I have not included my more directly political and peace-related essays, some of which are still available. Nor have I included essays on the romantic poets. I hope to make a collection of these later.

My thanks are due to Cambridge University Press, *Dissent*, *Essays in Labour History* (edited by John Saville), *Indian Historical Review*, William Morris Society, *New Society*, *London Review of Books*, *New York Review of Books*, *Radical History Review*, *Socialist Register*, *Past and Present Society* and *The Times Literary Supplement*.

E.P.T.

August 1993

Introduction

These essays were handed over for publication by Edward a fortnight before he died in August last year. During the previous six months he had been making a careful selection, and this, the order and the suggested title are all his. Most of these pieces have appeared over the years in a wide spread of journals, many of them now virtually inaccessible.

The division of the book into two parts, 'Persons' and 'Polemics', reflects two aspects of Edward's writing. On the one hand re-examination and rehabilitation of the lost or misinterpreted figures in history – from William Morris to the voiceless agricultural protesters of the eighteenth century. On the other the polemical attacks, brilliant and unforgettable, on fellow historians with whom he differed – in this collection seen in 'Happy Families' or 'Peterloo', elsewhere in his famous demolition of Louis Althusser.

Reference is made in Edward's preface to a collection of essays on the Romantics, the preparation of which was fairly advanced at the time of his death. One of the essays, 'Hunting the Jacobin Fox' appears in the current issue of *Past and Present* (Spring 1994); the complete volume will appear in due course. Other as yet unpublished or uncollected material, including a volume of poems, is in preparation.

One project should be especially mentioned here. Edward was a prolific letter writer; for him letters were an important form of communication, as friends and colleagues will recall. Many of his most creative ideas as well as his humorous and relaxed comments are to be found in his letters. We are asking anyone who has letters from him to let us know and if possible to let us have either the originals or copies. At some future date it is hoped to publish a selection.

Dorothy Thompson
Martin Eve
26 May 1994

Persons

Mary Wollstonecraft

On the day after Mary Wollstonecraft first made love to William Godwin she retreated in concern and self-doubt: 'Consider what has passed as a fever of your imagination ... and I will become again a Solitary Walker.' Claire Tomalin, in her bright new biography, gives us this passage, but not that other haunting sentence: 'I perceive that I shall be a child to the end of the chapter ...'.

We are all, every one of us, in some part of ourselves children to the end of the chapter. Wollstonecraft didn't always manage her personal life wisely. Nor, when one comes to think of it, did Coleridge, De Quincey, Wordsworth, Hazlitt ... need one go on? I have no objection to reminders that persons of genius share all the infirmities of other mortals. The particular infirmities to which they were liable, often help us to understand also their genius. But it is, in the end, the plus of genius, and not the lowest common denominator of infirmity, which gives their lives importance.

I do object, on Wollstonecraft's behalf, to the inequitable treatment which she has received at the hands of historians and critics. She is seen less as a significant intellectual, or as a courageous moralist in an exceptionally exposed position, than as an 'Extraordinary Woman.' And the moral confusions, or personal crises, of a woman are always somehow more interesting than those of a man: they engross all other aspects of the subject. As, indeed, from the inexorable facts of the woman's 'situation' they often tend to do. Wordsworth 'had' an illegitimate daughter in revolutionary France: he carried her around intermittently for a few years as a private guilt, but his daughter didn't encumber him in more practical ways. Wollstonecraft also 'had' an illegitimate daughter in revolutionary France; but the having was a rather different matter, and thereafter she carried her around (with the help of a loyal maid) through France, England, northern Europe. It was not a carefully guarded secret, to be turned up by biographers in this century. Out-facing the 'world,' she walked with Fanny through the London streets.

A different matter. And it makes her life a subject peculiarly difficult to handle. We are all interested in sexual relations; we are all willing to moralise about them at the drop of a hat. And the mention of Wollstonecraft's name is like the collapse of a whole hat-shop: it turns up the moralising volume-control somewhere in our intestines. We have scarcely begun to establish the facts before we begin to mix them up with our own moralising additives: scandalised, or apologetic, or admiring or condescending. What we make of her is already mixed up with what we have made of ourselves; it is something different from her own taut, unrelenting self-making.

There have been perhaps a dozen serious biographies: the first, by William Godwin, appeared within a year of her death. None of them wholly satisfies. One reason is that Wollstonecraft presents not one subject, but two: and it would take unusual versatility to unite both in a single study. From one aspect, she was one of the five or six truly significant ultra-radical intellectuals in England in the 1790s: she must be placed beside Paine and Godwin: beside the Coleridge of the *Watchman*: Flower of the *Cambridge Intelligencer*: or Thelwall of the *Tribune* and the *Rights of Nature*. In this company, she requires no manner of condescension because she happened also to be a woman. Nor did she ask for such. It was her notion that 'mind has no sex': she measured herself as an equal in the republic of the intellect.

But from another aspect, Wollstonecraft was reminded by every fact of nature and of society that she was a woman. She was not a mind which has no sex, but a human being exceptionally exposed within a feminine predicament. Long before she died, she was seized upon by friend and by enemy as an exemplar. She noted this in her late *Letters from Sweden*:

> All the world is a stage, thought I; and few are there who do not play the part they have learnt by rote; and those who do not, seem marks set up to be pelted at by fortune; or rather as signposts, which point out the road to others, whilst forced to stand still themselves amidst the mud and dust.

Not many men are expected to justify in every encounter of their lives their published professions. The author of the *Vindication of the Rights of Woman* was exposed in her every motion. The 'world' observed her successively as a mannish journalist: as a rejected lover (of Fuseli); as a soured spinster (the 'wrong side' of 30); as a discarded mistress (of Imlay); as the mother of an illegitimate child; as an attempted suicide.

> 'What' said I within myself, 'this is Miss Mary Wollstonecraft, parading about with a child at her heels, with as little ceremony as if it were a watch just bought at the jeweler's. So much for the rights of women,' thought I ....

The characteristic response is that of Archibald Hamilton Rowan, the Irish patriot. It is fair to add that he became her friend, and perhaps was thus educated a little out of his prejudices.

The final episode of her life has much of the contrivance of fiction. When she married William Godwin it was much as if De Beauvoir, soon after writing *The Second Sex*, had married Sartre at the zenith of his reputation, and then had died in childbirth. What a temptation her life provides for the nudge-nudge sort of biographer. And what materials survived her. After her death, Godwin – candid, benevolent, and stricken (perhaps for the only time in his life) by emotions which he could not rationalise – thought it an act of piety to publish her *Posthumous Works*, including her letters to her feckless and foot-loose lover, Imlay. It was not an act of piety. She could not have wished it so. No rejected lover, man or woman, imploring for love in the face of equivocation or indifference could wish to be so exposed.

But there was more. Wollstonecraft's marriage to Godwin, in her last year, was conducted from independent neighbouring establishments. Godwin objected to marriage on principle, and Wollstonecraft accepted his views up to a point: they were each to continue to conduct an independent life, received friends (of either sex), and visit socially as independent persons, not as man-and-wife. Hence domestic arrangements were conducted often by letter: usually affectionate, sometimes loving, sometimes querulous or recriminatory, sometimes just arrangements for dinner or the theatre. And all that lot survives also. This is fortunate again for biographers. But I doubt how far any of us would wish to be judged – or judged in a public sense – on evidence of this casual, and essentially unconsidered kind.

So there are two possible subjects here, and the best two biographies, hitherto, have taken opposite courses. The standard academic biography by Ralph Wardle is painstaking and, on occasion, pedestrian; but it maintains a seriousness towards its subject's intellectual identity, examining her writings with care but turning its back upon any sustained analysis of her sexual predicament. Wollstonecraft, one feels, might have approved this approach. More recently, Margaret George has published in the United States, but not, so far as I am aware, in Britain, a highly-intelligent analysis (*One Woman's 'Situation,'* Illinois, 1970) of her subject's personal evolution and predicament. Both books are to be strongly recommended, although neither, in my view, even when taken together, give a full view of Wollstonecraft's originality and stature.

I had hoped to welcome Claire Tomalin's book, and in a way I do. The books by Wardle and George are better. But Tomalin has attacked her subject with zest. She has turned up a few new facts, although her documentation is (deliberately) so sloppy that it is difficult see what is new and what she has borrowed from Wardle and others. She has read around her subject to place her in a context: the placings succeed on occasion, when they concern personalities and not ideas. The chapter on Wollstonecraft's experiences as governess to Lord and Lady Kingsborough is perceptive – the best treatment of this which I have read. And the book flows along nicely – an inquisitive feminine narrative which readers will enjoy. The book will certainly go: it is a calculated book club choice.

It is this fact which relieves me from an inhibition against saying that I dislike it a good deal. It is a book which diminishes the stature of its subject. And, by a sick irony, it does this in ways which are supposedly characteristically feminine. Wherever Tomalin deals with central political or intellectual issues, her manner and her matter is commonplace, personalised, or crassly philistine. Her French revolution is a madly-interesting scene with swinging intellectuals followed by a predictable plebeian Terror. (In England, it was 'the signal for everyone to rush to extremes'.) Tomalin is against extremes, and, as the book proceeds, it becomes apparent that no one is wholly balanced and mature except the author: certainly not Wollstonecraft, for whom she is always making sophisticated psychological allowances. After all, Wollstonecraft did not have the benefit of reading Freud, Durkheim or Kenneth Tynan. The political philosophy of Godwin and of Holcroft is sketched in boldly: 'their enthusiasm for perfectibility was such that they envisaged the end of all superstition, crime, war, illness and even ... sleep and death itself.' Any attentive reader of Jilly Cooper's weekly column will know herself wiser than that: and, since this is so, Tomalin need carry her investigation of Godwin's thought no further.

It follows that Tomalin is very little interested in Wollstonecraft's thought either. She underestimates the *Rights of Man*; condescends to the *Vindication*; and she scarcely discusses the late (and important) *Letters from Sweden* at all. By contrast, she hovers lingeringly above each personal encounter or private letter, and pokes around knowingly for hidden sexual motives. While only a few lines of the *Vindication* are cited, we have passage after passage of the letters to Imlay, some of them provoking the most *interesting* questions: could there be 'an allusion to a flirtation with another man here'?

The basis of Wollstonecraft's precarious independence, and the very precondition of her ever writing the *Vindication*, was secured when she was befriended by that very remarkable Dissenting publisher, Joseph Johnson, who provided her with regular work, an income, and lodgings. This is the only episode in her subject's life which has Tomalin baffled. Johnson (49) was befriending 'Mary,' 'youngish' (28). And yet there is no evidence as to even a putative sexual encounter. For Tomalin, this is utterly improper. She implies (with no evidence) that perhaps Johnson was a homosexual; or, when he invited 'Mary' to work for him, 'perhaps he was in a manic moment such as come to certain asthmatics.' At any rate, 'Johnson's interest in women as anything other than friends was either extremely discreet or, more probably, non-existent.' And (a final solution) 'they played at fathers and daughters'.

'Women as anything other than friends' – could our sexually

hyperconscious age condemn itself more clearly than this? We
know nothing about Johnson's sexual inclinations and (one might
add in passing), since we do know nothing, speculation on the
subject is more suited to a gossip column than a history book.
What we do know about Johnson is that he was a good judge of
authors; he published ultra-radical and feminist books throughout
the 1790s; he was the friend of other writers with feminist
sympathies – Mary Hays, William Frend, George Dyer – and his
loyalty to these people and causes led him in the end to prison.
When Wollstonecraft arrived on his doorstep, Johnson needed a
reliable full-time editorial assistant: his need and her ability and
predicament matched each other. Is it not conceivable that they
actually became *friends*, agreeing to set aside or distance Tomalin's
obligatory 'anything other than'? It is even possible that they were
'playing at' being comrades in a common political and intellectual
endeavour – a game which I fear our own sophisticated world
would regard with knowing disbelief.

But it was this game of egalitarian comradeship for which
Wollstonecraft attempted to image the rules. Against Rousseau's
sophistry, that educated women would lose their power over men,
she replied: 'This is the very point I aim at. I do not wish them to
have power over men; but over themselves.' To attempt this
self-determination in her own life, entailed a disregard for convention which required qualities which can easily be labelled as
domineering, wilful, egotistical. To attempt this also meant that she
must suffer in her own experience as she pressed against each one
of those boundaries which she had already defined in her writings.
As Margaret George has written: 'With that determination to be
"free" Mary proceeded to successive revelations of the limits –
external and self-imposed – of her freedom'. With extraordinary
tenacity, she herself sought to bring those two subjects – her
philosophy and her biography – into one: as Godwin wrote, she
'had through life tramped on those rules which are built on the
assumption of the imbecility of her sex'. She was bound to suffer;
and her suffering, expressed in letters never intended for publication, and in a style of self-dramatising, over-articulate 'sensibility'
nurtured by Rousseau's *Confessions* and the *Sorrows of Werther*, is
altogether too 'heavy' for the flip insensibility of our own times.

So Wollstonecraft has become a bit of a bore. Each generation does her over again in its own image. The anti-Jacobins did her as a prostitute. The bourgeois feminists did her as a bourgeois feminist. More recently, in 1947, two American Freudians (one, shamefully, a woman) did her over as a bitch motivated by penis-envy: 'the shadow of the phallus lay darkly, threateningly over all that she did.' As against this, Tomalin's doings are greatly preferable. Wollstonecraft – or 'Mary', as she must always call her – is now seen as a premature inhabitant of our own literary and feminine north London: premature not only in the fact of living in the 1790s but also in displaying manifest immaturities which, from the composure of our advanced civilisation, we may easily detect, smile at, but make allowances for. Every mature professional woman today, who has 'worked hard at' her relationships, 'come to terms with' her sexuality, and who is never manic or extreme in her feminism, can recognise instantly in Tomalin's Mary that exasperating neighbour, or old college friend, who is always getting into muddles and – in the moment of denouncing us for our conventionality – falling flat on her own face. And every uninformed male reviewer can see Tomalin's Mary equally clearly. For the *Daily Telegraph Magazine*, this is the 'book of the week': Mary had 'an acute shortage of worldly wisdom'; 'she fell in love with charming rotters'; she 'gave birth to a tragic bastard' – 'a magnificent and touching failure.' Predictably, she leads *The Times* review page as 'Poor Mary': her life is seen as a 'comedy' which (we are chivalrously warned) it is too easy to laugh at.

I do not find Wollstonecraft's life funny. Nor can I see it as any kind of failure. I see her as a major intellectual, and as one of the greatest of Englishwomen. There were scores of thousands of women in the 1790s who were domineering, or who professed sensibility excessively, or who got into personal muddles; just as there were scores of thousands of men who were vain, cock-sure and who drank too much. But there was only one Wollstonecraft, just as there was only one Paine. It is the plus that matters. Large innovations in thought and sensibility often arise after so many and so prolonged premonitions that they appear to us, in retrospect, as mere commonplaces. Paine's *Rights of Man* and Wollstonecraft's *Vindication* both have this air: it is a puzzle that no one had written them before.

But no one had. And, once written, the terms of argument were forever changed. It is difficult to know which book proposed the larger claims: but since women make up one half of the species, the honours may rest with Wollstonecraft. Her arguments, in this book and in other places, could have been made with more system. But they were not negligible: they could be repressed, but they could not be expunged. Nor were they repressed as utterly as Tomalin, in her final chapter, proposes. She has simply looked in the wrong places. She should have looked, instead, at the Shelleyan tradition carried through to Thomas Hardy and William Morris: or at Anna Wheeler and William Thompson: at Owenites and free-thinkers.

Nor is this all. Paine's book is better written, better structured. But Wollstonecraft's is the more complex sensibility. She by no means swam along easily with the current of 18th century rationalism: she often struck across it, creating within it a romantic and critical eddy. She had suffered too much in her own human nature – and she had experienced, very closely, Paris at the height of the Terror – not to have reservations about Godwinian optimism. More than this, in the very moment of the annunciation of 'bourgeois feminism' she was one of those most alert to the limitations of bourgeois political thought. As a woman, she had fully experienced the force of property rights, both in personal and in social life; and she knew the hollowness of programmes of merely-political emancipation to people held in economic dependency. Hence her writing always showed an alertness to social injustice, and – as in her *Letters from Sweden* – a disgust at ascendant commercialism. In this way, she spliced together feminism and social radicalism at the very start.

As for her life: I know that I would not have lived it so well, and I think it arrogant in any biographer to assume, too easily, that it could have been lived better. This was not, after all, north London in 1974. It was a rough time: and the place was less provided with our modern supportive amenities. (There was not, come to think of it, a Tavistock clinic to take one's horrors to, nor a social worker to advise her on her bastard child.) She fell into one or two holes: and she dug herself out, with her own nails. She never asked anyone to extricate her, except for Imlay, and she had

– or do we not allow this now? – a little claim on him. Even from Imlay she would accept – if affection had died – no alms or maintenance. She went on her own way, as a solitary walker. She not only took upon herself the full consequences of her convictions, in a world whose rules she had not made, but she had the resilience to get up (she, a deserted mistress fished out of the Thames) and resume her work of imagining the rules for egalitarian comradeship once more.

We have rarely seen her equal in our history. To Tomalin's mature assessment, I prefer infinitely the words of Virginia Woolf, where she speaks of 'the high-handed and hot-blooded manner in which she cut her way to the quick of life.' And as Woolf well knew, high-handedness brings down its revenges. Wollstonecraft was prepared for these: but what she does not deserve is the revenge of 'Poor Mary!' blazoned across a complacent press. She needs no one's condescension. She was poor in nothing. She was never beaten. And the final evidence lies in that part of her which remained a child to the end of the chapter. For that part of her – the refusal to become careful and 'knowing,' the resilient assent to new experience – is exactly that part which most of us are careful to cauterise, and then to protect with the callouses of our worldly-wise complicities.

From *New Society*, 19th September 1974, reviewing Claire Tomalin's *The Life and Death of Mary Wollstonecraft*, Weidenfeld & Nicholson

Eleanor Marx

This book has already received a generous welcome, and it deserves to do so. In my own view it does not fulfil the promise of the first volume (*Eleanor Marx: Family Life, 1855–1883*), published five years ago. But it is a work of vitality and of scholarship, and it draws more fully upon unpublished correspondence of Eleanor Marx and of Engels's circle than has ever been done before. So it is, and is likely to remain, an important study.

But it is not an objective study. The reader who does not like to be manipulated – to be nudged through the evidence towards a prescribed conclusion, now asked to turn his head this way and now ordered to close his eyes, and now shown only an approved portion of the evidence – such a reader will still prefer Chushichi Tsuzuki's ten-year-old biography.

Tsuzuki lays out very clearly, and sometimes tersely, the evidence, and invites the reader to form a judgement. Kapp does not. She is wholly entitled to write a very different, and (as she supposes) less 'academic' biography. This will be, for many readers, the virtue of her book. It is, without any pretence, engagingly partisan. She seeks to enter without reserve into the consciousness of her heroine – or hero (for in the longest, 180-page section of the book, Engels displaces Eleanor as the central figure). She quotes liberally from her (or his) letters, sees the world (usually an obtuse and intractable world) through their eyes, enters with wit and malice into their quarrels, encounters the *dramatis personae* of the British and European socialist movements (usually a bungling or treacherous, and always a politically-backward cast) as Eleanor or Engels encountered them, and generally she lays about her with zest and humour.

All this is good fun, and sometimes it really is. The very interesting (if sad) long section on Engels is called 'The Last Lustre of the General'. We must certainly hope that this is far from the last, but it must certainly be a late lustre of Yvonne Kapp; and it is the lustre of an indomitable and loyal orthodox Communist who is possessed of the superb confidence and maturity gained by standing in one place while an obtuse and intractable world persists in its wilfully treacherous and backward courses. Eleanor's suicide, she implies, was influenced – if not provoked – by her lack of preparedness for a similar experience. 'The mainstream of the British working-class movement – her native element – was flowing ever more swiftly, broadly and deeply into channels far removed from Marxism, to leave her in a rivulet whose current would not be strong enough to bear her forward.' Eleanor, who was 'political from top to toe', 'had thought to see the dawn of a new world. For her the light receded and she would not stay.'

This is not convincing. But that suicide has now been discussed a good deal before a British public which has even witnessed it on television. It might be more respectful to this very political and gifted English daughter of Marx to comment on her contribution to the early socialist movement. And here the good fun of Kapp's polemic does not take us so far. For one thing it cannot be sustained without doing repeated injustice to all fellow socialists who lay outside the immediate guidance of the Engels family circle. For another it requires situating ourselves totally within this circle and accepting it at its own valuation.

One is irritated less with 'Tussy' (Eleanor), whose loyalty to 'the General' is wholly forgivable than with Engels himself: and also with Kapp. By the time of his 'last lustre' Engels had lived *for fifty years* in England; and yet, inside his residence in Regent's Park Road, he might have been living inside some time-warp in the Tardis. The English shadows which flitted outside remained (as they did not for Marx) *'them'*. 'Their art seems rather better than their literature and their poetry better than their prose', he remarked in a generous mood in 1884. By 1894 he was ten years more grumpy and less generous: when Dr Ludwig Freyberger (soon to marry Louise Kautsky and move into Regent's Park Road) turned up from Vienna, Engels announced to Sorge that he had 'already shown the English that more medicine is learnt on the Continent than here', 'the clumsy people here cannot come up to the Vienna standard', British practitioners were inferior in physiology, pathology, surgery, etc etc. Yvonne Kapp snorts at this, but when Engels

repeatedly offers judgements as to the British Socialist movement
and its personnel of a similar ill-informed and rancorous levity, she
neither snorts nor hems nor haws. She receives his writ with the
dedication of a devotee.

Now let us put the record down a little more coolly, and take a
closer view. Eleanor Marx Aveling and Edward Aveling were on
the Executive of the SDF in 1884 and formed part of the 'cabal'
which, provoked by Hyndman's dictatorial methods, resigned to
form the Socialist League. In this secession (which may have been
a tactical error) they were fully supported by Engels, on the
grounds that 'the whole Federation was really nothing but a
swindle.' This general (but not very precise or political) judgement
suffices as a guide for Kapp for the next 600 or so pages:
Hyndman and all the SDF are dismissed (until in 1896 the
Avelings rejoin it) as a swindle. We have Engels's authority for
this, after all.

Next the Avelings (for at this stage they acted together) served
on the executive of the Socialist League. Engels advised that the
League was strong enough only to run a monthly journal; William
Morris (and the majority) wanted a weekly journal around which
they could build the League. After 15 months Morris had his way,
and 'Eleanor and Aveling took the opportunity to withdraw'.
Eleanor wrote to her sister, Laura: 'An awful mess they'll make of
it e'er long. By dint of much arguing the General and I induced
Ed[ward] to give up the sub-editorship.' Edward 'really has not the
time ... and more important, there is no one here really dependable
to work with ... we have *no-one*.' The position – a frequent cry –
'was impossible'. 'Here all is a muddle', chorused Engels: 'The
turning of *Commonweal* into a "weekly" – absurd in every respect
– has given Edward a chance of getting out of his responsibility
for this now incalculable organ .... It would be ridiculous to expect
the working class to take the slightest notice of these various
vagaries of what is by courtesy called English Socialism,' etc. etc.
etc. Kapp evidently approves their political realism and sagacity,
noting that Aveling was replaced by Bax, and that Eleanor's
'International Record' was taken over by May Morris 'who had not
quite the same facilities as Eleanor to gather detailed news from all
over Europe, including Russia, as well as both North and South

America.' Exactly so: the new socialist weekly (and, as it proved to be for at least two years, very much the best socialist weekly appearing in Britain) was as a deliberate act of policy deprived of Eleanor's services and Engels's incomparable information.

Next the Avelings were off (in the autumn of 1886) for their lecture tour of the United States, to which another story attaches. Returning, they gave up time and effort to lecturing at Radical Clubs. This was useful work, but did it really entitle Engels to write, like a gushing aunt, that 'at present the Avelings are doing more than anyone else here, and being more effective ...'? 'If all goes well,' he crowed, ' it will push the Social Democratic Federation as well as the Socialist League into the background.' This is odd, since members of both those bodies, as well as the indefatigable Fabian, Bernard Shaw, were busy lecturing to Radical Clubs in the same period. (But Engels, inside the Tardis, could not be expected to know that). Next, the 1887 Annual Conference of the League, which, after a finely-balanced argument, voted to abstain from parliamentary action. I have argued, in my *William Morris*, that the 'parliamentarians' forced the wrong issue in the wrong way, thereby forcing Morris into anarchist arms. The decision, Kapp notes, 'came dangerously near to rendering the Socialist League impotent. Neither Eleanor nor Aveling allowed their names to go forward for election to the Central Council.'

My point is that the tactics of the Avelings (forced on at every stage by Engels) were self-fulfilling. Whenever political disagreements arose, the Avelings withdrew from engagement and drove their allies into their opponents' arms. Everyone else was always 'impossible': 'we have *no-one*' (although Ernest Belfort Bax, the only prominent English Socialist who was sometimes admitted to the Tardis on Engels's sociable Sunday nights, was sometimes acclaimed as *'ours'*). So the Avelings fall back on the Bloomsbury Socialist Society. Now if anyone else had fallen back on a society with such a name, Yvonne Kapp would have split our sides with the bolts of her sarcasm. But on this occasion she tells us almost nothing about this society (and less than Tsuzuki) and does not even mention the activities of Alexander Karley Donald, its leading political light, a solicitor, litterateur and heavy political 'realist', who once had the temerity to advise William Morris to 'lower his moral tone', thereby occasioning a very distinct *heightening* of the moral atmosphere.

Some eight years and 400 pages later, by which time the Avelings have been in and out of other organisations, including the ILP (and very little light is thrown on this episode), Kapp makes this remarkable summary:

> By now there is no need to labour the point that Eleanor, as a genuine Marxist and thus the least dogmatic of any for her time and place, did not really give a fig for these sects as such even when she worked with them in a disciplined fashion. Always she had homed her way unerringly to such groups in which she sensed this 'instinctive urge' to socialism: to any zone where her words would fall on fertile ground. By the late '90s, the SDF appeared to her more 'socialist' – and to have more influence – than any other existing organisation, so she rejoined it.

But this is the problem. We most of us have difficulties in choosing, and in sticking to our chosen organisations, even when we suppose ourselves to be 'genuine Marxists' or other kinds of superior pigeon with unerring homing instincts. But it is difficult to work loyally with *any* organisation – or to be regarded as a loyal comrade – if we 'do not really give a fig' for them. And this was, very specifically, Eleanor Marx's problem, and one which was bequeathed to her by her father and by Engels. She had the vices entailed by her birth and her virtues. The loyalty which she gave abundantly to her father's memory, to 'the General', and, with tragic tenacity, to Aveling, led her to feel that she and this immediate familial circle (sometimes even called 'the party') allowed her to dispense with lesser loyalties to her comrades in the English movement. If these made mistakes (and she, and Engels, sometimes identified these mistakes very tellingly) she was absolved of any duty to stand by them, or seek to correct them. She and Aveling simply had to home their way unerringly to their next abode.

The 'instinctive urge' of 'the party', however, sometimes seems more like a wholly subjective gut-reaction.

It included, for historical reasons dating from the break-up of the First International, an instinctive horror of anything showing even toleration towards anarchism – a horror which Kapp fully shares. This horror alienated Eleanor from William Morris, Domela Nieuwenhuis, and even (later) from Keir Hardie and Tom Mann. Engels and Eleanor kept the French, German, Dutch and American comrades informed as to the sins of the British movement in correspondence which is both bitchy and lacking in any political propriety. Undoubtedly they felt deeply, in their familial bones, that the international revolutionary socialist movement was something that they owned, as an inheritance from 'Mohr'.

When Lafargue, having been bombarded for years with letters as to Hyndman's unspeakable vices, neglected to invite him to an organising conference to plan the international conference of 1889, he was hauled over the coals by Engels: 'the Federation is unquestionably more important than the League ... Hyndman would not have harmed any of you.' But, Yvonne Kapp, adds, 'Lafargue had added to his folly by writing to William Morris personally ... Eleanor had something to say about this': 'Paul's writing to Morris was a great mistake,' (she ticked off her sister, Laura Lafargue): 'Morris is personally liked, but you would not get a 1/2 dozen workmen to take him seriously.' Paul would have done better to have left all the invitations to be drawn up in the Tardis. But then, perhaps, it would have turned out that 'we have *no-one.*'

Yvonne Kapp has released so much more damaging trivia from the Bottigelli archives that it is extraordinary that she should rage so sardonically at those who speak of 'a Marxist clique' within the international movement, or who argue (with Bax – who had every opportunity to observe) that Engels sought to 'foist' Aveling as a leader upon the English movement. Her evidence confirms both points, although I don't think that either point strikes a death-blow at Engels or at Marxism. Engels was ageing, very set in his ways, very German, and exceedingly busy with 101 important and significant intellectual tasks, as well as a few insignificant and meddlesome ones. When he really put his mind to a problem, and informed himself adequately, his political judgement was always weighty and sometimes superb. But when he did not he was opinionated, obstinate, and arrogant. The British movement had long been his blind spot, since he could never forgive the working class for abandoning the Chartists of his youth. As R. Page Arnot, a Communist scholar older than Yvonne Kapp and as loyal as her, if not as orthodox, has noted: 'Apart from those admitted to his immediate family circle, there is no Englishman or Scotsman for whom Engels had a good word to say.' But to any who were so admitted Engels was more pliant. As Eleanor wrote in panic to her sister Laura in Engels's last year (when the Freybergers moved in on him) 'you know very well that anyone living with the General can manipulate him to any extent.'

The Avelings did not live with Engels, although it would appear (Kapp is unable to clarify the point) that there must have been times when they, like the Lafargues, were living *off* him. They were his main informants on the English movement (information which, with his own uncharitable additives, he relayed around the socialist world), and they stood between him and that movement. 'On account of Aveling,' Bernstein – who had every opportunity to observe – later recalled, 'many people kept away from Engels's house.' One such person was Mrs Schack, who had been active in the German women's movement. Kapp nudges us towards a hilarious and satirical view of this officious lady: 'She was strongly opposed to the introduction of State licensed and supervised brothels and very keen on what Engels designated "Free Trade in whores".' Are we to suppose from this that State licensed brothels are a correct Marxist demand, objected to only by 'pious bourgeois women'? Perhaps we are not; we are only supposed to see Mrs Schack as hysterical and ridiculous. This is an example of Kapp's common game of playing both ends against the middle. One end is the absolute priority of political over personal criteria and the absolute political authority of Engels and of 'Tussy'; while Kapp acknowledges Aveling's sexual and financial offences, these are seen as something quite distinct from his political soundness – Aveling 'was always to be found on the correct side of the political fence.' The other end is the assumption that almost all the personal attacks on Aveling were caused by anti-Marxist political motivation, and a readiness to use any kind of personal gossip to devalue Aveling's critics. If the gifted socialist agitator J.L. Mahon also refused to work with Aveling (and it is clear that Engels made this a condition of his support for Mahon's propaganda) then we are allowed by Kapp to suppose that this was only because he was a self-respecting worker with a 'puritanical streak' who was shocked by the Avelings' common-law marriage.

When I first wrote my study of *William Morris* over twenty years ago I inclined to Kapp's judgement, and gave both Eleanor and Engels the benefit of the doubt. But since that time the Engels–Lafargue correspondence has become available, and I have consequently sharpened my own judgement in revision. Engels's lofty dismissal, in 1887, of the existing socialist movement in Britain as 'a number of small cliques held together by personal motives', comes uneasily from a man who was at the centre of the smallest and most personally-motivated clique of all. The Avelings, having hurried on the split in the SDF, failed then to give a full commitment to the Socialist League, formed a faction within it, and forced on a further split which destroyed their own creation. Engels, who indignantly rebutted each and every attack on Aveling as the malicious slander of political enemies, was both the captive of Aveling and his political mentor. His personal motives (loyalty to 'Tussy') were admirable. But in the result he contributed in a small way to the confusions of the early movement and to the disrepute into which 'British Marxism' fell.

Aveling (it seems) surrounded himself with bouncing cheques and left other people to settle his bills and to comfort his discarded mistresses. The notion that these private vices can be segregated from his public and political virtue will not hold ice. His was the behaviour of an élitist, who made a tolerable and entertaining living for himself in the top storey of a poor movement. But what of that other notion, so prevalent now that it may be called a stereotype, that Eleanor all along was the noble and innocent victim of his abuse? Her suicide projected this interpretation backwards, across the previous fifteen years; by killing herself as she did, in a final protest against him, she rejected the name she had long chosen – Eleanor Marx Aveling – and re-entered a purified history as Eleanor Marx.

But I do not think this notion will do either. Eleanor also first entered the movement as a special person, an élitist, the daughter of 'Mohr'. She could not possibly have been other. She was spoiled by Engels and invited instantly into the control-room of the Tardis. His

sardonic contempt of those bungling English socialists rubbed off on
her. She was an enthusiastic Bohemian who shared Aveling's theatri-
cal ambitions and who enjoyed his round of one-act plays, sentimental comedies and *soirees*. It is difficult not to see 'the Avelings' in the
1880s except as a double act. If Dr Aveling enraged the American
socialists by charging them 25 dollars for 'corsage bouquets', Mrs
Aveling was the one who wore them. I think it probable that in these
early years she found Edward's flouting of bourgeois financial
proprieties to be daring and amusing. She learned, to her grievous
cost, otherwise. But in those days they certainly appeared to outsiders
as a marital package. When Bernstein spoke in the advanced Fabian
household of the Blands of the Avelings, 'there was suddenly a
suspiciously unanimous chorus of praise of them. "Oh, the Avelings
are very clever people." "Oh, everybody must admit that they have
been of great service to the movement," and so forth.' It is always
remembered that Shaw's Dubedat ('as natural as a cat, he moves
among men as most men move among things') is derived from
Aveling; it is less often recalled that (in Bernstein's view) 'the
deliberate blindness and deafness of Mrs Dubedat in respect of all
that was said to the detriment of her husband' is equally derived from
Eleanor:

> Of course when he says he doesn't believe in morality, ordinary
> pious people think he must be wicked. You can understand,
> can't you, how all this starts a great deal of gossip about him,
> and gets repeated until even good friends get set against him?

The important word is 'deliberate'.
    In her socialist propaganda work in the 1880s Eleanor was an
enthusiast. I find in an old notebook a letter of hers proposing in
October 1885 that a Christmas Tree be organised for the children
of the Socialist League:

> We cannot too soon make children understand that Socialism
> means happiness. Perhaps some friends (I tremble a little at the
> thought of Bax) will object to a *Christ*mas tree. If they or he
> shd I will only remind them of the origin of the Christian
> festival – of the beautiful old Pagan feast that celebrated the

birth of light. Let us, like the Christians, adopt this old story to our purpose. Is not Socialism the real 'new birth', & with its light will not the old darkness of the earth disappear?

This is the Eleanor whom Marxists have always cherished, the passionate daughter of Marx who disproves in all her life the libelling of the family as cold-blooded materialists. Yet we have also to remember that the enthusiastic comrade, who combines a ready resource of emotion with an absolute conviction of her own political integrity, can sometimes be an unsettling, even disruptive, fellow worker. Yvonne Kapp gives us a curious insight into the aftermath of 'Bloody Sunday' (1887). The demonstrators were prevented from entering Trafalgar Square by over 4,000 police and 600 guardsmen. The Radical, Irish and Socialist crowds were ingloriously routed, 200 of them to hospital. The next question for the movement was what to do next week – whether to rush the Square once more or whether to demonstrate in Hyde Park. Eleanor, writing to sister Laura, had not a moment of doubt:

> We shall urge going to the Square, but I fear many will funk .... If we can induce them to go next Sunday, it will mean very warm work. Last Sunday the troops had ammunition ready and stood with fixed bayonets. Next Sunday I think it very possible they will actually fire. That would be *very* useful to the whole movement here. It would complete the work some of us have been doing this long while past, of winning over the better Radical element to Socialism.

A delegate meeting of Radical clubs was called to take the decision, and a witty Radical reporter noted:

> In front of the platform sat Lady Macbeth Aveling and the redoubtable Edward, D.Sc. They were of course in favour of a spirited dash at Trafalgar Square; and very fine it was to see the lofty scorn of Lady Macbeth when any speaker on the pacific side rose to address the meeting. When the resolution proposing the Hyde Park meeting was read Lady Macbeth turned to Edward, D.Sc., and hissed 'C-o-w-a-r-d-s!' between her teeth.

Among those whom Eleanor implied to Laura were 'funks' was William Morris, since he was less than convinced that the unleashing of the military upon an unarmed crowd would be *very useful to the whole movement*'. And Yvonne Kapp notes approvingly: 'While Eleanor learnt from Bloody Sunday that the working class had not yet enough experience of struggle, Morris drew the conclusion that it had not yet enough education or organisation to engage in struggle.' This is untrue, as Kapp must know, since she has just quoted Morris's own judgement on the matter: he proposed that the demonstrators should immediately learn to struggle *more effectively*, by organisation, crowd discipline and drill, and 'a due system of scouts, outposts and supports ...'

Eleanor maintained this faith in the educative value of a severe defeat, which would make the real class struggle apparent and bring recalcitrant Britain into line with the Continent. In the last year of her life, while assisting the engineers in their long lock-out, she admitted in a letter to Natalie Liebknecht that 'we are hopelessly beaten'. 'It is true – ... entre nous – the beating may, in the long run be as useful to our cause, more useful perhaps, than a half-hearted "victory" ...' This did not prove to be true, and, in general, too many of Eleanor's political judgements are spoiled by this kind of warm-hearted and wilful political emoting.

Eleanor Marx was not the incomparable paragon and the all-wise Marxist homing pigeon that Yvonne Kapp would have her to be. Such hagiography ends up by diminishing the subject. She was, however, a very remarkable and gifted socialist, whose gifts and whose services grew greater in her later years. The difference can be seen during the New Unionism, from late in 1888 onwards, when Eleanor identified especially with the Gasworkers and General Labourers Union. In doing so, she ceased to act as an élitist, a special person, and ceased to skate in circles on the surface of the movement. She also disengages clearly from the figure of Aveling, being clearly accepted in her own right by Will Thorne and his brethren. And also by the sisters of the union, whom she played a most significant part in organising and then in assisting with the humdrum chores of weekly union work.

One must always admire 'Tussy' for her fight, her warmth, her enthusiasm and her loyalties. I have argued that we cannot and should not always admire her for her political judgement and actions, because this entails injustice to her fellow socialists and (more seriously) an almost religious belief in the all-wise guardian-ship of some Truth in the Marx and Engels circle. But we can, after 1889, increasingly admire her for her judgement also, as well as for a new humility which she learned in the course of her own personal tragedy. Much of her international work, not only for the large International but also for smaller conferences of miners and glass-workers, was tedious, backstage, and unrewarding: endless translations, much correspondence, interpreting and hosting of delegates. Her practical work among the profoundly exploited women of the East End remains to us as an example. Her many lecturing trips in the 1890s (sometimes still with Aveling) to branches of the ILP or SDF in the North of England, Scotland and Wales were warmly received and selflessly given. There were no 'corsage bouquets' to be gained in Aberdeen, but much good and reciprocal comradeship.

The greatest tragedy, as it seems to me, is that when she came to her end – and she had a right to choose that end – she did not realise how much she had come to be loved and honoured in the movement, and how clearly her many friends dissociated Aveling from her. She felt more apart from that British movement than she needed to have felt. As to the suicide itself, there is still something unexplained. There is that curious letter, six months before the event, to her half-brother, Marx's natural son, Freddie Domuth: 'I am so alone, and I am face to face with a most horrible position: *utter* ruin – everything, *to the last penny*, or utter, open disgrace.' But even after that letter she took Aveling back and nursed him through an operation. And when Freddie called on her, she could not bring herself to tell him what the crisis had been. Certainly 'utter, open disgrace' could not have referred to the fear that she would be left alone, exposed as Aveling's discarded mistress. She was long innured to that kind of gossip, and anyway – as she demonstrated in that year by coming to the help of Edith Lanchester – she had not changed her views on 'free marriage'. As Kapp suggests, some new but major default by Aveling upon political or trade union funds, offering the alternative of full repayment or his imprisonment, might fit the letter; and yet, if that had been so, surely Aveling's enemies would have forced the matter into the light?

Something had happened, which even her contemporaries could not know about or gossip about. Tsuzuki hints, but Kapp does not, at what this could have been. 'Tussy's' deepest secret, which she had only learned on 'the General's' death, was that Freddie was, not Engels's, but her own father's natural son. Kapp's earlier volume gives the fullest account of these circumstances, and the shock of their disclosure. This disclosure injured Eleanor at the centre of her psyche – her loyalty to 'Mohr' and her cherished image of a blissful family life. She could easily, in her first emotional response, have sobbed about it on Aveling's shoulder. Now, like a cat moving among women as most men move among things, Aveling might have offered an ultimatum: your money or I tell. The 'utter, open disgrace' would not be for Eleanor, but for what she cared for even more, the honour of her father, the family, the party, the movement. How Mohr's enemies, across the continents, would rage and lampoon and, even worse, would laugh. And so, indeed, they might in those days have done. She would certainly have preferred to die – maybe even did die – rather than that this could come about. If so, she did not withold that secret for ever, but she withheld it for a further fifty years; and with that she would have been satisfied.

In all this the evidence presents a gap which, as Yvonne Kapp writes, 'can be filled only by pure guesswork.' For many other gaps in Eleanor's life guesswork no longer is needed: Kapp's two overflowing volumes have more than filled them up. I have argued with some of her conclusions and against some of her methods. But I must insist once more: these volumes are a notable achievement of scholarship and of lively exposition, and are worthy of their subject.

From *New Society*

Homage to Tom Maguire

As the writing of labour history becomes more professionalised, so the centre of interest shifts from front-line engagements to the disputes and strategical plans of GHQ. In the Colindale Library, the Public Record Office, the national archives of trade unions, the Place or Webb Collections, the techniques proper to a constitutional or economic historian can be employed. The dubious reminiscences of local worthies can be disregarded (unless required for 'colour'), the regional skirmishes can be dismissed with an irritable footnote, and the historian can get down in earnest to national minute-books, Congress proceedings, intrigues among the leadership, and under-hand political agreements.

And yet – how far are the techniques of the political or constitutional historian adequate to deal with the tensions and lines of growth in movements which (until the highly bureaucratised post-1945 era) have always been exceptionally responsive to problems of local social and industrial context – local splits and breakaways – ground-swells of opinion at the rank-and-file level?

The national historian still tends to have a curiously distorted view of goings-on 'in the provinces'. Provincial events are seen as shadowy incidents or unaccountable spontaneous upheavals on the periphery of the national scene, which the London wire-pullers try to cope with and put into their correct historical pattern. And provincial leaders are commonly denied full historical citizenship; if mentioned at all, they are generally credited with various worthy second-class abilities, but rarely regarded as men with their own problems, their own capacity for initiative, and on occasions a particular genius without which national programmes and new political philosophies can never be wedded to movements of men. Hence labour historians tend to fall into a double-vision; on the one hand, there are the mass movements which grow blindly and spontaneously under economic and social pressures: on the other, the leaders and manipulators – the Places, the Chartist journalists, the Juntas and parliamentarians – who direct these elemental forces into political channels. And where this superficial national approach is beginning to give way to a more mature school of local history, employing sociological techniques, nevertheless we still find that the national and local pictures are rarely put together.

The early years of the ILP provide a striking example of this. The ILP grew from the bottom up: its birthplaces were in those shadowy parts known as 'the provinces'. It 'was created by the fusing of local elements into one national whole. From the circumference its members came to establish the centre ... '[1] Its first council seat was won in the Colne Valley: its first authentic parliamentary challenges came in Bradford and Halifax: its first conference showed an overwhelming preponderance of strength in the North of England:[2] its early directories show this strength consolidated.[3] When the two-party political structure began to crack, and a third party with a distinctively socialist character emerged, this even occurred neither in Westminster nor in the offices of Champion's *Labour Elector* but amongst the mills, brickyards, and gasworks of the West Riding.

Unless we register this fact, it is futile to speculate on the true origins of the ILP. Certainly Hardie and Burgess and Blatchford were the foremost propagandists for an independent party of labour. Certainly Champion worked for it, and so did Mahon, the Avelings, and the Hoxton Labour League: so – for that matter – did Hyndman when he first founded the Democratic Federation, and Engels in his *Labour Standard* articles of 1881, and the pedigree is a great deal longer than that.[4] Indeed, there was no lack of prophets. The problem was to translate prophecy into stable organisation and mass enthusiasm. Moreover, local grievances, severe industrial disputes, mass disaffection amongst Liberal voters – these in themselves were not sufficient to bring the thing about. The 1880s saw more than one false dawn – the crofters' struggle, the socialist propaganda among the Northumberland miners during the strike of 1887, the municipal revolt at Bolton in 1887.[5] In every case the socialist pioneers threw their hats in the air; in every case they retired disappointed and puzzled, as the electorate swung back to old allegiances, the new organisations crumbled, the councillors were re-absorbed by the Great Liberal Party.

The customary national picture of the West Riding break-through attributes the emergence of the ILP to one event – the great strike at Manningham Mills, Bradford. Pressed forward blindly by economic hardship and the effect of President McKinley's tariffs, the good-hearted Nonconformist Yorkshire workers turned instinctively to the arms of 'Nunquam' and Keir Hardie. But this will not do at all. It does not explain why a strike at one firm could have become the focus for the discontent of a whole Riding. It does not explain the nature of this discontent. It does not explain why the Yorkshire ILP was so deeply rooted, so stubborn in face of Liberal blandishments, so competently led. It passes over incidents of equal importance to the Manningham strike. It implies an appalling attitude of condescension towards these provincial folk who are credited with every virtue except the capital human virtue of conscious action in a conscious historical role.

If we must counter-pose to this legend our own propositions, then they are these: the two-party system cracked in Yorkshire because a very large number of Yorkshire working men and women took a conscious decision to form a socialist party. The fertilisation of the masses with socialist ideas was not spontaneous but was the result of the work, over many years, of a group of exceptionally gifted propagandists and trade unionists. This work did not begin with street-corner oratory and end with the singing of the 'Marseillaise' in a socialist clubroom, although both of these activities played their part; it required also tenacity and foresight, qualities of mass leadership and the rare ability to relate theory to practice without losing sight of theory in the press of events. And if we must have one man who played an outstanding role in opening the way for the ILP, that man was a semi-employed Leeds-Irish photographer in his late twenties – Tom Maguire.

I

Of course, an individual does not create a movement of thousands: this must be the product of a community. And the West Riding woollen district, in the 1880s, was a distinctive community, with common characteristics imposed by its staple

industries, geographical isolation, and historical traditions. Although the population was rapidly swelling and absorbing immigrants,[6] Yorkshire traditions were vigorous, local dialect almanacs
still thrived, the *Yorkshire Factory Times* made a feature of
dialect stories and verses, and in the more isolated areas, like the
Colne and Calder and Holme Valleys, memories were long. In
such communities, an 'alien agitator' from outside would make
little headway; but once the local leaders moved, the whole
community might follow. Leeds, on the western edge of the
woollen district, was a more cosmopolitan city, with more
diverse industry, a larger professional and clerical population, and
a recent influx of Jewish workers into the ready-made clothing
trade.[7] New ideas, new national movements, tended to extend
their influence to the woollen districts, not directly from London
but by way of Leeds; the textile workers' leaders learnt their
socialism from the Leeds and Bradford Socialist Leagues; Ben
Turner, the dialect poet from Huddersfield, was initiated into the
movement when he 'flitted' for two years to Leeds.[8]

It is important to recall how far 'independent labour' was already,
in the mid-1880s, part of the structure of this community. In one
sense, the ILP gave political expression to the various forms of
independent or semi-independent working-class organisation which
had been built and consolidated in the West Riding in the previous
thirty years – co-operatives, trade unions, friendly societies, various
forms of chapel or educational or economic 'self-help'. Among these,
the co-operative societies were strongest;[9] George Garside, who won
the first ILP seat in the Colne Valley, was a prominent co-operator.[10]
The trade unions were the weakest. In the late sixties or early
seventies trades councils existed in Leeds, Bradford, Halifax, Huddersfield, and Dewsbury; but by the early eighties all had disappeared
except for those at Leeds and Bradford, and these survived in
attenuated form through the support of skilled and craft unions.[11]
When the Bradford Trades Council invited the TUC to meet in their
home town in 1888, one of the reasons given was 'the fact that the
work-people engaged in the staple industries of the district are in a
very disorganised state';[12] a Bradford Congress would boost local
morale – as indeed it did, although in unexpected directions. Ben
Turner's history of the early years of the textile union is a record of

erratic spurts of organising, followed by dissolution and apathy; 'We were all poor folks with poor incomes and poor trade and hadn't the vision that we ought to have had'.[13]

If the 'independence of labour' found expression in some parts of the community's life, there was little evidence of this in the early eighties in the political complexion of the West Riding. It required a new generation, and the new militant unionism, to twist 'self-help' into socialist campaigning. The prevalent tone of the earlier years is one of surfeited, self-satisfied Liberalism. Local papers were busy celebrating the improvements in standards of life since the hungry forties, and recalling for the hundredth time the wisdom of the repeal of the Corn Laws. Local historians, with genuine feeling, commended the passing of the sanded floors and cellar-dwellings and oatmeal diet of the days of the 'poverty-knockers'; and some looked back, almost with nostalgia, to the fiery wool-combers and the Chartist weavers with their torchlight meetings.[14] In March 1885 a gathering of Chartist veterans took place in a Halifax temperance hotel; after an 'excellent repast' and an address reviewing the progress of the people since 1844, the best thanks of the meeting were moved 'to Mr Gladstone and his government for passing into law those principles which we have endeavoured during a long life to enjoy'. The motion was seconded by George Webber, at one time the most intransigent of physical force leaders. 'The majority of those attending the meeting', the report concludes, 'have become men of business and in some cases employers of labour'; and the reporter could not pass over the opportunity for taking their lives as a text for a small piece on the rewards of 'economy, industry, and temperance'.[15] Even Ernest Jones's Chartist stalwarts had found their place in Smiles's Valhalla.

Indeed, it is difficult to recognise the Bradford of Jowett's recollections – squalid back-to-back, open privy middens, an infant mortality rate (in some districts) of over one in four[16] – in the complacent compilations of a committee originated by Sir Jacob Behrens to inquire into the Condition of the Industrial Classes in 1887.[17] Here the statistics are carefully compiled, the rise in the wages of the skilled workers abundantly proved, the abolition of some of the worst abuses of the forties noted. And yet, less than three years later, not only the *Yorkshire Factory Times*, but also local Liberal and Conservative papers carried exposures of decaying slums, insanitary conditions, appalling social evils.[18] What made the difference?

It is true that a new generation was arising which demanded more of life than had contented their parents. In the 1850s the cramped blocks of back-to-backs were at least a step forward from the cellars, and the warren-like 'folds' of earlier days; in the nineties the ending of all back-to-back building was to be a leading point in ILP municipal campaigns.[19] But too much influence in this change of outlook should not be attributed to the Education Act of 1870. The ILP strongholds, Bradford and Halifax, were also the strongholds of half-time working; children went into the mills at the age of 10, on passing Standard III, and in Halifax, by a little-known local exemption clause, they could commence work when barely literate.[20] Moreover, in the previous twenty years the enforcement of the Factory Acts in the West Riding had been notorious for its laxity.[21] 12 per cent of those married at Bradford Parish Church in 1887 still signed their names with a cross.[22]

Nor should too much weight be placed upon the argument that the general improvement in trade in the later eighties emboldened the textile workers and placed them in a strong position for strike action and organisation. This was certainly a factor in the success of the Leeds unskilled agitation among the bricklayers' labourers and others. But the textile industry presents a very different picture. The West Riding woollen trade provides a notoriously dangerous field for generalisation, owing to its manifold subdivisions, local variants, and specialised markets; where American tariffs might create chaos in the fine worsted industry of Bradford they would leave Batley, the new 'shoddy-opolis', unaffected.[23] Nevertheless, certain common features may be indicated. (1) Yorkshire employers had been 'spoiled' by the abnormal boom years, 1870–74, a boom to which they looked back, even in the nineties, with nostalgia; during this period there was a spate of mill-building, inflated valuations, and profits were admitted to be 'inordinately large'.[24] (2) In the ensuing ten years, tariffs (especially in Germany and USA), keener world competition, and the onset of the 'great depression', led to a marked decline in profits, sharp local competition, and readjustments within the industry;[25] but despite a falling-off in overtime, and the onset of periods of short time, the volume of trade continued to expand and (as a Leeds observer noted) 'in many trades the *sum of profits* has been to some extent kept up by the *increased volume* of trade'.[26] Between 1886 and 1890 (the year of the McKinley tariff) problems of competition and readjustment were intensified. (3) Throughout these fifteen years (1875–90) we have nothing approaching a depression of the kind met by the cotton industry in the inter-war years of this century. Vast fortunes continued to be amassed, and the brunt of the crisis was borne by the textile workers whose wages declined throughout the period.[27] This decline was effected through direct wage reductions; increased mechanisation and intensification of labour; and the increasing proportion of women to male workers in the industry. (4) Thus we have in the wool textile industry of the late eighties an extreme example of the gulf which opened between the labour aristocracy and the unskilled workers at this time in other industries. Despite a few pockets of organised male aristocrats – power-loom over-lookers, card setters, warp dressers, and the like[28] – the bulk of the labour force endured a stationary or declining standard of living. The high proportion of women and juvenile workers, and the variations and jealousies between town and town, mill and mill, and even shed and shed, placed almost insuperable difficulties in the way of trade-union organisation.[29] Men's wages were continually forced down to the level of the women, and throughout the district the custom of the 'family wage' prevailed. (5) In these conditions, general trade unionism could scarcely 'get off the ground' unless backed by exceptional resources. The skilled trade unionists cannot be blamed for indifference; in 1876 the Bradford Trades Council made a sustained attempt to organise the dyers, but only ten workers attended a well-advertised meeting.[30] The Weavers' Union, consolidated after the Huddersfield strike of 1883, hung on for several years only by the skin of its teeth.[31] It was the enormous publicity provided by the *Yorkshire Factory Times*, founded in 1889, by the successful struggles of the unskilled

workers in London and (above all) in Leeds, and the indefatigable activity of socialist and new unionist propagandists which
provided the catalyst for the movement of 1890–93.

Even so, a paradox must be noted: it was not the success,
but the partial failure – the impossibility of complete success –
in the trade-union field, which turned the textile workers into the
channels of independent political action. Had the Manningham
Mills strike ended in victory, like the struggles of dockers,
gasworkers, and building workers, then Bradford night not have
been the birthplace of the ILP. Defeat at Manningham, and the
precarious nature of the partial organisation achieved elsewhere,
were a spur to political action – and for three leading reasons:
First, the bitter indignation aroused by economic oppression and
social injustice, against which industrial action appeared to
provide no effective remedy, was bound to break out in the
demand for an independent class party opposed to the parties of
the employers. Second, if the causes of poverty could not be
removed, its *effects* could be tackled by resolute independent
action in the field of local government: hence the great
importance of the early campaigns of the ILP in the West
Riding on unemployment, against the half-time system, for 'fair
contracts', school milk and medical services, on sanitary problems
and artisan's dwellings, nursery schools and slum clearance.[32]
Third, the complexity and subdivisions of the textile industry,
and the preponderance of women and juvenile workers, together
with the sub-contracting and 'sweat-shops' in the Leeds tailoring
industry – all these gave overwhelming point to the demand for
the Legal Eight Hour Day. Political action was seen as the only
effective remedy for industrial grievances.[33]

The appeal of the Legal Eight Hour Day had a massive
simplicity; it appeared to offer at one blow results which
trade-union action could only hope to achieve after many years
of hazard and sacrifice; it might go some way towards relieving
unemployment as well. Moreover, the demand was in the direct
line of the strongest West Riding traditions: Oastler and the Ten
Hours Movement: the more recent campaign of the Factory Acts
Reform Association, whose efforts to win the nine-hours day
resulted in the 56½ hour week in 1874. The experience of half a

century had led Yorkshire workers to believe that arguments that a shorter working day would lead to lower wages and loss of trade to foreign competitors, were no more than employers' propaganda points.[34]

Here we have some of the ingredients from which the West Yorkshire ILP was made. A close-knit community, in which the independence of labour found social, economic, religious expression. An industry facing readjustment and competition. Declining wages and appalling social evils. Tremendous problems in the way of effective trade-union organisation. A strong tradition of campaigning for legal protection in industry and limitation of hours. And to this tradition, another must be added: the tradition of the *political* independence of labour. The Chartist organisation had survived in West Yorkshire as long as in any part of the country. Halifax was Ernest Jones's 'constituency', and while Chartist sentiments were appeased by the adoption of Stansfeld, the friend of Mazzini, as one of the two members in 1859, the flame broke out afresh during the Reform League agitation. Jones stumped the West Riding, addressing enormous crowds; he was invited to stand both in Dewsbury and Halifax, and although he preferred Manchester, the Halifax men revolted against one of their sitting members, the local mill-owner Akroyd, and sponsored the independent candidature of E.O. Greening, the Co-operator, who achieved the very respectable poll of 2,802.[35] This was in 1868: lads in their 'teens at the time would be scarcely 40 years of age when the ILP was formed. When John Lister contested Halifax for the ILP in 1893 his election manifesto appealed to 'Radical Halifax', and his supporters recalled the traditions of Greening, Jones, and (local veterans) Ben Rushton and John Snowden, and demanded indignantly whether a 'Whig' should be allowed to sit for such a borough.[36]

All the same, we should not seek for an unbroken independent labour tradition, from Chartism into ILP. On its dissolution Greening's election committee handed on its funds to the Halifax Liberal Electoral Association; and were not those man-eating tigers, Geo. Webber and Ben Wilson, toasting Gladstone in lemonade in 1885? In 1884 19-year-old Tom Maguire was writing to the *Christian Socialist*, warning that land nationalisation might prove a

diversion from the main assault on the bastions of capitalism, as
Corn Law Repeal had proved before:

> Do you not remember, good folk, the Bright and Cobden cry of
> 'Free Trade and Corn Law Repeal', which along with capitalis-
> tic combination, annihilated Chartism, the only genuine political
> movement of modern times in favour of the people? ... Ernest
> Jones and Bronterre O'Brien are forgotten, ridiculed, out of
> history. John Bright and Richard Cobden are household words.[37]

The surviving Chartists, and many of their sons, had come to terms
with Liberal Radicalism; they were (as Engels said) the grandchil-
dren of the old Chartists who were now 'entering the line of
battle',[38] rediscovering Chartist traditions from family or local
folk-lore or published reminiscences.[39] A quite remarkable proportion of the young men and women prominent in the early
Yorkshire ILP claimed Chartist forebears or the influence of
Chartist traditions in their childhood.[40] 'Eh, love, you cannot
understand now', one Chartist great grandfather said to a little girl
who was to become a leader of the Bradford textile workers, 'but
when you get to be a big girl I want you always to think for the
people, and live for the people, for it will be a long time before
they can do it for themselves.'[41]

One further ingredient must not be overlooked: Radical Nonconformity. We may leave on one side the futile and unhistorical
argument that goes by the name, 'Methodism or Marxism?' The
attempt to suggest that the ILP was founded by a slate of Methodist
parsons and local preachers is even more wildly inaccurate than the
attempt to attribute it to the single-handed efforts of Engels and
Aveling. Of those prominent in its formation in Yorkshire, Tom
Maguire was an atheist with an Irish-Catholic background; Isabella
Ford a Quaker; Ben Turner and Allan Gee (a late convert from
Liberalism) were secularists;[42] Alf Mattison was a disciple of Edward
Carpenter; John Lister a Catholic; Walt Wood, the gasworkers'
leader, would appear to have been a happy pagan – as may have been
Paul Bland and Tom Paylor;[43] only Jowett, W.H. Drew, and perhaps
Balmforth of Huddersfield, among the initiators of the movement,
suggest themselves as active Nonconformists. In truth, Radical Non-

conformity had become a retarding social and political influence in
the eighties, its face set in a perpetual grimace at the Established
Church and the Anglican landed aristocracy; the face was, only too
often, the face of a mill-owner, like Alfred Illingworth, the Nonconformist worsted-spinner, whom Tillett fought in West Bradford. The
Bradford textile workers owed their socialism no more to the Methodist Church than the peasants of South Italy owe their communism
to the Catholic; and if the socialists succeeded in sweeping whole
chapel-fulls of the former into the movement, by their broad, unsec-
tarian, ethical appeal, the credit is due to them and not to the
Nonconformist 'Establishment' which fought the ILP every inch of
the way.

Once the break-through had been made, it is true that the
movement gained a moral dimension; that Radical Christian
tradition, which had been seen before on a Luddite scaffold and in
Chartist chapels and camp meetings, swept the West Riding like a
revivalist campaign; we meet again the full-toned moral periods,
the Biblical echoes, the references to the Sermon on the Mount.[44]
It is not a question of creed, belief, or church, but a question of
language, a question of moral texture. It was as much a revolt
against organised Christianity as a form of Christian expression.
The Yorkshire ILP was a sturdy cross-bred. Its leaders owed much
of their theory to Marxist propagandists; but they preferred the
moral exhortations of William Morris to the doctrinaire tones of
Hyndman, and they were happier with 'Nunquam' than with
Quelch. When they found out that Tillett was a Congregationalist,
it made a fine propaganda point with the electorate.[45] But this was
not among their reasons for their choice of him as candidate; he
was selected as a prominent new unionist and a socialist.[46]
Nonconformity – 'Radical' Nonconformity – was outraged. The
Bradford and District Nonconformist Association passed a unanimous resolution of confidence in Alfred Illingworth, MP, the
'widely-esteemed Nonconformist', and a correspondent to the
Bradford Observer wrote of the ILP's intervention in terms that
suggest they were guilty of sacrilege:

A humble but ardent supporter of a politician whom I regard as
a constant and sagacious servant of God and the people, how

could I see without sorrow, and I may say horror, the entrance of Mr Ben Tillett to fasten like a viper on his throat?[47]

Mr Illingworth's throat now and, the implication runs, God's throat next. The Nonconformist Association called a public meeting in support of both, with a pride of reverends on the platform. Tillett's followers packed the meeting, and Drew and Pickles intercepted Jowett – on his way to a Co-operative meeting – with the cry: 'You are just the man we want'. At the public meeting, Briggs Priestley, MP, presided, fresh from an unpopular piece of parliamentary sabotage against a Factory Bill. One after the other, two reverends were shouted down; then the audience stormed the platform, pushing up Jowett, Minty, and Pickles (dubious 'nonconformists', these last two), and remaining in uproar until Jowett was allowed to move an amendment. Impressively he warned the clergy: 'If you persist in opposing the labour movement there will soon be more reason than ever to complain of the absence of working men from your chapels':

> The labourers would establish a Labour Church (cheers and 'Bravo Jowett') and there they would cheer for Jesus Christ, the working man of Nazareth (cheers).[48]

The Labour Churches in Bradford and Leeds, when they were established, were not only undenominational; it is also difficult to describe them as Christian or religious in any sense except that of the broad ethical appeal of the 'religion of socialism' whose text was Morris's 'Fellowship is Life'. They retained sufficient ceremonial forms, and a sufficient admixture of Christian speakers, for the Nonconformist members to feel at home; but the 'hymn' might be Maguire's 'Hey for the Day!' and the 'sermon' might be by Edward Carpenter from a text from Whitman. Carpenter's friend and disciple, Alf Mattison, was first secretary of the Leeds Labour Church, while the 'sermon' at the Bradford Labour Church, on the occasion of the foundation conference of the ILP, was preached by George Bernard Shaw – a tactful but uncompromising address which ended with the avowal that he was an atheist.[49] We must not underestimate the importance of the religious associations drawn upon in the speeches of Hardie or Tillett; these reverberated in the hearts of a generation who had picked up their little education in Sunday school or chapel. But these owed little to any doctrine of personal salvation or personal sin; the sin was the sin of the capitalist class, and salvation must come through the efforts of the working class itself, expressed through solidarity and brotherhood, and aspiring towards a co-operative commonwealth. Tom Mann, when he stumped Yorkshire, had little Christian charity to spare for non-union men or blacklegs, even though he was willing enough to employ the parable of the Good Samaritan as a scourge on the back of the Ossett Corporation which had let out its scavenging by contract.[50] The broad ethical appeal was the same, whether it was voiced by the Quaker Isabella Ford, or Margaret McMillan ('Educate every child as if it were your own'), or by the free-thinker Charles Glyde: 'I wish to treat all poor as I would my own father, mother, sister, or brother'.[51] In the early nineties this ethical appeal gave fervour, self-confidence and stamina to the movement; later, when it was taken out of its direct social context and transformed into platform rhetoric by such men as Snowden and Grayson, it was to smudge political understanding and weaken the movement. But in 1892 this authentic moral revolt was one of the first indications to a close observer that the ILP had come to stay: 'it is of the people – such will be the secret of its success'. The letter is from Tom Maguire to Edward Carpenter:

> Now the mountain, so long in labour, has been delivered of its mouse – a bright active cheery little mouse with just a touch of venom in its sharp little teeth ... Our mouse though young in the flesh is old in the spirit, since to my own knowledge this is its third reincarnation ....
>
> You will find in your travels that this new party lifts its head all over the North. It has caught the people as I imagine the Chartist movement did. And it is of the people – such will be the secret of its success. Everywhere its bent is Socialist because Socialists are the only people who have any message for it.[52]

II

No man had worked harder for this than Maguire. Of poor Irish-Catholic parentage, singled out by the priests for his intelligence, he had found his own way to secularism at the age of 16, joined the Democratic Federation at 17, was finding his feet as an open-air propagandist and a lecturer in the debating clubs and coffee taverns in his 18th year.[53] J.L. Mahon was in Leeds for a period in 1884, and struck up a friendship with him. When the split in the SDF took place, Maguire sided with Morris and was placed on the Provisional Council of the League. He commenced the work of building a small Leeds branch, while also giving aid to Bland, Minty, and Pickles in Bradford.[54] By October 1885 there were sixteen Leeds socialists in good standing: most were young industrial workers, unemployed or on short time.[55]

He went through the whole gamut of experiences which made up the lives of the 'pioneers'; the open-air work, the occasional big meeting for Morris or Annie Besant, the attacks – especially from his old Catholic associates ('we shall live their narrow fury down', he wrote to Mahon[56]), the weekend outings when propaganda and pleasure were combined,[57] the excitement when the first premises were opened, the songs and camaraderie of the fervent sect.[58] A poet, and a man of great intellectual vigour and curiosity, he was naturally drawn to William Morris's side of the movement. But more than most Socialist Leaguers, he knew that the early propaganda was too abstract to achieve a wide popular appeal. As early as 1884 he singled out the Eight Hours' Day demand as of prime importance;[59] although – as a photographer's assistant – he was not a trade unionist himself, he was directing the Socialist League, in 1885, towards work among the miners and the ASE.[60] From the maturity of his late twenties he looked back tolerantly upon these years. 'We were kindly, well-disposed young chaps,' he wrote, whose object was 'the Internationalisation of the entire world.' As time went by, and no progress was made (after four years' propaganda the League branch was only 30 strong), the socialists began to divide:

> Some thought that we might advantageously limit the scope of our ideal to the five continents, while directing our operations more immediately to our own locality. Others were strongly of the opinion that our ideal was too narrow, and they proposed as the object of the society the internationalisation of the known and

undiscovered world, with a view to the eventual inter-solarisation of the planets .... They entirely ignored the locality to which, for the most part, they were comparative strangers ....[61]

The division so parodied followed closely the division between the anarchists and parliamentarians in the national Socialist League. In the wrangles of 1887 and 1888, the Leeds branch sided with the parliamentarians; after 1888, while the Leeds and Bradford Leagues maintained their link with the national body, sold their quota of *Commonweal*, and regarded William Morris with undiminished affection, they took less and less notice of London goings-on. They subscribed now to Keir Hardie's *Miner*; 2s. 6d. was scraped together for the Mid-Lothian election fund; and while Maguire still contributed poems and articles to *Commonweal*, he also maintained a link with Mahon, who had now broken with the League and who produced in 1888 his blueprint for a labour party, *The Labour Programme*.[62] After the Bradford TUC of the same year, the Yorkshire Socialist Leaguers directed their energies towards the two main objectives: the conversion of the trade unions, and propaganda for an independent party of labour. 'A definite step is now being taken towards the formation of a Socialist Labor Party in Leeds', declared a handbill of autumn 1888, which announced lectures by Maguire on 'The Need of a Labour Party', and by Tom Paylor, on 'The Lesson of the Trades Congress'.[63] When Mahon and H. A. Barker launched their Labour Union, Maguire and Pickles (of Bradford) were among the signatories.[64] After Maguire's death, a correspondent in the *Yorkshire Factory Times* commented on the breadth of his reading and the volume of propaganda work which he undertook in these years – 'Three lectures each Sunday, and two, and occasionally three, in the course of the week, in addition to articles, poems, and letters to the press'.

The propaganda gained growing audiences in the coffee taverns, Radical clubs, and at the 'open-air spouting place' – Vicar's Croft. But the Leeds Trades Council was a stronghold of the Liberal skilled unionists, and – except in the ASE – no headway could be made. The break-through, when it came, came in spectacular fashion. Some bricklayers' labourers, attending an open-air meeting, stayed on to discuss their grievances ('rather aimlessly') with

Paylor and Sweeney. The Leaguers offered their clubroom for a committee meeting of the men on the next Sunday. On 30 June 1889 3,000 labourers attended a meeting at which they were addressed by Maguire, Paylor, and other socialists; 200 names were handed in for the new union; a committee elected; within a week several thousand labourers were on strike for a 1/2d. an hour (from 5d, to 5½d.); within five weeks the union was 800 strong, and the strike had ended in victory.[65] A week later the great Dock Strike in London began.

It is a comment upon the divorce between the skilled unionists and the unskilled that the labourers turned to the socialists rather than to the Leeds Trades Council, on which the skilled building unions had long been represented. From the outset the skilled unionists in Leeds regarded the socialist intervention with undisguised hostility, while even the *Yorkshire Factory Times* published a grumbling, suspicious editorial.[66]

The socialists for their part were elated, and were not above rubbing salt in the wound: 'We are endeavouring to organise the unskilled labourers in all branches of industry in the town, since the aristocrats of labour take no steps in organising them'.[67] But no one anticipated the nearly incredible surge of unskilled agitation which engulfed the West Riding in the next twelve months. Trade was brisk, and Maguire repeatedly urged the workers to seize their opportunity; in December he was addressing a demonstration of the newly formed Leeds section of the Gasworkers and General Labourers Union (embracing already gasworkers, maltsters, draymen, general labourers, dyers, and claiming a membership of 3,000) and urging them to press home their advantage while the employers 'could not afford to tarry';[68] a month later he was exhorting a meeting of clayworkers and brickyard labourers 'to go with the flowing tide'.[69] Mattison, the young skilled engineer, helped out the Gasworkers as secretary; he recalled later the shock of surprise when Will Thorne came up to help, with his heavy navvy's boots and knotted red handkerchief.[70] Week after week, Maguire, Paylor, Sweeney, Cockayne, and Turner attended demonstrations, assisted strikes, presided at the formation of new unions: tramway workers, blue dyers, corporation workers, plasterer's labourers, paviour's labourers, mechanic's labourers, axle workers. In October 1889 900 girls struck at Messrs. Arthur's tailoring works, against the deduction of 1d. out of every 1s. earned in payment for motive power on their sewing-machines; despite the selfless assistance of Isabella Ford[71] and Maguire, and the ambiguous support of the Trades Council,[72] the strike ended after the sixth week in a sad collapse.[73] But the defeat scarcely checked the advancing wave of unionism. In late October 1889 the Leeds Tailors' Union (catering at first chiefly for Jewish workers) was formed, with Maguire in the chair.[74] The Tailoresses' Union continued to grow, with the particular assistance of Isabella Ford. When some 3,000 tailoring workers went on strike, Maguire was adviser, organiser, and poet, writing for them 'The Song of the Sweater's Victim', 'the singing of which by several hundred Jews in their broken English may be better imagined than described':

> ... every worker in every trade,
>   In Britain and everywhere,
>   Whether he labour by needle or spade,
>   Shall gather in his rightful share.[75]

In March these new unions still remained outside the Trades Council, and had grouped in a new body called the 'Yorkshire Labour Council'.[76] The first May Day in Leeds was celebrated by this Council, in association with the Gasworkers. The procession alone was estimated at 6,000, headed by the banner of the Leeds Jewish Tailors, Pressers, and Machinists: a band playing the 'Marseillaise': 1,100 Jewish tailors: 900 slipper-makers: 800 gasworkers: dyers, maltsters, teamsters, and labourers. Between the slipper-makers and the gasworkers there marched the smallest and proudest contingent – 40 members of the Leeds Socialist league. Maguire presided at the main platform, where the demonstration was swelled by several thousand, and a resolution passed endorsing the 'necessity of an Eight Hour Day ... as the first step towards the abolition of national and industrial war; the overthrow of race hatred; and the ultimate emancipation of Labour'.[77] The Annual Report of the Leeds Trades Council for 1890 mentions neither May Day nor the gas strike, but recorded the Council's resolution in October (on a small majority vote) 'that a general Eight Hour's legislative measure is impracticable'.[78]

Maguire, Paylor, Mattison – all were in their early twenties when this sudden elevation from the status of a sect to that of leaders and advisers to the unskilled of half a populous county took place. They had no national advisers. Morris was retiring in disgust from the anarchist playground which the London League was becoming; anyway, he was writing 'News from Nowhere', which his Leeds followers read eagerly in the odd half-hours spared from union organising[79] – although he found time to deliver his last notable address for the League, on 'The Class Struggle', in Leeds in March 1890. It is a noble and far-seeing lecture, but its only practical proposal was that a General Strike for socialism might be the best next step – for which advice Maguire and Paylor moved a hearty vote of thanks.[80] Forty miles away, at Millthorpe, Edward Carpenter watched events with awe; he had no advice to offer, and his influence upon the Leeds socialists made itself felt in other ways.[81] Cunninghame Graham helped with a fleeting visit, as did Thorne. The only national figure who kept his finger on events in Leeds was Maguire's old friend, J.L. Mahon of the Labour Union; and his reputation was much tarnished by the failure of the London Postmen's Union.[82] The Leeds and Bradford socialists were virtually detached from London and thrown upon their own resources; in May 1889 they held a joint demonstration at the famous Chartist meeting-spot, Blackstone Edge, with the Lancashire branches of the SDF;[83] in July of the same year a Yorkshire Socialist Federation was set up.[84] But their own resources were not slender. The years of seemingly fruitless propaganda, when the joint forces of Leeds and Bradford socialism had tramped like a group of youth hostellers, spreading 'the gospel' in villages and singing Morris's songs in country lanes,[85] had not been wasted. Maguire and Jowett, in their very early twenties, both showed astonishing maturity; they had gained a fund of experience, a clear theory of politics, and a self-confidence and *élan*, which prepared them for those vintage years, 1889–92, when (in Ben Turner's words) 'it was not alone a labour of love, but a labour of joy, for the workers seemed awake'.[86]

The climax to Leeds new unionism, and the final proof of the

ability of Maguire's small group, came in the gas strike (or
lock-out) of June–July 1890. The rapid organisation of the previous
winter had won, without a struggle, sweeping gains for the men,
including the eight-hour day. In the summer of 1890, when the
demand for gas fell off, the Gas Sub-Committee of the Liberal-
dominated municipal council, determined to counter-attack with all
the forces at its command, and to enforce the withdrawal of certain
concessions.[87] A short, but violent and extremely ill-tempered,
struggle ensued. The Gas Committee alienated general working-
class and much middle-class sentiment by its stupid and high-
handed tactics, particularly its elaborate attempts to displace local
men by blacklegs imported (often under false pretences) from great
distances and at great cost to the ratepayers. Worse, it made itself
ridiculous in a hundred ways; the villain in the public eye was its
chairman, Alderman Gilston, well known for his Radical Home
Rule speeches and his claims to be a 'friend of the working
classes'; another Liberal councillor set Leeds laughing by his
renderings of 'Rule Britannia' for the entertainment of blacklegs
temporarily housed in the Town Hall crypt. Ridicule grew as those
few blacklegs who were transported to the gasworks turned out to
be incapable of performing the work, or asked to be sent home at
the town's expense. At the height of the struggle, a ludicrous
procession moved through the surging crowds in the town centre;
several hundred blacklegs, headed by cavalry, surrounded by a
double file of police, and a file of military, and followed by the
Mayor and magistrates. As they passed beneath the Wellington
Road railway bridge, coal, sleepers, bricks, bottles, and assorted
missiles were hurled down by pickets and sympathisers upon the
civic procession. Arriving in the new Wortley gasworks in a 'very
excited and exhausted state', the blacklegs at once held an
indignation meeting in protest against their inadequate protection.
Then – when pickets climbed on the walls to shout – they fled
over the rear walls 'by the dozen' until only 76 remained inside.
For several days the town was like an armed camp. On one side,
Hussars with drawn swords patrolled the streets in defence of the
Liberal Gas Committee; on the other, railwaymen, corporation
workers, and even (it would seem) individual policeman, combined
to give information to the pickets. When the strikers returned, with

almost complete victory, it was estimated that the affray had cost
the town £20,000.[88]

Maguire and Paylor, and their leading converts among the gasworkers, Walt Wood and Cockayne, bore the brunt of the struggle.
They tried

> to get the crowd into peaceful ways, but blood was shed
> nevertheless. In the morning after the first night of the riots, it
> was a sight to see the leaders of the union telling the members
> off to duty, arranging picketing work, and getting the men who
> had been deceived ... off home.[89]

Maguire, rather than Thorn, deserved the copy of *Capital* which
Engels gave to the victor of the struggle.[90] Moreover, in the height of
the struggle he saw his political opportunity, and struck home hard.
He addressed both of the mass demonstrations on the two Sundays of
the strike, and drove home the lesson of the independence of labour.
If the Leeds Gas Committee persisted in their course, he said, 'the
Liberal party of the town would get such a knockdown blow as they
would never recover from ... ' How long (he asked) are the working
classes of this town 'going to return people to the Council who, when
returned, use the forces of the town against the working classes?'[91]
From this point on, many skilled unionists in Leeds began to turn
away from Liberalism.[92]

If the first strong link in the chain which led to the ILP was forged
in the gas strike, it also led to the breaking of the last link which
bound the Leeds socialists to the Socialist League. The occasion was
a quarrel in the local club. 'Those of us who had to do with the
gasworkers, in response to the men's wishes and in accordance with
our ideas of policy, considered a Labour Electoral League should be
formed', Maguire wrote to Carpenter. 'Our Anarchist friends, who
were conspicuous by their absence in the gas fights', 'told the people
that no policy should be entertained but physical force':

> I admit the Labour Electoral move is not all to be desired, but it
> seemed the next immediate step to take in order to keep the
> Labour unions militant, and to emphasise the conflict of the
> workers and the employers.

The incident disgusted him: 'as usual with Socialists when they fall out, all kinds of personal attacks and insinuations have been the order of the day'.[93]

The majority of the Leeds socialists went out with Maguire, to be followed, shortly after, by the Bradford Socialist League. Both groups formed socialist clubs, and soon, as a more stable form of organisation, these adopted a Fabian disguise; over the next year a rash of Fabian Societies spread across West Yorkshire, until the London Fabians became quite uneasy at the threatened permeation.[94] But the Fabian Society offered no more prospect for turning the mass industrial unrest into political channels than had the Socialist League; and it was only with the formation of the Bradford Labour Union that the political wing of the movement got under way. 'I thought of a new move', recalled James Bartley, then a sub-editor on the *Workman's Times*, who initiated the first meeting:

> On Sunday, April 26th, 1891, I took the first steps for putting it into operation. That particular Sunday ... was a bright sunshiny day. I went to Shipley ... in order to consult Mr W.H. Drew. ... He was attending anniversary services at Bethel Baptist Chapel, but during a lull in the proceedings I called him out to the chapel-yard. Here we talked over the situation ....[95]

When the Bradford Labour Union was finally founded in May it was under the heading Independent Labour Party. 'Suddenly a name was coined that hit off the genius of the English people', Maguire later said. From this moment it 'went like wildfire'.[96] Why was its birthplace Bradford and not Leeds?

III

Leeds was to provide a remarkable example of arrested development. Despite its early vigour, the movement met repeated barriers; the first authentic ILP councillor in Leeds was not elected until 1906, when Jowett had already done fourteen magnificent years of service on the Bradford Council – eight miles away! But if we note the social and industrial contrasts, some of the reasons become apparent. Leeds was not as close-knit a community as other West Yorkshire towns: its industries were more diverse. The unskilled male workers were in general successful in improving their conditions as a result of the new unionism, and some of their discontent was dispersed: the gas strike was short, sharp, and victorious where that at Manningham Mills was long, humiliating, and a defeat. Social antagonisms were modified by the interpolation of many intermediate strata between the mass of the workers and employers, including those skilled workers who owed a traditional allegiance to Lib-Labism.

It is this last fact, above all, which accounts for the failure of the Leeds ILP to gather the momentum of Bradford. Although the new unions affiliated to the Trades Council after the gas strike, and the Yorkshire Labour Council was dissolved,[97] the old guard on the Trades Council maintained a controlling influence. In September 1891 they seemed to be drawing together, with a successful mass demonstration addressed by Mann and Tillett; and a Labour Electoral Union was sponsored by the Council, on independent lines.[98] But the Trades Council insisted on maintaining the right of veto over the Labour Union, and the old guard sought to exercise this in the Liberal interest; finally, in 1892, it severed its connection with the Union, which became the Leeds ILP.[99] Hence the impressive unity between Trades Council and ILP which was the leading feature of developments in Bradford, Halifax, and the heavy woollen district was never to be found in Leeds.

This political friction was only to be expected in a centre where the Trades Council had a history covering a quarter-century, and the leaders of the skilled unions had a place in the Liberal firmament. But the problem was aggravated by socialist errors and accidents of person. In 1890 Maguire's old friend, J.L. Mahon, returned to Leeds. Maguire had defects as a political leader – he was without personal ambition and incapable of political guile. In the intervals between storms (when necessity drove him to the front) he preferred to advise from the background.[100] He allowed Mahon – who shared none of his dislike of the limelight – to assume the leadership of the Leeds movement; perhaps he was glad to be relieved of the responsibility he had borne for so long.

Mahon was a man of great ability: the idea of Labour Unions

was largely his. He had done stalwart service for the Socialist
League in the past. But now his many defects were gaining on his
virtues. He was vain, incurably quarrelsome, and given to intrigue,
and he inspired neither loyalty nor trust. It would be tedious to
recount the rows that gathered around him between 1890 and 1893.
He wrangled inside the Gasworkers' Union:[101] he was prominent in
a sensational row between the Gasworkers and the Trades Council
over the School Board election of November 1891:[102] he allowed
himself to be drawn into a long and unsavoury public quarrel with
John Judge, the leader of the old unionists.[103] Finally, he allied
himself wholeheartedly with Champion's attempt to 'nobble' the
ILP in 1892. He flaunted Tory 'sympathies' in an attempt to shock
Liberal working men from their allegiance.[104] With Champion's
money, and under Champion's day-to-day direction, he stood as
Independent Labour candidate for South Leeds in September 1892
– a by-election which ended in riot and anticlimax, but which did
as much as anything to raise the well-justified taunt of 'Carlton
Club money' which hung around the ILP at its foundation
conference.[105] 'What a cunning chap he is,' Carpenter wrote to
Mattison, – 'I can't say I like him. I wonder how Maguire feels
about it all.'[106] But Maguire's opinions are not recorded. Mahon
and Champion between them nearly succeeded in smashing the ILP
on the eve of its foundation; and yet Maguire's old friendship for
Mahon, and his hatred for personal rancour and intrigue, led him to
retreat into his shell.[107]

In the woollen districts the development was quite different.
Here the origins were less spectacular: but when the movement
began in earnest, the entire trade-union movement swung round
behind it. In 1886 that other remarkable young Yorkshire socialist,
Ben Turner, could only get two other members for a Huddersfield
branch of the SDF.[108] The Bradford League, in its early years,
depended a good deal upon speakers and guidance from Leeds; it
paid serious attention to the trade unions only after the Bradford
TUC of September 1888.[109] The extant minute-books of the
Bradford Trades Council have a hiatus between July 1889 and
January 1893. As the former minute-book closes, the Trades
Council claims to represent 3,000 workers, mainly outside the
textile industry. Its secretary, Sam Shaftoe, is a prominent unionist

of the old Lib-Lab school, and the Council is still negotiating
humbly with the Liberal Association for a member on their School
Board Eight. When the latter minute-book commences, the Council
claims 10,000 members, Drew of the weavers is on its executive,
Shaftoe has disappeared, Cowgill – an ILPer from the ASE – is
secretary, and the Council is functioning in close alliance with the
ILP.[110]

Three events dictated this transformation; the publication of the
Yorkshire Factory Times, the influence of the Leeds unskilled
agitation, and the events surrounding the Manningham Mills strike.
Andrews, the proprietor of the *Cotton Factory Times*, started the
Yorkshire journal largely as a commercial venture; it was his
policy to employ the local union men as correspondents, and Drew,
Bartley, Turner and Gee were placed on the staff, with Burgess as
the first editor. Its influence achieved in a few months what the
painstaking efforts of organisers had failed to achieve in years. Its
dramatic effect in the woollen districts, as propagandist for trade
unionism, has been described in the vivid pages of Ben Turner's
reminiscences.[111] Bad masters were exposed, grievances aired,
successes advertised. With the textile workers on the move, the
unskilled struggles in Leeds spilled over into the towns and
villages to the West, swelling the tide. Maguire, Paylor, Turner,
Mattison, organised the gasworkers and clayworkers at Halifax,
where 9,000 were claimed at a demonstration in the autumn of
1889.[112] Railwaymen were organised in other towns. In December
1890 the Manningham strike commenced.

This strike, which at its peak involved nearly 5,000 workers and
which dragged through a bitter winter until the end of April 1891
has often been described. Here we may select only certain features
for comment. (1) Contrary to the general impression, it was not the
most-depressed but the better-paid workers – velvet and plush
weavers – who initiated the strike. The several thousand unskilled
women and girls who later thronged the streets came out in
sympathy or were forced out by the firm in order to embarrass the
strike fund.[113] (2) Sympathy was aroused for the strikers, not only
by their inexperience and pitiful plight, but also by the explanation
of S.C. Lister that it was necessary to bring down their wages to
continental standards, and peg them to the rate paid at his mills in

Crefeld. This 'continental threat' the *Yorkshire Factory Times* took up as 'a distinct challenge to all the textile workers in the two counties of Lancashire and Yorkshire'.[114] (3) The outstanding organisers of the strike – Turner, Drew, and Isabella Ford – were proclaimed socialists; Turner, living in Leeds, was in constant contact with the Leeds socialists, although his earlier experiences in West Yorkshire, where he had received generous assistance from Liberal unionists of the old school, led him to take up a mediating role. (4) It was the repeated attempts by chief constable, watch committee, town clerk, and Mayor to prevent the strikers and sympathisers from holding meetings, at first in halls, and then in customary open-air meeting-places (thus provoking the famous riots in Dockers' Square) which, willy-nilly, forced to the very forefront the question of independent political action. It was this struggle which induced the strikers to fetch up Ben Tillett for a great protest meeting; and he voiced their sentiments when he declared that 'at election times the people can teach would-be Caesars – town clerks and Mayors and watch committees – a salutary lesson'.[115] After the strike was defeated, the *Factory Times* commented:

> The operatives have from the first been fought not only by their own employers at Manningham but by the whole of the monied class of Bradford. From the highest dignitary down to the lowest corporate official 'law and order' has been against them.[116]

'In future,' warned Drew, when presenting the balance sheet of the strike, 'capitalists will have to reckon with whole communities of labour rather than sections.'[117]

This, then, was the background to Bartley's discussion with Drew in the yard of the Bethel Baptist chapel. Even so, the formation of the Bradford Labour Union was only one in a chain of similar attempts, each of which had been re-absorbed within the Liberal Party;[118] and at any time in the next year the Labour Union might have met with the same fate. Its programme, like that of the Colne Valley Labour Union, was largely a list of radical-democratic demands, adapted from Mahon's

Labour Programme of 1888 which clearly provided the model.[119] Despite the admonition, 'Workmen, Remember November' placarded in the streets from the time of the Manningham strike, only one Trades Council nominee was successful in the 1891 municipal elections, and he was the staunch old unionist, Shaftoe, who – when he had done his duty by securing guarantees from the Council for the right of public meeting – fell back into the Liberal Party, which rewarded him with nomination to the bench.[120] Moreover, the Bradford and Colne Valley Labour Unions had the utmost difficulty in finding suitable candidates to nurse the constituencies. Tillett and Mann were up to their necks holding the Dockers' Union together, and beating off an employers' counter-attack; Shaw said the Bradford working men should choose one of their own number, and not run after the 'tall hats and frock coats'.[121]

At length Blatchford was persuaded to nurse East Bradford, only to withdraw, without an apology to the electors, when the launching of the *Clarion* absorbed all his time.[122] Tillett was persuaded to stand for Bradford West only when presented with 1,000 electors' signatures, and after a deputation from the Labour Union had visited the Dockers' Annual Congress.[123] Mann, when invited by Colne Valley, held aloof longer; he was wondering about permeating the Church; he had his eye on the ASE; he was doubtful about parliamentary action; he thought the Colne Valley men should get down to trade unionism and municipal action before they talked of Parliament.[124] The Yorkshire men had to solve their problems on their own.

In truth, it was a miracle that the Labour Unions survived into 1892, and multiplied so fast. This could not have been done without a resolute and capable local socialist leadership, aided by the inflexibility and stupidity of the local Liberal employers. It was a longer step than we realise from the running of occasional Labour candidates for council or school board, even against official Liberal nominees, to the formation of an independent party, pledged to a socialist programme. The Labour Union men was assisted by the uncompromising advocacy of Blatchford and Burgess; by the proportional representation system operating in local board elections, which enabled them to win spectacular and morale-building victories;[125] but above all, by the advance of the Trades Council movement.

The Trades Councils, even more than the Labour Unions, were the organisational unit upon which the West Yorkshire ILP was based. Among Trades Councils re-formed or formed at this time were Halifax (1889), Huddersfield (1890), Keighley (1890), Brighouse (1892), Spen Valley (1891), the Heavy Woollen District (Dewsbury & Batley, 1891); the Yorkshire Federation of Trades Councils – the first county federation – was founded in 1893.[126] In almost every case, these were formed by socialists and new unionists with the direct aim of promoting independent political action; in some cases, the Trades council formed the local ILP as its political arm.[127] The socialists no longer sowed their propaganda broadcast or at thinly-attended meetings; they directed it first and foremost at the unionists, urging them to take political action, at first in the field of local politics.

> Men of an antagonistic class [declared Maguire, addressing a demonstration of 2,000 gasworkers and labourers at Dewsbury in July 1891], were sent upon their various public bodies to manage their town's affairs. Men who polluted rivers and filled the air with smoke from their chimneys were sent to their Council chambers to carry out the Acts of Parliament to prevent the pollution of rivers and the air.[128]

Since the Trades Councils were young, the socialists encountered little opposition. At Bradford, Shaftoe was too good a trade unionist to stand aside from the tide of new unionism; he played his full part, speaking often alongside Paylor, Turner, and Drew, becoming secretary of the newly formed Woolcombers' Union, and although he was known to oppose the ILP he held his silence during Tillett's 1892 candidature.[129] At Halifax the Liberals delivered themselves into the hands of the ILP by an act of crass stupidity. Beever, the President of the Trades Council, had been converted to socialism and was taking an active part in the local Fabian propaganda in late 1891, but another prominent and influential member, Tattersall, was still a member of the Liberal executive. In 1892 both Beever and

Tattersall were sacked, one after the other, by the same firm; the reason given, 'they did not want anyone in their employ who was engaged in setting labour against capital'.[130] It was well known in the town that the most influential partner in the firm was also a leading member of the local Liberal caucus, and the indignation in the town was so intense that testimonials were raised, demonstrations held, a Labour Union formed – the month after Tattersall's dismissal – on the initiative of the Trades Council, and a month later Keir Hardie was addressing a mass meeting which resolved that 'the time has come when a national and independent Labour Party must be formed'.[131] Two months later again, in November 1892, Beever, Tattersall, Lister, and one other ILP candidate were swept on to the town council, while in January 1893, in the ILP's first parliamentary by-election, Lister, the local squire, mine-owner, and Fabian, who had come to socialism by way of Marx's *Capital* and Tom Maguire, polled 3028 votes against the Liberal 4,617 and the Tory 4,219.

Indeed, this last incident points the pattern which can be seen throughout the West Riding. At Leeds the Liberal Gas Committee. At Colne Valley, the sitting Liberal member, Sir James Kitson – the 'Carnegie' of the West Riding, whose firm ex-Royal Commissioner of Labour Tom Mann described as having 'worse conditions ... than could be found in any other engineering firm in ... Leeds'.[132] At Halifax the Liberal employer, sacking the Trades Council leaders. In a dozen boroughs and urban districts Liberal councillors refusing trade-union demands for 'fair contracts' or artisan dwellings. In Holmfirth the Liberal Association which rejected the eight-hour day to the disgust of the miners' delegates who forthwith resigned.[133] In Shipley the Liberal caucus, where three men were 'ruling the roost', which held down Radical contendents.[134] In Bradford the worsted-spinning Liberal Nonconformist MP and the Liberal Watch Committee. In every case social and industrial agitation on questions in the immediate, everyday experience of the working people, confronted the face – sometimes complacent, sometimes oppressive, sometimes just plain stupid – of established Liberalism. As the people recoiled in confusion and anger, the socialists seized their opportunity and founded the ILP.

IV

How far was the Yorkshire ILP an authentic socialist party? How far was it a late product of Liberal-Radicalism, carried by a temporary tide of industrial and social unrest into independent political channels? The evidence is conflicting. Lister, in his 1893 contest at Halifax, went out of his way to emphasise that he was a labour, and not a socialist, candidate.[135] Calculations at Halifax and Bradford suggest that a fair number of votes were drawn from former Conservative electors, but undoubtedly the majority came from Liberal electors or from young men voting for the first time.[136] In 1897 Tom Mann fought a by-election at Halifax, polling 2,000 votes. In an after-the-poll speech he paid tactful and generous tribute to Lister, but –

> most excellent man as he was ... his particular appreciation of Socialism, his method of advocating Socialism, his speaking of it as advanced Liberalism ... was one of the chief reasons he had succeeded in getting the number of votes he had. (Cheers.) In his judgement the Socialist movement generally, and the Independent Labour Party particularly, did not at the last fight reach that particular stage when the issues were sufficiently clearly defined .... He contended that there were more Socialists in Halifax today than there were when Mr Lister polled 3,800. (Cheers.) [137]

The first years of the Halifax ILP bear out this judgment; endless bickering and defections in the 600-strong branch called upon the time of Hardie, Mann, and even the Annual Conference and revealed how many disgruntled Liberals and even Tories had been swept into the movement in 1892.

No doubt this was true elsewhere, and helps to explain a certain decline in support in the late nineties. It is true also that socialist demands were sometimes tacked on to liberal-democratic demands in an almost ludicrous manner, to disarm opposition or as a casual afterthought.[138] But this is only half the truth, and the less important half. The Yorkshire ILP was a party of youth; its leaders – Maguire, Ben Turner, Jowett – were young; the men and women who staffed the Labour unions and clubs, the Labour churches, the trade unions and Trades Councils, were often in their twenties. And the young people were socialists – ardent followers of Hardie, Morris, Blatchford, Tillett, Mann. When Blatchford accepted the East Bradford nomination he was uncompromising in his socialist advocacy: 'the earth and all that the earth produced – the tools they used, the land and all the capital belonged to the people'. The *Yorkshire Factory Times* commended this doctrine in its editorial, as

> the foundation upon which the Independent Labour Party must be built. It is a rock, and is irremovable. It is as firmly fixed as the earth itself. It is a line of demarcation over which neither Liberal nor Tory may pass and retain his creed.[139]

It was this socialist conviction which prevented the Bradford men from surrendering to Liberal blandishment, when Tillett was offered a straight fight with the Tory in West Bradford.[140] The young socialist delegates gave an overwhelming rebuff to Mahon's attempt to draw the socialist teeth of the ILP at its first conference. In October 1894 the delegates at the Yorkshire Federation of the ILP were dissuaded from voting for a change of name to the 'Socialist Labour Party' only by the advocacy of Maguire who (at 29) was 'as old a Socialist as any in the room'.[141]

In private – it is true – Maguire had his doubts. There were troubles enough in the early ILP – enough to make him wish to concentrate on his writing for the *Factory Times* and *Labour Leader*, or to prefer a part in the unemployed agitation to 'your damned party politics and silly quarrels'.

> People call themselves Socialists [he wrote to a friend], but what they really are is just ordinary men with Socialist opinions hung round, they haven't got it inside of them .... It's hard, very hard; we get mixed up in disputes among ourselves ... and can't keep a straight line for the great thing, even if we all of us know what that is.[142]

No doubt, as a confirmed atheist, he distrusted the spell-binding

'Come to Jesus' appeal which the new men like Snowden were
bringing into the movement. [143] His early maturity seemed to be
giving way to a premature middle-age, hastened by illness and
perhaps by the lurking awareness that he was soon to 'be eternally
elbowed out of place after one small scrappy peep at the big
show'. Not yet 30, he was to be found more and more often
drinking in the Leeds Central ILP Club, telling stories of the 'old
days' like an old-timer, and entertaining the company with
anecdotes and songs. He continued his part in the unemployed
agitation, 'concealing from everybody the fact that he was practically one of the unemployed himself'. Early in March 1895, in his
thirtieth year, he collapsed with pneumonia; his comrades found
him without food or fire in the house; he died on 8 March,
refusing the services of a priest: 'I will stand or fall on the last
twelve years of my life and not on the last five minutes'. His
funeral was attended by a demonstration almost as large as those of
1889–90, in which Jewish tailoring workers and Irish labourers,
gasworkers and ILP councillors, all joined. With his death a phase
of the movement comes to an end. [144]

The young men of the Yorkshire ILP owed much to Maguire.
He had been the point of junction between the theoretical
understanding of the national leaders, the moral teaching of Morris
and Carpenter, and the needs and aspirations of his own people.
Nothing in history happens spontaneously, nothing worthwhile is
achieved without the expense of intellect and spirit. Maguire had
spent his energies without restraint. A poet of real talent, his
feelings had been assaulted by the filth of Leeds; the rag, shoddy,
and wool-combing industries, with their toll of disease and the
dread anthrax. His bitter experiences while organising the tailoresses were recorded in his *Machine Room Chants*; sometimes in
the moving tales of poverty:

No, I wouldn't like to die, sir, for I think the good Lord's hard
On us common workin' women; an' the like o' me's debarred
From His high, uncertain heaven, where fine ladies all go to.
So I try to keep on living', though the Lord knows how I do.

sometimes in humorous sketches of the problems of the organiser:

'They say I am cutting the other girls out
Who work for their bread and tea – no doubt;
　　But, thank you! England's free,
　　　　　　　　　　　　　Te-he!
I will do as I like as long as I dare,
What's fair to me is my own affair,
And I'll please myself anyhow – so there!'
　　　　　Says the Duchess of Number Three.
And the Number Three Department girls
They copy her hat and the cut of her curls –
　　'Tis a touching sight to see,
　　　　　　　　　　　　Dear me!
Her slightest word is their sacred law,
They run her errands and stand her jaw,
Content to find neither fault nor flaw
　　　　　In the Duchess of Number Three.

If many of the Yorkshire young people had in fact got socialism 'inside of them', then something of its quality – the hostility to Grundyism, the warm espousal of sex equality, the rich internationalism – owed much to Maguire. It is time that this forgotten 'provincial' was admitted to first-class citizenship of history, and time also that we discarded the theory of the spontaneous combustion of the Yorkshire ILP.

Notes on the South Leeds Election

On the resignation of the Liberal member for South Leeds in August 1892, J.L. Mahon at once wrote to Champion for his support in financing an Independent Labour Candidate in a three-cornered contest. 'I am rather sick of helping backboneless people into Parliament', Champion replied (27 August 1892). However, after various possible candidates had been approached without success (Mann, Hammill, Clem Edwards, Solly), Champion urged Mahon to stand himself. Champion saw his own part as that of an authoritative Parnell, and wrote to Mahon (5 September 1892): 'If as I am rather inclined to do, I go in for

taking hold of the ILP and running it for all it is worth, I mean
to have as lieutenants men who won't scuttle at the first shot
and will agree with me that our only chance is to go for the
Liberals all along the line without gloves. It is possible, given
pluck to put out 50 Liberals at the next election by running men
in 10 seats and voting Tory in the other 40. That will cause
some little fuss, and will probably put in a Tory Govt. holding
power at the sweet will of the ILP. But it will make the Labour
question in general and 8 hours in particular what the Irish
question has been made by similar tactics ... ' While Champion
scoured the London clubs for money, Mahon implemented this
policy and mounted a campaign on aggressively anti-Gladstonian
lines. From his letters Champion would appear to have been
suffering from delusions of grandeur: he wrote of his conversa-
tions with Chamberlain; his financial resources; his 'personal
adherents' in various towns; his intention of sending the Liberals
'back to opposition'; of buying control of the *Workman's Times*;
of 'exposing' all new union leaders who refused to speak for
Mahon. He sent a strong-arm man from Liverpool (14 September
1892): 'the handiest man with his fists of my acquaintance ...
very good tempered doesn't drink, and never hits anybody first.
But he knows his business and will half kill the biggest
Irishman in Leeds in two minutes.' Votes were not a serious
consideration – 'the main thing is to stoke up the anti-liberal
feeling for the future'. When Keir Hardie came up to help
Mahon, Champion wrote (20 September 1892) 'please assure him
from me, that if he will come and see me on his arrival in
London, I shall be able, and willing, to render him independent
of any attacks he may meet in his Constituency for helping
you.'

Mahon's election manifesto was a long anti-Gladstonian ha-
rangue, culminating in a series of Radical (but not socialist)
demands. The provocation offered to Liberal electors was only
too successful. Mahon's main election meeting was packed with
Gladstonian supporters – with the Irish most prominent; neither
the candidate, nor Tom Maguire (the Chairman), nor H.H.
Champion himself, could gain a hearing; and the meeting ended
in violent riot (*Leeds Mercury, Sheffield Daily Telegraph*, 19

September 1892). Three days later Mahon was disqualified from standing owing to an error in his nomination papers, and the incident ended in general ill-will.

Champion and Mahon remained in correspondence and confidently expected to dominate the first ILP Conference: on 4 November 1892 Champion was writing 'there will practically be none there – outside the local men – but my men.' Even Hardie was marked down as 'going on all right ... If he goes on as he is, I would help him and forgive him his "in-and-out-running" just after the election.' Mahon, for his part, was advising Yorkshire audiences to support those in favour of Chamberlain's 'Labour Programme' unless the Liberals brought out a better one (*Keighley News*, 10 December 1892). His final action in the Yorkshire ILP was to denounce John Lister's candidature at Halifax in February 1893. This curious combination of Parnellite tactics, Tory money, arbitrary intrigue, an apparently 'pro-Tory' interventions, helps to explain the set-back suffered by the Leeds ILP, the bitterness of feeling between old and new unionists on the Leeds Trades Council, and the profound suspicion with which some Socialists (who knew of Champion's and Mahon's strategy) regarded the first year of the ILP.

From *Essays in Labour History*, ed. John Saville

Notes

In collecting material for this essay I am indebted to Mrs Florence Mattison (the widow of Alf Mattison), Miss Norah Turner (daughter of Sir Ben Turner), and Mr A.T. Marles, first secretary of the Leeds Fabian Society, for help, information, and the loan of documents. Among other debts I must mention the kindness of the librarians or officials of the Brotherton Library, Leeds; the Bradford Trades Council; the Bradford Independent Labour Party; and the Colne Valley Labour Party.

1   J. Clayton, *The Rise and Decline of Socialism in Great Britain* (1926), p. 82.
2   Of 115 delegates, 24 came from Bradford, 8 from Leeds, 6 from Huddersfield, 3 from Halifax, and 8 from other parts of West Yorkshire. *Report of the First General Conference, ILP* (1893).

3 Of 305 branches listed in the 1895 Directory, 102 were in Yorkshire, followed by Lancashire (73), Scotland (41), London (29). Of Yorkshire's share we find Bradford (29), Colne Valley (11), Spen Valley (9), Leeds (8), Halifax (8), Huddersfield (8), Dewsbury (5). *ILP Directory* (Manchester, 1895).

4 For Champion, see especially H. Pelling, *The Origins of the Labour Party 1880–1900* (1954), pp. 59–64. For Mahon, see E.P. Thompson, *William Morris, Romantic to Revolutionary* (1955), pp. 614–16, where, however, the direct influence of Mahon's 'Labour Union' model upon the Yorkshire labour unions is under-estimated. For forerunners of the 'independent labour' pattern, see above, p. 271, note 1, and his 'Land and Labour League', *Bulletin of the International Institute of Social History, Amsterdam,* 1953.

5 For Northumberland, see Thompson, *op.cit.* pp. 517 ff. For Bolton, see Dona Torr, *Tom Mann and His Times* (1956), i, pp. 251 ff.

6 Census figures: Leeds (1851) 172,000, (1901) 429,000; Bradford (1851) 104,000, (1901) 280,000.

7 See Joan Thomas, *History of the Leeds Clothing Industry* (Yorkshire Bulletin of Economic and Social Research, 1955), Chapter Two.

8 Ben Turner, *About Myself* (1930), pp. 78–9. Turner had made contact earlier with the SDF and had been attached to a London branch.

9 Amongst the voluminous local literature, the following are of value in marking the 'independent' tradition: G.J. Holyoake, *History of Co-operation in Halifax* (1864); Owen Balmforth, *Huddersfield Industrial Society* (Manchester, 1910); and the reminiscences of John Hartley (*Todmorden & District News*, July 1903) and Joseph Greenwood (*Co-Partnership*, September 1909) – both of the strong Hebden Bridge Society.

10 Garside, born 1843, had a long record in the ASE, radical politics, and co-operative productive ventures, before his election to the County Council for Slaithwaite in March 1892: *Yorkshire Factory Times* (hereafter referred to as *YFT*), 26 February 1904.

11 Shaftoe, secretary to the Bradford Trades Council, was a skep and basket-maker; Bune, the Leeds secretary, was a brush-maker. In 1880 the Bradford TC represented Warpdressers, Stonemasons, Joiners, Plumbers, Lithographers, Engineers, Letterpress Printers, Tailors, Moulders, Hammermen, Dyers, Brush-makers, Skep & Basket-makers, Coach-makers, and Coopers. But six monthly meetings in 1881 were abandoned with 'no quorum' or 'desultory conversation'. (Bradford TC Minutes, 24 September 1880 *et seq.*) The Leeds TC had 33 societies affiliated in 1883; 25 in 1887. (*Annual Report,* 1894, p. 3.)

12 Circular, dated 1887, in Shaftoe Cutting-book (in possession of the Bradford TC).

13 Turner, *op. cit.* p. 93.

14 J. Lawson, *Letters to the Young on Progress in Pudsey* (Stanningley, 1887); F. Peel, 'Old Cleckheaton' in *Cleckheaton Guardian*, 25 January to 4 April 1994.

15 B. Wilson, *The Struggles of an Old Chartist* (Halifax, 1887), 40 pp., p. 40.

16 See Jowett's foreword to F. Brockway, *Socialism over Sixty Years* (1946), pp. 13–24.

17 W. Cudworth, *Condition of the Industrial Classes of Bradford & District* (Bradford, 1887).

18 See, *e.g., Halifax Guardian* for 12 articles on 'The Slums of Halifax' commencing 17 August 1889. Tom Maguire contributed a series of articles on 'Insanitary Leeds' to the *Leeds Weekly Express*, and see also Maguire and other contributors to *Hypnotic Leeds* (Leeds, 1893), edited by A. Marles.

19 Turner's election address for Batley in 1893 in Turner, *op. cit.* p. 171; 1893 Manifesto of Leeds ILP in T. Paylor, *Leeds for Labour* (Leeds, 1905), etc.

20 In 1885, 18,312 half-timers worked in the worsted industry alone, 92 per cent in Bradford district (Cudworth, *op. cit.* p. 10); in 1898, 6,887 half-timers were employed within the Bradford borough boundaries, and 4,086 within Halifax (*The Trade Unionist*, November 1898). On the question of the local exemption standard see the evidence of R. Waddington, secretary of the Half Time Committee of the NUT before the *R.C. on Labour*, 1892, xxxv, Group C, 3662 *et seq.*; and of G.D. Jones, 3855 *et seq.*

21 An old Birstall lady recalled: 'The mill-owners were very cute in dodging factory inspectors .... They had a big whisket handy in the sheds, and when they expected the inspector, we young girls were popped underneath the baskets until he had gone.' *Heckmondwike District News*, 14 August 1926.

22 Cudworth, *op. cit.* p. 20.

23 In 1885 North America did not feature among Batley's markets but was the second export market for Bradford's worsteds. *R.C. on Depression of Trade and Industry* (1886) I, pp. 75, 78.

24 Evidence of Mark Oldroyd of the Dewsbury and Batley Chambers of Commerce, *ibid.*, iii, 14, 105–7.

25 Evidence of H. Mitchell of the Bradford Chamber of Commerce, *ibid.*, ii. 3764 *et seq.* The export of raw material and semi-raw material (tops) was compensating for the decline in worsted stuffs.

26   *Ibid.*, ii. 6494 *et seq.*

27   The amount of the decline was an endless source of controversy; but friendly and unfriendly sources agree upon the fact. Cudworth, *op.cit.* p. 41: 'During the past ten years deductions have been made in wages and quietly submitted to by the workpeople'. See *YFT*, 20 September 1889 (Leeds wage tables, 1872–89); 10 July 1891. *R.C. on Labour*, 1892, xxxv, C, evidence of Gee, Turner and Drew, *passim*, especially 5092, 5124, 5389–411, 5675; 5554 (family wage); 5469, 5548–9 (Manningham Mills). For a summary of evidence presented by the weavers' leaders before the Royal Commission, see Tom Mann, *An Appeal to the Yorkshire Textile Workers* (Huddersfield, n.d., ? 1893).

28   Minutes of power-loom overlookers in possession of Bradford Trades Council; Minutes of Card Setters and Machine Tenters in possession of existing union.

29   It is important to note that even on the crest of the new union wave, with the assistance of the *Yorkshire Factory Times*, only 2 in 9 of the Huddersfield weavers were organised; 1 in 13 in the heavy woollen district; and 1 in 16 in the Bradford district. *R.C. on Labour*, 1892, xxxv, C; evidence of Gee (4790); Drew (5455–8); Turner (5682–3); see Drew's comment (5499) 'when people get down to the pitch to which the textile operatives are in the W. Riding, they have very little heart for anything [and] ... cannot afford even ... the subscription.'

30   Bradford TC Minutes, 29 November 1876. See also Walter Bateson, *The Way We Came* (Bradford, 1928) for the assistance given to the dyers by Shaftoe, who 'worked alongside of them as if he was a dye-house worker himself, and not a member of ... an exceptionally skilled trade – skep-making'.

31   B. Turner, *Heavy Woollen Textile Workers Union* (YFT, 1917), pp. 61–3.

32   The best accounts are in Brockway, *op. cit.* Chapter Two, and M. McMillan, *The Life of Rachel McMillan* (1927), *passim*.

33   The comparison with the cotton industry, with its strong unionism among the male spinners, and the union leaders' opposition to the Legal Eight Hour Day, is instructive.

34   See the evidence of J.H. Beever, secretary of the Halifax Trades Council, when questioned by Mundella at the Royal Commission: 'Well supposing you lost the trade? – Which I do not think probable. Suppose you did and you had passed an Act of Parliament, what would you do then? – Past experience does not send us in that direction.' *R.C. on Labour*, 1892, xxxv, C, 10,040–10,047.

35 Minutes of the Election Committee for Messrs Greening and Stansfeld, 1868 (in our possession).

36 John Lister, 'The Early History of the ILP Movement in Halifax', MSS. in the Mattison Collection, Brotherton Library; and Election Manifesto and copy of *Halifax Free Press* in the same collection.

37 *Christian Socialist*, September 1884.

38 K. Marx and F. Engels, *Selected Correspondence* (1943 edn.), p. 469.

39 Ben Wilson, *op, cit.* was published in 1887; J. Burnley's Chartist novel, *Looking for the Dawn* (Bradford, 1874); Frank Peel, *Risings of the Luddites, Chartists and Plugdrawers* (Heckmondwike, 1888). A gentleman named Aurelius Basilio Wakefield, one-time secretary to the Leeds committee of the Labour Representation League, was indefatigable in the 1870s and 1880s, delivering lectures on Ernest Jones.

40 C.L. Robinson, first ILP councillor in Bradford, had imbibed Chartist principles as a boy, was an admirer of Ernest Jones, and founder of a Republican Club in Bradford in 1870 (*YFT, 15 January 1904*). See also Tattersall, *YFT*, 22 July 1892; Ben Riley, *YFT, 17 June 1904; Ben Turner, About Myself*, pp. 28–9, 66; Philip Snowden, *An Autobiography* (1934), i. pp. 18–19.

41 *YFT, 22 July 1904.*

42 Ben Turner came to regard himself as an undenominational (or perhaps Benturnerite?) Christian, but he never 'belonged' to any Church (information from Miss Norah Turner). For Gee, see *YFT, 15 July 1892.*

43 *YFT, 5 February 1904, and Labour Leader*, 20 April 1901, for biographies of Wood and Bland.

44 At the mass execution of Luddites in 1813, the prisoners sang Methodist hymns on the scaffold. The outstanding West Yorkshire Chartist leader, Ben Rushton, was an expelled local preacher.

45 See *YFT, 17 July 1891: 'Ben is a deep Christian – an earnest, everyday Christian .... He is at home teaching trades unionism or preaching the religion of Christ.'*

46 When Tillett at first refused to stand, J. Bedford (of the General Railway Workers), E.D. Girdlestone, and G.B. Shaw were each invited to stand. *YFT, 15, 22, and 29 May 1891.*

47 *Bradford Observer*, 9 and 13 June 1892.

48 *Ibid.* 14 June 1892; Brockway, *op. cit.* pp. 40–1.

49 *Bradford Observer*, 16 January 1893.

50 *Dewsbury Reporter*, 8 June 1895.

51 *YFT, 14 October 1904.*

52 Isabella Ford (ed.), *Tom Maguire, A Remembrance* (Manchester, 1895), p. xii.

53 *Ibid.* pp. ix–x, xiii: Mattison Letterbook.

54 For the early history of the Leeds and Bradford Leagues, see also Thompson, *op. cit.* pp. 488, 491–4, 496.

55 Correspondence of the secretary, Socialist League, in the International Institute of Social History, Amsterdam; Maguire to Mahon, October and November 1885.

56 *Ibid.* September 1885.

57 See E. Carpenter, *My Days and Dreams* (1916), pp. 134–5; Mattison Notebooks.

58 'The Socialist League stood definitely for a brotherhood built on pure comradeship .... The Paris Commune and Chicago Martyrs anniversaries we used to look forward to .... Songs and speeches were a feature of those gatherings.' W. Hill to A. Mattison, n.d. in Mattison Letterbook.

59 *Christian Socialist*, September 1884.

60 See Maguire, 'The Yorkshire Miners', *Commonweal*, November 1885.

61 *YFT*, 4 November 1892.

62 *Commonweal*, 28 April 1888; Thompson, *op. cit.* pp. 614–15. Jowett was advocating an independent Labour Party in 1887 (*Bradford Observer*, 8 February 1887).

63 Handbill in Mattison Collection.

64 Thompson, *op. cit.* pp. 615–16.

65 Maguire's notes in *Commonweal*, 10 August and 16 November 1889; Thompson, *op. cit.* pp. 618–20; *YFT, 2 August 1889. Tom Paylor was at this time an insurance agent; Sweeney a boot and shoe worker.*

66 It complained at the new unions which accepted as leaders 'outsiders who may have some other object in view than the sole interest of the workers. Joined by a few malcontents from other associations these are organizing attacks on the old and tried officials of the Congress.' *YFT, 30 August 1889.*

67 *Commonweal*, 6 July 1889.

68 *YFT, 13 December 1889.*

69 *Ibid.* 20 December 1890.

70 *Leeds Weekly Citizen*, May 1931.

71 I.O. Ford came from a wealthy Quaker family at Adel Grange, near Leeds. She had helped Miss Paterson with the Women's Provident League. In the summer of 1888 she assisted the Weavers' Union during a strike in Leeds, and from that time forward was associated

with all the new union struggles involving women. *Report ana Balance Sheet of the West Riding Power Loom Weavers Association*, September 1888; and *YFT, 1 November 1889.*

72 *YFT, 1 November 1889, and (for Sweeney's criticisms of the Trades Council officials) 10 January 1890.*

73 *YFT, 25 October 1889 to 27 December 1889.*

74 *Ibid.* 1 November 1889.

75 *Tom Maguire, a Remembrance*, p. xvi; slide of the song in Mrs. Mattison's possession.

76 *YFT, 7 and 28 March 1890.*

77 *Ibid.* 9 May 1890; *Leeds Weekly Citizen*, May 1931.

78 Leeds TC *Annual Report* for year ending 31 May 1891, p. 6.

79 It appeared in instalments in *Commonweal* throughout 1890.

80 *Leeds Mercury*, 26 March 1890; Thompson, *op. cit.* pp. 632 ff.

81 On 12 March 1890, in the midst of the new union struggles, Carpenter was writing to Mattison: 'An interesting book has turned up, by Havelock Ellis, called The New Spirit – on Whitman, Tolstoi, Ibsen, Heine, & others. Everything seems to be rushing on faster & faster. Where are we going? Niagara, or the Islands of the Blest?' Mattison Collection.

82 See Thompson, *op. cit.* pp. 652–3. Mahon and Donald addressed the first demonstration of the Leeds gasworkers, *YFT, 13 December 1889.*

83 *Commonweal*, 4 May 1889; *Leeds Weekly Citizen*, 29 April 1929.

84 *Ibid.* 10 August 1889.

85 See F.W. Jowett, *What Made Me a Socialist* (Bradford, n.d.).

86 Turner, *About Myself*, p. 80.

87 For the full case of the Gas Committee and the union's reply see the letters exchanged between Ald. Gilston, and Tom Paylor in the *Leeds Mercury*, 27 and 28 June 1890.

88 The best accounts of the strike are to be found in the *Leeds Mercury*; *Commonweal* also carried (very strident) reports written by an anarchist.

89 *YFT, 5 February 1904; Tom Maguire, a Remembrance* p. xv.

90 W. Throne, *My Life's Battles* (1925), p. 131 f.

91 *Leeds Mercury*, 30 June 1890.

92 Arthur Shaw of the ASE, President of Leeds Trades Council in 1894 and 1896, relates how – before the gas strike – he 'worked with ardour and perseverance for the success of the Liberal Party'. During the strike he witnessed a Liberal Councillor and 'professed friend of Labour' entertain the blacklegs 'with "Britons never shall be slaves"'. Other Liberals provided them with beer and tobacco,

while at the same time the Leeds gasworkers were provided with military, as another mark of Liberal friendship. This decided me. I vowed I would never again assist either of the Political Parties.' J. Clayton (ed.), *Why I Joined the independent Labour Party* (Leeds, n.d.).

93 *Tom Maguire, a Remembrance*, p. xi.

94 By the end of 1892 there were Fabian Societies at Batley, Bradford, Copley (near Halifax), Halifax, Holmfirth, Huddersfield, Leeds, and Sowerby Bridge; Castleford and Dewsbury were added before May 1893. *List of Members* (Fabian Society, October 1892) and *Tenth Annual Report* of Fabian Society, April 1893. A correspondent in the *Labour Leader*, 20 April 1901, notes that the Bradford Socialist League 'afterwards merged into the Bradford Socialist Society and finally became a branch of the Fabian Society'. The Halifax Fabian Society was especially effective in its propaganda; see Lister MSS. History.

95 *Labour Leader*, 13 April 1901.

96 *Dewsbury Reporter*, 13 October 1894.

97 At the same time the Leeds TC changed its name to the Trades and Labour Council.

98 Leeds Trades Council, *Annual Report*, 1892, pp. 1–2, 6. This was the successor to the Labour Electoral Association which had been founded after the gas strike, with Maguire as secretary and the formidable old unionist, Judge, as treasurer. *YFT, 18 July 1890, and for Judge, 1 July 1892.*

99 *Annual Report*, 1893, p.5.

100 'I'll retire into the corner and write poetry', he declared after the gas strike (*Tom Maguire, a Remembrance*, p. xii). See also letter quoted in Thompson, *op. cit.* p. 703 n. 1: 'Tom .. sinks his own individuality and allows other people to run away with his ideas', etc.

101 Mahon was elected paid assistant secretary of the Yorkshire District of the Gasworkers on a slender majority vote in July 1891. *YFT, 10 July 1891.*

102 *YFT, 20 November 1891.*

103 *Ibid.* 26 February 1892.

104 Information from Mr A.T. Marles.

105 See Note on the South Leeds Election, pp. 315–6.

106 Edward Carpenter to Alf Mattison, 2 October 1892, Mattison Collection.

107 On the occasion of the first National Conference of the ILP Carpenter wrote to Mattison (13 January 1893): '(I see that old

fraud Mahon has got there – Champion too!) I am glad you didn't yield to Mahon about going, and Tom M. I think in his heart cannot be sorry that *you* were elected.' Mattison Collection.

108 Article by Turner in *Yorkshire Evening News*, 1924, in Mattison Cutting-book.

109 Obituary of Paul Bland, *Labour Leader*, 20 April 1901.

110 Bradford TC Minutes, in possession of Bradford Trades Council.

111 Turner, *Heavy Woollen Textile Workers Union*, pp. 65–7: 'The paper opened up a new vista. We scoured Yorkshire textile areas for members, and the Union grew from a few hundreds to a few thousands.' See also Paylor on its effect, in *YFT, 25 December 1891.*

112 *Commonweal*, 19 October 1889; John Lister, a learned antiquarian, was later to write: 'I learned many useful, practical lessons from some of these "agitators" who ... knew far more about the industrial history of our country than I'. Lister MSS. History.

113 *YFT, 19 December 1890, 16 January 1891.*

114 *Ibid.* 6 February 1891. But a German manufacturer wrote to the *Bradford Observer* from Crefeld and claimed that their average wages were *higher* than those in Lister's mills.

115 *Ibid.* 24 April 1891.

116 *Ibid.* 1 May 1891.

117 *Ibid.* 17 July 1891.

118 The Bradford Trades Council was 'considering' contesting East Bradford with a Labour candidate in 1885 (TC Minutes, 10 February 1885). But in 1888 the Liberal Association could only be persuaded with great difficulty to admit a Trades Council nominee to the 'Liberal Eight' for the School Board. (Minutes, 6 November, and entries to 4 December 1889). However a Labour Electoral Association had been formed in 1888, and socialists like Bland, Cowgill, Conellan and Bartley were making themselves felt on the Council. But the LEA was hamstrung by Liberal-Socialist disagreements, and Jowett, who was secretary, let it die. *Labour Leader*, 20 April 1901; Brockway, *op. cit.* p. 31.

119 For Mahon's *Programme*, see Thompson, *op. cit.* p. 615, note 2. For the Bradford Labour Union programme, see *Labour Union Journal*, 30 June 1892. For Colne Valley, see Mann, *op. cit.*

120 Bills and election leaflets in Shaftoe Cutting-book.

121 *YFT,* 29 May 1891.

122 *Ibid.* 15 and 22 January 1892.

123 *Minutes of 2nd Annual Congress of Dockers &c.* (September 1891), pp. 25–6. The signatures have been bound and are preserved by the Bradford Trades Council.

124 Minutes of Colne Valley Labour Union (in possession of C.V. Labour Party). For an example of Mann's views on the priority of trade union and municipal work over parliamentary, see the *Trade Unionist & Trades Council Record*, 5 September 1891; for an example of a reproof aimed at Mann, see editorial, 'Tom Mann and the Representation of Labour', *YFT, 28 August 1891.*

125 *E.g.* at Huddersfield in February 1891, when Balmforth topped the poll in the School Board elections.

126 *YFT, 10 February 1893.*

127 The Heavy Woollen District Trades Council was formed in July 1891, with Ben Turner as secretary, and in only two months was intervening in local elections. Minutes, 15 September 1891 (in possession of Miss Nora Turner).

128 *YFT, 10 July 1891.*

129 *Bradford Observer*, 14 June 1892.

130 *YFT, 1 July 1892. The firm was Clayton, Murgatroyd & Co.*

131 Lister MSS. History and cuttings in Mattison Collection, and *YFT, 20 November 1891.*

132 *Trade Unionist & Trades Council Record*, 7 November 1891.

133 *YFT, 7 August 1891.*

134 *Ibid.* 14 August 1891.

135 Election Manifesto and Lister MSS. History; *Halifax Free Press*, January 1893.

136 Snowden, *op. cit.* i. p. 69: 'the ILP was attracting in the main the young men who were not yet voters'.

137 *Halifax Guardian*, 6 March 1897.

138 In February 1894 a resolution was passed at the Yorkshire Federation of Trades Councils urging the government to 'take up at once the question of the nationalisation of the land, minerals, railways, and all the means of production and distribution, as a means of helping to solve the unemployed question'. *YFT, 16 February 1894.*

139 *YFT, 10 July 1892.*

140 See Burgess in the *Labour Leader*, 20 April 1901.

141 *Dewsbury Reporter*, 13 October 1894.

142 *Tom Maguire, a Remembrance* p. vi.

143 Snowden, *op. cit.* i, p. 82.

144 *Tom Maguire, a Remembrance*; T. Maguire, *Machine Room Chants* (1895); J. Clayton, *Before Sunrise* (Manchester, 1896); miscellaneous cuttings in Turner and Mattison Scrapbooks, and Mattison Notebook.

William Morris

I have in no way altered my opinion that – if we are to acknowledge William Morris as one of the greatest of Englishmen – it is not because he was, by fits and starts, a good poet; nor because of his influence upon typography; nor because of his high craftsmanship in the decorative arts; nor because he was a practical socialist pioneer; nor, indeed, because he was *all* these; but because of a quality which permeates all these activities and which gives to them a certain unity. I have tried to describe this quality by saying that Morris was a great moralist, a great moral teacher. It is in his moral criticism of society (and which of his actions in the decorative arts, or in Anti-Scrape, or the renewal of interest in Icelandic Saga, was not informed by a fundamental criticism of the way of life of his own time?) – and in the crucial position which this criticism occupies in our cultural history at the point of transition from an old tradition to a new [1] – that his greatness is to be found. And this greatness comes to its full maturity in the political writing and example of his later years. I have gained the feeling that – perhaps through fear of controversy and out of respect for admirers of William Morris who do not share his political convictions – this Society has tended to be reticent on this matter. But Morris was one of our greatest men, *because* he was a great revolutionary; a profoundly cultured and humane revolutionary, but not the less a revolutionary for this reason. Moreover, he was a man working for *practical* revolution. It is this which brings the whole man together. It is this which will make his reputation grow as the years advance.

English revolutionaries in the past 100 years have been men without a Revolution. At times they have convinced themselves of the Revolution's imminence. H.M. Hyndman, when he founded the Social Democratic Federation in 1882, looked forward to 1889 as the probable date of its commencement. For a time Morris (whose thinking was greatly influenced by the Paris Commune) shared this cataclysmic outlook. But when he founded the Socialist League in 1884 he had already grown more reticent: 'our immediate aim should be chiefly educational ... with a view to dealing with the crisis if it should come in our day, or of handing on the tradition of our hope to others if we should die before it comes'.

Five years later again, when writing *News from Nowhere*, Morris postponed the commencement of the Revolution to 1952. In the sixty years that would intervene he foresaw much 'troublesome and wearisome action', leading to the triumph of 'demi-semi-Socialism', which would improve the *condition* of the working-class while leaving its *position* unchanged. At the end of this vista of reform he still saw an ultimate revolutionary confrontation; and in one of his last lectures – delivered in 1895, the year before his death – he avowed:

> I have thought the matter up and down, and in and out, and I cannot for the life of me see how the great change which we long for can come otherwise than by disturbance and suffering of some kind .... We are living in an epoch where there is combat between commercialism, or the system of reckless waste, and communism, or the system of neighbourly common sense. Can that combat be fought out ... without loss and suffering? Plainly speaking I *know* that it cannot.

He was a revolutionary without a Revolution: more than that, he *knew* that he did not live within a revolutionary context. He did not, like Cromwell, have Revolution thrust upon him; nor did he, like Lenin, build a dedicated party within a society whose revolutionary potential was apparent. In the eyes of his opponents he was the very type of the socialist 'trouble-maker' or (as they would phrase it today) the maladjusted intellectual. He wanted to stir up revolt where no revolt was. He wanted to make contented men discontented, and discontented men into agitators of discontent: 'it is to stir you up *not* to be content with a little that I am here tonight'. And he spent his energy recklessly during the last fifteen years of his life, with the aim of creating a revolutionary

tradition – both intellectual and practical – within a society unripe
for Revolution.

This is, of course, the role for which the romantic poet is cast,
and many have been content to dismiss Morris, the revolutionary,
with this platitude. The late romantic poet, author of *The Earthly
Paradise*, and the utopian dreamer, author of *News from Nowhere*,
are confused in the same sentimental – or irritable – portrait of
baffled unpractical idealism.

The portrait is false. For one thing, the convention supposes an
effervescent iconoclastic youth, succeeded by premature death or by
a respectable and pedestrian middle-age. This was not the course of
Morris' life. Certainly, he rebelled in his youth. It was a moral
rebellion, stemming from the romantic tradition, nourished by
Carlyle and Ruskin. The enemy was 'bourgeoisdom and philistinism'. The tilting-grounds in his 'holy warfare against the age' were
the visual arts. The battle was joined with fervour, but it had
scarcely started when – as happened with more than one Victorian
rebel – the enemy opened its ranks to receive him with acclaim.
Morris, in his late thirties, seemed doomed to enter the family
album of Victorian men of letters. That tedious poem, *The Earthly
Paradise*, was taken into the bosom of that very 'bourgeoisdom
and philistinism' against which Morris had risen in revolt. So
costly were the products of the Firm in the decorative arts that it
was forced to depend upon the custom of the wealthy. And while
the Morris fashions began to penetrate the drawing-rooms of the
select, the Railway Age and the architects of Restoration continued
to desecrate the outside world.

This was the first time that success spelt failure to Morris: he
savoured the futility of his revolt like gall. 'Am I doing nothing
but make-belief then, something like Louis XVI's lock-making?' he
asked. And – when supervising work in the house of the Northern
iron-master, Sir Lowthian Bell – he turned suddenly upon his
patron 'like a wild animal' and declared: 'I spend my life in
ministering to the swinish luxury of the rich'.

He repudiated success as other men repudiate calumny. He
plunged into more intricate problems of craftsmanship at the Firm.
He sustained his 'hatred of modern civilisation' by translating
Icelandic saga. He deliberately sat on his top hat. He launched his

great campaign for the protection of ancient buildings. He opened his morning paper and was astonished to find that Britain was on the eve of a major war, on behalf of the Turkish Empire. His response was to become an agitator.

This agitation was to carry him, by way of an acute personal and intellectual crisis, into the embryonic socialist movement, which he joined in his fiftieth year. From this time forward he was to see war – whether overt, imperialist and bloody, or stealthy, respectable and bloodless – as the authentic expression of the Victorian ethos. It was from the circumstances of war that he was to draw one of his most evocative images of capitalist society:

> Do not be deceived by the outside appearance of order in our plutocratic society. It fares with it as it does with the older forms of war, that there is an outside look of quite wonderful order about it; how neat and comforting the steady march of the regiment; how quiet and respectable the sergeants look; how clean the polished cannon ... the looks of adjutant and sergeant as innocent-looking as may be; nay, the very orders for destruction and plunder are given with a quiet precision which seems the very token of a good conscience; this is the mask that lies before the ruined cornfield and the burning cottage, and mangled bodies, the untimely death of worthy men, the desolated home.

This second rebellion was at one and the same time the consummation of his youthful revolt and the genesis of a new revolutionary impulse within our culture. This time there was to be no reconciliation. The Victorian middle-class, which dearly loved an idealist reformer, was shocked not so much by his rebellion as by its practical form of expression. 'Mr Morris ... is not content to be heard merely as a voice crying in the wilderness,' complained one aggrieved leader-writer, 'he would disturb the foundations of society in order that a higher artistic value may be given to our carpets.'

For Morris broke with the conventional picture of the rebellious romantic in another respect. In everything to which he turned his hand he demanded of himself *practical* mastery. As he turned to the dye-vat and to the loom, so he turned his hands to the work of making a Revolution. There is no work which he did not take upon himself. He spoke on open-air pitches, Sunday after Sunday, until his health broke down. He addressed demonstrations of miners and of the unemployed. He attended innumerable committee meetings. He edited *Commonweal*, and sold it in the streets. He appeared, as prisoner and as witness, in the police courts. 'I can't help it,' he answered a reproof from his closest friend, Georgie Burne-Jones. 'The ideas which have taken hold of me will not let me rest .... One must turn to hope, and only in one direction do I see it – on the road to Revolution: everything else is gone ....'

And yet, for all this evidence of practical personal commitment cannot the charge of misguided romanticism still be sustained? While Morris accepted almost *in toto* the economic and historical analysis of Marx, he always avowed that his 'special leading motive' in becoming a revolutionary socialist was 'hatred of modern civilisation'. 'It is a shoddy age,' he roared at a *Clarion* reporter. 'Shoddy is King. From the statesman to the shoemaker all is shoddy!' The reporter concealed his boots further beneath the table: 'Then you do not admire the common-sense John Bull, Mr Morris?' 'John Bull is a *stupid, unpractical oaf,*' was the reply. Nothing infuriated Morris more than the complacent philistinism of the 'practical man', unless it was the complacent philistinism of the *un*practical one. 'That's an impossible dream of yours, Mr Morris,' a clergyman once declared, 'such a society would need God Almighty Himself to manage it.' Morris shook his fist in reply: 'Well, damn it, man, you catch your God Almighty – we'll have Him.'

But as we draw further from his time, it is Morris, and not his critics, who appears as a realist. He was a healthy man, living in a neurotic society. I speak of *moral* realism, not the realism of the practical revolutionary. As leader of the Socialist League he made blunders enough – Engels had justification for his irritable characterisation of him, in private letters, as a 'settled sentimental socialist'. But Engels underestimated the vigour of that long tradition of moral criticism which was Morris' inheritance. With his rich historical experience, and his concrete response to social reality, Morris had astonishing insight into the lines of growth, the elements of decay, within his culture. In lectures, speeches, passing notes in *Commonweal*, he cast his eyes forward to our time. He foresaw (in 1887) that the opening up of Africa would lead to the ending of the Great Depression, followed by 'a great European war, perhaps lengthened out into a regular epoch of war'. He foresaw Fascism. He foresaw (and regretted) the Welfare State.

The enemy, as in his youth, was still 'bourgeoisdom and philistinism'. But now he stood appalled before the destructive urges which he sensed within the Victorian middle classes, whom – he said – 'in spite of their individual good nature and banality, I look upon as a most terrible and implacable force':

> The most refined and cultured people ... have a sort of Manichean hatred of the world (I use the word in its proper sense, the home of man). Such people must be both the enemies of beauty and the slaves of necessity . . .

The utilitarian, competitive ethic he now saw as the ethic of Cain; he had always known that it murdered art, he had come to understand that it murdered man's dignity as a creator in his daily labour, he now discovered that it could murder mankind. He spoke in a lecture of 'the strength of that tremendous organisation under which we live .... Rather than lose anything which really is its essence, it will pull the roof of the world down upon its head'. He was consumed with the urgency of the socialist propaganda. If capitalism were not to be displaced by a clear-sighted constructive revolutionary movement, if it were to end in mere deadlock and blind insurrection, then 'the end, the fall of Europe, may be long in coming, but when it does, it will be far more terrible, far more confused and full of suffering than the period of the fall of Rome'.

In this tormented century such insights are worth more than a pedantic sneer. It is as if Morris had cast his eye over Gallipoli and Passchendaele, over purge and counter-purge, over concentration camps and scorched earth, over the tragedy of Africa and the other tragedies to come. At times one feels, indeed, that he deduced from the acquisitive ethic within class-divided society an Iron Law of Morality no less rigid than Lassalle's Iron Law of Wages. Into the maw of the Age of Commerce 'honour, justice, beauty, pleasure, hope, all must be cast ... to stave off the end awhile; and yet at last the end must come'. He might have found the proof, the culminating logic, of such a Law in our own ingenious devices for annihilation.

Morris was sceptical – especially in his last years – as to the tendency towards the immiseration of the masses within capitalism. But he was convinced of the tendency towards the moral immisera-tion of the dominant classes. Whence was this terrible diagnosis derived? It came, by one road, from Carlyle's denunciation of a society where cash-payment is the sole nexus of man with man; by another road, from his own study of the conditions of nineteenth century labour and productive relations; by yet another, from Marx's moral indignation, and its foundation in the manuscripts of the early 1840s. Morris did not use the term 'alienation', which has regained currency today; but he was – and remains – our greatest diagnostician of alienation, in terms of the concrete perception of the moralist, and within the context of a particular English cultural tradition. From these economic and social relationships, this moral logic must ensue.

And this logic demanded that the ethic of atomised, acquisitive society be opposed by the ethic of community. As between these two there could be no shadow of compromise. It was this logic which drove Morris to the street-corners, to play the fool's part as revolutionary agitator in the complacent streets of Gladstone's England. And here we meet with the second great irony of Morris' career. For a second time his rebellion met with success; and for a second time success was flavoured with gall.

This is not to say that Morris' section of the movement – the Socialist League – was successful. It petered out into anarchist tomfoolery, leaving Morris stranded in his Hammersmith Socialist Society. But, indirectly, the propaganda helped to set a mass movement in motion: and, indeed, the direct political influence of Morris is often under-rated. By the early 1890s men whom Morris had helped to convert were leading dynamic popular movements: Tom Mann and the new unions: Blatchford and *Clarion*: the Socialist Leaguers, Jowett and Maguire, who were architects of the Yorkshire ILP. And yet this was not the success for which Morris had looked.

Here lies the dilemma of the revolutionary within a society unripe for revolution. If he stands aside from the main currents of social change, he becomes purist, sectarian, without influence. If he swims with the current, he is swept downward by the flow of reformism and compromise. In the 1880s Morris had hoped that the propaganda would *'make Socialists* ... cover the country with a network of associations composed of men who feel their antagonism to the dominant classes, and have no temptation to waste their time in the thousand follies of party politics.' At that time he was an uncompromising anti-parliamentarian. A parliamentary socialist party would, he thought, enter into a path of compromise and opportunism: it would 'fall into the error of moving earth and sea to fill the ballot boxes with Socialist votes which will not represent Socialist *men.*' The 'rollicking opportunism' of the Fabians, and especially of Sidney Webb, met with his absolute opposition. Webb's mistake (declared Morris) was 'to over-estimate the importance of the *mechanism* of a system of society apart from the *end* towards which it may be used.'

The *end* he himself always described as Communism. When, in the nineties, the whole movement set in the direction of piecemeal reform, eight-hour agitation and parliamentary action, he welcomed this as a necessary process in awakening the aspirations of the workers. But, in his last lectures, he asked repeatedly 'how far the betterment of the working people might go and yet stop short at last without having made any progress on the *direct* road to Communism?

> Whether ... the tremendous organization of civilized commercial society is not playing the cat and mouse game with us socialists. Whether the Society of Inequality might not accept the equasi-socialist machinery ... and work it for the purpose of upholding that society in a somewhat shorn condition, maybe, but a same one .... The workers better treated, better organized, helping to govern themselves, but with no more pretence to equality with the rich ... than they have now.

Herein lies his realism, overlapping his own circumstances, and searching the dilemmas of our own time with a moral insight so

intense that it can be mistaken as callous. When the prospect of
'the capitalist public service ... brought to perfection' was put
before him, he remarked that he 'would not walk across the street
for the realisation of such an "ideal"'.

The nub of the question lies in the concept of community.
Webb and the Fabians looked forward to Equality of Opportunity,
within a competitive society: Morris looked forward to a Society of
Equals, a socialist community. It is not a small difference that
divides these concepts. In one – however modified – the ethic of
competition, the energies of war. In the other, the ethic of
co-operation, the energies of love. These two ethics Morris
contrasted again and again by the names of False and True Society:
False Society, or Commercial War: and 'that true society of loved
and lover, parent and child, friend and friend ... which exists by its
own inherent right and reason, in spite of what is usually thought
to be the cement of society, arbitrary authority.'

It was the greatest achievement of Morris, in his full
maturity, to bring this concept of community to the point of
expression: to place it in the sharpest antagonism to his own
society: and to embody it in imaginative terms and in the
'exalted brotherhood and hope' of the socialist propaganda. To
this he summoned all his resources – his knowledge of medieval
and of Icelandic society, his craftsman's insight into the processes of labour, his robust historical imagination. He had no time
for noble savages, and even less for the Fabian nostrum of State
bureaucracy. No amount of mechanical manipulation from above
could engender the ethic of community; 'individual men' (he
said) 'cannot shuffle off the business of life onto the shoulders
of an abstraction called the State.' Contrary to the prevalent
opinion, Morris welcomed all machinery which reduced the pain
and drudgery of labour; but decentralisation both of production
and of administration he believed essential. In True Society, the
unit of administration must be small enough for every citizen to
feel a personal responsibility. The community of Communism
must be an organic growth of mutual obligations, of personal
and social bonds, arising from a condition of practical equality.
And between False and True Society there lay, like a 'river of
fire', the Revolution. It was the work of a realist to indicate

where that river ran, and to hand down to us a 'tradition of hope' as to the lands beyond those deadly waters.

In conclusion, if there is one part of my long study of Morris which – in the light of the political controversies of recent years – would seem to be a fruitful area of re-examination, it is in those passages where I seek to relate the basis of Morris' moral critique of society to the Marxist tradition. The question is complex, and leads into an intricate succession of definitions. I feel now – as I did then – that Morris' and Marx's critique of capitalism are complementary and reinforce each other. There can be no question of disassociating the two. Moreover, I would wish to retract nothing of what I have written of Morris' profound debt to the writings of Marx; these gave to his own criticism much of their form and some of their force.

But I have tended at certain points to suggest that Morris' moral critique of society is *dependent upon* Marx's economic and historical analysis, that the morality is in some ways secondary, the analysis of power and productive relationships primary. That is not the way in which I look upon the question now. I see the two as inextricably bound together in the same context of social life. Economic relationships are at the same time moral relationships; relations of production are at the same time relations between people, of oppression or of co-operation: and there is a moral logic as well as an economic logic, which derives from these relationships. The history of the class struggle is at the same time the history of human morality. 'As I strove to stir up people to this reform,' Williams Morris wrote in his Preface to *Signs of Change*:

I found that the causes of the vulgarities of civilization lay deeper than I had thought, and little by little I was driven to the conclusion that all these uglinesses are but the outward expression of the innate moral baseness into which we are forced by our present form of society ....

This is the phrase – 'innate moral baseness'. And if capitalist society in Britain today displays fewer of the extreme hardships and oppressions of Morris' day, the innate moral baseness of the acquisitive ethic, and of exploitive rather than co-operative social relationships, gives rise to new inhumanities, to the atomisation of social life, and to the greater international idiocies.

There is nothing here which contradicts Marx's analysis. What I am insisting on is not only that Morris' discoveries are complementary to those of Marx, but also that they are a *necessary* complement, that without this historical understanding of the evolution of man's moral nature (to which Marx scarcely returned after the 1844 MS) his essential concept of the 'whole man' becomes lost, as it has so often been lost in the later Marxist tradition. A generation is now arising to whom the moral critique of society makes a more direct appeal than the traditional analysis of economic causes. For this generation, Morris' writings have lost, in the passage of years, none of their pungency and force. And as socialists see Marx's genius in transforming the traditions of English economic theory and of German philosophy, so they should see how Morris transformed a great tradition of liberal and humane criticism of society, and how he brought this into the common revolutionary stream. And if this achievement had been more widely recognised, perhaps fewer Marxists would have been found who could have supposed that the overthrow of capitalist class power and productive relationships could – by itself – lead on to the fruition of a Communist community: that, if the forms of economic ownership were right, the rest would follow. They would have realised – as Morris proclaimed in all his work – that the construction of a Communist community would require a moral revolution as profound as the revolution in economic and social power.

It is because William Morris, in imaginative and in day-to-day polemical writing alike, sought to body forth a vision of the actual social and personal relations, the values and attitudes consonant with a Society of Equals, that he remains the greatest moral initiator of Communism within our tradition.

A lecture to the William Morris Society, 1959.

Note

1   A position which has recently received a fresh and penetrating appraisal in Mr Raymond Williams' *Culture and Society*.

Christopher Caudwell

I

Christopher St. John Sprigg (Christopher Caudwell) was killed in action, forty years ago, on February 12th, 1937, on the Jarama River, covering with a machine-gun the retreat of his fellows in the British battalion of the International Brigade. He was then twenty-nine years old. He was unknown to the intellectual world, even of the Left. All his significant works – *Illusion and Reality, Studies in a Dying Culture, Further Studies, The Crisis of Physics*, and *Romance and Realism* [1] – were published posthumously.

All these works were written in two years, 1935–36, years in which his output included also poems and short stories (mainly unpublished), freelance journalism, detective novels. He also joined, at the end of 1935, the Poplar branch of the Communist Party, and took an active part in branch life.

There was also, throughout this period, a voracious ingestion of new reading. Caudwell was 'self-taught': he had left school (for journalism) before he was fifteen, and he was never exposed to formal advanced education.

Caudwell defies the usual stereotypes of the literary Left of the Thirties. These stereotypes are, in any case, of questionable validity. Even so, Caudwell does not belong to the ambience of *Left Review*, the Left Book Clubs or Unity Theatre; and he had avoided public school and university altogether. He disliked, and avoided the company of intellectual circles, even (perhaps especially) of the Left. He appears to have had few friends, and to have developed his thought in isolation. His style, with its polemical attack, its lack of any reverence for the demarcation-lines of disciplines, its impatience of scholarly apparatus, must appear strange, even 'vulgar', to today's practitioners of the Marxism of the Academy. And there can be no doubt that Caudwell wrote too much and wrote too fast; some parts of *Illusion and Reality* were written (in the summer of 1935 in Cornwall) at the rate of 5,000 words a day. This book, at least, he was able to prepare for the press. All the remainder was left in manuscript (sometimes corrected, sometimes requiring further revision) when he left for Spain. We cannot be certain as to the author's own intentions with these unfinished manuscripts.[2]

All this is unpromising. It is not difficult to see Caudwell as a phenomenon – as an extraordinary shooting-star crossing England's empirical night – as a premonitory sign of a more sophisticated Marxism whose true annunciation was delayed until the Sixties. But we would be foolish to expect much more of such a brief, intense and isolated intellectual episode. The image which comes to mind, involuntarily, is that of fire: a consciousness too bright and self-consuming – images of burning, of ignition, of phosphorescence, came readily to Caudwell's own pen. That being said (and tribute having been paid) it is easy to tidy Caudwell away, as an episode in the pre-history of British Marxism.

I cannot accept this conclusion. Some part of Caudwell's thought seems to me more significant than this, and its impulse is not yet exhausted. *Studies in a Dying Culture* played a significant part in the intellectual biography of my own generation. Recent studies by younger scholars seem to me to misunderstand what were Caudwell's central and most creative preoccupations. Moreover, as our own preoccupations change, so Caudwell's work presents itself for a new kind of interrogation. In his Foreword to *Studies* Caudwell asked, rhetorically, for an explanation of the 'anarchy' of bourgeois intellectual culture: 'Either the Devil has come amongst us having great power, or there is a causal explanation for a disease common to economics, science, and art.' But in the past two decades the Devil has come amongst Marxists, having exceeding great power, productive of a comparable anarchy. It is no longer possible to suppose a Marxist orthodoxy against which Caudwell can be judged, confirmed or found wanting. We can no longer ask whether Caudwell was or was not 'correct'; we have to approach his work with a renewed attention, and examine whether he may have offered solutions to difficulties which are far from being resolved. This changes the whole character of the necessary investigation.

II

But to write about Caudwell's thought brings one, at once, face to face with a problem of unusual difficulty: what was Caudwell's thought about? The question seems to call for two quite easy answers. First, Caudwell was centrally concerned with problems of aesthetics and of literary criticism. A serious recent study assumes (but does not show) that *Illusion and Reality* was his 'major work'; 'indubitably' it was 'his most important production.'[3] This is the received view; it has not been contested; and one suspects that younger Marxists today do not read Caudwell at all unless they are interested in aesthetics, and that those who do content themselves with an impatient survey of *Illusion and Reality*.[4]

If Caudwell's central work was about literary criticism, in any of its generally accepted connotations, then we must accept the judgement that this work remains of interest only in a disconcerting, admonitory way. Raymond Williams noted, in *Culture and Society*, that Caudwell 'has little to say of actual literature that is even interesting': 'his discussion is not even specific enough to be wrong.'[5] I do not wish to contest this judgement.[6] Nor do I think that it can be evaded by shifting our attention from Caudwell's criticism to his 'aesthetics'. Certainly, Caudwell was concerned with 'the function of literature', and he developed interesting arguments from cultural anthropology which bear upon aesthetics. But I cannot see that large claims can be made for Caudwell's 'aesthetics' if it cannot be shown that he was engaged in any close way with the study of literary artefacts. The arguments remain as assertions, insecurely grounded upon unexamined evidence. So that we are now forced back upon the second, and easier, answer to our question. Caudwell's thought – so runs the answer – was about a great many things. He was 'brilliant' and 'versatile'. He moved eloquently among problems of physics, philosophy, literary criticism, anthropology, neurology, psycho-analysis, and so on. He said, perhaps, nothing definitive about any of these. But we have – as Professor J.B.S. Haldane noted in an early review – 'a quarry of ideas'. With singular unanimity, commentators on Caudwell have grasped at this conclusion. It is the consensus (sometimes grudging) reached in the famous 'Caudwell controversy' in *The Modern*

Quarterly in 1950–51. It is a conclusion also of Mulhern: 'Caudwell's work is best seen not as a system to be appropriated as a whole, but as a copious source of insights and arguments needing critical reflection.'[7]

But here the difficulties enlarge. One quality in Caudwell which attracted, and sometimes bemused, his contemporaries was the extraordinary width of his intellectual range. But what if this width went along with error and shallowness in each field which he touched? This would appear to be another conclusion in today's received wisdom. Eagleton has expressed it with eloquence:

> Insulated from much of Europe, intellectually isolated even within his own society, permeated by Stalinism and idealism, bereft of 'a theory of superstructure', Caudwell nonetheless persevered in the historically hopeless task of producing from these unpropitious conditions a fully-fledged Marxist aesthetic. His work bears all the scars of that self-contradictory enterprise: speculative and erratic, studded with random insights, punctuated by hectic forrays into and out of alien territories and strewn with hair-raising theoretical vulgarities.[8]

This passage might usefully be examined. We have, once again, the 'quarry of ideas' ('studded with random insights'); but, with 'random', we must suppose the quarry to produce many kinds of stone as well as much useless shale. It is, again, assumed (but not shown) that Caudwell's project was to construct 'a Marxist aesthetic'. But how far can that other assumption (now widely accepted as a revealed truth) as to the utter poverty and provincialism of the thought available to a British Marxist in the Thirties be sustained? In the bibliography to *Illusion and Reality* (over 500 titles) one is struck by the pre-eminence of anthropology,[9] an attention appropriate in a work which was sub-titled, 'A Study in the Sources of Poetry'.[10] Psychology and neurology also take a prominent position. How far was this enterprise 'insulated from much of Europe'? Allowance must be made for changing fashions and for the slow establishment of certain reputations. But it may be noted that the bibliography includes works by Bukharin, Cassirer, Croce, Durkheim, the Gestalt psychologists,

Levy-Bruhl, Malinowski, Piaget and Saussure, as well as Freud, Jung, Adler, Pavlov, Van Gennep, Planck, Ribot, Roheim, Sapir and so on. There are gaps, of course, but this can scarcely be described as 'insulation'.

But the most striking phrase in Eagleton's summary is 'punctuated by hectic forrays into and out of alien territories'. The bibliography suggests that the territories which Caudwell inhabited most securely while writing *Illusion and Reality* were anthropology and psychology (with neurology) and that, if anything, the forrays were into literature and linguistics. But what is that word *alien* doing there? Must genetics, anthropology, mathematics, neurology and physiology be alien to literary pursuits, irrelevant to an investigation into the sources of poetry? One fears that this is, indeed, the implication.

The dissociation between 'science' and 'art' was, in Caudwell's view, a prime symptom of the crisis in bourgeois culture. Indeed, he argued that this culture could be seen to be dying because of its inability to hold together in any one philosophic place a unitary world-view. His argument here was strenuous, even obsessive, and we can scarcely meet him, in his own chosen terms, if we disregard it. But yet, how far did Caudwell himself really succeed in straddling the two halves of our culture, and how are we, who fall within one or the other, to decide?

Whatever virtue exists in *The Crisis in Physics* and in two of the *Further Studies* rests upon their general competence in areas which are normally *terra incognita* to poets, critics, historians and sociologists. I am certainly unable to judge this virtue. Moreover, certain of Caudwell's arguments rest not only upon the supposition that he has correctly understood the knowledge of the science contemporary to him, but also – as in his argument about the cortex and the unconscious in 'Consciousness' – upon whether the science then available to him has stood the test of the past forty years. To sit in judgement on these copious insights we are forced to convene an inter-disciplinary committee. But the experts, as always, fail to speak with a united voice. When his work was first presented it was commended by scientists as eminent as Haldane. But there followed, in 1951, a devastating judgement from a scientist of unusual breadth of knowledge, J.D. Bernal: 'It is

largely on account of his use of the language of popular science
that Caudwell's work has had ... such an appeal to intellectuals,
particularly to literary intellectuals.' His formulations, Bernal argues, were not only schematic or, sometimes, plainly wrong,[11] but
they were accompanied by a capitulation to 'contemporary bourgeois scientific philosophy.'

This would seem to leave us with a negative judgement of
finality. And yet, embedded in Bernal's critique (to which no other
scientist had an opportunity to reply [12]) there is a large reservation
which has gone unnoticed: 'It is true that Caudwell criticised,
brilliantly and destructively, the philosophical conclusions of bourgeois scientists ...' So Caudwell's criticisms of bourgeois science
was (his sternest critic allows) 'brilliant', and it is not easy to see
how a mere populariser could mount such a critique. And are we
entitled to absolute confidence in the judgement of Bernal (and of
other critics in that controversy) as to what was, or was not,
'bourgeois' about the science or the psycho-analysis of their time?
For these same critics were, at that same time, apologising for or
applauding Zhdanov's crass interventions in Soviet intellectual life,
Stalin's masterful solution of the problems of linguistics, and the
revolutionary character of Lysenko's genetics. Indeed, this may
have been one reason why the 'Caudwell Controversy' ever broke
the surface of the British Communist Party's normally monolithic
press. In those worst years of the intellectual Cold War the
international Communist movement had embarked on a rigorous
campaign to correct or expose all 'bourgeois' heresies, and the
assault on Caudwell was perhaps seen, by the directors of the
Party's press, as a small purgative exercise in the Zhdanov mode.

I suggest, with hesitation, that Caudwell's scientific incompetence
has not been finally shown. If the vocabulary of neurology,[13] of
physics, and of linguistics have been revised since his time, the
problems which he pointed towards (with an inadequate vocabulary)
may still remain. As we shall see, Caudwell's preoccupations within
the sciences were not substantive but epistemological. Even so, just
as we cannot reasonably offer Caudwell as a literary critic, so we
cannot suffer him as 'a scientist'. Perhaps, then, he was no kind of
specialist, but should be seen simply as a creative Marxist, or a
Marxist philosopher, who could deal 'brilliantly and destructively'

with the methods and conclusions of bourgeois scientific or literary study? But this leads us into further difficulties again. For it raises at once the question: *was* Caudwell a Marxist at all? And, if so, of what kind?

Undoubtedly Caudwell supposed himself to be a Marxist. He was also an active Communist, and his commitment led him to that death on Jarama Ridge. That death, in its turn, threw light retrospectively upon his intellectual commitment, authenticating it beyond interrogation. But, while honourable, his political judgements are not thereby shown to have been always wise or philosophically well-founded. His *Studies* assume throughout an orthodox antinomy between a dying bourgeois culture, on one hand, and an ascendant and healthy Soviet and Communist culture on the other. The Soviet Union appears, not as a subject for enquiry, but as a rhetorical affirmative antithesis to the maladies of the capitalist world; and these rhetorical flourishes date his work as surely as the rhetorical anti-Jacobinism dates the later work of Burke or much of the work of Coleridge. We must agree that this is so, although in none of these cases does this 'dating' altogether disallow or overthrow the ulterior argument. But, in Caudwell's case, it has often been asked whether this ulterior argument was Marxist at all?

Once again, it is Raymond Williams who defines the problem with the most accurate touch. He shows, with reference to *Illusion and Reality* and *Further Studies*, that certain of Caudwell's definitions appear to revalue Marx's basic conception of the relation between social being and social consciousness. This might (he adds in passing) be 'an improvement of Marx', but the question is left unresolved: it is 'a quarrel which one who is not a Marxist will not attempt to resolve.' Williams, whose relation to Marxism has become increasingly close and complex, would not (one supposes) take the same exit today; indeed, he has recently signalled that his views of Caudwell have undergone some revision.[14] For it is a point of some substance. If Caudwell had in fact offered 'an improvement of Marx', and opened the way to a resolution of rather familiar difficulties, then this would raise immensely the interest of Caudwell's work. At the time when *Culture and Society* was written, Williams was mainly concerned with identifying these difficulties and defining these contradictions. Today we should be more concerned with moving on to resolutions.

That was not, however, the spirit in which, several years before, the 'Caudwell Controversy' had been conducted. As one might expect, in that place and at that time, the argument was initiated (by Maurice Cornforth) on the grounds of whether Caudwell was or was not a proper and orthodox Marxist, according to an orthodoxy increasingly petrified by Stalinist doctrine.[15] Despite the efforts of Caudwell's defenders,[16] the argument never succeeded in escaping from the terms in which it had at first been set.

We are in difficulties. Caudwell (it is agreed) was a poor critic. His credentials as a theorist of aesthetics, as a scientist, and as a Marxist have all been questioned. His political judgement was honourable but naive. But in this train of argument something has been left to him, and this has not (to my knowledge) been adequately examined. I will not go over my tracks again. Instead, I will propose, assertively, a different way into Caudwell's work.

This must commence by down-grading *Illusion and Reality* very severely. But then we must up-grade, equally firmly, *Studies in a Dying Culture*, some part of *The Crisis in Physics*, and several of the *Further Studies*. The strengths found here will enable us to retrieve a part, but only a small part, of *Illusion and Reality*. Only this procedure can lead us to Caudwell's central theoretical concerns.

Caudwell was an anatomist of ideology. He was obsessed with the characteristic illusions of the bourgeois epoch, with the logic of these illusions (their epistemological expression and their epistemological consequences), and with the way in which, possessed by these illusions, we 'stand in our own light'. Caudwell's insights were not only copious: they were connected by unitary preoccupations. These preoccupations carry him quite far into significant questions in cultural anthropology, linguistics, psychology, philosophy, and also, possibly, in physics and neurology. Insofar as certain of these same ideological illusions had penetrated deeply into orthodox Marxism also, so that what went by the name of Marxism was standing in its own light, Caudwell was potentially a heretic within the orthodox Marxist tradition. He may or may not have known this: we should at least note that his dismissal of conventional Marxist reflection theory was blunt, even brutal, and suggests a conscious polemic. His heretic potential was, anyway, sensed subsequently by the orthodox and by fellow heretics alike: this alone can explain the sudden blossoming, at the zenith of ideological Stalinism, of the 'Caudwell Controversy', like a crimson cactus in flower in the sand-hills of *The Modern Quarterly*. For that argument was, at root, a displaced and ill-conducted argument between dogmatic and creative Marxism, for which the structures of the Communist Party offered no other outlet. And, finally, it will be argued, Caudwell's heresy, or his creative impulse, is not exhausted yet.

III

Let us, then, enter Caudwell's world from a new direction. *Illusion and Reality* is in no respect to be seen as his major work. It was written while Caudwell was undergoing a self-conversion to Marxism, from late 1934 to the autumn of 1935. I do not wish to labour its deficiencies, but will assert these as I find them. Despite an impression gained from the chapter-headings, of massive and complex organisation, it is an ill-organised, involuted, and repetitive book. In the first two chapters, and thereafter in passages in the later chapters, Caudwell draws on occasion to advantage upon the findings of anthropologists as to the function of song and verse in primitive and tribal societies. This proper junction between anthropology and aesthetics was not original, but Caudwell gave a new emphasis to this junction within terms of a Marxist exposition. The creative possibilities of this approach were realised, less in Caudwell's own work than in that of those most directly influenced by him: notably, in George Thomson's *Aeschylus and Athens* (1941) and in his lucid *Marxism and Poetry* (1945).

There follow four chapters on the development of English poetry – chapters (and a notorious 'table') which have only been a source of embarrassment to Marxist critics. Then we pass, by way of some uneven (but sometimes interesting) passages on language and epistemology, to those chapters ('The Psyche and Phantasy', 'Poetry's Dream-work') in which Caudwell seeks to come to terms with contemporary psychoanalysis. In general, Caudwell's nose is pressed too closely against the window-pane of his recent reading, and the interval between ingestion and critical reflection has been too brief for him to get his thoughts into order. Finally, we come to some euphoric conclusions about Communist art, in which the influence of Bukharin's optimistic public rhetoric (1934) [17] can be clearly seen. Assertively throughout the book 'the bourgeois' (an epochal noun) has been denounced, but since the denunciation lacks specificity, the tone becomes overbearing and pharasaical.

It is a bad book. Cornforth and Mulhern have correctly indicated certain deforming weaknesses, and in particular the analytic preference for simplistic binary oppositions: Man/Nature: Science/Art: Instincts (or 'genotype')/Society. Other criticisms, as to Caudwell's 'idealism', are (I will argue) less well-founded.

The relation between *Illusion and Reality* and the *Studies* still needs clarification. I have always supposed that the *Studies* are the later work; many passages in both works are clearly and closely related, but in every case the statement in the *Studies* is more lucid and more cogent. The account given by Caudwell's latest editor confirms this sequence. [18] Caudwell commenced *Studies in a Dying Culture* late in 1935, shortly before joining the Communist Party, and a first draft was completed in April 1936. All the studies (including *Further Studies*) were part of a single conception. Caudwell had planned to use, as an epigraph to all the studies, a quotation from Lenin: 'Communism becomes an empty phrase, a mere facade, and the Communist a mere bluffer, if he has not worked over in his consciousness the whole inheritance of human knowledge.'[19] This is a quite extraordinary project, to undertake in real earnest and to commit to paper. During the summer and autumn of 1936 revision and expansion continued: the study on physics was expanded (in *The Crisis in Physics)* to book-length. *Romance and Realism* is another expanded study, and a further study, on biology, remains unpublished. It is not possible to say how far Caudwell considered any of the work to be completed: some part clearly stood in need of revision, and has suffered from inexpert editing. [20]

So the studies are, not the mature Caudwell, but as mature as Caudwell became. For opposing reasons they were deprived of the full light of critical attention when they appeared. *Studies in a*

Dying Culture (1938) was obscured, as by a magnesium flare, by the illumination of his self-sacrifice in Spain: friends were elegaic, critics were subdued. *Further Studies* (1949) appeared in some of the worst ideological moments of the Cold War; damned or ignored by an ascendant conservatism, it aroused the suspicion of a consolidating Stalinism. Nor was this suspicion without some basis. For Caudwell's reputation had by then begun to acquire a kind of underground, proto-revisionist status.

Caudwell's *style* was one occasion for this suspicion: it has often been thought to be difficult. Initiating the debate in *The Modern Quarterly*, Cornforth argued that the difficulty arises 'because his thought is nebulous, shifting, eclectic and inconsistent; because he clothes simple things in a veil of obscure phrases, and drags with him the confusions of bourgeois ideology. Caudwell's style ... is not yet the style of a Marxist.' Let us take, from the first few pages of *Studies in a Dying Culture*, a sample of this style: Shaw (he is arguing) fails because he represents human beings 'as walking intellects':

Fortunately they are not, or the human race would long ago have perished in some dream-fantasy of logic and metaphysics. Human beings are mountains of unconscious being, walking the old grooves of instinct and simple life, with a kind of occasional phosphorescence of consciousness at the summit. And this conscious phosphorescence derives its value and its power from the emotions, from the instincts; only its form is derived from the intellectual shapes of thought. Age by age man strives to make this consciousness more intense, the artist by subtilising and intensifying the emotions, the scientist by making fuller and more real the thought form, and in both cases this is done by burning more being in the thin flame. Shaw, however, is obsessed with the 'pure' flame, phosphorescence separate from being ...

This mixed thought and feeling of consciousness is not the source of social power, only a component of it. Society with its workshops, its buildings, its material solidity, is always present below real being and is a kind of vast reservoir of the unknown, unconscious and irrational in every man, so that of everyone we

can say his conscious life is only a fitful gleam on the mass of
his whole existence. Moreover, there is a kind of carapacious
toughness about the conscious part of society which resists
change, even while, below these generalisations, changes in
material and technique and real detailed being are going on.

It is the tension 'between man's being and man's consciousness,
which drives on society and makes life vital.' (SDC, 5–7).

Two comments spring to mind. First, this is not the style of 'a
Marxist', in the conventions sanctioned as 'correct' in Communist
publications of 1946–56 (but very much less in the Thirties): it is
Caudwell's own style. He has thrown away the crutches of
authorised texts, and is walking on his own. Everything that he
writes is thought through afresh and is expressed in his own way.
But (the second comment) it is not always thought through
consistently. For the passage exposes him to the criticisms expressed by Cornforth. 'Nebulous': are we to take 'the emotions'
and 'the instincts' (from which consciousness 'derives its value') as
being, ultimately, the same effects? 'Shifting': is 'being' to be
taken as 'instinct and simple life' or as 'society', which is 'always
present below real being'? 'Inconsistent': is the tension which
'drives on society' between being and consciousness, or between
social being and social consciousness (two different propositions),
and can a 'tension' drive society unless some ulterior dynamic
gives rise to this tension?

Caudwell's style is fluent, cogent and assertive. There are repeti-
tions – repeated nodal points of argument to which we return again
and again: notably, the compulsive nature of market relations in
contradiction to the bourgeois illusion of freedom. There are also
lesions of logic, shifts and jumps: there are long views which are
sometimes very much too long – whole historical epochs character-
ised in a paragraph, or passages of scientific allusion which are not
always apt. There is also, on occasion, a millenarial or messianic
tone. It is a dying culture, and the alternative – Communism –
appears clear, absolute and immanent. Caudwell is throughout impatient of mediations; the passage from economy to ideology is swift
and compulsive. Above all, the dialectical mode of analysis in his
hands leads to an over-readiness to propose binary oppositions: there

are, frequently, only two forms or two choices; we move always among antinomies, and society or ideology arrange themselves around two 'poles'. Even the passage we have considered moves always between being/consciousness: value/form: the artist/the scientist: instinct (emotion)/thought.

But the passage prompts a third comment. It succeeds, in places, in conveying a metaphoric meaning which is not co-incident with its apparent rational argument. Caudwell is polemicising against Shaw's belief in 'the solitary primacy of thought'; his emphasis falls upon the immense inertia of habit, custom and tradition ('mountains of unconscious being, walking the old grooves of instinct and simple life'), upon the social determination of thought ('Society ... with its material solidity .... a vast reservoir of the unknown, unconscious and irrational in every man'), upon the precariousness of consciousness ('occasional phosphorescence') and yet upon the ardour and consuming force of the intellectual enterprise ('burning more being in the thin flame'). The passage has, as it were, a dual life: a rational argument, imprecise and shifting in its terms, and a metaphoric and allusive life, persuasive and suggestive and of greater vitality. That the two lives do not cohere should properly arouse suspicion: logic is becoming subservient to rhetoric. But the vitality of the metaphoric life – which is the signature of all of Caudwell's best writing – suggests a different kind of confidence in handling ideas, and a capacity to precipitate abstractions into concrete images. Where the two lives *do* cohere (and they often do in the studies) the imagination seizes upon the concept and endows it with passion.

What then is communicated is not just a new 'idea' (or an old idea freshly communicated) but a new way of seeing. For such images may be both concrete and conceptually ambiguous, in the sense that they cannot easily be slotted into the categories which we have prepared in our minds to receive them: 'mountains of unconscious being', 'phosphorescence'. Hence they prompt unease, they generate further enquiry, they challenge habitual mental routines. It is this kind of challenge which Caudwell presented to his generation, and we cannot understand this if we discard his metaphors, disregard his antithetical figures, reduce his thought to expository precis, and then measure it beside a precis of Marx or

Stalin or Althusser. For what we have then lost, with Caudwell's 'style', is Caudwell's way of seeing.

His way of seeing, his mode of apprehension, was 'dialectical'. This tells us little: the term can cover as many sins as virtues. It can indicate mere schematism, barren and wilful paradox, inflated mystification, as well as the binary oscillations and polar antitheses of which we have already convicted Caudwell. These certainly are present, but they are not all that is present. He also has a way of seeing coincident and opposed potentialities within a single 'moment' and of following through the contradictory logic of ideological process. This strength is not only a way of seeing, it is a way of teaching others how to see. After Blake and Marx, this faculty of dialectical vision has been rare enough for us to regard it with a special respect. Nor was this vision easily attained. It was attained, although only insecurely, in his final year of writing, and it was the product of a cogent and clearly-developed interactionist epistemology. This is what we must now examine.

IV

To attempt to work over 'the whole inheritance of human knowledge' would be to go on a fool's errand if one did not suppose there to be some uniting structures or qualities to be found in this inheritance. Caudwell supposed these to be epistemological and ideological. He studied thought, less in its products than in its process. He watched himself as he thought. He watched himself as he loved. He even watched love as he loved –

A wind impalpable that blows one way
All the mind's stiff and treelike qualities ...

To be in love, when 'flesh usurps the brain's forsaken zone', prompted a sense of epistemological crisis:

When I could bite my tongue out in desire
To have your body, local now to me,
You were a woman, and your proper image
Unvarying on the black screen of the night,

What are you now? A thigh, a smile, an odour:
A cloud of anecdotes and fed desires
Bubblingly unfolds inside my brain
To vex its vision with a monstrous beast ...[21]

Fulfilled love, by breaking down the distance between subject and object, proposed questions, not about loving, but about knowing.

We recall also the references to the 'occasional phosphorescence' of consciousness, and to the artist and scientist 'burning more being in the thin flame'. The images appealed to him. But we should go on to note that they were something more than a gesture of rhetoric. In 'Consciousness' he asks: 'What governs the tiny localisations of conscious light in the vast Arctic night of the cortex?' (FS 192–3). A good question, perhaps, but not one to which we should anticipate an answer. But Caudwell does, then, go on to propose an answer, in terms of the relation between the thalamus and the cortex. This is decidedly unsettling to a literary consciousness, which does not like to be seen in such a material aspect. And it is interesting that it lies almost wholly outside the terms of today's dominant Marxist consciousness also – at least of that part which has been defined as 'Western Marxism'. It is one thing to assert, as an abstract proviso, that all matter, society and culture are mutually related or mutually determining; it is quite another thing to examine, or even to argue about, their mediations and determinations; and another thing again to take this argument into the privacy of our own theoretical heads, and to suggest that even Theory itself may be composed of 'the affective "heating" of cortical traces'. This is, presumably, an example of a 'hectic forray' into 'alien territories'.

For much Western Marxism has been able to dispense with material (and sometimes even historical) determinants of thought, unless in a 'last instance' way, as a kind of pre-theoretical proviso. By obscure and not-always-acknowledged routes (one being phenomenology) this Marxism has arrived at the oddly-idealist conclusion that all that can be known to thought are thought and its ideal materials: we may correctly examine a category but not a cortex. To examine a cortex, during the course of an epistemological enquiry, would be, according to this

orthodoxy, to surrender to the most vulgar positivism or behav-
iourism.

Yet, oddly enough, Caudwell himself polemicises stridently and
even repetitively against mechanical materialism and positivism.
And (what is equally odd) the burden of the criticism brought
against him in the *Modern Quarterly* controversy of 1950–51 was
that of 'idealism'. It is necessary to situate Caudwell's writings
against the background of epistemological 'reflection-theory', that
intellectually-constrictive orthodoxy which, descended in some part
from *Materialism and Empirio-Criticism,* had been congealed by
Stalin and dispersed throughout the international Communist movement as doctrine. In his summation to that controversy, Maurice
Cornforth (who subsequently wrote some better philosophy than
this) expressed the common-sense of his own orthodox generation:

> It is a fundamental idea of materialism (I quote Stalin and add
> my own italics) 'that the multifold phenomena of the world
> constitute *different forms of matter in motion,*' and 'that matter
> is *primary*, since it is the *source* of sensations, ideas, mind, and
> that mind is *secondary, derivative*, since it is a *reflection* of
> matter, a *reflection* of being.'[22]

What is implicit here is that 'mind' affords some kind of *copy* of
'matter', although a copy distorted by ideological illusions. A
uniting theme of all the studies (of which *The Crisis in Physics*
was originally one) is a critical examination of exactly this
proposition. Although I cannot recall any place where these are
cited, Caudwell might well have been exploring the consequences
imposed by Marx's first two theses on Feuerbach.[23] These consequences were detected equally in the arts, the sciences, and in
philosophy. 'The bourgeois, brought up on a diet of dualism,
cannot conceive that subject and object are not mutually exclusive
opposites,' But in fact, 'complete objectivity brings us back to
complete subjectivity and vice versa.' (*R&R* 56).

'The chief defect of all hitherto existing materialism', Marx had
written, 'is that the object, reality, sensuousness, is conceived only
in the form of the *object* or *contemplation*, but not as *human
sensuous activity, practice*, not subjectively. Thus it happened that

the *active* side, in opposition to materialism, was developed by idealism – but only abstractly, since, of course, idealism does not know real sensuous activity as such.' With Stalin Marx's *'human sensuous activity, practice'* have been forgotten, and the subject/object dualism has returned ('mind is *secondary, derivative'*) with the additional authority of being the doctrine of the First Proletarian State. Now Caudwell does not waste breath denying that being is historically prior to thought: 'Thought guides action, but it learns *how* to guide *from* action. Being must historically and always precede knowing, for knowing evolves as an extension of being.' (*SDC* 4) But neither matter/mind nor being/knowing can be seen in terms of 'primary' and 'secondary' ('derivative') relations; dialectical materialism recognises the 'mutually determining relations between knowing and being' – 'knowing is a mutually determining relation between subject and object' (*FS* 254–5). A central passage in 'Reality' must be cited at more length:

> The question of which is first, mind or matter, is not ... a question of which is first, subject or object. Every discernment of a quality (mind, truth, colour, size) is the discernment of a two-term relation between a thing as subject and the rest of the Universe. Mind is the general name for a relation between the human body as subject, and the rest of the Universe .... Going back in the Universe along the dialectic of qualities we reach by inference a state where no human or animal bodies existed and therefore no minds. It is not strictly accurate to say that therefore the object is prior to the subject any more than it is correct to say the opposite. *Object and subject, as exhibited by the mind relation, come into being simultaneously. Human body, mind, and human environment cannot exist separately, they are all parts of the one set.* What is prior is the material unity from which they arise as an inner antagonism.
>
> We can say that relations seen by us between qualities in our environment (the arrangement of the cosmos, energy, mass, all the entities of physics) existed before the subject-object relationship implied in mind. We prove this by the transformations which take place independent of our desires. In this sense nature is prior to mind and this is the vital sense for science. These

qualities produced, as cause and ground produce effect, the synthesis, or particular subject-object relationship which we call knowing. Nature therefore produced mind. But the nature which produced mind was not nature 'as seen by us', for this is importing into it the late subject-object relationship called 'mind'. It is nature as known by us, that is, as having indirect and not direct relations with us. It is nature in determining relation with, but not part of, our contemporary universe. Yet, by sublation, this nature that produced mind is contained in the universe of which the mind relation is now a feature; and that is why it is known to us.

Such a view of reality reconciles the endless dualism of mentalism or objectivism. It is the Universe of dialectical materialism. (*FS* 228–9), (my italics).

What is remarkable in Caudwell is the tenacity with which he explored outwards from this central insight, into the materiality of thought ('Consciousness', 'Freud') and into the ideality of 'nature' ('Reality', *The Crisis in Physics*). The 'crisis' in physics had arisen, in his view, as a consequence of the inadequacy of the categories of mechanical materialism: 'When the bourgeois considers matter as the object of cognition, he is unable to conceive of it except under the categories of mechanism.' (*C in P* 29). Mechanism had 'stripped Nature, the object of all qualities which had in them any tincture of the subjective.' (*Ibid.* 55) 'Thus nature ... appears as the object *in contemplation*, the object as it is in itself, measured in terms of its own necessity,' an object 'quantitative, bare of quality.' (*Ibid.* 45).

At first matter is only stripped of colour, sound, 'pushiness', heat, which all prove to be modes of motion. Motion, length, mass and shape are however believed to be absolutely objective qualities, independent of the observer. However they prove one after the other to be relative to the observer. Thus matter is left finally with no real i.e. non-subjective qualities, except those of number. But number is ideal, and hence objective reality vanishes. Matter has become unknowable. (*Ibid.* 46)

But, in a parallel movement, bourgeois philosophy underwent a process 'in which man or mind, figuring as active, sensuous subjectivity, was stripped of all those qualities which had an objective component in them.' This stripping left mind 'as bare as matter when it was stripped of all subjective quality. Matter was left with nothing but mathematics existing in the human head. Subjectivity was left with nothing but the Idea ...' But 'the Idea existing apart from the brain is objective reality and therefore enters the category of matter. Idealism has become materialism, just as mechanical materialism when it ended in mathematics, had become idealism.' (*Ibid*. 56–7)[24]

Positivism attempts to resolve this crisis but is dismissed by Caudwell as 'a confused, amateurish and dishonest philosophy':

> Consciousness (phenomena) is a relation between Man and Nature, but positivism attempts to take the relation without the terms.... It is impossible to have real activity without two terms, without a contradiction, and a unity of opposites whose activity springs from their interpenetration. Hence consciousness becomes a mere passive 'reflection' of the world; its function becomes merely to be a pale copy of existing practice. The relation of knowing ceases to be an active and mutually determining relation, and becomes a godlike apprehension separate from material reality. (*Ibid*. 65)

But reflection-theory must lead on 'to a regretful admission that it is a "misleading" reflection', since 'all the known subjective qualities (colour, scent, shape, mass, pushiness, beauty) are merely symbolic ciphers for the thing in itself.' (*Ibid*. 65) Consciousness 'has become a screen'.

It is not my intention to attempt any judgement as to the adequacy of Caudwell's account of 'bourgeois' philosophy or of 'bourgeois' physics. I will say that I consider his account has merits, and, in particular, his diagnosis of a phenomenon repeatedly witnessed within bourgeois culture: that is, the repeated generation of idealism and mechanical materialism, not as true antagonists but as pseudo-antitheses, generated as twins in the same moment of conception, or, rather, as positive and negative aspects of the same

fractured movement of thought: 'It is not Berkeley who fights
mechanical materialism, but Berkeley who generates it.' (*FS* 212)
But my main intention is simply to present Caudwell's epistemological preoccupations (which were consistent and which inform all
his work) and to assert – contrary to a well-known stereotype –
that these cannot be reduced to the dominant reflection-theory of
that time.

It is true that in *Illusion and Reality*, when discussing language,
Caudwell uses the term 'reflection' unselfconsciously:

> By means of the word, men's association in economic produc-
> tion continually generates changes in their perceptual private
> worlds and the common world [i.e. common perceptual world],
> enriching both. A vast moving superstructure rises above man's
> busy hands which is the reflection of all the changes he has
> effected or discovered in ages of life. Presently this common
> world becomes as complex and remote from concrete social life
> as the market, of which its secret life and unknown creative
> forces are the counterpart.
>
>   This is the shadow world of thought, or ideology. It is the
> reflection in men's heads of the real world. It is always and
> necessarily only symbolical of the real world. It is always and
> necessarily a reflection which has an active and significant
> relation to the object, and it is this activity and significance, and
> not the projective qualities of the reflection, which guarantee its
> truth. (*I&R* 160–1)

This passage reveals, once again, some strain between the apparent,
rational argument and the metaphoric meaning. At the first level
Caudwell's attention is slack: 'thought' is bluntly equated to
'ideology': 'reflection' suggests 'shadow world'. But at the second
level ('a vast moving superstructure rises above man's busy hands')
he is intent upon conveying a complexity of relationship which
cannot be sustained by the image of 'reflection'. For Caudwell,
even when writing about language, remains a student of the
sciences. And 'reflection' recalls to his mind the strict definition of
projection in geometry. But how can a 'shadow' or 'reflection',
when considered in its projective qualities, have 'an active and

significant relation to the object?' The question is left unresolved; it is not even clearly posed.

By the time that he wrote the *Studies* Caudwell's emphasis upon the 'active and significant relation to the object' (and his implicit hostility to orthodox reflection theory) has hardened:

> Social consciousness is not a mirror-image of social being; If it were, it would be useless, a mere fantasy. It is material, possessed of mass and inertia, composed of real things – philosophies, language habits, churches, judiciaries, police. If social consciousness were but a mirror-image, it could change like an image without the expenditure of energy when the object which it mirrored changed. But it is more than that. It is a functional superstructure which interacts with the foundations, each altering the other. There is a coming-and-going between them. (*SDC* 25)

This is an argument from the sociology of ideas, and, as I think, a legitimate one. But Caudwell argues the point also in more strictly epistemological terms. In *The Crisis in Physics* there is a significant passage:

> When I say 'reflection' I mean that the same general development has taken place in the sphere of social relations as in ideological categories, because the latter are merely subtilizations, qualitatively different, of the former .... Of course it is not suggested that physical theory is a mirror-reflex of social relations. It gives information about non-social reality. But it gives such information *to* society. The knowledge is conscious knowledge. It has therefore to be cast into the categories of society.

These categories are not like Kantian categories, eternal and given in the nature of the mind, a set of tools which work up into a cognizable shape the unknowable thing-in-itself. Man interpenetrates actively with Nature .... This struggle is not merely physical – practical – it is also theoretical, a relation of cognition. (*C in P* 27–9)

It is (we recall) Caudwell's principal accusation against positivism that it reduces consciousness to a passive reflection of the world, 'a pale copy of existing practice.'

I fear that I am labouring a point. But perhaps it requires to be laboured. For according to one widely-accepted stereotype, British Marxism – at any time before the annunciation in this island of 'Western Marxism' in the Sixties – was subdued to a vulgar epistemological positivism. It can be seen that this was not true of Caudwell, nor of his considerable influence upon the Marxism of the Forties. Sebastiano Timpanaro has directed a polemic against the idealism of 'Western Marxism', which has managed to shuffle off concern with material (physical, biological) determinants as 'vulgar materialism' or 'positivism'.[25] If Timpanaro is right (and I think that on many points he is) then Caudwell's astonishing attempt at epistemological synthesis is in need of attention. For we may have been witnessing within the heart of the Marxist tradition itself a reproduction of that phenomenon which Caudwell diagnosed within bourgeois culture: the generation of those pseudo-antagonists, mechanical materialism and idealism. The same subject/object dualism, entering into Marxism, has left us with the twins of economic determinism and Althusserian idealism, each regenerating the other: the material basis determines the superstructure, independent of ideality, while the superstructure of ideality retires into the autonomy of a self-determining theoretical practice.

It is true that the majority Marxist tradition had been invaded by positivism by the Thirties. It is also true that the forerunners of 'Western Marxism' resisted this invasion, but at a very heavy cost. This cost is now evident in what passes today as a fashionable Marxist epistemology which has become locked into an idealist theoretical practice which, in its turn, constitutes a serious regression from the positions occupied by Caudwell. These positions might have been an elaboration of Marx's second thesis on Feuerbach.[26] The relation between being and knowing, Caudwell asserted, 'can only be understood in a dialectical manner' (*SDC* 13). But dialectics is not a formal logic, 'a machine for extracting the nature of reality from thought':

It is a recognition of the mutually determining relations between knowing and being .... Thought is knowing; the experience is being, and at each step new experience negates old thought. Yet their tension causes an advance to a new hypothesis more inclusive than the old. (*FS* 254)[27]

In this interactionist epistemology, there could never be tolerated that bleak theoretical closure (or confusion of empirical engagement with *empiricism*) which has been imposed by Althusser:

Truth always appears as a result of man's successful interaction with his environment .... To attempt to find it in a mere scrutiny of the conscious field, by 'pure' thought, results not in truth but in mere consistency. The contents of the mind are measured against themselves without the incursion of a disturbance from outside, which disturbances in fact, in the past history of the field, are what have created it. (*FS* 95)

Knowledge arises in a continual passage between conceptualisation and empirical observation, hypothesis and experiment, just as, in its origin, it arises from a similar interaction in the heart of the labour process: 'The plough is as much a statement about the nature of reality as the instructions how to use it. Each is useless without the other; each makes possible the development of the other.' (*FS* 96) At points Caudwell demands a test of theory by the praxis of experiment which has a Popperian ring:

No hypothesis, religious or scientific, can have any meaning unless it can give rise to a crucial test, which will enable it to be socially compared with other hypotheses. (*SDC* 164–5)

These arguments are all resumed in his study of 'Reality':

Our active contact with reality ensures a continual dialectical change in thought and perception, and the constant ingression of the new as a result of our changing relations with it. Thought therefore only needs to go out in action to remain dialectical; hence the dialectical nature of scientific hypotheses: The hypothesis goes out in the experiment, and, as a 'result', become changed, and returns upon the hypothesis to alter it ...

Whenever we see thought becoming non-dialectical and logical, there must be a breach between thought and action. Instead of preoccupying itself with the changing subject-object relation, mind preoccupies itself with the forms of that symbolism which, in the past, has contained old dialectical formulations of realities .... Thought has become introverted. (*FS* 253–4)

Thus Caudwell was able to write the epitaph of theoretical practice before it had even been imagined.

V

This interactionism was carried over, in a somewhat modified form, from epistemology to historical and cultural analysis. In his study of religion, 'The Breath of Discontent', he noted that religious ideas 'are causally linked with material reality, and are not only determined but also determine, in their turn exerting a causal influence on their matrix.' (*FS* 18) And in 'Reality'.

Thus thought is naturally dialectic in so far as it is part of the process of society. At each stage thought and material being are flung apart and return on each other, in mutual determinism, generating the new qualities of society. (*FS* 248).

But what meaning are we to give here to 'determine' and to 'mutual determinism?' And is this a 'dialectic' or merely a barren oscillation which, escaping the problem of determinism, simply leaves us with an antithetical model?

I do not think that Caudwell was consistent in this part of his thought. But what he offers is not a barren paradox but a fruitful contradiction, a tension which he leaves unresolved. This contradiction was greatly superior to the flat resolutions offered by most of his contemporaries. Nor was it a naive contradiction. One should recall that a great part – from chapter VI to the end – of *The*

Crisis in Physics is committed to the discussion of determinism and causality. Some part of that argument is relevant only to the natural sciences, and more than a part of it is too specialised for me to follow with confidence. But we should note that Caudwell distinguishes between determinism and predeterminism or 'absolute' determinism; and that by the former he indicates not pre-emptive or predictive 'law' but the given character and properties of an entity, occupying a given 'space', and hence setting limits upon the 'space' of other entities and thus determining their properties also. All properties in nature are, in this sense, mutually determining; Caudwell reaches for the image of the pool and the crevice, the river and the river-bed;[28] and this might be understood, in contemporary terms, as a structuralist argument. This corresponds to one sense of 'determination', as defined recently by Raymond Williams: the setting of limits.[29]

But if we transfer the term to social and cultural analysis, what are we left with? If 'thought and material being' are 'in mutual determinism', then we may say that 'social being determines social consciousness', but we must add that 'social consciousness determines social being'. Since (as Williams insists) 'in practice determination is never only the setting of limits: it is also the exertion of pressures', it would seem that we are left with an alternating current of interaction. But 'a Marxism without some concept of determination is in effect worthless',[30] and mutual interaction is scarcely determination. We are pulled back (I think) by Caudwell from a merely interactionist historical theory in several ways. First, in a certain epistemological priority afforded to being. 'I live, therefore I think I am' (*FS 239*): *Vivo, ergo cogito sum*. There is no sense in which either *sum* or *cogito* can be 'prior' to each other, since both are part of the same relation of being/cognition. But *sum* (when taken together with *vivo*) is always in the process of change, of becoming; and it is becoming ('experience') which thinking is *about* (*FS* 240); 'consciousness is therefore change, it is the ingression of the new.' (*FS* 92). Second, the source of this change, this becoming, is always situated by Caudwell primarily in the labour process: 'From the very start the labour process, by the society it generates, acts as a mediating term in the generation of truth.' (*FS* 96–7) 'Thought flows from being,

and ... man changes his consciousness by changing his social
relations, which change is the result of the pressure of real being
below those relations.' (SDC 11) The argument is muddy here
(does consciousness change social relations or vice versa, and what
is the 'real being' below both?), but clearly determination, in the
sense of 'the exertion of pressures' is moving from being to
consciousness. Third, when discussing class society, Caudwell
continually shows the exertion of determining pressure in the form
of ideological distortions of consciousness, as expressed in the very
categories within which thought is ordered. To this point we will
return.

But Caudwell cannot be said to be consistent. In the polemical
passages of *Studies in a Dying Culture* he ascribed, with wit and
even with sympathy, brutal class determinations to the products of
the bourgeois intellect. Loosely in *Illusion and Reality* and with
more precision and sophistication in *Further Studies* he exalted the
role of the artist and the scientist, who have in some way detached
themselves from 'the bourgeois'. And he introduced the concept of
'inner energy' which, more than anything else, brought (some years
after his death) the 'Caudwell Controversy' about his head.

It was on this count that Cornforth assailed Caudwell for his
'idealism'. He cited these lines from *Illusion and Reality*:

Energy is always flowing out to the environment of society, and
new perception always flowing in from it; as we change
ourselves, we change the world ....(I&R 296)[31]

And Cornforth comments:

Where Marx said that by acting on and changing the external
world we develop our powers and change ourselves, Caudwell
puts it the other way round .... From him, evidently, this 'energy
flowing out' has not its source in the external material world,
but comes from somewhere within us .... This idealist notion of
'inner energy' plays no small part in his writings.[32]

And in his reply to the discussion, a year later, Cornforth added:

The energy of man is itself a form of the motion of matter, just as the consciousness of man is a reflection of matter. Any other idea of energy or consciousness is idealism and mysticism.[33]

We have come a long way from those happy days of Marxist certainty. Of course, the energy of man may be seen as 'a form of the motion of matter' (Caudwell himself took more pains than most writers to see it in this aspect), but this does not settle, finally, the question of the directions in which it moves. As Williams remarked, in *Culture and Society*:

It is clear that many English writers on culture who are also, politically, Marxists seem primarily concerned to make out a case for its existence, to argue that it is important, against a known reaction to Marxism which had established the idea that Marx, with his theory of structure and superstructure, had diminished the value hitherto accorded to intellectual and imaginative creation.[34]

Cornforth reminds us that this known reaction' was not only outside the Marxist tradition (among Marxism's critics) but also deeply entrenched within it. Perhaps Williams mistook whom the English Marxist critics of the late Thirties and Forties were arguing *with*? When Alick West (in defence of Caudwell) noted that Marx also referred to 'inner energy', Cornforth replied that Marx must have been thinking of 'the minimum of food necessary' if the capitalists were to be able to exploit the workers: 'To imagine some inner store of human energy is to think of man and of his energies and powers in a merely abstract, idealist way.'

The entire body of Caudwell's work may be read as a polemic against mechanical materialism of this kind, masquerading as Marxism. Men can do nothing significant without consciousness and passion: all that they do is passionate and conscious. In *Illusion and Reality* he is 'making out a case' for the part played by the arts in the generation and organisation of spiritual energies; indeed, poetry, and the arts come to be shorthand for almost all of culture that is not-science. This is one valid criticism of his work: in making a general case for culture, he lost sight of the particular case of art, and of the particularity of each art product. And I have already indicated that I have such extensive criticisms of this apprenticework (*Illusion and Reality*) that I consider it to be beyond the repair of close criticism. But my criticisms certainly do not extend to the propriety of the project itself: that is, the renewed emphasis, within a Marxist problematic, upon human *subjectivity* and (in consequence) upon the arts.

The difficulty of Caudwell's project was greatly enhanced by the positivism, indeed philistinism, of the Marxist tradition within which he worked. Cornforth was especially incensed at Caudwell's careful (and rational) definition of poetry as 'irrational': 'So poetry does not, as Marxists had hitherto supposed, portray in poetic images the reality of the world and of our own life in it.' 'The reactionary theory that poetry "is irrational" and is concerned, not with the real world, but with some "underworld" of emotions' is one which Marxists should reject 'with indignation'. It must have been comforting, in those distant days, to have known with such assurance what was the 'real world' (a world somehow distinct from that of the emotions?), and to have had such ready reserves of indignation for all who strayed from the truth. But it must also have been a difficult and discomforting time for Caudwell, and, perhaps also, for Fox, for West, for Rickword and Slater and Swingler, and other pioneers of socialist cultural theory and practice.

What Caudwell has to say about effective culture is cogently argued and always suggestive, although the proposals in the studies are generally superior to those in *Illusion and Realty*. It is not my business to rehearse these arguments again; they are familiar and readily available, have been explored by Margolies and Mulhern, and perhaps should now be re-examined by anthropologists as well as by critics. What I wish to stress is that Caudwell's insights (however disorderly) were bought at a cost which orthodox Marxism was unwilling to pay. For Caudwell argued:

> The value of art to society is that by it an emotional adaptation is possible. Man's instincts are pressed in art against the altered mould of reality, and by a specific organisation of the emotions thus generated, there is a new attitude, an *adaptation*. (*SDC* 54)

'All art is produced by this tension between changing social relations and outmoded consciousness.' (*Ibid.* 54) Art modifies the subject's 'general attitude towards life ... Viewed from the society's standpoint, art is the fashioning of the affective consciousness of its members, the conditioning of their instincts.' (*Ibid.* 50) So that we are, once again, within an interactionist field: art, operates *upon* men and changes them affectively. Pseudo-art, the commercialised product, is 'simply affective massage. It awakens and satisfies the instincts without expressing and synthesising a tension between instinct and environment.' (*FS 107*)

The critical problem, when situating Caudwell within the Marxist tradition, lies in his recourse to the concept of the 'genotype'. This is by no means a casual or carelessly-introduced concept. Caudwell's central notions of cultural adaptation and of the function of the arts rests upon the concept of an unchanging genotype in friction with changing social environment. This is no elision of thought: it is a deliberate and repeated proposition:

> This contradiction between instinct and cultural environment is absolutely primary to society ... (*I&R* 137)
>
> [Great art is expression of] the timelessness of the instincts, the unchanging secret face of the genotype which persists beneath all the rich superstructure of civilisation. (*Ibid.* 228)
>
> All art is emotional and therefore concerned with the instincts whose adaptation to social life produces emotional consciousness. Hence art cannot escape its close relation with the genotype whose secret desires link in one endless series all human culture. (*Ibid.* 231)

While Caudwell's treatment of the 'instincts' becomes refined in the subsequent studies, he nowhere disclaims the concept of the genotype.

Now it is necessary to identify, not only what the difficulty is, in Caudwell's use of 'genotype', but also what the difficulty is *not*. For a common response, among historical materialists, is immediately to identify the concept of genotype with that of 'human nature', and to dismiss the argument unheard as 'reactionary'. There has been, and still is, for observable and honourable reasons, a deep hostility in the Marxist tradition to any such concept of human nature, and Cornforth's reaction is typical of the common-sense of the tradition:

> The whole idea of the genotype and the instincts is a piece of made-up idealist metaphysics. For it supposes that something exists within the organism – the genotype and the instincts – which is not susceptible to change; which is not born and modified and developed in the course of the life of the organism, but which precedes it and stamps its own pattern on it.
>
> Applied to human affairs, this is a singularly reactionary theory. It teaches that human nature never changes .... Timeless human nature, the instincts of the savage, persist unchanged and unchangeable beneath the developing social and cultural 'super-structure'; civilisation is but a thin veneer covering the volcanic underworld of primitive instincts ...
>
> Marxism does not explain society and its development in terms of eternal genotypical instincts. It rejects these reactionary hypotheses of bourgeois biology and psychology. [35]

But, of course, Caudwell does not 'explain society and its development' in terms of the genotype either. This is, exactly, what he does *not* do, for if he could have explained social development in this way, then no function would have been left for the arts. Nor is it correct that the genotype is synonymous with 'human nature'. The genotype gives us, rather, 'brute nature' – the nature of man as a brute, prior to his or her acquisition, through socialisation and culture, of humanity, or human nature. The 'constancy of man' Caudwell sometimes illustrated in a figure of the feral child:

> By constancy we mean his constancy as bare individual. If a Melanesian, an ancient Athenian and a modern English babe were allowed to grow up in a wood ... none would share any of the characteristics of its parents' culture – either their language, their economic production, or their consciousness. They would grow up sub-human. This shows that man remains through the ages relatively unchanged, or that at least his genetic change is

in no way proportioned to his change as a member of contemporary society. (*FS* 137–8; see also *I&R* 151)

It is not clear to me that this is shown (for the 'sub-human' genotype cannot then be described as 'man'), and the experiment is unlikely to be made. But it is clear that Caudwell intends the concept (or hypothesis) of the genotype to stand, not for human nature, but for pre-human nature, a common biological and instinctual ground, persisting relatively unchanged through historical time, prior to acculturation. So far from being a 'reactionary' thesis, which seeks to reduce all change to a timeless human nature, it emphasises that *everything* that is 'human' arises within society and culture.

Indeed, it is not so much a concept as a commonplace. Without further definition it offers little more than the hypothesis that brute, pre-human nature remains the nature of brute *homo* and not that of the dog or the ape. And what alternative concepts could be proposed? One might be that cultural adaptations are genetically transmitted, and that every babe is born, in some part, a Melanesian, an ancient Athenian, a Cockney, or, perhaps, an Aryan or a White Anglo-Saxon Protestant. Another might be that every babe is born without any genetically-transmitted species-inheritance: that is, as a natural blank. Neither concept offers an improvement on that of the genotype. The problems arise when we attempt to define this genotype, with its attendant instinctual ground, and then employ the concept in historical or cultural analysis.

The genotype is a concept which Caudwell took from biology, and we do not know what clarification is offered in his still-unpublished further study on that theme. But clarification is to be found in other studies. These suggest that it is unfair to characterise Caudwell's theory as 'a psychologism', or to suggest that his concept of 'the instincts' remains undefined.[36] 'The innate responses of an organism, the so-called instincts, as such are unconscious, mechanical, and unaffected by experience.' They are the concern, not of psychology, but of physiology (*SDC* 184):

Instinct is what we call a simple repetition of hereditary habits, the mechanical reappearance of the old. Such simple responses to external or internal stimuli change from age to age, but, in relation to the rapid tempo of social life, there is a consistency about them which leads us to separate them *as hypothetical entities* [my italics], the instincts. Situations which, while evoking instinctual responses, do not permit their emergence unchanged, but cause a suspension or interruption of the pattern, produce affects or emotions. The result of such a situation is the transforming, or conditioning (Pavlov), repression or sublimation (Freud) of the response. (*FS* 90)[37]

It is in the study of 'Consciousness' that we have Caudwell's most sustained critique of 'instinct psychology', and, precisely, of psychologism, in which 'the drama of the instincts ... becomes a kind of bourgeois novel, in which the heroes are the instincts; and their experiences, mutual struggles and transformations generate not only all psychical but also all cultural phenomena':

What in fact are these instincts? They are innate patterns of behaviour automatically elicited by stimuli. They are therefore inevitable recurrences amid the sea of change, like the seasons. They are determined in fact (predetermined) by past events.

The bourgeois however sees them 'as freely striving for unconscious goals, and psychology becomes the adventures of the free instincts in their struggles against the restraints of the *environment* (in Freud, of *society*) which impede and cripple their freedom':

The magnificent story of human culture becomes ... simply the tragedy of the crippling of the free instincts by the social restraints they have freely created .... Experience, art and science are in this psychology the fetters of the instinctive energy; all experiences are the scars of the wounds to this freedom (inhibition and repression). Moreover the unconscious plays a strange role. Since experience is in this inversion of life's story the prison house of the free instincts, consciousness (the most recent and least innate products of the psyche) acts the part of gaoler to the unconscious (the most archaic and least conditioned psychic products). Quite a little coercive State reigns in the psyche, complete even to the Censor. Abominable things are done to the instincts; screams (dreams and obsessions) issue from time to time from the dungeons where the noble bourgeois revolutionaries are being tortured by the authorities. It is a picture in the best anarchist style ....

But 'the instincts are not free springs of connation towards a goal. They are, so far as they can be abstractly separated, unconscious necessities, as Kant realised. They are unfree.' Above all,

They are changed in human culture. As a result of this change, these necessities become conscious, become emotion and thought; they exist for themselves and are altered thereby. The change *is* the emotion or thought, and now they are no longer the instincts ... (*FS* 179–82)

Caudwell, then, is retaining the concept (or 'hypothesis') of the instincts and of the genotype, while flatly rejecting 'instinct psychology'. He is placed in a difficulty in that the dominant available psychological vocabularies offer conditioning (Pavlov) and repression or sublimation (Freud), whereas the change he wishes to express is that of transformation and exfoliation. Socialisation, by transforming the instincts, by changing the pre-social and pre-human genotype into the human, is a process of realisation. 'Man, as society advances, has a consciousness composed less and less of unmodified instinct, more and more of socially-fashioned knowledge and emotion.' (*SDC* 217) 'Emotion, in all its vivid colouring, is the creation of ages of culture acting on the blind unfeeling instincts. All art, all education, all day-to-day social experience, draw it out of the heart of the human genotype and direct and shape its myriad phenomena. Only society as a whole can really direct this force in the individual.' (*SDC* 183) Hence psychology,

can only have for its material all those psychic contents that result from the *modification* of responses by experience. It is this material that changes, that develops, that is distinctively human, that is of importance, and psychology should and in

practice does ignore the *unchanging* instinctual basis as a cause.
(*SDC* 184)

Well and good. The genotype stands for the genetic transmission of
pre-human nature, a ground of instincts or innate responses (a
predetermined programming) which remains relatively constant
through historical time, but which, in the absence of repeated
'Mowgli' experiments, can only be inferred as a hypothesis. The
genotype signifies the genetic transmission of whatever is left when
we have subtracted all that is culturally or socially acquired. There
does not appear to be anything inherently reactionary, or idealist, or
anti-Marxist in such a concept. It is, however, a singularly weak
and indefinite concept; everything depends upon how it is put to
use, and how the 'innate' instincts are defined. Moreover, the term
entails once again that dislocation between a rational and a
metaphoric meaning which we have noted before in Caudwell's
writing: but in this case the rational signification (when taken
together with his critique of 'instinct psychology') is greatly
preferable to the metaphoric drift. This drift arises, in large part,
from the use of a *singular* concept – *the* genotype – to describe a
clump of genetically-transmitted physical properties and instinctual
propensities. By assimilation into this singular noun, the particular
components of the typical genetic complement become lost to view,
and with the least imprecision or lapse of attention – as in the shift
from 'genotype' to 'man' – the metaphor drifts towards an
unchanging human nature. More than this, the metaphor, in its
singular sense, is then brought into conjunction with the collective
noun, 'society'; and we have then drifted back towards the very
position which Caudwell sought to reject – that of the unchanging
instinctual extra-social 'individual' type facing a changing society.[38]
    Caudwell is guilty, especially in *Illusion and Reality*, of this
kind of inattention. There are times when he slides carelessly
between the notion of instinctual responses, inherent in the
genotype ('man'), and affects or 'emotions', which are seen as
belonging to a common perceptual and affective world (adhering to
the affective properties of language itself), the product of complex
processes of cultural formation. But what is critically wrong is the
use to which he put the concept in cultural and historical analysis.

There is surely a contradiction between Caudwell's argument that 'psychology should ... ignore the *unchanging* instinctual basis as a cause', and the central place which he invoked for the genotype in his theory of art. For the accurate definition of the human genetic inheritance (even if only as ever-more-precise hypotheses) might appear to be a valid concern of physiology, neurology, and thence by extension of psychology or linguistics; but only thence by further extension, and through these mediations, of aesthetics. And in general, in historical and cultural analysis, the extension becomes so remote that the genotype or pre-human nature must remain an unknowable and unobservable entity, and hence a concept not so much false as without meaning. As I argued in these pages four years ago:

> The bare forked creature, naked biological man, is not a context we can ever observe, because the very notion of man (as opposed to his anthropoid ancestor) is coincident with culture .... Thus to propose the investigation of 'man' apart from his culture (or his lived history) is to propose an unreal abstraction, the investigation of non-man.[39]

Caudwell was seeking to hold in one place a materialist theory of art which took into serious account the evidence of physiology, neurology, psychology, anthropology. The intention was valid, and the enterprise should not be abandoned. But the concept of the genotype obscured rather than clarified the linkages. If this clumpish singular concept is broken apart, then the way is open to the scrupulous examination of particular (biological, instinctual, mental) links and determinations. As these knowledges advance, so they may be brought together again in a 'natural history of man' (or, as I would prefer, of natural determinants within history) to which even historians may give a hesitant recognition. But Caudwell proposed an unmediated conflict between instinct and social environment, not as some original hypothesis (a primeval cultural 'contract'), but as an operation continuing throughout history, in which the original instincts, freshly renewed with each genetic transmission, must be socialised by 'art'. The difficulty is, first, that Caudwell places far more upon 'art' and 'poetry' than

they can bear. And, second, that in his practice, he must often
attribute to the genotype or the instincts an active, assertive
presence ('secret face', 'secret desires') which is at odds with his
more careful definitions in the studies.

In the following passage both difficulties are presented:

> Man himself is composed like society of current active being
> and inherited conscious formulations. He is somatic and psychic,
> instinctive and conscious, and these opposites interpenetrate. He
> is formed, half rigid, in the shape of the culture he was born in,
> half fluid and new and insurgent, sucking reality through his
> instinctive roots. Thus he feels, right in the heart of him, this
> tension between being and thinking, between new being and old
> thought, a tension which will give rise by synthesis to new
> thought. He feels as if the deepest instinctive part of him and
> the most valuable is being dragged away from his consciousness
> by events. (*SDC* 26)

Once again, we have a conflict between a rational and metaphoric
meaning. But in its rational argument the passage does, after all,
merit the term, 'psychologism'. The 'somatic' and the 'instinctive'
become 'being', the 'roots' through which reality is sucked into
consciousness. This not only contradicts all that Caudwell has to
say, in his more measured appraisals, as to the instincts as innate
behaviour patterns, prior to culture and to social being: it also
inverts the argument of 'Consciousness', for, with 'rigid ...
insurgent ... new being and old thought', it appears that the
instinctive life alone is 'active' and that culture is resistant to
change and 'inherited'. The passage exemplifies the tendency of his
concept of the genotype to escape from his own controls.

What have become lost in this passage are the concepts of
social being and of culture. Caudwell has forgotten that the
instincts 'are changed in human culture .... The change *is* the
emotion or thought.' And that social being is as remote from 'the
instincts' as an agrarian system is from hunger. The genotype was
used by Caudwell (and here I am in agreement with Mulhern) in
an essentialist and often reductionist manner. By identifying one
essential, basic function for the arts ('man's instincts are pressed in

art against the altered mould of reality') Caudwell is continually reducing his analysis to a circulation within his original terms. But if man's instincts are pressed against the mould of reality, this finds expression not only in art but in every form of acculturation and socialisation; indeed, by the time the child ventures to lisp its first nursery rhyme, it has acquired, through language and socialisation, a character in which the genotype is already masked or transformed beyond recall. Language is already naming and changing instincts into emotions; and the contradiction, or tension, which arises is less between the instincts and reality than between inherited cultural modes and fresh experience. The conflict arises, not between pre-culture and culture, but *within culture itself.*

In Caudwell's hands the concept of the genotype becomes a blunt instrument which he wielded monotonously, like an unhoned scythe with which he tried to hack a way through a dense undergrowth of other mediations to reach some ever-present original source. But the source, unless as aboriginal hypothesis, was never there. Caudwell's failure to elaborate any concept of value or of value-system (for values cannot be comprised in a vocabulary of instincts, emotions or affects) is the inadequacy in his conceptual terms which has the most serious practical consequences. His theory offers instincts adapted into emotions or even attitudes, but the ordering of feeling can only be understood in terms of value. And when we consider value and poetry, concepts so large as Man's Struggle with Nature (a debilitating and repetitious concept, and yet a necessary correspondent concept to that of the genotype and culture), obliterate where all the significant questions lie. For value will be found, most often, in particular historical contexts, and in particular men and women's struggle with, or adjustment to, or love for, other particular women and men. All this escapes from Caudwell's view, just as, in his essentialist paradigm, he often loses all sight of the real historical contradictions, in social being, of social class.

This enforces a severe judgement upon that part of Caudwell's enterprise. But reservations must be entered. Marxism's resistance to the concept of 'human nature', however deployed, may be proper. But the resistance may also cover, as I think it did with Cornforth, an ulterior flight from the subjective. Caudwell is not to be pilloried because he found poetry 'irrational', nor because of his emphasis on the operative, transforming role of the arts. Nor is he to be dismissed as 'idealist' because of his notion of 'inner energy' (even if his proper emphasis upon subjective 'energy' sometimes confuses instinctual drives and internalised cultural resources); nor yet (in my view) because of his arguments as to the mutually-determining interaction between social being and social consciousness. This remains the most critically-difficult area of any general Marxist theory of history and of culture, and if Caudwell did not resolve the problem he is to be commended for not tidying it away, in the conventions of his time, and for placing it upon the agenda of theory. Indeed, his emphasis upon active subjectivity, and his fruitful ambiguity as to being/consciousness, accounts in large part for his liberating and 'heretical' influence.

The terms of Caudwell's attempted revision are often unsatisfactory: the conceptual vocabulary which he inherited or which he invented from diverse disciplines sometimes broke apart in his hands: but the Marxism of his time offered him no other. And I am less confident than some others that 'Western', or any other, Marxism has subsequently resolved these problems. I would prefer to accept the judgement of Williams, the first half of whose *Marxism and Literature* is the most substantial work of critical reflection upon the terms of Marxist analysis to appear from any English thinker since the time of Caudwell: all these problems still remain on the agenda.

A further reservation may be entered. I have been over-severe when I suggested that Caudwell was trapped in his cultural theory in an oscillatory passage between Man/Nature, genotype/social environment. True, he fell back into this far too often; but there are middle terms in his more extended arguments; for the first, the labour process; for the second, language. And on both he had significant ideas to offer.

For the labour process, we will simply report his argument. It is, once again, presented more cogently in the further study, 'Beauty', than in *Illusion and Reality*:

The nature of fields and plants imposes on the organism specific types of co-operation in sowing and reaping and determines the shape of the plough. It imposes on them language, whereby they signify to each other their duties and urge each other on in carrying them out. Once established the labour process, extending as remotely as the observation of the stars, as widely as the organisation of all human relations, and as abstractedly as the invention of numbers, gathers and accumulates truth. (*FS* 96–7)

Not only truth, but also the arts (or 'beauty') are generated in the labour process:

In primitive civilisation this intimate generation of truth and beauty in the course of the labour process and their mutual effect on each other is so clear that it needs no elaboration. The harvest is work, but it is also dance; it deals with reality, but it is also pleasure. All social forms, gestures, and manners have to primitives a purpose, and are both affective and cognitive. Law is not merely the elucidation of a truth in dispute, but the satisfaction of the gods, of the innate sense of rightness in man's desires. Myths express man's primitive instincts and his view of reality. The simplest garment or household utensil has a settled beauty. Work is performed in time to singing, and has its own fixed ceremony. All tasks have their lucky days. Truth and beauty, science and art are primitive, but at least they are vitally intermingled, each giving life to the other.

It is the special achievement of later bourgeois civilisation to have robbed science of desirability and art of reality. (*FS* 105–6)

The passage presents the usual essentialist difficulties ('*Innate* sense of rightness?' 'Man's primitive instincts?') but these are not so severe as to disqualify the argument.

In *Illusion and Reality* Caudwell argued persuasively for a derivation of the arts within the heart of the labour process, in adapting and organising human attitudes in co-operative ways, in summoning up necessary psychic energies in expectation of harvest or in mimesis of the hunt; and, by extension, he derived myth from the labour process also:

> The dead and the not-dead are the two great divisions of
> primitive society which seem almost to stand to each other in
> the relation of exploited to exploiting classes. The living owe
> their productive level to the capital, the instruments of produc-
> tion, the instruction, the wisdom, and the transmitted culture of
> the dead who therefore continue to live in the interstices of the
> society they have departed from in body. This half-life of the
> dead, constantly recalled to the living by their instructions, their
> leavings and their social formulations, is the other-world sur-
> vival of the dead in all primitive societies .... This immortality
> of the dead is a fantastic reality. The dead really live on
> socially in the inherited culture of society, but to the primitive
> they live fantastically, clothed in the affective and concrete
> images of his dreams in another, ghostly world. (*FS* 32)

All these arguments – although some have been refined since
Caudwell's time – continue to command our sympathetic attention.
But while Man and Nature are mediated by the labour process, the
mediation is only provisional, and the two parties to the relation
are sometimes offered, inexplicably, as implacable antagonists:

> The war between man and nature is waged on more and more
> fronts; and it is precisely this undying hostility, this furious
> antagonism, which produces a greater humanisation of the
> environment by man and a greater environmentalisation of man
> by nature. (*FS* 27)

This is perhaps an example of a lapse in Caudwell's style into the
dominant 'Soviet' rhetoric of the mid-Thirties: the military vocabulary of the opening, the barren antithetical epigram of the
conclusion, and the central proposition, then acclaimed in Soviet
orthodoxy, that in socialist society the struggle between classes
would give way to the more basic struggle between men and
nature: massed battalions of tractors, each flying a red flag, waging
furious war upon the virgin steppes.

   Even when the middle term, the labour process, is held to, it is
held in terms of struggle or war. (Men might – a gardener or a
stock-breeder might argue – co-operate with nature). A certain kind

of drama is insisted upon which colours Caudwell's view of art.
And we are in danger of replacing one essentialist paradigm with
another, only slightly more refined. Caudwell's move from primitive to modern society is so swift that (despite passing references
to class) it allows for the interposition of only one new important
concept: that of the market, and of commodity-fetishism:

> Labour now becomes, not labour to achieve a goal and to attain
> the desirable, but labour for the market and for cash. Labour
> becomes blind and unconscious. What is made, or why it is
> made, is no longer understood, for the labour is merely for cash,
> which now alone supports life. Thus all affective elements are
> withdrawn from labour, and must therefore reappear elsewhere.
> They now reappear attached to the mythical commodity which
> represents the unconscious market – cash. Cash is the music of
> labour in bourgeois society. Cash achieves objective beauty.
> Labour in itself becomes increasingly distasteful and irksome
> and cash increasingly beautiful and desirable. Money become the
> god of society. Thus the complete disintegration of a culture on
> the affective side is achieved, and has resulted from the same
> causes as its disintegration on the cognitive side. (*FS* 107–8)

The thought is pressed forward powerfully, like a logical imperative; it is derivative from Marx and also, perhaps, from Morris;[40]
but it is, once again, essentialist – the rapid delineation of the deep
process of a whole epoch – and it has no location within the
complexity of particular historical and cultural formations: what
happened (one wonders) in the interval between 'primitive' and
'later bourgeois civilisation?' The 'complete disintegration of a
culture' comes through as a kind of swearing at 'the bourgeois'.

What Caudwell says about language is less clear. His approach to linguistics was more amateurish than was his approach
to anthropology, physiology, psychology. None of his studies was
centrally concerned with language, and the treatment in *Illusion
and Reality* is glancing and unsystematic and is diverted into
consideration of the polar antitheses of language's cognitive and
affective attributes ('science'/'art'). What may be more significant
than anything which he says is the number of vulgarisations and

reductions which he *avoided* making. Williams has noted that the
dominant Marxism from the late nineteenth to the mid-twentieth
century tended to neglect language theory, and to group practical
language activities 'under the categories of "ideology" and "the
superstructure".' What was lost was the understanding of language as 'practical consciousness' or as 'practical, constitutive
activity':

> Language ... became a tool or an instrument or a medium taken
> up by individuals when they had something to communicate, as
> distinct from the faculty which made them, from the beginning,
> not only able to relate and communicate, but in real terms to be
> practically conscious and so to possess the active practice of
> language.[41]

There are times when Caudwell writes of language as a simple
medium of exchange ('the expression of a transfer between one man
and another' (*I&R* 160); but this medium is not supposed as an
exchange between already-formed, pre-given individual consciousness. For it is through language that consciousness is generated. The
'elaborate activities' of primitive economic production –

> Can only be co-ordinated by an elaboration of affect and word
> organisations which thus contain within their interstices a *social*
> view of outer *reality* and a *community* of emotionally tinged *ideas.*
> Thus any picture of the individual consciousness at the start
> detaching itself as a simple ego from all reality, and acquiring its
> own presentations and organising them, is false; for consciousness
> emerges as the concomitant of economic production, as part and
> parcel of man's interpenetration with outer reality. The interpen-
> etration generates consciousness, which is therefore full of the
> impress of both. The formation of consciousness is an active
> process, now and historically .... (*FS* 23–4)

'We can never prove consciousness in terms of the theory of the
common perceptual world because it is entirely that world.' (*I&R*
192) Language generates consciousness by creating a common
perceptual world and also a common affective 'ego': the conscious

'I' is always, through language, a social creation. Caudwell is content to describe this world as 'symbolic', and to enquire into its operation very little further. Language is always more rigid ('the mind's stiff and treelike qualities') than the changing reality which it stands for:

> The socially accepted pictures we make in words of reality cannot change as if they were reflections in a mirror. An object is reflected in a mirror. If the object moves the reflection moves. But in language reality is symbolised in unchanging words, which give a false stability and permanence to the object they represent. Thus they instantaneously photograph reality rather than reflect it. This frigid character of language is regrettable but ... it is probably the only way in which man with his linear consciousness, can get a grip of fluid reality. Language, as it develops, shows more and more of this false permanence .... This permanence is part of the inescapable nature of symbolism, which is expressed in the rules of logic. It is one of the strange freaks of the human mind that it has supposed that reality must obey the rules of logic, whereas the correct view is that symbolism by its very nature has certain rules, expressed in the laws of logic, and these are nothing to do with the process of reality, but represent the nature of the symbolic process itself. (*SDC* 50–1)

That is an odd passage. In moving away from 'reflection', Caudwell seems to be about to discuss the 'autonomy' of language and its rules. But he seizes, instead, upon 'photograph', which defeats his purpose.[42] And then, by stressing the rules of logic rather than grammar, he diverts attention from language to its products. But the confusion arises from an inadequate linguistic theory, and not from an assimilation of language to ideology or to superstructure. Moreover, in evading attention to the symbolic structure of language Caudwell was also evading (perhaps deliberately) Saussurian structuralism.

We cannot say that Caudwell had even an incipient, unformulated theory of language. Rejecting the theories available to him, he was concerned with skirting around their traps and with offering certain affirmations. If we accept Williams's analysis of the problem, then Caudwell's notion of language remained stubbornly 'constitutive', a 'practical consciousness' which 'is saturated by and saturates all social activity.'[43] He does not place 'the individual' here and a linguistic system there; his cumbersome notions of a common perceptual world and a common affective ego entail an insistence that language is 'the means of realisation of any individual life.'[44] Language is seen both as a medium of communication and as internalised, the very stuff of consciousness. He attends more carefully to the affective than to the cognitive properties of language. Writing of the 'mimic representation', not of language but of art, he argued:

> The emanation is *in* us, *in* our affective reaction with the elements of the representation. Given in the representation are not only the affects, but, simultaneously, their organisation in an affective *attitude* towards the piece of reality symbolised in the mimicry. This affective attitude is bitten in by a general heightening of consciousness and increase in self-value, due to the non-motor nature of the innovations aroused, which seems therefore all to pass into an affective irradiation of consciousness. (*SDC* 49)

Caudwell commonly ascribed to 'art' functions and properties which might more properly be ascribed to language, and thence to culture. There is, more than once, the suggestion that the affective are the fluid and dynamic properties of language, as opposed to the 'frigidity' and false 'permanence' of its cognitive symbolism. 'In the fashioning of consciousness the great instrument is language. It is language which makes us consciously see the sun, the stars, the rain and the sea – objects which merely elicit *responses* from animals.' (*I&R* 192) Men inherit through their language particular modes of consciousness:

> The primitive does not see seas, but the river Oceanus; he does not see mammals, but edible beasts. He does not see, in the night sky, blazing worlds in the limitless void, but a roof inlaid with patines of bright gold. Hence all natural things are artificial. (*FS* 111)

In the same way:

> a civilised man's view of outer reality is almost entirely built up of the common perceptual world: he sees the sun as a fiery star, cows as animals, iron as metal, and so on. The extraordinary power and universality of language guarantees this. But it is just as true that his whole emotional consciousness, his whole feeling-attitude to the sun, iron, cows and so forth, is almost entirely built up from the common ego which enables us to live in close relation as men. (*I&R* 167)

But whereas the cognitive system of language's symbolism finds expression in fixed (frigid) categories, which can only be broken down and reconstructed in the course of strenuous intellectual conflict (this is one theme of *The Crisis in Physics*), the *concrete* properties of poetry can reach deeply into the inherited affective modes transmitted by language, conveying directly 'an experience' which modifies 'the subject's general attitude towards life', thus also modifying the common affective ego which is thence transmitted to the future. (*SDC* 49) It is this direct, concrete, operative power of poetry which continues to afford a challenge, the possibility of revolutionising inherited modes of consciousness.

I do not offer all this as any kind of systematic theory. We slide around too much between language, culture, art and poetry. But I do not think it is all nonsense either. At least, it leaves open doors which, as Williams has shown, the Marxism of Caudwell's time was closing or whose existence it refused to acknowledge. And Caudwell declined also to take another available exit (which has currently become more fashionable) in which men are seen as 'acting out the laws and codes of an inaccessible linguistic system.'[45] Caudwell's was a way of muddling through, among shifting terms. But what was saved, in the midst of this muddle, was not negligible; it was a sense of the nobility and import of poetry among the arts. The attack upon Caudwell in 1950–51 assumes some of its significance from this, and must be seen alongside Zhdanov's attack on Pasternak and that of Revai on Lukács. It is not just that Stalinism feared poets as heretics; there was an ulterior fear of consciousness itself, in its active and

creative attributes, of which poetry is the sign. Hence poetry must
be allocated an inferior, reflective function – to 'portray in poetic
images the reality of the world' – a reality that was 'objective' and
given independent of consciousness. In defending poetry from this
relegation Caudwell was also defending a view of human creativity.
But with creativity must also go uncertainty: failures in prediction,
failures to conform to objective law, threats to a positivist 'science'
of society. Such threats were intolerable. The Party, guided by
Marxism-Leninism-Stalinism, should be able to decide what was
'reality', and then poets could set reality to rhyme. It was for these
reasons – and not because Caudwell had failed in some parts of his
enterprise – that his whole work came under official attack. Yet the
attack was not (as we have seen) without some legitimate basis,
and Caudwell's own confusions, in *Illusion and Reality*, inhibited
the defence.[46] By the time the dust had settled, his work had fallen
into general disrepute.

VI

And should it now be rehabilitated once again? That is not the
intention of this essay. I hope to have shown that Caudwell's work
was more interesting, more complex, and more heretical than has
been supposed. But nothing that he wrote is of a maturity or
consistency to merit election as a Marxist or any other kind of
'classic'.

Yet if we replace the *Studies* where they should always have
been – at the centre of Caudwell's work – then we are entitled to
make a favourable revision of the accepted judgement. In the
transition from *Illusion and Reality* to the *Studies* more had
changed in Caudwell than could be expected in the passage of one
year. After completing that book in Cornwall, he had moved to
Poplar, where he soon became a member of the local branch of the
Communist Party, sharing rooms with several of his new comrades.
Until this time he seems to have been withdrawn and introverted,
within the protection of his kindly older brother Theodore, and
with few friends apart from Paul Beard, a school-fellow and critic,
and his wife, Elizabeth, a writer. Now, developing late, he
discovered in himself new resources of sociability. He had almost
nothing to do with the intellectuals of the Party (he attended some

lectures on Marxism and Literature by Alick West and Douglas Garman), but in a year of activity which included battles with the Blackshirts he won the comradeship of his fellow Poplar Communists.[47] It is evident, in the *Studies*, that he had found a new style and a new sense of audience; there is a new fluency of polemical attack and a new self-confidence. He also focussed his mind in a new way upon one central problem: that of ideology.

Even here Caudwell's work does not allow for a simple judgement. We may set aside the sectarian stridency, which belonged to a strident (and critical) historical moment. But we meet, once again, the old problem of Caudwell's 'essentialist' tricks of mind, his tendency to intellectualise the social process. Every critic, from Cornforth to Mulhern, has noted that in his work any real sense of history is missing. In Williams's view, 'To describe English life, thought, and imagination in the last three hundred years simply as "bourgeois", to describe English culture now as "dying", is to surrender reality to a formula.'[48] There is nothing in Caudwell's writing which speaks to the actual texture and mediations of social and cultural process; if he explored the consequences of Marx's first two theses on Feuerbach, he failed to take the point of the sixth.[49] His study on history ('Me and Nature') is quite the worst in *Further Studies*, and his interesting study of religion ('The Breath of Discontent') is suddenly made ridiculous by a jejeune sectarian political parable on the life of Christ (Jesus was a premature social-democrat, and 'by his treatment of the vital question of workers' power, Jesus had from the start ensured the defeat of his communist programme'). The study is in fact very much more interesting in its comments on magic than in any part of its treatment of religion. (see *FS* 30)

While Caudwell encounters and despatches various kinds of philosophical idealism, idealism re-enters into his history: first, as a transcultural idea of progress – Man/Nature/Progress – which, while showing men as being irredeemably stunted and thwarted by class division and ideological illusion, nevertheless always hypostasises a Man who is progressively enriched and fulfilled. Second, idealism returns as the epochal idea of 'the bourgeois', who maintains across centuries an archetypal ideal character, imposing its ideal logic upon the historical evolution of the epoch:

> The absolutist Tudors are only a phase of the bourgeois
> revolution .... The full bourgeois state comes later into being as
> a democratic constitutional state. The bourgeois has then
> achieved his desire, which is that there should be no overt
> dominating relations over himself. There are only to be dominat-
> ing rights over property .... (*R&R* 42)

Thus the democratic state is seen as the fulfilment of some primal
and constant bourgeois idea. This idea is seen to arc across time,
from those unlikely bourgeois, the Tudors, to the Thirties, disclosing its consecutive logic, from a rich individualist protest at its
origin to its final loss of identity within the compulsive and unfree
anarchy of uncontrolled market relations, of Fascism and of war.

But this epochal idealism, I would argue, is a vice attendant upon
significant virtues. I suggested earlier that Caudwell should be seen as
an anatomist of ideology. He was preoccupied centrally in all his
work with ideology, and above all with its own authentic *logic*. If he
was wrong to afford to this logic autonomy – an idea imposing itself
on history – he was not wrong to identify this logic as an authentic
element within the social process. He was concerned with the
characteristic 'illusion of the epoch'; the 'deep structure' of myth; the
generation of modes of intellectual self-mystification.

In this preoccupation Caudwell anticipated some part of 'Western Marxist' thought. He gave a similar primacy to the ways in
which the mind becomes estranged from reality through its
self-imprisonment in its own categories. The categories of the
critic, he remarks in *Romance and Realism*, are 'generated below
the surface by one developing thing, bourgeois social relations. As
all the critic's other categories are bourgeois, he could never see
this; it is like trying to look through himself ....' (*R&R* 33) He
carried this central concern into every area of his studies: literature,
psychology, physics. He noted, in a criticism of functional anthropology which anticipates much subsequent debate:

> The view of human society taken by this school is not really
> functional, for it does not include, as functions of society, the
> 'civilised' equipment the observers themselves bring to the
> survey of primitive society. (*FS* 17)

Or, in *The Crisis in Physics*, 'the social relations are reflected in all the products of society (including the ideology of physics) as categories' (*C in P* 29):

> The genius does not escape from the categories of his age, any more than man escapes from time and space, but the measure of his genius consists in the degree to which he fills these categories with content – a degree which may even result in their explosion. This explosion is, however, in turn dependent on a certain ripeness in the categories. (*Ibid.* 25)

In suggestive comments on the limitations of bourgeois feminism he remarked: 'The woman revolts *within* the categories of bourgeois culture.' She finds herself an alien in 'man's world', for 'this world is a vast cognitive expression of man's notion of reality.' But if her revolt does not transcend these categories, then it 'is bound to fail, because it asserts woman's right to be man, in other words to enslave herself to masculine values.' (*R&R* 72, 113)

The *Studies* then are each in different ways explorations of the illusion of the bourgeois epoch, and of the deforming or limiting character of bourgeois categories. The method is assertive; the judgements hard and sometimes ungenerous; the temptation to marshall evidence in binary oppositions is too often taken; and the tone is at some points pharasaical. 'The bourgeois', in Caudwell's essays, is always tripping up on his own categories and falling full length in the epistemological mud, but somehow, despite these repeated exposures to ridicule, someone called Man is advancing in knowledge and producing great art. But these polemical vices were perhaps the inevitable concomitants of a venture which was, in Caudwell's time, original and arduous. He was attempting to offer, not an alternative view in one special area (economics or politics), but to effect a rupture with a whole received view of the world, with its vocabulary and its terms of argument:

> When categories are first imposed, they seem arbitrary, violent, the expression of individual personalities .... When one is born into these categories, so that from childhood one's mind is moulded by them, they seem reasonable, peaceful and impersonal. (*R&R* 42)

Caudwell's acrid style expresses the violence and novelty of
exactly such an encounter.

The method of the *Studies* seemed to me, when I first read
them, and still seems to me today, to have been productive.
Caudwell understood the nature of ideology better than it is
generally understood today, and his work developed this understanding in new directions. This follows in some part upon his
'heretical' rejection of reflection-theory. Ideas, art, intellectual
artefacts do not appear to Caudwell (as they did to some of his
contemporaries) as sociological symptoms expressed (inconven-
iently) in other terms, or as simple reflections of class interests.
Nor did he (as is often still done) use 'ideology' as an
indiscriminate and replaceable term for any system of beliefs.
Ideology gives the 'characteristic shape' to a society's intellectual
culture; it is 'a basic world-view', with attendant categories, which:

> Is only revealed on analysis as an unseen force, not explicit in
> the formulations of that culture, but acting like a pressure from
> without. It gives to that culture a characteristic distortion which
> is not visible to those who still live within the framework of
> that economy. (*FS* 116)

The 'carapacious toughness' of 'the conscious part of society'
consists in the fixity of the categories into which knowledge is
sorted, and these categories 'always reflect in a class society the
particular conditions of functioning of the ruling class as felt by
them' (*C in P* 89) But these categories, while resistant to change,
are not inert; they also exert 'a pressure', they direct intellectual
interests in certain directions (*C in P* 53). They determine a certain
drift of the mind which is, ultimately, itself determined in class
ways. We can observe this pressure, this drift, by observing the
way in which in different historical periods, similar illusions
reappear within quite distinct fields of thought. Hence we may
legitimately analyse ideology not only as product but also as
process; it has its own logic which is, in part, self-determined, in
that given categories tend to reproduce themselves in consecutive
ways. While we cannot substitute the ideological logic for the real
history – capitalist evolution is not the acting out of a basic

bourgeois idea – nevertheless this logic is an authentic component of that history, a history inconceivable and indescribable independent of the 'idea'.

The bourgeois illusion of freedom is the central character of all the studies. 'The deepest and most ineradicable bourgeois illusion', upon which all others are built, is that 'man is free not through but *in spite of* social relations' (*SDC* 69). 'This demand of bourgeois culture was in fact unrealisable', since 'man cannot strip himself of his social relations and remain man.' 'Freedom is secreted in the relation of man to man' (*SDC* xxi). But repeatedly the logic of bourgeois ideology enforces a refusal to acknowledge social determinations. 'The bourgeois by his position is committed to the belief that a dominating relation to a thing (private property) is not a dominating relation at all'; 'the relation between a man and his property is a relation between man and a thing, and is therefore no restraint on the liberty of other men' (*FS* 167; *SDC* 100). Throughout the studies the bourgeois is seen as a man 'standing in his own light':

> As a bourgeois he had been unconscious of any necessity determining his action, for the bourgeois law of social action is 'Do as you will'. It forgets to state whether (a) you *can* do as you will; (b) you can *will* what you will. (*FS* 168)

As the growing complexity of economic organisation, the rise of the State, and the threat of the working-class movement make older bourgeois notions of social liberty come to appear increasingly unpracticable, nevertheless the bourgeois illusion continued to reproduce itself in the arts and the intellectual disciplines. It reappears, with astonishing vigour, in modern psycho-analysis (see 'Freud', 'Love, 'Consciousness'); it supports the ineffectual pacifism of the Thirties; it diverts D.H. Lawrence from the sources of his own genius; above all, it is stubbornly defended in the bourgeois self-image:

> The bourgeois cannot admit himself to be a determined individual – to do so would be to uncover the determining relations which are all social relations .... Thus the bourgeois

reserves for himself an area of spontaneity or non-causality in
all values in which the human mind is concerned, and since
there is no determinism there, they are all arbitrary and might
be anything (*FS 72).*

Ideology, as seen by Caudwell, is not a cunning and wilful class
imposition, as mask to disguise social realities and to mystify the
oppressed. It is, in its most essential effects, a form of self-mystification, a drift of the mind and of the sensibility. But it does also
mystify the oppressed, impose an approved view of social reality,
and, hence, enforce the hegemony of the rulers. About this – and the
institutional consolidation and reproduction of ideology in its dominative aspects – Caudwell has less to say. But he does, repeatedly, jab
at the central legitimating notion of the 'freedom' of market relations,
a notion astonishingly regenerate in the capitalist world today:

> Man is completely free except for the payment of money. That
> is the overt character of bourgeois relations. Secretly it is
> different, for society can only be a relation between men, not
> between man and a thing, not even between man and cash.
> (*SDC* 151)

This way of seeing ideology is of course derived from Marx, but
Caudwell has thought it through once again, and has made it his
own. I find it congenial, and also contagious. It has influenced
by own historical thinking, although the imbrication of ideology,
with its own authentic logic, within particular social contexts
whose logic need not be congruent, presents problems both of
reciprocal determination and of contradiction of a complexity
which Caudwell's epochal analysis glosses over. And I must also
confess to another area in which Caudwell influenced me, an
area in which his thought is unclear, ambiguous and perhaps
heretical. This concerns the relations between 'basis' and 'superstructure', between needs and norms, between 'economy' and
value-system or 'morality'.

Caudwell does not often employ the basis/superstructure analogy,
and if he does so it is clearly as a figure-of-speech. He is more
concerned to close than to force open the gap between social being

and social consciousness; one is not seen as primary, the other as derivative. Yet at the same time he is given to statements that intellectual artefacts are 'economic products'. 'Religion', he notes at one point, is 'like the consciousness of which it is a part, an economic product.' (*FS* 18) And again, 'man's inner freedom, the conscious will, acting towards conscious ends, is a product of society; it is an economic product' (*SDC* 216). If religion and free-will are economic products, what then is the economy? Caudwell has an answer to this too:

> By economic production we mean an active interpenetration of organism with nature that is not innate, is not genetically inherited, but is transmitted by external means, and yet is not environmental in the biological sense. It is cultural. (*FS* 27)

So we are in a circle. Religion and free-will are economic products. What is economic production? It is cultural. But this is not the word-spinning of an ideologue. Caudwell is not shuffling his papers at random, and grabbing at whatever term comes to hand. It is true that he may be trying to shock us out of certain received bourgeois (or Marxist?) categories, in which the purity of culture can never be sullied by vulgar 'economics' or in which economic production is substantial 'material reality' and culture an insubstantial accessory. That the assimilation is meditated and deliberate, and is of a piece with his interactionist epistemology, is made clear in his study of 'Love'. Love 'is man's name for the emotional element in social relations':

> If our definition of love is correct, it is true that love makes the world go round. But it would be rather truer to say that the society going round as it does, makes love what it is. This is one of those relations like that of knowing and being, which can only be understood in a dialectical manner. Thought guides action, yet it is action which gives birth to consciousness, and so the two separate, struggle, and return on each other, and therefore perpetually develop. Just as human life is being mingled with knowing, *society is economic production mingled with love*. (*SDC* 130–1) (*My italics*).

Thus Caudwell is refusing to allow us to place 'economics' in a
conceptual basis, and consciousness and affective culture in a
conceptual superstructure. Needs and norms must be taken together,
and knowledge must be taken with them, as part of a unitary
process in which men in particular forms of association (mode of
production) produce both goods and culture. This may be seen
clearly in primitive society: 'as the researches of anthropologists
show, economic production is inextricably interwoven with social
affection.' (*SDC* 150) The dichotomy between 'economy' and
'love' has no transcultural heuristic value: it is historically-specific
to capitalist society.

> The bourgeois was determined to believe that the market was
> the only social relation between man and man. This meant that
> he must refuse to believe that love was an integral part of a
> social relation. He repressed this tenderness from his social
> consciousness. (*SDC* 152)

In all distinctive bourgeois relations 'it is characteristic that
tenderness is completely expelled, because tenderness can only exist
between men, and in capitalism all relations appear to be between a
man and a commodity' (*Ibid*. 151). 'Economics', in short, is a
category *invented* by the bourgeois, in his utilitarian stage; and the
same category imposes a particular, limited and instrumental view
of human motivations and satisfactions which excludes all needs
and faculties which are not responsive to the stimuli of the market,
or subject to its operations:

> To our generation the association of economic relations with
> sexual love seems arbitrary, not because our idea of love is too
> rich but because our notion of economic relations is too
> bourgeois. Bourgeois civilisation has reduced social relations to
> the cash nexus. They have become emptied of affection. (*Ibid*.
> 148)

But 'economic' is not a category which Caudwell rejects. He holds
onto it, as a very general term for men and women in association
producing the means of life, and at the same time producing

themselves and their own culture, and he tries to stuff back into it those qualities which the bourgeois category has excluded:

> The misery of the world is economic, but that does not mean that it is cash. That is a bourgeois error. Just because they are economic, they involve the tenderest and most valued feelings of social man. (*Ibid.* 156).

('They', I take it, refers not to 'misery' but to a missing term, 'social relations'). This thought carries him on to his apocalyptic conclusion:

> Today it is as if love and economic relations have gathered at two opposite poles. All the unused tenderness of man's instincts gather at one pole and at the other are economic relations, reduced to bare coercive rights to commodities. This polar segregation is the source of a terrific tension, and will give rise to a vast transformation of bourgeois society. They must, in a revolutionary destruction and construction, return in on each other and fuse in a new synthesis. This is communism. (*Ibid.* 157)

This is powerful as a parable, but the parable is too neat. Metaphor and logic are slipping in different directions, rhetoric is dominant, the idea is imposing itself on the social process, old errors (man's a-historical 'instincts') reappear. Moreover, on the previous page Caudwell had sketched an alternative scenario: displaced societal feelings might equally reappear in the form of social neuroses – 'hate, patriotism, fascism', anti-semitism, 'absurd and yet pathetic Royal Jubilee enthusiasms', or 'mad impossible loyalties to Hitlers and Aryan grandmothers.'[50] All this is forgotten or brushed impatiently aside. 'Emotion' (affirmative) will 'burst from the ground in which it has been repressed with all the force of an explosion .... This is a revolution.'

The conclusion, then, will not do, although I confess that I was long attracted by its metaphoric vitality. It is not altogether spurious, for it serves to remind us, forcibly, that the injury which capitalist process inflicts on us is not only that of economic exploitation. It is also that of defining us, in this abbreviated way, as economic creatures at all. And men and women do, continually find ways of resisting these definitions. And this resistance has often proved to be more difficult for capitalism to accommodate than the direct resistance of exploited economic men, which can often be bought off in economic ways. So that the 'tension' upon which Caudwell builds his parable is not of his invention.

But the conclusion is less significant than the train of argument which led up to it. This is not without difficulty, of several kinds. It is possible to ask, for example, why *love* should be the distinctive emotional element in social relations, and not hate, greed, envy, aggression, &c. To this Caudwell has, implicitly, his own answer; if society is dependent upon men and women associating co-operatively in economic production, then only the adhesive affective qualities are functional, and these we decide to call 'love'; greed, aggression, &c., are dysfunctional. This answer scarcely suffices. But the ulterior methodological problems are, to the dominant Marxist tradition even greater. The assimilation of 'economics' and 'culture', and of social affection to the productive base, are plainly heretical. And if the notion that the misery of the world is economic, in the sense of cash, is 'a bourgeois error', it is also an error which has penetrated very deeply into the interstices of the Marxist tradition. And where in all this 'dialectical' interaction ('society is economic production mingled with love') are we to insert – as Caudwell elsewhere does insert, sometimes brutally – the determining pressure of social being? Have we not lost sight of the critical concept of society organised according to a specific and structured mode of production?[51]

Caudwell does not resolve these questions. I have already said that his thought in this area was unclear and ambiguous. There was a time, a very recent time, when to ask such questions and to receive an irresolute answer would have been to have courted dismissal. Marxism – or the people who spoke most loudly and authoritatively in Marxism's name – already knew the answers. I am glad that this intellectual iron age is now passing; one has waited for a long time for it to go by. Caudwell, in my view, was asking questions which had to be asked, and his ambiguity was a fruitful ambiguity. In refusing the orthodox closures offered by reflection theory, by the basis/superstructure model, and by the allocation of 'economics' to the base and norms, or affective culture, to the superstructure, he was holding open a door to a more creative tradition.

VII

Some of us strayed through that door, hesitantly and with many backward looks. That is, I suppose, one reason for my writing this essay. Caudwell's insights and Caudwell's confusions were imprinted upon many of my generation. I hope that I may have shown – and Caudwell, if Promethean, was by no means an isolated figure – that the Marxism available in England as we entered the Forties was more complex than is often supposed. But I may only have confirmed, in the eyes of modern critics, the poverty and confusion of our resources. Even so, one should not swing from one fashion to the next without making some settlement of intellectual accounts.

In these accounts I still feel myself to be in Caudwell's debt. The examination has proved to be more difficult than I anticipated. I now find that very much of Caudwell's work, perhaps ninety per cent, must be set aside. It no longer affords any point of entry. But there is a residue, a ten per cent, which still holds an extraordinary, searching vitality. Above all, Caudwell was walking abroad in the intellectual world of his time, encountering the largest ideas and issues of his contemporary culture. He was not, as sometimes happens today, retreating into the introverted security where Marxists speak only to Marxists in a universe of self-validating texts. His enterprise – to work over in his consciousness 'the whole inheritance of human knowledge' – was impossible ambitious, but it is not for that reason discredited. *Studies in a Dying Culture* remains, with Hazlitt's *The Spirit of the Age* (with which it bears, at some points, comparison), an outstanding diagnosis of a particular moment of intellectual history.

This moment was not just 'the Thirties'. It was a particular point within the Thirties. One of his editors, recalling the year (1935–36) when the studies were written, has summarised it thus:

It was a good time to be a left-wing idealist: during that year Hitler occupied the Rhineland, Abyssinia fell to the Italians, and the Spanish Civil War began. In London, troops of Sir Oswald Moseley's British Union of Fascists made their most serious effort to invade the East End, and were repulsed by the workers, and the Hunger Marchers from Jarrow arrived in Westminster ....[52]

It was, moreover, a time of sustained and exalted illusion about Soviet reality. The major purges and trials had yet to come. At the first Soviet Writers Congress (1934), whose proceedings were translated when Caudwell was completing *Illusion and Reality*, Bukharin, in one of his last public appearances (but who could know that?), had appeared to offer a charter to the poets endorsing their creative autonomy.[53] Whether or not it was 'a good time' to be a left-wing idealist, it was a time in which one might easily take one culture to be dying and another to be coming of age.

Caudwell's utopian vision of Soviet Communism leaves a dusty taste in our mouths today, and inevitably this must date some part of his writing. But the poles and oppositions between which he made culture and history swing were not by any means factitious. He lived at a time when bourgeois individualism did, in extremity, effect alliances with Fascism; when peaceful *laissez-faire* did undergo a transformation into armed imperialism; when the commercial degradation of art did appear to gather at one pole and self-contemplating aestheticism at the other; when eminent scientists were proclaiming the rediscovery of God and of free will in the indeterminacy of physical laws; when ascendant psycho-analysis was presenting society as the prison-house and culture as the warden constraining the nobility of the free expressive instincts. That crisis was not imaginary. It imposed itself 'like a pressure from without' upon his acrid style and within the antinomies of his thought. At length it imposed itself upon his life, and took him to his death in Spain. His body was never recovered. The unfinished manuscripts which were recovered [54] represent the most heroic effort of any British Marxist to think his own intellectual time:

I see a man
Last heard of alive on a hill-crest
In Spain, expecting to die at his gun,
Alone, his youth and work all over,
His stars and planets
Reduced to yards of ground,
Hoping others will harvest his crop.[55]

From the *Socialist Register,* 1977

Notes

I am grateful to those who have read or heard different versions of this essay for their critical comments: these include Philip Corrigan, Alan Dawley, Martin Eve, Dorothy Thompson, Raymond Williams, the editors of the *Socialist Register*, and members of the Birmingham University Caudwell Society.

1. *The Crisis in Physics* (1939); *Illusion and Reality* (1937); *Romance and Realism: a Study in English Bourgeois Literature* (Princeton, 1970); *Studies in a Dying Culture* (1938); *Further Studies in a Dying Culture* (1949). My references in the text are to these editions, abbreviated as *C in P, I&R, R&R, SDC, FS.* In 1965 Lawrence and Wishart issued a selection from Caudwell's writings as *The Concept of Freedom.* There is a *Monthly Review* paperback edition (1972), of *SDC* and *FS* within a single cover.
2. Biographical evidence is patchy and sometimes contradictory: see the biographical note in Christopher Caudwell, *Poems* (1939); and material in Stanley E. Hyman, *The Armed Vision* (New York, 1948) and David N. Margolies, *The Function of Literature: a Study of Caudwell's Aesthetics* (1969). The most informative account is undoubtedly in Samuel Hynes's introduction to *R&R.* Since writing this essay, I have had a sight of an unpublished biography by George Moburg, 'Christopher Caudwell: The Making of a Revolutionary', which is based on letters and manuscripts in the possession of Caudwell's brother, Mr Theodore Sprigg. Mr Moburg's study fully confirms the account given by Samuel Hynes.
3. Francis Mulhern, 'The Marxist Aesthetics of Christopher Caudwell', *New Left Review*, 85, May/June 1974, pp. 37–58. While I disagree with Mulhern on many points I welcome his careful and thoughtful study.

4. See Terry Eagleton, 'Raymond Williams: an Appraisal', *New Left Review*, 95, January/February 1976, p. 7: 'Who is the major English Marxist critic? Christopher Caudwell, *hélas*. It is in such pat question and answer that the problem of a Marxist criticism in contemporary Britain is most deftly posed. For though Caudwell is the major forebear – major, at least, in the sheer undaunted ambitiousness of his project – it is equally true that there is little, except negatively, to be learnt from him.'

5. Raymond Williams, *Culture and Society* (Penguin edition, 1961), p. 272, 269.

6. It should, however, be noted that the late essay, planned as one of the *Studies*, and published only in 1970 as *Romance and Realism*, reveals a quite new specificity of judgement, a more watchful eye and a more attentive ear, notably in its treatment of Meredith, Hardy, Kipling, Moore and Virginia Woolf. This suggests reserves of critical power only casually drawn upon in Caudwell's earlier writings.

7. Loc. cit., p. 58

8. Loc, cit., p. 7

9   A rough-and-ready breakdown into categories gives us: Linguistics, 14; Mathematics, 14; Philosophy, 33; General science (including genetics, physics), 37; Ancient civilizations (Egypt, Greece, Rome), 39; Marxism, 39; History, economics, general politics, 64; Literary criticism and the arts, 75; Psychology and neurology, 78; Anthropology and archaeology, 122. A few titles evade even these classifications. And there are two or three volumes of poetry.

10. Caudwell at first intended to call the book *Verse and Mathematics – a Study of the Foundation of Poetry:* see *R&R*, p. 10. Caudwell in fact disavowed any claim to have studied aesthetics: 'to deal fully and appreciatively with [aesthetic] values in one author alone would perhaps occupy several books.' His concern was, rather, with 'the social generation of art', and at a time when 'a culture disintegrates' this must be a prior concern: *R&R*, 139–40.

11. Bernal's criticism (*Modern Quarterly*, Vol. 6, no. 4, Autumn 1951, pp. 346–50) does not in fact identify specific errors in Caudwell's scientific writing, although he indicates one passage (*FS* 243) as 'word-spinning': i.e. an overstrained analogy rather than an error of fact.

12. The discussion was closed with Cornforth's reply (loc. cit., Autumn 1951), with the remark that it would 'have to be continued elsewhere'. But there was, in the conditions of that time, in the Party's control of its own press and in the virtual absence of any independent journals interested in Marxist discussion, nowhere else for its continuance. The number of contributions to that discussion (Summer and Autumn

1951), often heavily edited and cut (as well as other contributions which never appeared?), indicates the very general interest that had been aroused. In my view the 'controversy' was editorially controlled throughout and directed to a foregone conclusion.

13. A neurologist, B.H. Kerman, added some helpful footnotes to the study of 'Consciousness' in *Further Studies*, which offered corrections to Caudwell in the light of subsequent research: but it is also made clear that these corrections did not undermine his basic argument, and, indeed, his argument 'brilliantly anticipates a whole trend which is now discernible in modern neuroanatomy': *FS 11.*

14. See Raymond Williams, *Culture and Society*, pp. 269, 271; *Marxism and Literature* (Oxford, 1977), p. 30.

15. Maurice Cornforth, 'Caudwell and Marxism', *Modern Quarterly*, Vol. 6, no. 1, Winter 1950–51. In describing this orthodoxy as 'Stalinist' I of course employ hindsight, but not complacent hindsight. There were a good many frustrated proto-revisionists in the Communist Party in those days; in my own circles we designated the enemy as 'King Street' and as 'Jungle Marxism', of which we increasingly came to see *Modern Quarterly* as the leading intellectual organ. For a superb example of Jungle Marxism, see (in the same number as Cornforth on Caudwell), Dr. John Lewis (the review's editor) on 'The Moral Complexion of our People', from which we learn, *inter alia*, that 'the militant worker exemplifies kindness, courage, comradeship, mercy, integrity and truth to a degree not known before.' The spectacle of Althusser going hammer-and-tongs at Lewis (King Street's leading lay preacher of the most vulgar orthodoxy) as an idealist and revisionist heretic defies one's sense of the ridiculous.

16. Caudwell's leading defender was George Thomson ('In Defence of Poetry', *Modern Quarterly*, Vol. 6, no. 2, Spring 1951). I have been told by Professor Thomson that he was given an exceedingly short time – only a few days – to prepare his reply to Cornforth; perhaps this explains why he was driven to defend Caudwell mainly by trading quotations from Marx. It seems that it had been the intention that Cornforth's article should go uncontested, as an *ex cathedra* statement of the 'correct' view on Caudwell's work. Only an outcry among Party members, and the high standing of several of them – including George Thomson (who had been on the Party's Executive Committee) – forced the discussion to be opened.

17. N. Bukharin, 'Poetry, Poetics and the Problems of Poetry in the U.S.S.R.', in *Problems of Soviet Literature: Reports and Speeches at the First Soviet Writers Congress*, 1934, ed. A. Zhdanov, N. Bukharin, K. Radek, &c (1935). Margolies, op. cit., pp. 86–91,

discusses the influence of Bukharin's ideas on Caudwell. But he fails to convey the intelligence, flexibility and soaring confidence of this report.

18. See Hynes, 'Introduction', *R&R* Earlier editors and critics had supposed that *Studies in a Dying Culture* preceded *Illusion and Reality*.

19. Hynes, op. cit., pp. 13–14.

20. See below, note 54. Several of Caudwell's works are marred by evident misreadings or mis-transcriptions of the manuscripts, notably *The Crisis in Physics*, with 'defendant' for *dependent* (p. 11), 'conscience' for *conscious* (p. 20), 'ethers' for *ethics* (p. 74), 'denominated' for *denominator* (p. 81), 'with' for *without* (p. 150), 'sun' for *sum* (p. 220) , and so on. Such errors reduce whole sentences to nonsense.

21. *Poems*, p. 41.

22. *Modern Quarterly*, Vol. 6, no. 4, Autumn, 1951.

23. The 1886 edition of Engels, *Ludwig Feuerbach*, is cited in the bibliography to *I.&R.*

24. A related argument appears in *I&R*, pp. 164–5 and in 'Beauty', *FS*, p. 93.

25. Sebastiano Timpanaro, 'Considerations on Materialism', *New Left Review*, 85, May/June 1974; *On Materialism* (New Left Books, 1975).

26. 'The question whether objective truth can be attributed to human thinking is not a question of theory but is a practical question. In practice man must prove the truth, i.e. the reality and power, the "this-sidedness" of his thinking. The dispute over the reality or non-reality of thinking which is isolated from practice is a purely scholastic question.'

27. Compare *C in P*, p. 58: 'Dialectics can only be filled with content by activity upon the object – that is, by practice and experiment. since the object did not exist for Hegel, his dialectic could never be filled with realistic content, and remained a beautiful and intricate mill grinding the air of theory and producing nothing but his prejudices and aspirations.'

28. See e.g. *C in P*, pp. 126–7, *FS*, p. 247.

29. *Marxism and Literature*, p. 85.

30. Ibid., pp. 83, 87.

31. The passage continues: 'as we change the world we learn more about it; as we learn more about it, we change ourselves ....'

32. Loc. cit., p. 18.

33. Loc. cit., p. 356.

34. Loc. cit., p. 266.
35. Loc. cit., pp. 22-3.
36. As Mulhern suggest, op. cit., p. 54.
37. Cf. *SDC*, pp. 135–7: 'An instinct is a certain innate behaviour-patter or chain of reflexes, conditioned or modified by experience'; we must 'rid our mind of mythological entities of these separate instincts, like distinct souls, planted in the animal or human breast ....'
38. See Raymond Williams, *Marxism and Literature*, p. 87. In a private communication to me, Williams suggested the way in which the metaphor 'drifts'.
39. 'Open Letter to Leszek Kolakowski', *Socialist Register*, 1973, p. 67.
40. Morris's *Hopes and Fears for Art* is included in the bibliography of *I. & R.*
41. *Marxism and Literature*, p. 30.
42. The image of 'photograph' appears in a more complex form in *I&R*, p. 161: 'Words are tied to percepts which are photographic memory-images of bits of reality. These percepts are fused into concepts, are organised and ordered in the broadest and most abstract way. Or, more accurately, out of the broad humming chaos of "existence" – the simplest percept, other concepts and percepts arise by differentiation and integration.'
43. Williams, op. cit., p. 37.
44. Ibid., pp. 41–2. See Caudwell's comment on Russell, *SDC*, p. 214: 'Language filled his head with ideas, showed him what to observe, taught him logic, put all other men's wisdom at his disposal, and awoke in him affectively the elementary decencies of society.'
45. *Marxism and Literature*, p. 36.
46. The most helpful contributions to the controversy (*Modern Quarterly*, Vol. 6. no. 3, Summer 1951) were from Montagu Slater and Geoffrey Matthews, both of whom accepted extensive criticism of Caudwell. Matthews wrote (p. 272): 'Caudwell's great weakness as a Marxist literary critic is surely not that he invented the bourgeois illusion within which all the modern English poets have written, but that he does not study these poets from any other angle than that of the illusion.'
47. Moburg, cit. supra., note 2.
48. *Culture and Society*, p. 273.
49. 'The human essence is no abstraction inherent in each single individual. In its reality it is the *ensemble* of the social relations.'
50. In this notion of displaced 'love' as social neurosis, Caudwell may have been influenced (like Auden) by Gestalt psychology.
51. The difficulty appears in a passage in 'Love' (*SDC*, p. 132): 'What

does matter to men is the emotional element in social relations ... which makes man in each generation what he is. *This emotion is not separate from but springs out of the economic basis of these relations*, which thus determine religion. Man's quality in each age is determined by his emotional and technological relations, and *these are not separate but part of the one social process.*' I strongly assent to the implications of the words which I have italicised. But what 'springs out of' a basis must be inherent in this basis and these relations, and hence the analogy of basis/superstructure has only a limited (and often misleading) analytic use. What then is 'economic' about this basis? Is 'economic' the same as 'technological?' What Caudwell has failed to elaborate is the concept of a *mode of production*, which entails *both* 'economic' and normative correspondent attributes: the priority afforded to 'economy' is historically-specific to capitalist market relations. There is nothing about a mode of production which demands our attributing priority to the (bourgeois) category of 'economics' as opposed to the norms, affective qualities, and social relations (of power, domination and subordination) without which that mode of production would be inoperative and inconceivable. All are part of the one set. On these points I find helpful Maurice Godelier, *Perspectives in Marxist Anthropology* (Cambridge, 1977), esp. chapters one and two. Godelier still maintains a concept of infrastructure/superstructure, which is, however, almost dissolved in his rich and scrupulous analysis. I understand that his thought is still developing in this area, and we must await his conclusions with interest.

52. Samuel Hynes, in *R&R*, p. 12.
53. Bukharin's eloquent and affirmative report (cit. supra., note 17) came to a climax with the slogan: 'Culture, culture and yet again culture!' (p. 257). It was received by the delegates with ecstatic excitement, as the signal of reconciliation between the Soviet regime and the intelligentsia: for the circumstances, see Stephen F. Cohen, *Bukharin and the Bolshevik Revolution* (1974), pp. 355–6.
54. In a letter to Elizabeth and Paul Beard (cited by Moburg, above, note 2), which constitutes his literary testament on leaving for Spain, he referred to *Studies* as 'imperfect hasty sketches', and 'only drafts'. They would 'all have to be rewritten and refined ... it needs refining, balancing, getting in it the movement of time, ripening and humanising.'
55. R.F. Willets, 'Homage to Christopher Caudwell', *Envoi*, no. 15, 1962.

Polemics

In Defence of the Jury

It was nice to be awoken on 12 November by the BBC informing us that the Queen's Speech would announce measures 'to strengthen the jury system'. It is, after all, a very ancient English institution for which we feel a ritualistic affection. And it is good to know that our betters are taking care of it.

There have been a lot of measures to 'strengthen the jury system' in recent years. In 1967 the Criminal Justice Act abolished the unanimity rule and introduced a majority verdict (at ten to two). This was presumably to bring the jury in line with the metric system and the decimalisation of money. Then measures were taken to rationalise the archaic system of defence challenges and to reduce their effectiveness. The number of peremptory challenges allowed to the defence had already, in 1948, been reduced from 20 to seven. In the Criminal Law Act of 1977 they were further reduced to three. Meanwhile, in 1973, the Lord Chancellor, Lord Hailsham, by an Order in the law vacation, had struck out the ancient practice of listing the occupations of jurors summoned onto the panel.

Two further measures were taken in the compendious 1977 Criminal Law Act. In an unobtrusive clause (which eluded Parliamentary notice) the most ancient form of jury in English history – the jury of inquest – was shorn of effective powers. And in a sweeping series of clauses, the option of trial by jury – or, in the old language, 'putting oneself on one's country' – was removed in many categories of case where the option had previously been open. Such cases, which include many offences against public order, in which, of course, the evidence of the Police is usually decisive, are now tried summarily before the stipendiary magistrates.

Few cases have been more important in the history of jury rights than what is known as Bushel's Case (1670). This is the

case of the Quakers, Penn and Mead, indicted at the Old Bailey in
that they did preach and speak to persons in the street assembled,
by reason whereof a great concourse and tumult of people a long
time did remain and continue, in contempt of the King and his
law, and to the great terror and disturbance of his liege subjects.
Bushel was the intransigent juror who refused to allow his fellow
jurymen to be intimidated into bringing in a verdict of guilty in
those terms, but would bring in a verdict of guilty of preaching
only. Mr Bushel was directly bullied by the whole bench:

> Alderman Sir J. Robinson: I tell you, you deserve to be indicted
> more than any man that hath been brought to the bar this day ...
>
> Mr Justice May: Sirrah, you are an impudent fellow ...
>
> The Recorder: You are a factious fellow: I will set a mark on
> you ...
>
> The Major: I will cut his nose ...

This did not sufficiently strengthen the jury, so they were hauled
off to prison for the failure to convict. On appeal, the jury was
vindicated, and the precedent was established of the jury's power to
determine its own verdict, free from the threat of punishment. But
if William Penn were to preach at Gracechurch Street today, Mr
Bushel and his fellows would be unable to afford him the
protection of their special verdict, since the case – as a public
order offence – would not come before a jury at all.

The ink of the Criminal Law Act, 1977, had scarcely dried
before an even more remarkable resource of jury-strengthening was
disclosed to a startled British public. I must suppose that the 'ABC
Case', under the Official Secrets Acts, is sufficiently fresh in
memory for me to be able to dispense with rehearsing the details.
There was never any question of the three defendants (the
journalists, Crispin Aubrey and Duncan Campbell, and the former
signals corporal, John Berry) meditating passing any information to
'the enemy' – except (an important qualification) insofar as the
British Security Services have always regarded the British public as
the enemy. The ABC Trial was intended to be a sensational public
show trial, and a condign warning against the 'whistle-blowers'. In
the event, it was (for the prosecution) a sensational anti-climax.

One reason for this was the scandal occasioned by the revelation of jury-vetting.

What occasions surprise is not the fact that vetting had taken place, but the shamefaced way in which the fact came out. On the opening of the trial, the distinguished counsel for the defence, Jeremy Hutchinson QC, visited the court to obtain a sight of the panel. In a casual conversation with a court officer Lord Hutchinson learned that – more than two months before – the prosecution had applied privately to a judge in chambers for the panel list, in order to scrutinise the members. In the face of pressure from the legal profession the Attorney-General suddenly released to the *Times* 'guidelines' authorising jury-vetting, which he had secretly issued four years before to senior police and the Director of Public Prosecutions – without the knowledge of Parliament or the Bar.

These guidelines instructed the Police that there were 'certain exceptional types of case of public importance' in which, in order to 'ensure the proper administration of justice', jury-vetting might take place. Such cases were gestured at as those involving terrorists, criminal gangs, or 'serious offences where strong political motives were involved'. In these cases it was held proper to identify and remove from the jury persons of 'extreme political beliefs'. Checks to identify such persons should involve the use of the data banks of the central criminal records computer at Hendon (which has a capacity for storing records on a mere forty million people); a check on Special Branch records; and further checks on jurors by the local CID.

What vetting signifies became a little clearer in the autumn of 1979 at the opening of the trial of four anarchists. The trial judge authorised jury-vetting by the prosecution, and allowed the defence to engage private detectives (out of legal aid funds) to undertake its own investigation of the panel. When this unsavoury business became too expensive, he ordered instead that an edited version of the prosecution's information gained from police records (but not from Security records) should be passed on to the defence. The gleanings of the police computer were duly leaked by some responsible person to the press, and the public had a brief glimpse of the extraordinary miscellany of fact, trivia and malicious gossip stored at the taxpayer's expense. Of a panel of 93, more than one-fifth had entries on central police files. Some were for trivial and long-expired offences which could never have constituted disqualification for jury service – for example, a 14-year-old fine of £5 for a minor theft at work. Others were dignified in the records because their children or kin were reputed to have had associations with 'criminals'. Another was listed as having resided at an address reputed to be a squat. Yet others were listed because they had been the victims of a crime, or had made complaints against the Police.

It was left to the incoming Conservative Attorney-General to regularise the procedures of jury-vetting by a Practice Direction, to introduce a few emollient formalities, and to lower the profile of the issue so that it is now accepted as 'normality'. It can be seen that this is not a party-political question. No one can be accused of partisan zeal. 'Ensuring the proper administration of justice' is a consensual duty in which Lord Hailsham and Labour's Attorney-General Sam Silkin laboured alongside each other, while the pupating leadership of the SDP (then in Mr Callaghan's Cabinet) averted their faces – or perhaps did not. All have shared in the work of 'strengthening the jury system' by diluting the unanimous verdict, removing offences to summary jurisdiction, limiting the challenges of the defence, and extending the scrutiny of the panel by the prosecution (with the aid of police information-storage of a miscellaneous and uncontrolled kind).

The new measures in the Criminal Justice Bill, published on 13 November, are therefore strictly on course. They will strip from jury trial more categories of offence, including criminal damage and common assault and battery (Clauses 24 and 25). Clause 83, the right to challenge jurors without cause (when selecting the jury from the panel), is now to be abolished. The legally illiterate – that is, most of us – will suppose this to be even-handed. In fact, this is a unilateral pre-emptive strike against the defence's 800-year-old right to peremptory challenge. For (as we shall see) the Crown does not have a right to peremptory challenge, but, instead, an equally effective right of 'stand-by', which is to remain unlimited and uncontrolled.

These measures are introduced with the awesome authority of the Roskill Committee. We can be assured that everything has been looked into, all evidence taken, and that the jury system will be strengthened accordingly. Yet one must note that here a little transplant operation has been done. For the Roskill Committee was, in fact, the Fraud Trials Committee, and its brief was to recommend 'just, expeditious and economical disposal' of 'criminal proceedings in England and Wales arising from fraud'.

Fraud is a complex area, and in these days of City and computer crime becomes every year more complex. I am unqualified to comment on the Roskill Committee's exertions in this area. But the extensive attention given to the jury's role (two chapters out of eight in the Report, as well as a supplementary volume of confected studies) takes it far beyond its brief – perhaps on the prompting of the Lord Chancellor? The Committee does not, in fact, offer *any* evidence to show that juries in complex fraud cases have returned incompetent or perverse verdicts. Instead, it marshals hypotheses from simulated situations to present a plausible case that a random jury might not have the powers of comprehension or skills in numeracy to sustain its functions. These arguments, which led towards the need for expert assessors and the recommendation of a special Fraud Trials Tribunal, are relevant to the issue of fraud and to fraud alone. I will leave this issue aside, noting only that the Law Society and other expert bodies emphatically dissent from any measure which would abolish jury trial in fraud cases. Their arguments, summarised in the Report by Mr Walter Merricks in a Note of Dissent, seem to me to be sound. The point which concerns me is that, even if a case might be made for the replacement of jury trial by assessors in certain categories of fraud case – proposals which do not find a place in the Criminal Justice Bill – the arguments for this have no bearing whatsoever upon the jury in its other roles and functions.

The transplant operation was done in the White Paper 'Criminal Justice', Command Paper 9658. This commended the 'powerful analysis' of the Roskill Committee, and extended its recommendation that the defence's right of peremptory challenge should be abolished in fraud trials to all jury trials. Not a scintilla of evidence in support of this extension of the particular into the general has been offered. 'The Government,' Command Paper 9658 intoned benevolently, 'has no desire to interfere unnecessarily with a long-established right', and then proceed to recommend measures for exactly such unnecessary interference.

The justification for these measures, if any, must be looked for in the special findings of the Roskill Committee. Seven members sat with Lord Roskill: an eminent chartered accountant, an information-technology expert, a former Chief Inspector of Constabulary, a circuit judge, a former chairman of Courtauld's, and the vice-chairman of Shropshire County Council. The seventh was Mr Walter Merricks, secretary of the Professional and Public Relations Committee of the Law Society, whose most cogent Note of Dissent on all the Committee's findings regarding the jury has already been mentioned: I will graciously allow him to stand by for the rest of these proceedings.

Without doubt Lord Roskill's Committee was eminently qualified to consider complex fraud. The members knew much about offences against the rights of money. Their qualifications to survey and make recommendations on the long-established rights, practices and traditions of the English and Welsh peoples are less evident. Not one of them appears to be qualified as a historian, and I do not notice any historians who were called to give evidence. (An exception should be made for Lord Devlin, whose contributions to legal history have been distinguished, and whose evidence – which has not been published – appears to have run directly contrary to the Committee's recommendations.) Of course, the historical profession may be faulted for not volunteering to come forward. But then we supposed that the Committee was concerned with its purported brief – contemporary complex fraud – and did not know that a transplant operation was in progress, by which its findings would be fraudulently employed against our liberties. The rest of what I have to say must therefore be a belated submission to a defunct committee.

The Roskill Committee found historical matters to be tedious, and meriting less than a page in their Report. They also found them to be a source of irrelevant passions: 'Our task has been to look at this emotive topic dispassionately in the light of the evidence presented to us.' Since history might be 'emotive', it could be excluded from evidence. The level of historical reference may be exemplified by a footnote (p.125) where the Report is discussing the defendant's right of peremptory challenge. This reads: 'At common law each defendant charged with a felony could make up to 35 challenges; over the years it declined from 20 in 1509, to seven in 1948 when the right of challenge was extended to misdemeanours.' The casual eye receives the notion of a steady 'decline'. In fact, the level of defence challenges without cause remained stable at 20 – not, I think, from 1509 but from 22 H. 8c. 14 (1541–2) – for over four hundred years. During which long and often tempestuous period the administration of justice did not fall apart. The erosion of jury rights and the intrusion upon its practices belong to the past four decades, and especially to the last fifteen years. Our betters prefer to take very brief views of history.

The jury is a very ancient creature, almost as old as the Monarchy and as old as Parliament. It is also a very odd beast. No one would even dream of inventing such an institution today, least of all a Roskill Committee. There is no single, A to Z, exhaustive and scholarly history of the jury, partly because it is a chameleon-like creature, which has altered its colour and shape in differing contexts. Excellent local studies are now being done, in the burgeoning history of crime and legal practice. Perhaps the most ambitious attempt to present jury history as a whole is Thomas Andrew Green's *Verdict according to Conscience*.

The book is subtitled 'Perspectives on the English Criminal Trial Jury, 1200-1800'. It sets out briskly and well in difficult Medieval terrain, begins to falter in the 17th century, and collapses in a heap with exhaustion – an exhaustion which the reader shares – in the 18th century. This is partly because Professor Green's 'perspectives' keep shifting their bearings. In Medieval England he is concerned to examine both theory and practice; he interrogates the existing scholarship with respect, and adds his own interesting samplings of the records. He reveals an institution with surprising vigour, which the Crown (with its slender administrative resources) was forced to come to terms with, and which played a remarkable role in softening the inelastic laws of homicide. Thereafter his point of view becomes more theoretical and ideological. There are some valuable sections (for example, on the Quaker cases after the Restoration): but he is increasingly inattentive to the actual composition of juries, their modes of summoning, their practices, and prefers to rehearse the arguments in Whig and Tory tracts. His treatment of the critically important libel and sedition cases of the late 18th century is an anti-climax – he appears to be at a loss in the political and social context, and even to lose confidence in his own theme. As for the practice of 17th and 18th-century juries, we will do better to go directly to the scholars whose work he has borrowed from – Cockburn, Langbein, Douglas Hay, and especially J.M. Beattie's *Crime and the Courts in England, 1660-1800.*

Never mind. *Verdict according to Conscience* gathers a great deal together in one place, has many shrewd pages and much patient exposition. It will be a resource for many historians, and Professor Green deserves our thanks. His recurrent theme – that of 'jury nullification' of the rigours of the law (a practice sometimes tolerated or even connived at by the Bench) – is profoundly relevant to the current debate. But, strangely, he omits to follow his own insights through into any explicit engagement with Patrick Devlin's brilliant Blackstone Lecture. 'The Power without the Right', published in *The Judge* (1979), which ought to be the bench-mark from which any discussion of the jury's role must start.

We have got our noses pressed too close against the window-pane, as historians often do. Let us stand back and take the scene in. The jury system is, to a social historian, a very remarkable institution. Beginning as a group of knowledgeable persons (or 'inquest'), who could report their findings to the officers of the Crown, it has survived immense changes in political life and administration – not as a fictive or vestigial sign but as an active element in the judicial process.

During its 800-year life it has shed some functions and acquired others, evincing a quite unusual flexibility – from ancient juries of presentment, the homages of courts leet and baron, and the Regarders and homage of forest courts, to the formalities of the jury box today. Even more remarkable, it is an institution, or presence, or tradition – which is it? – which is in some part secret and impervious to research. The actual deliberations of the jury may not be disclosed, and sustained accounts of them are few and imperfect.

What, indeed, is the jury? A legal expert may tell us how it is summoned, and, less exactly, what are its powers. But a social historian cannot be so certain. To be a juror is to have thrust upon one a temporary office, to which is attached an inherited weight of rules, practices and expectations; and this weight transforms an office into an imposed (and often internalised) role. This role is exercised for a day, or a week, or for three months, and then as suddenly as it was adopted, it falls away once more. Seen in this way, the jury is less an institution than a practice, or a place amidst adjacent judicial practices: a place through which generation after generation flows, inheriting the practices of their forerunners, yet inheriting these with little formal instruction, and practising the role in the light of expectations brought with them into the jury box and shared by the public outside.

When considered in this aspect, the jury may be viewed in two ways, as theatre and as expectations as to role. The emphasis, in theatre, is upon the practice, and in expectations it is upon the inherited political culture. By 'theatre' I don't only mean the evident theatre of the courtroom process – and the space allocated to the several parties (judge, prisoners, counsel and jury). Despite the theatricality of some 17th and 18th-century trials, the jury's space could be surprisingly informal in this. Early 18th-century form prescribed only that 'these Twelve Men standing near may hear all that is said and produced on either Part, and may ask what Questions they please of the Witnesses'. Or, in an account of 1767: 'as the custom is now, they sit among the crowd, undistinguished, and it is not easy to know them from the rest of the spectators.' This promiscuous arrangement occasioned inconvenience 'when they consult on giving their verdict without going out of court'. Yet this very inconvenience emphasised that part of their role in the theatre which had to do with their being members of the general audience of the public, albeit members especially qualified with voices.

The place in the theatre has been that of a lay presence conferring legitimacy upon the process, but sometimes at a cost which authority has found it hard to bear. For by their very presence (and the power of their verdict), they have profoundly modified the entire play. Judge, prosecution, defence, have addressed their words to them, sought to overawe or confuse them, or to move them to mercy: and this has shaped the form of the drama and dictated its lines. Because of the jury's presence, the mysteries of the law must be broken down into lay language – law must be made to appear rational and even, on occasion, humane. This is so deeply assumed that its importance may easily be neglected. Take the jury away – in 1686 or 1796 or 1986 – and the entire judicial process would have been – or would still be – altogether re-cast.

John Lilburne, the leader of the Levellers in London, had a superb sense of the theatre's possibilities. On his third trial for his life, in 1653, 'he called them his honourable Jury, and said they were the keepers of the Liberties of England; and will make it appear that the Jury are the Judges of the Law as well as of the Fact.' In his previous trial, in 1649, he had played the jury against the judges in a drama which explicitly solicited the applause of the audience in the theatre. When Lilburne claimed that the jury were judges of law as well as fact, the presiding judge interposed a denial. Swinging upon the bench, Colonel Lilburne replied: 'You that call yourselves judges of the law are no more but Norman intruders.' And when he closed his defence, he returned to the point: 'You judges sit there, being no more, if the jury please, but ciphers to pronounce the sentence, or their clerks to say Amen.' The audience in the court 'with a loud voice cried "Amen, Amen" and gave an extraordinary great hum, which made the judges look something untowardly about them, and caused Major-General Skippon to send for three fresh companies of foot soldiers'.

It is inadvisable, if you are on trial for your life, to treat judges in this way. Grand drama in this style was possible only in a period of revolutionary ferment, when the legitimacy of Parliament, law and judges were all in question. And perhaps honest John Lilburne was a little fortified, in 1653, by the knowledge that outside the courtroom there were said to be six thousand London citizens, many of them former soldiers of the New Model Army, who had thoughtfully provided themselves with bludgeons and cutlasses to use upon judges and jury if the verdict should displease them. Not even Securicor could be hired for such a service today.

Lilburne's acquittals remind us that a trial of sensitive political moment attracted an audience, not only in the courtroom, but in the nation outside. When the jury foreman pronounced the verdict of not guilty in 1649, 'the whole multitude of people in the Hall, for joy of the Prisoner's acquittal, gave such a loud and unanimous shout, as is believed was never heard in Guildhall, which lasted for about half an hour without intermission; which made the Judges for fear turn pale, and hang down their heads; but the Prisoner stood silent at the bar, rather more sad in his countenance than he was before.' The acclamations spread to the streets, and bonfires were lit throughout the city. Similar scenes were witnessed on the acquittal of the Seven Bishops (1688), the acquittal of printers and publishers of Junius's Letters (1770), and the acquittal of Thomas Hardy and his fellow reformers in 1794. Jurors in such cases could be drawn in triumph through the streets, feasted and toasted, or be commemorated on medals and token coinage.

Enough of 'theatre'. By 'expectations' I mean the notions of the jury's role and responsibilities handed on over successive genera-tions which flow through this place or theatre. This belongs, clearly, to political culture. It is a culture in which people are socialised in a hundred formal – but mainly informal – ways: by parents, teachers, discussions in alehouses or coffee-bars, in trade unions or political parties, by reading trial reports or watching Perry Mason or *The Rockford Files* on TV – perhaps even historians pass on a little. But this is not the same as the casual response which might be made by the man or woman in the street to questionnaire on jury rights. Most people would like to wriggle out of the duty. But selection for actual jury service can concentrate the mind amazingly; presence in that theatre can be fiercely educative; and people discover within themselves capacities to fulfil a role which they had never anticipated.

This political culture is, of course, always changing. Memories of rights are lost and are then rediscovered. And I may have entered this discussion from an over-optimistic perspective. The record of the 'humanising' role of the jury over centuries is incontestable; jury 'nullification' or the mitigation of the offence by 'pious perjury' in criminal trials – finding a verdict of guilty but of a lesser offence than would have been capital – must have saved tens of thousands from the gallows. Moreover, the uncertainty as to a jury's verdict must have prevented more thousands of oppressive prosecutions from ever being launched. But since William Hone's acquittals in 1817, juries in cases with a markedly political tone have disappointed civil libertarians more often than they have cheered them. Radicals, Chartists, Freethinkers, trade-unionists, socialists, suffragettes, Communists – all had reason to complain of the partiality of British juries.

This is because real juries (as distinct from jury theory) have operated in a real context of class perceptions and conflict. It would be absurd to say that the jury was invented by 'bourgeois liberalism' to suit the convenience of the bourgeoisie, for it was invented at a time when the bourgeoisie was not yet a glint in feudalism's eye. But the assumption by the jury of a new and critical role – that of inhibitor of oppressive process and defender of the subject against the Crown or the organs of the state – was the expression of a particular moment (which stretches from the 17th to the early 19th century) when the middling sort of people (from whom juries, and especially London juries, were drawn) found themselves to be repeatedly at issue with the aristocracy and Court.

The stubborn jury which acquitted Lilburne in 1653 – and then defended its verdict before the Council of State – was made up of two haberdashers, two woollen-drapers, a leather-seller, salter, bookbinder, grocer, brewer, tallow-chandler and two undescribed. For some hundred and fifty years London juries in politically sensitive cases continued to have a profile like this: they were empanelled from lesser gentry, shopkeepers, master tradesmen, merchants and dealers – a social stratum which included many with some 'independence' from the lines of interest and patronage. The jury which acquitted of treason one of the London Corresponding Society leaders, Dr Robert Crossfield, in 1796 was made up of two merchants, two masons, a corn factor, sugar baker, wine merchant, coachmaker, carpenter, bookseller, distiller and tailor. While the members of working trades represented on such panels were not journeymen or labourers (who were debarred by property qualifications), some may have been small masters or contractors. The London jury reached down to the 'petty bourgeoisie', among whom – contrary to stereo-types – Radical and Painite ideas moved strongly.

Already a sour note of dissent can be heard, however. The post-Waterloo Radical movement was bringing into action a class of persons who had no more chance of being called for jury service than had the blacks in Mississippi. When Brandreth and his follows awaited trial at Derby for their part in the Pentridge Rising of 1817 – all of them stockingers and disfranchised working men – the political theorist among them was Thomas Bacon, an old 'Jacobin' of the 1790s. A correspondent wrote in alarm to the Home Secretary: 'Old Bacon has been telling the prisoners they are not tried by their Peers, but by men of property. I name this to show you what dreadful principles these men have taught their unfortunate children.'

The unfortunate children of the poor taught their own children the same dreadful principles, and so alternative expectations about juries – as promoters of class injustice – were formed within the political culture of the working class. Twenty years on, and the situation was rank with class antagonism. Chartists expected (and sometimes received) more fair play and mercy from judges than from juries, made up – in the country – from farmers and publicans, and in the towns from the 'shopocracy'. When John Frost and his fellows were convicted, in 1840, for their part in the rising of Chartist miners at Newport, there was of course no miner on the jury – nor was it likely that a miner would serve as a juror for the next hundred years. The jury which convicted Frost was made up of five farmers, and a haberdasher, butcher, ironmonger, baker, miller, grocer and coachmaker.

Freethinkers in Victorian times equated trial by jury with 'trial by bigotry'. It should therefore occasion no surprise that Chartist, free-thought, trade-union or early Labour publications are not filled with panegyrics of the system: nor should we expect them from suffragettes who always faced all-male juries. What is perhaps surprising is that the principle of jury trial – as trial by one's peers or equals – was still generally upheld by the disenfranchised. The Chartists of North-East England in 1839 declared: 'We have made up our minds ... to stand by the trial by jury as constituted by Alfred the Great.' When William Cuffey, a black tailor (the son of a slave) and respected London Chartist leader, was tried for treason in 1848, he objected that 'the jurors were not his equals, as he was a journey-man mechanic.' After conviction, and while awaiting his sentence of transportation, he addressed the court with the greatest composure: 'This has not been a fair trial, and my request was not complied with to have a jury of my equals. But the jury as it is I have no fault to find with; I dare say they have acted conscientiously.' Throughout his trial he appealed to 'the rights of the working classes' to enter into full citizenship. It did not occur to him to notice the matter of his colour.

Thus in the years after 1832 the political culture of Britain acquired a new working-class dimension, but the social profile of the jury remained unchanged. A jury of the middling sort of people, which in 1649 or 1794 still watchfully confronted the 'Crown', now turned itself about and confronted the challenge of democracy from their social inferiors. Perhaps this may explain why the jury survived into the 20th century almost immune from the rationalisations imposed by Utilitarians in other areas. The jury's ancient legitimacy proved to be a useful resource in the control of working-class movements.

And so it remained, for most purposes, until 14 years ago. Until 1972 qualification for jury service came with the payment of rates (£30p.a. in London, £20 elsewhere). This tied jury service to householder-ratepayers, excluding wives, lodgers, co-habiting adults including adult children, and many categories of non-rate-paying tenant. The English and Welsh jury until 1972 excluded the majority of the adult population and was, in Lord Devlin's admirable account in 1956 (*Trial by Jury*), 'predominantly male, middle-aged, middle-minded and middle-class'. (Before the admission of women householders in 1919 it had of course been exclusively male.) In 1972, some special categories apart, admission to jury service became in effect co-terminous with admission to the electoral roll.

A great deal can be explained by this. Many senior police and some judges and politicians faced this inrush of vulgar democracy into the courts with ashen faces and palpitating hearts. We were told, by Sir Robert Mark, by the Association of Chief Police Officers (ACPO) and others, that the rate of acquittals was rising steeply, that jurors were being suborned by Mafia-like gangs, and that professional criminals were becoming immune from effective prosecution. Subsequent inquiry has shown much of this 'evidence' to have been flawed (or even faked). There is no dramatic disparity between the record of jury performance before and after 1972. Of course, like every human institution ever studied by historians, the jury is not immune from frailties and improper pressures (whether from criminal gangs or from the Crown). But the anti-jury lobby has functioned incessantly since 1972, and has scored repeatedly with those measures to 'strengthen' the jury which I have already reported. The Roskill Committee's fraudulent transplant operation and the current Criminal Justice Bill are the latest products of this exercise. After eight hundred years our betters have decided to bring the jury under their condign control.

* * *

In the previous article we discussed the unusual concern of the past 14 years to 'strengthen' (or subdue) jury practices, some of which date back hundreds of years. There has always been another resource of jury-'strengthening', which is jury-packing. A disquisition on this ancient British practice would require a further essay, much longer than the present one. Jury-vetting is not the same thing as jury-packing, although the first may prepare for the second. Whether packing does or could take place in contemporary English practice is a matter remarkably obscure. The Police may properly inspect the panel against their records, in order to remove disqualified persons, and in the course of this scrutiny much other information will come to light, which may or may not be passed on privily to the clerk of the court or to the prosecution. Of one thing we may be certain: the current monitoring of practice by the Director of Public Prosecutions (reported in Command Paper 9658) will tell us nothing that the Police (or ACPO) does not wish the public to know.

What panel scrutiny – or, in sensitive cases, the more elaborate investigations of vetting – allows is the exercise of the Crown's right of peremptory challenge or 'stand-by', to remove obnoxious jurors from the panel. The Report of the Roskill Committee is anodyne and confusing on the matter of challenge, largely because of the failure to present it in any historical perspective. It is my duty therefore to attempt a brief correction.

In looking into this matter I was intrigued to find that every one of the critical cases still cited today as precedents governing the contemporary practice of challenge and stand-by arose in the course of highly-charged political cases in the period 1790–1848. I refer in particular to *Rex v. O'Coigly* (1798), *Rex v. Edmonds* and ensuing appeal (1820, 1821), and to several Chartist cases in 1848.

Father James O'Coigly, a Catholic priest, was a United Irishman who, sometimes disguised as 'Captain Jones', was travelling in England in the year of the Irish rebellion, as courier to the 'Jacobin' underground. With Arthur O'Connor and others, he was arrested when about to board ship for France, and a sensationally seditious address was found in his pocket, welcoming a French invasion in support of British liberty. It led to a dramatic 'state trial', and there was much sparring by both sides in selecting the jury. The defence made several challenges for cause of potential jurors. One of these, Mr Raikes, was proved to have gone up to the prisoners before the trial, 'looked them all steadfastly in the face ... clenched his fist, and exclaimed "damned rascals!"' 'That is no cause of challenge,' exclaimed the Attorney-General (who led the prosecution): 'We are getting here into prodigious irregularity, and I feel it my duty to protect the Gentlemen of the Jury against this sort of attack.' In the end, Mr Raikes did not serve on the jury, but there was clearly a strong opinion among judges and counsel for the prosecution that to shake one's fist in the face of the prisoners before a trial did not constitute cause of challenge on grounds of 'unindifferency'. Any loyal gentleman, confronted with imputed Jacobins, should be expected to do much the same: but any gentleman must also be presumed to have that liberality of mind which would allow him to be persuaded in the course of the trial that the imputation of Jacobinism had been brought on these particular prisoners in error.

The course of this challenge was confused and did not establish a ruling precedent. *Rex v. O'Coigly* is remembered by lawyers now for its ruling on the adjacent issue of the Crown's right of challenge or 'stand-by', which was here argued at length and determined in a way which governs practice to this day. The

Crown was disallowed any right of peremptory challenge, but must always show cause: however, by a sweet legal fiction, it may postpone showing cause by calling on the juror to stand by to the end of the panel, and then challenging for cause only if the rest of the panel is exhausted – which seldom, if ever, takes place. In the result, the Crown was effectively awarded an unlimited number of peremptory challenges. As for Father O'Coigly, he was convicted and hanged.

As regards the defence, in the first half of the 19th century the position was this: it had, in its quiver, the right of 20 peremptory challenges. Thereafter it might only challenge for cause. And by a series of decisions it became established (in lay language) that such challenge – if in the matter of prejudice, bias, 'unindifferency' – may only be for particular bias against particular defendants. Prejudice of a more general nature might not be allowed as cause. Moreover, challenge for cause might only be allowed to proceed through the means of questioning a potential juror in court (an interrogation known as *voir dire*) if good reason for cause to question was first shown to the court, which, at its discretion, might then permit questioning. And, further, the proof of a juror's bias should be founded upon extrinsic evidence and not on interrogation alone.

It is notorious that English and United States court practice has handled this matter in different ways. If we take the procedural question out of its context, there is much to be said for the logic of the English resolution. Let us suppose the prisoner to be charged with arson. Now we cannot expect it to be likely that we will find a jury which has no opinion as to the rights and wrongs of arson. Therefore we should not permit a juror to be interrogated as to his opinion of this offence, under the implication that an adverse view of arson – or even of the particular episode of arson coming under trial – is evidence of bias against the prisoner. Unless the juror can be proved to have said that he or she believes the defendant to be a foul arsonist, a disgust for arson carries no imputation of bias.

In politically sensitive contexts this logic does not wear so well, however. Examine the case of *Rex v. Edmonds and Others* (1820). This was a trial for conspiracy, before a special jury, at Warwickshire Assizes. The defendants included the venerable Major John

Cartwright, the 'Father' of English Reformers; the editor of the Radical *Black Dwarf*, T.J. Wooler; and Edmonds, the secretary of the Birmingham reformers. Their offences arose out of the same context as the Peterloo meeting in support of manhood suffrage: seditious agitation, disorderly demonstrations, the election of a popular 'representative' for the unenfranchised city of Birmingham. The defendants were convicted, and either imprisoned or fined. There was an appeal to King's Bench in 1821. One ground of appeal concerned the defence's challenge for cause. At his trial Wooler had sought to examine jurors on *voir dire* as to whether they had expressed any opinion in the case. The court, presided over by the Lord Chief Baron, had refused to allow the questions. In judgement, Abbot, Lord Chief Justice, upheld the Lord Chief Baron. An opinion as to the general guilt of radical agitators, and as to the need to bring them to punishment, could in no way be shown to be a cause of disqualification. Only 'a preconceived opinion of their personal guilt, or a determination to find them guilty', could be shown as cause: and this must be proved by extrinsic evidence, not by *voir dire* interrogation.

I am not arguing the evident fact that arson and sedition are different orders of offence. I am pointing to a narrower fact, which is that bias expressed by jurors against Radicalism may be inseparable from a bias against particular defendants, in a way in which bias against arson may not. Arsonists, rapists, murderers and highwaymen rarely advertise, publish and demonstrate on behalf of their intentions before committing their offences, whereas Radicals, Freethinkers, Chartists, advocates of birth control, suffragettes, and so on, commonly did (or do): and it was often this advocacy, rather than any other overt act, which constituted, in the eyes of the law, the offence. There was no way in which Warwickshire jurors in 1820 could express hostility towards Racialism without also expressing a particular hostility against these notorious leaders of the cause of Reform.

The decision in *Rex v. Edmonds*, however, established the ruling precedent which is still cited in disputed cases to this day. It was enforced and further defined in two cases arising from the Chartist agitation of 1848, *Regina v. Cuffey* and *Regina v. Dowling*. In the year of revolutions, Chartism reached its last peak of agitational presence. In London a monster meeting was convened for 10 April, with the intention of presenting yet one more mass petition for universal male suffrage. The Government professed to believe that an insurrection was threatened and prepared for it in full military style. This included the raising of a prodigious number – perhaps a hundred and seventy thousand – special constables. This was a *levée en masse* of London's bourgeoisie and petty bourgeoisie, placed in arms and under orders against London's working class.

The prisoners at the trials which came up at the Central Criminal Court the following September were Chartists and Irish Confederates accused of insurrectionary preparations in the confused aftermath of 10 April. The clearest decision in the matter of *voir dire* arose in the case of Dowling, a young Irish portrait-painter. Kenealy, his counsel, declared that he wished to examine every one of the jurors on the *voir dire* to find out whether they had served as special constables:

Mr Justice Erle: Have you any cause?

Kenealy: That he does not stand indifferent.

Attorney-General: That is no cause. You must state a particular cause.

Kenealy: I have reason to believe that he is a special constable and has prejudged this case. It is perfectly notorious that the great majority of the inhabitants about here were sworn as special constables. I have no special instructions with regard to this gentleman ... and cannot therefore prove the fact *aliunde*.

Mr Justice Erle: Then I must refuse the application.

Kenealy: Am I to understand your lordship to say that I am not to be allowed to examine upon the *voir dire*? Am I to understand that the right is to be taken away from the people of England?

He was, indeed, so to understand. And this ruling was upheld on appeal. Dowling was duly convicted by a jury of special constables, and sentenced to 20 years' transportation.

The cases – *O'Coigly* through *Edmonds* to *Dowling* – are those cited in Halsbury and in all compendiums of contemporary law, as establishing the rule as it lies today. Each of these decisions came out of a context of political conflict, in which the authorities sought to 'strengthen' the operation of the jury system in the interests of 'the better administration of justice'. When we are told – as the Roskill Committee tells us, and as without doubt Conservative Law Officers will argue in coming debates on the Criminal Justice Bill – that the defence is losing little in losing its ancient rights of peremptory challenge (to be reduced now from three to nil), since the right of challenge for cause remains unimpaired, it is essential to remember, first, that the law's definition of 'cause' excludes all general prejudice (political, racial, gender, religious etc), and, second, that since the defence is barred from questioning the juror on *voir dire* (unless with prior cause shown), it is unlikely that cause can ever come to light.

American practice is vastly different. Our jury systems are like a tree with a strong common trunk, but on one side a bough has been lopped off, so that today only a vestigial challenge for cause is allowed to the English defence, while on the other side is a flourishing American branch, heavily-laden with challenges on *voir dire* examinations. Thus jury selection in England became a formal and expeditious matter, rarely occupying as much as an hour, in which *voir dire* is rare, whereas on the other side of the Atlantic there was, by the late 19th century, a heavy branch of practice indeed. In the Haymarket case (the 'Chicago Anarchists') selection of a jury involved examination, mainly on *voir dire*, of 981 panellists, over a period of 21 days; and in the trial of Jacob Sharp, in the New York Aldermanic corruption cases of 1886–7, 2,100 panellists were summoned, 1,196 were examined, and 22 days were spent in jury selection. These procedures, only a little abbreviated, continue in many states today.

This has altered the jury system, when considered within the expectations of our political future. And altered it irrevocably. We cannot go back. We could not now import protracted *voir dire* procedures into English courts, because they would run athwart inherited expectations. The jurors, every woman and every man, would have their backs put up by such interrogation. They would feel it as an insult to their integrity, as well as a breach of British reticence as to the privacy of opinion. Any attempt in this direction can be counter-productive for the defence. When Lilburne was on trial in 1649 and was presented with a juror whom he did not know by person or report, he scanned him closely and then said: 'He is an honest man, and looks with an honest face: let him go.' The juror, so flattered, was the more ready to acquit. It is a trick which counsel still understand today. There is, moreover, some suggestion that clumsy exercises in vetting can also be counter-productive. Vetted juries returned acquittals in the 'Anarchists' (1979), Cyprus signalmen and Clive Ponting cases. Perhaps they were put on their mettle to show that they were not cat's-paws of the Crown?

We may take the point of expectations further than that. Because jury selection in England has been procedurally abbreviated, the dominant expectation in our political culture has become this: the jury is, or ought to be, a random selection of our peers. That is what 'a fair trial' is now thought to be. Now an exact historian might argue that American practice is closer to ancient precedent: the selected 12 must be 'good men and true', 'of good repute', 'men of a clear reputation'. Moreover, it was 12 men from whom, by an elaborate system of challenge, it was possible to remove persons of known bias against or affiance to either party.

The history is not, then, if we are exact, one of merely random selection. That is why the poor old Roskill Committee got itself so confused. For the record is this. Trial by jury, drawing upon a limited pool of male householders in the much smaller communities of the past, allowed both sides to find out a great deal about the panel; and it was upon this investigation that instructions to challenge could be made. When Lilburne's jury was in selection in 1649 he asked the court: 'I do not know the faces of two of the men that were read to me ... Will you let me have some friends by me that are citizens of London, that know them, to give me information of their qualities and conditions? For without this, truly, you may as well hang me without a trial.' Move on a hundred and fifty or two hundred years. In politically sensitive trial after trial, it can be observed, from the Treasury Solicitor's papers or from the trial record, that both sides were busily employed in investigating the panel. The Crown's resources were of course greater, and their inquiries more thorough. But even in John Frost's trial in 1840 defence counsel had inquired into all but five of the panel of 318, and had noted objections to 160. This amounted to an exhaustive survey or canvass, and there was no suggestion that this involved any impropriety.

The scrutiny of the panel is, then, ancient and venerable practice. So what is all this present pother about? It is this. The opportunity for the defence to scrutinise or influence the selection of the jury is being closed, while the prosecution's scrutiny and means of influence are enlarged. In England the number of peremptory challenges open to the defence has been reduced from 20 to seven, to three and now nil. But challenge for *cause* (which we are grandly told remains untampered with) was lopped off and sealed by 1848, when *voir dire* interrogation was limited to a vestigial survival, and the definition of 'cause' excluded matters of general bias. Meanwhile the constituency from which panels are drawn has changed out of recognition. Gone are the close communities in which a householder's reputation might be quickly learned. Panels today are drawn from vast and anonymous catch-ment areas: the defence is presented with faceless names drawn from an electoral list, a meaningless swathe of names and addresses, from which the one point of purchase – the 'additions' or occupations – was struck out in 1973 by Lord Hailsham's pen. The defence today is blindfold, unless it should resort to hiring expensive 'private eyes' to lurk around the streets and ask questions of neighbours – a practice prohibitive in cost and offensive to our privacy. For this reason, in recent years, the peremptory challenge has been used rather rarely by experienced counsel, and – if used at all – most often in an effort to adjust the number of women or perhaps of blacks or of young or old people on a jury.

For the prosecution it is a different question altogether. ACPO, the DPP and successive Attorney-Generals have come up with jury-vetting, with scarcely a reproof from the judiciary. As the resources of Police and Security enlarge, more and more sophisti-cated methods of machine-storage and retrieval of records are available to the prosecution. At the press of a few keys, the Police can routinely open a huge and crazily-distorted screen to view the panel: a squatter, an associate of Trotskyists, the mother of a girl supposed to associate with 'criminals', or a citizen who has committed the aggravated offence of actually complaining about the Police. This information may routinely be passed on, with a nod and a wink, to the prosecution or the officers of the court. In politically sensitive cases, where the Attorney-General's and ACPO's Practice Directions authorise vetting, there may be added the impertinent and often erroneous records of the Special Branch, CID and perhaps Security Services, which may be fed to the prosecution, enriched by the products of Britain's growth industries: spying, mail-interception and telephone-tapping.

Meanwhile, the Crown's right of peremptory challenge (disguised as 'stand-by') remains unlimited: that is, its ability, upon secret and prejudicial information, to water the jury. Even the Roskill Committee, for all its gross confusions, must be acquitted of such partiality. It suggested that if the defence's right of peremptory challenge were to be abolished, then the occupations of jurors should go back on the lists, and the prosecution's right of stand-by (without cause) should also be abolished: 'Unquestionably, in our view, it would be necessary for both sides to be treated in the same way.' But our betters these days have no patience with even the fictions of fair play. Neither recommendation will be found in the Criminal Justice Bill. In truth, they are frightened by a democratic jury. They are afraid that it might shy at oppressive prosecutions, and throw the DPP into the ditch. It did so, after all, in the Cyprus signals trial and the Clive Ponting case. This is the real occasion for these measures in the Bill.

Well, that is it. The fraudulent operation of the Roskill Committee is over. On the prompting of a committee of judges, senior police and accountants, another portion of our liberties is to be chipped away. As Mr Walter Merricks said, in his admirable Note of Dissent in the Roskill Report, 'my colleagues seem to find trial by jury an anomaly.' In fact, the Report of the Roskill Committee is more explicit: 'Society appears to have an attachment to jury trial which is emotional or sentimental rather than logical.' The Committee itself shows a marked preference for summary jurisdiction and trial by tribunals, and for verdicts 'delivered by persons qualified by training'. We are to be governed by experts for our own good.

One must grope back in our history – perhaps for several hundred years – to come upon a time which had less true respect for the values of democracy than we – or our 'experts' – have now. The defence's peremptory challenge, Mr Merricks notes, may be 'difficult to defend in strict logic: it is but one feature of a complex and not wholly logical system in which the checks and balances have evolved over a long period.' What enrages our betters is that some of these checks inhibit *them*.

They do not like old things. They are the 'projectors and adventurers, the alchymists and empirics', of modern times. They are concerned with 'the proper administration of justice' a thing to be administered by them to us. They are the Gradgrinds of government offices and the Militants of the MoD or MI5, commuting from Richmond and from Sussex villages to their departments, meditating benignly on more expert measures of social control. They are the Fordists of bureaucracy, who wish to engrave over the portals of our law courts: 'History is bunk.'

They are the culturally-deprived of our time, and it would be unfair to mock them for their disabilities. Two basic propositions of democracy are so bizarre to their atrophied faculties that they really cannot comprehend them. The first is that there could be occasions when laws are judged by the public to be oppressive, or when the subject requires a defence against the Crown (or organs of the state). In our history it is at precisely such moments that the jury has interposed the power of its verdict. Clive Ponting's case has shown this function to be not wholly obsolete.

The defence of the subject against the over-mighty state was once regarded – by such men as Sir William Blackstone and Thomas Jefferson – as a crucial function of the jury, elevating it to a high place among the defining institutions of a political democracy. For Alexis de Tocqueville the American jury was an 'eminently republican element in government' which 'places the real direction of Society in the hands of the governed'. I know of only one old judge, long retired from practice, who even understands this language today. And he – Lord Devlin – now writes in elegiac tone. Thirty years ago he could still say that 'the jury is the lamp that shows that freedom lives.' In 1978, he warned of the gathering signs 'that the jury has another half-century or so of life to be spent in the sort of comfortable reservation which conquerors, bringing with them a new civilisation, assign to the natives whom they are displacing.'

The second proposition is beyond the comprehension not only of our betters but of almost any of us in these latter days. It is the quaint archaic notion that anyone – randomly selected – might be able to perform a human-sized office or role. We have less sense of ourselves than villagers in Medieval times, who rotated parish offices, or 18th-century tradesmen who could find it in themselves to defy the Attorney-General and the Bench. The jury is perhaps the last place in our social organisation where any person, any citizen, may be called upon to perform a fully adult role. It has not been shown that our fellow citizens have failed, when placed in the jury box. They appear, when they find themselves there, to undergo some inexplicable reversion to pre-modern modes, and to find in themselves resources to fulfil the responsibility. But the very idea of it is 'illogical' and absurd. Only a crank could possibly suggest such a direct exercise of democracy today. Indeed, although as a historian I have to confess that the thing has worked, I can scarcely comprehend it myself.

As for the matter of challenges, no doubt our betters will have their way. For decades only a handful of MPs have shown any zeal for our rights or liberties. All major parties have shared in the complicity. Nor could we try to fight our way back by importing *voir dire* across the Atlantic. The defence could never compete with the Hendon Police Computer and the data banks of Security. Our only way now is to opt for the random jury, with defined rights of peremptory challenge equal to both sides (and the abolition of the fiction of stand-by). The panel should be selected by statistical criteria of randomness. There should be impartial scrutiny of court practices, and penalties imposed for collusion between the Police and the prosecution (or court officers) in manipulating the panel. How this could be best effected I must leave to qualified persons, who would not include ACPO or the DPP. In politically or racially sensitive cases we might experiment with some *voir dire* interrogation for a trial period.

But I am no 'projector or adventurer'. I would trust a little in the devices inherited from our ancestors. I will be satisfied with the abolition of vetting, the closing-down of their infernal data banks, the dismantling of their invasive devices for the interception of our privacy, the restoration of the powers of the jury of inquest, the return of certain excluded categories to the option of trial by jury, and the regeneration of some sense of independence (or at least some sense of shame) amongst the judiciary. This might best be effected by a Commission to Inquire into Serious Fraud upon the People's Rights and Liberties, from which politicians, police and judges would be disqualified.

This is not to say that the old system was beyond all possibility of reform. There could be more preparation for our rights and our duties as jurors in our schools. It may be argued that 18 is too young to fulfil the role, that literacy qualifications might be more scrupulous, or even that, for some modern types of case, qualifications might be required in numeracy. And education might go further still. Aspirant judges might be transported for a probationary period to New South Wales, to sit at the feet of Mr Justice Powell, and study notions of truth and of impartiality now obsolescent in our island courts. I would be willing, for a modest fee, if the Lord Chancellor so wishes, to prepare an annual examination for all the judiciary in the people's rights and precedents, although I fear that a great many vacancies would ensue upon the Bench. And the Attorney-General has my permission to circulate, gratis, a copy of this article to all electors, not forgetting the Police. But these notions savour a little of the zealot. For the moment, randomness – and confidence in our fellow citizens – is enough.

Published as two articles in the *London Review of Books*, 4th and 18th December 1986.

Peterloo

Peterloo, 1819. A Portfolio of Contemporary Documents. Manchester Public Libraries.

Joyce Marlow: *The Peterloo Massacre*. Rapp and Whiting.

Robert Walmsley: *Peterloo: The Case Reopened*. Manchester University Press.

The 150th anniversary of the massacre at St. Peter's Fields, 1819, saw the appearance of three new publications, two of which may be described as occasional. The first is a well-presented folder of plans, prints, and broad-sides, prepared by the Manchester Public Libraries. The second is a popular account ('the first book for the general reader', as the blurb has it) by Miss Joyce Marlow. The bias of her book appears to be, like her maternal descent, of 'Radical, Unitarian, small mill-owning stock': and the general reader may sometimes find that her folksy narrative – 'Bamford's wife, Mima, a sterling character, made determined efforts to ascertain what had happened to "our Sam" ...' – tends to cloy. Miss Marlow offers some general background to explain what led up to Peterloo: this is second-hand and generally over-simplified: but her narrative of the events of the day itself is closely observed; well-written, and deftly employs a little original material. On this account her book deserves to find some readers: although the *first* book for the general reader must remain, as it has always been, Samuel Bamford's *Passages in the Life of a Radical*.

Bamford's evidence is not, of course, privileged and beyond reach of examination. He was one of the crowd ridden down by Yeomanry and Hussars – a thing likely to induce bias in the victims. And he was later found guilty before a special jury at York Assizes for 'assembling with unlawful banners, at an unlawful meeting, for the purpose of inciting the subjects of our

Lord the king, to contempt and hatred of the government', and sentenced to one year's imprisonment. This clear decision in an impartial court of justice suggests him not only as a biased but also as a compromised witness. No matter such as this escapes the watchful eye of Mr Robert Walmsley.

Mr Walmsley's *Peterloo: The Case Re-opened* is not so much occasioned by the anniversary: it is, in itself, an occasion, and is – the blurb tells us – 'the fruit of half a lifetime's research'. The 585 pages of this fruit swing from the impeccable bough of the Manchester University Press. Mr Walmsley, a Manchester antiquarian bookseller, first had his interest in Peterloo aroused some thirty years ago during the course of research into the family history of the Hultons of Hulton. William Hulton (1787–1864) was chairman of the magistrates who overlooked the field of Peterloo and gave to the Yeomanry the fatal order to advance. In the course of his researches Mr Walmsley became convinced, not only that William Hulton had been unfairly treated by historians, but that he and his fellow magistrates were the victims of nothing less than a Radical conspiracy to falsify the events of that day – a conspiracy fostered by Hunt, Bamford, and Richard Carlile, furthered by Archibald Prentice (author of *Historical Sketches of Manchester*) and John Edward Taylor (before he sobered down and founded the *Manchester Guardian*), and in which John Tyas (the correspondent of *The Times* who witnessed events from the hustings), the Rev Edward Stanley, and dozens of others were witting or unwitting accessories – a conspiracy so compelling that even Donald Read, in his sober and by no means radical study of *Peterloo* (1957), failed to detect it.

It is necessary to make clear what Mr Walmsley's book is not, as well as what it is. It is not a general interpretative account of Peterloo within its political or local background. Nothing is said of radicalism or reaction before January, 1819; very little is said about the government of Manchester in 1819, or to explain the character, role, or reputation of such important actors as Joseph Nadin or Henry Hunt before they emerge on the 1819 stage. This is not a book for the general reader, unless he has taken the precaution of reading (at least) Bamford – or Prentice – and Dr Read beforehand. Nor is it, altogether, a book for the scholar, although it has competent scholarly apparatus, adequate footnotes and bibliography, and a very good index. It is not based on extensive newly discovered evidence, although Mr Walmsley introduces interesting new material from the Rev W.R. Hay (the prominent clerical magistrate) and from William Hulton himself. In particular there has been no new search of Home Office, legal, or military papers in the Public Record Office.

Such new material as there is relates largely to the Hultons of Hulton. We learn not only that there was a Ranulph Hulton who was sub-deacon at Manchester Collegiate Church in 1465 but (more interestingly) that William's mother's horse 'Church and King' won the Kersal Moor races in 1749; and we are given a most revealing view of William himself, addressing the anniversary dinner of the Manchester Pitt Club two years before Peterloo, proposing the toast. 'The Pride of Britain and the Admiration of the World – Our Glorious Constitution', and rolling around the room the unabashed and unalloyed clichés of the British ancien régime: Under this vast aegis repose our liberties, encircled with wisely-ordained laws, and blessed with the sanction of a pure religion .... Shall we then, sell the black-letter volumes of our great charters for any spurious editions printed with type of the National Convention, for Co-chrane, Burdett and Company?

If Mr Walmsley had confined himself to writing a brief biography of William Hulton he would have served historians well. It would have seemed somewhat quaint and provincial, smelling of fine vellum and reverence; and in such a work an exculpatory chapter on Peterloo would have passed without remark. But this chapter has expanded to become some 500 pages of Mr Walmsley's text, and it cannot pass without remark. Nor has it. One of the book's more ecstatic reviewers (in the *Daily Telegraph*) has declared that Mr Walmsley's 'massive research challenges the accepted version', his book 'leaves no fact unchallenged and uncorroborated, no document unread *in full*, no source unchecked', and that it 'utterly discredits' the accounts in Prentice and Bamford. Not very many readers, perhaps, will struggle their whole way through the book; and of those who do even fewer will follow, point by point, its exceedingly repetitious, but at the some time involuted apologetics. But all – or nearly all – will come from it with a bemused impression that, in all this turning and wheeling around a few points, something must have been proved, somebody must have been exposed. And as such the book will enter the folklore of history.

Mr Walmsley is interested, chiefly, in the events of the day of Peterloo and even more closely in the events of one half-hour of that day – between 1.15 and 1.45 p.m. – from the time when Henry Hunt arrived on the hustings to the time when the field was empty of all but shawls, bonnets, sticks, and cavalry adjusting their saddle-girths. Obsessively he rides up and down that field and its environs, obsessively he rides up and down the five or ten minutes between the arrival of the Yeomanry at the edge of the field and the dispersal of the crowd, summoning witnesses in the newspaper press of the weeks following, dragging them back by their collars, making them pace over the yards before and behind the hustings, cross-examining reminiscences and confronting them with conflicting depositions, galloping off into the suburbs of the twentieth century to interrogate suspicious stragglers, like F.A. Bruton, the author of the careful *The Story of Peterloo* (1919).

At the centre of his obsession is this: what happened on that day was unintentional, and the crowd (or part of it) was the first aggressor. The magistrates in their house overlooking the hustings were justly alarmed by the proceedings, both by tumults which had preceded August 16 and by the radical rhetoric and military array of the crowd on the day. With a nice sense of legalistic propriety they waited until Hunt and his fellow speakers were on the hustings and then ordered the constables to arrest them; this Joseph Nadin, the deputy-constable, refused to do without military aid; the magistrates sent for Yeomanry and Hussars, and the Yeomanry arrived first, fortuitously; the Yeomanry were ordered to support the constables in the execution of the warrant, and they advanced in reasonable order and without aggressive intention or action into the crowd; but the crowd then closed in upon them in a menacing manner and the Yeomanry were assailed, at some point close to the hustings, by brickbats and sticks hurled by a portion of the crowd; most of the Yeomanry kept their heads until Hunt and his fellows had been arrested, and then, increasingly assailed by brickbats and hemmed in on all sides by a threatening crowd, were forced to beat off their attackers (with the *flats* of their sabres) in self-defence. The magistrates, observing their predicament in the midst of a threatening multitude, were forced to order the Hussars to come to their rescue and to clear the field. All followed on. And the radicals have made party-political propaganda out of their own aggression ever since.

One needs a book like this, every now and then, to recall that the patron saint of historians is St. Sisyphus. Before we enquire what facts he has actually adduced, Mr Walmsley must be acquitted of one charge. He is certainly not guilty of wilful suppression or distortion, although there are many inconvenient facts unmentioned and others which are bludgeoned into unrecognizable pulp. He could not have written this book unless he believed in its truth, obsessively. No one but a true Church-and-King believer, an authentic descendant and vindicator of the shopkeepers on horseback who made up the Manchester Yeomanry, could have cantered, brandishing his sword of polemic, into so many blind alleys of argument as he has. The printed – and, to historians, long known and readily available – documents which he quotes, he quotes repetitiously and in full.

Yet the fact is that Mr Walmsley has *no* new facts to adduce about this half-hour. His book is a sustained essay in special pleading about minutiae, in which he is very much disposed to believe that A did happen and very much disposed to believe that B did not happen. Such a conviction, sustained over 500 pages, is bound – whatever the press of defenceless facts against it – to reach the hustings in the end and to cut down the 'radical' flags. Nevertheless, let us follow Mr Walmsley on to his chosen part of the field.

Did the Yeomanry ride quietly up to the hustings to effect the arrests, or did they (as 'radicals' mythologise) begin to strike out with their sabres from their first entry into the crowd? Were they attacked, before they reached the hustings, by sticks and brickbats? The overwhelming majority of witnesses to these events may be suspected of 'prejudice', as parties to the event, since the greater part belonged to the crowd who were ridden into, and the remainder belonged to the magistracy, special constables, and the Yeomanry who did the riding. Their evidence is not therefore worthless, since they were subject to cross-examination in the

courts, and betrayed the customary signs of veracity or inconsist-
ency. However, historians, from 1819 until 1969, have attempted to
simplify the extreme difficulties of sifting this evidence (and the
reports of partisan newspapers, on either side) by looking for
witnesses who cannot be accused of belonging, in any obvious
sense, to either contesting party. There *are* a few such observers:
uncommitted and merely curious spectators on the fringes of the
crowd: householders whose windows overlooked the field: and
(notably) several press reporters who were afforded places on the
hustings – John Tyas of *The Times*, John Smith of the *Liverpool
Mercury*, Edward Baines of the *Leeds Mercury* – and the Rev.
Edward Stanley, a clergyman who had private business on that day
with Mr Buxton, who owned the house which the magistrates
chose as their headquarters, and who stayed on to observe the
whole affair from a window directly above the magistrates.

Mr Stanley, in a careful account written within a few months
of the affair, was unequivocal. On the brickbats, for example: 'I
indeed saw no missile weapons used throughout the whole
transaction, but ... the dust at the hustings soon partially
obscured everything that took place near that particular spot.' Mr
Walmsley seizes upon this honest statement as merely negative:
Stanley could not see the brickbats because of the dust. (He does
not notice that, if he accepts Stanley's testimony here, he must
for the same reason question Hulton's testimony at the trial of
Hunt: 'When the Yeomanry advanced to the hustings I saw
bricks and stones flying' – since Hulton's viewpoint was almost
identical to that of Stanley, and magistrates must peer through
the same dust as clergymen). Uncommitted witnesses, however,
can be found on the hustings, beyond the rising dust. Thus Tyas,
who was reporting from the hustings, on the Yeomanry's
approach to the hustings: 'Not a brickbat was thrown at them ...
during this period.' Mr Walmsley gets around this by quoting
Captain Birley, the scarcely impartial witness who commanded
the Yeomanry on the field, to the effect that the first attack was
made upon his men at the *rear* of the hustings, which Tyas
could not observe. Mr Walmsley does not report the evidence of
Smith (at Hunt's trial) who was over six feet high and had a
good viewpoint to the left of the hustings:

I saw no stone or brick-bat thrown at them; in my judgement, if any stones or brick-bats had been thrown I was in a situation likely to have seen it, my eyes and countenance were in a direction towards the military up to the moment of their reaching the hustings.

The question of the manner in which the Yeomanry approached the hustings is much the same. Smith declared in a letter to the Earl of Derby written two days after Peterloo that they 'rushed upon the people, cutting right and left', and repeated the same general testimony in Redford v. Birley three years later. He did not attest to the fact during the intervening trial of Hunt, presumably because, as he was led by counsel through his evidence, he was not asked this question; but Mr Walmsley finds the omission so significant as to be sinister and to discredit his whole evidence – he 'thought fit to modify' his 'first impressions' when under oath.

The Rev. Edward Stanley receives very much the same treatment. His testimony (which influenced the accounts of those two 'radical' writers, F.A. Bruton and Dr Read) was plain:

It has often been asked when and where the cavalry struck the people. I can only say that from the moment they began to force their way through the crowd towards the husting swords were up and swords were down, but whether they fell with the sharp or flat side, of course I cannot pretend to give an opinion.

Mr Walmsley demolishes this by showing that, three years later, in the action of Redford v. Birley, 'Stanley's testimony under oath was not the testimony given in his narrative':

Did you watch the advance of the cavalry from their place up to the hustings?
I did.
Did you see either sticks, or stones or anything of the kind used against the cavalry in their advance up to the hustings?
Certainly not.

Did you see any resistance whatever to the cavalry, except the thickness of the meeting?

None.

Do I understand you to say you saw them surround the hustings, or not?

Surround I could not say, for the other side of the hustings, of course, was partially eclipsed by the people upon it.

But you saw them encircle part?

Encircle part.

Did you see what was done when they got there? ...

I saw the swords up and down, the orators tumbled or thrown over, and the mob dispersed.

Mr Walmsley – and it must be insisted that this is a fair example of his method – is seized with the misapprehension that the juxtaposition of these two passages of Stanley's amount to an astounding discrepancy ('Bruton appeared quite oblivious that these discrepancies existed'), and he canters about the pages with it like a captured Cap of Liberty:

> In his printed narrative the 'swords were up and the swords were down' on their way up to the hustings. On oath, Stanley testified he saw 'swords up and down' when they got to the hustings.

But – oh, St. Sisyphus! – there is no discrepancy here at all. Stanley, being led by counsel, had to reply as exactly as he could to the exact question asked, which is, in this case, what he saw done *at the hustings*. And he uses the identical phrase which he had used in his earlier narrative because, being an accurate man (he was later a president of the Manchester Statistical Society), he was describing what he could actually *see* through rising dust at a distance of some hundred yards – the swords rising and falling.

Mr Walmsley allows that there were one or two other witnesses who shared Stanley's illusions, but he implies that the evidence is slender and unsupported. Such a conclusion is made possible only by the cavalier way in which Mr Walmsley passes by the evidence adduced in the inquest on John Lees of Oldham, at which at least nine witnesses testified to seeing the Yeomanry cut at the people on their way to the hustings:

Coroner: At what pace did they come?

Jonah Andrew (cotton spinner): I think it was a trot. It was as fast as they could get, and the constables were making way for them.

Q. Did you see them striking any one?

A. Yes; I saw them striking as they come along, and they struck one person when they were about twenty yards from me ... they squandered to the right and left before they came to me ....

Q. Well: What then?

A. Why they began to cut and hack at the people like butchers.

*

William Norris Buckley (merchant, and nephew to one of the active-magistrates): There was a complete convulsion when the soldiers rode their horses among the multitude, and they seemed to be laying about them with their swords, in their way to the hustings; and when they arrived there, they cut down the people that held the flags.

*

Coroner: Do you know anything of the death of John Lees?

Elizabeth Farren: No, I do not.

Q. Then why do you come here?

A. Because I was cut.

Q. Where were you cut?

A. On the forehead (Here the witness raised her bonnet and cap, as also the bandage over her forehead, and exhibited a large wound not quite healed).

The Coroner: I don't mean that, woman. Where were you at the time you were cut?

A. About thirty yards from the house where the Justices were, amongst the special constables ....

Q. Were you cut as the Cavalry went to the hustings, or on their return?

A. I was cut as they were going towards the hustings. I had with me this child (shewing the child she held in her arms). I was frightened for its safety, and to protect it, held it close to my side with the head downward, to avoid the blow. I desired them to spare my child, and I was directly cut on my forehead.

Q. What passed then?

A. I became insensible ....

None of this, or similar, evidence at the inquest on John Lees is cited by Mr Walmsley. The witnesses, and in particular the last one, were clearly highly prejudiced. The counsel for the family of the deceased offered to bring any number of further witnesses to prove the same facts, but were prevented by the coroner; the counsel for the Manchester constables brought forward several witnesses (including Joseph Nadin) who contradicted this evidence (and who saw the controversial brickbats) and could no doubt have brought forward others. All that can be said is that the witnesses for the former appear to be more various in their occupations and commitments and to offer more authentic testimony.

This is relevant to Mr Walmsley's large claim to have dispersed from the field all previous historians, since his neglect of the evidence presented at this inquest is in striking contrast to the exceptional weight which he places upon the evidence presented for the defence in Redford v. Birley. The Oldham inquest, upon a victim who died, most probably of injuries sustained at Peterloo, was a turbulent and ill-conducted affair, at which the reformers sought to bring forward evidence leading to a verdict of 'wilful murder' against the Yeomanry. But it was held within weeks of the event, when neither the authorised nor the unauthorised versions had congealed; the testimonies have authenticity and freshness, and the very breaches in legal formality lead to scores of revealing polemical encounters. Redford v. Birley, on the other hand, was held *three years* after Peterloo; it was a civil action for damages by one of the injured against the commander and several members of the Yeomanry. In the interval there had been the trial of Hunt, press outcry, parliamentary debates, demands for enquiry; memories

had dimmed and the evidence had been many times rehearsed; and
the Manchester authorities offered for the first time a unified and
well-drilled defence of their actions. Mr Walmsley has a touching
faith in the absolute historical verity of legal decisions (when they
confirm his own conclusions), and the fact that the jury found
against Redford appears to him to substantiate at every point this
tardily mounted official version and, moreover, to brand Prentice
and Bamford – who continued to pass on their own version – as
wilful deceivers of posterity.

This is central to his argument. The 580 pages of the Oldham
inquest are 'interminable proceedings'; which may be largely
discounted; but the 632 pages of three-year-chewed cud in Redford
v. Birley are commended as providing a 'cloud of witnesses' to
prove that it was not the Yeomanry at all but the *crowd* which
attacked. But it is characteristic of Mr Walmsley's polemical
method that he never does settle down, in any systematic way, to
examine what Redford v. Birley did, or did not, 'prove'.

In fact, an analysis of the trial gives these results: on the first
of Mr Walmsley's disputed points, twenty nine of Redford's
witnesses swore that they did not see brickbats, stones, or any form
of resistance by the crowd to the Yeomanry before they reached
the hustings, whereas seventeen of Captain Birley's witnesses swore
that they did. Among Redford's twenty-nine witnesses were seven
weavers, one fustian-cutter, one carver and gilder, two cotton
manufacturers, one pattern-drawer, one Church of England clergyman (Stanley), one dissenting minister, one Quaker surgeon, three
gentlemen, one salesman, four journalists (including Tyas, Baines
and Smith), one chemist, two householders overlooking the field,
and one member of the Manchester Yeomanry. Among Birley's
seventeen were the Deputy-Constable (Nadin), two of the committee of magistrates (Hulton and Hay), one merchant's agent, one
calico-printer, one policeman, two lawyers, one gentleman, one
farm steward, and at least six special constables. The former would
appear to be the more representative group, with the greatest
number of independently placed witnesses.

On Mr Walmsley's second disputed point – whether the
Yeomanry struck out with their sabres on the way to the hustings
– the honours are more even: rather more – and more various –

witnesses said they did than said they did not. The fact that the
jury (which was a special jury) found for Birley does not, in any
case, indicate anything about their judgment on these parts of the
evidence, since they were directed by the judge 'that if the
defendants were acting in the legal discharge of their duty, being
called upon by the magistracy to act, the verdict ought to be for
the defendants'. Since the fact that the magistracy ordered the
Yeomanry into the crowd is one of the few facts about Peterloo
which was never disputed, the jury had no alternative; but a verdict
reached on such a basis can have no binding power on the
judgment of posterity.

In contrast to his faith in the 'cloud of witnesses' in Redford v.
Birley, Mr Walmsley evidently found the more authentic evidence
given at the Oldham inquest too painful to read with precision. His
few, selective references to it are generally inaccurate. Here is an
example. He writes that one witness

> testified that he heard one of the Yeomanry say 'there is that
> villain Saxton: run him through,' which in the printed report of
> the proceedings is italicized, apparently to make it clear that it
> corroborated John Tyas's report in *The Times*. It did. The words
> were almost identical. Tyas had written: 'There is that villain
> Saxton: do you run him through the body.' This passage has
> been cited in modern times [footnote citing E.P. Thompson] as
> convincing testimony, without adding the information that this
> witness, 'muttering to himself', was dismissed from the court-
> room as an incredible one.

The passage deserves detailed criticism, as exemplifying Mr
Walmsley's pursuit of imaginary molehills and his ignorance of
tangible mountains. The suggestion that the words quoted were
italicized to indicate that they corroborated Tyas's report is pure
attribution; it is very much more probable that they were italicized
to distinguish quoted matter from the witnesses' own words. If Mr
Walmsley had been discussing evidence supporting the Yeomanry
he would probably have found that two witnesses corroborating
each other offered final proof; in this case he suggests that
corroboration suggests collusion. The witness, it is true, is reported

as withdrawing, muttering, but there is nothing in the report to suggest that he was dismissed as 'incredible'; he was dismissed because the coroner was out of patience, was seeking to abbreviate the proceedings, and was refusing to take evidence which did not bear directly upon the wounding of John Lees by the hustings; and the witness was muttering because he was not permitted to relate all the facts about the Yeomanry which he knew:

> Coroner: Do you mean to state, that you saw these two people, Harrison and Shelmerdine, wound any body?
>
> James Walker: I don't know that I saw Harrison wound any body, but I saw him attempt to wound both me and Mr Saxton; and if I had not jumped back, I am sure he would have cut me. I saw Shelmerdine inflict a wound upon a person afterwards.
>
> Q. Near the hustings?
>
> A. No.
>
> Q. Then this is the conclusion of your evidence, that you neither saw Shelmerdine or Harrison wound any person at the hustings? Which was it that attempted to strike you?
>
> A. Harrison.
>
> The Coroner: That is all I ask you.
>
> The Witness: But I have not stated all I know. I saw different men wounded after that.
>
> The Coroner: You are told, that is not evidence. Go about your business.
>
> (The Witness withdrew, muttering.)

The witness was not, in any case, the witness cited by E.P. Thompson, unless Mr Walmsley has access to an edition of *The Making of the English Working Class* which is unknown to us. Mr Thompson cites Nathan Broadhurst, who appears some 300-odd pages earlier in the inquest, and who also testified (collusively?) to the attack on Saxton, using the words: 'There's Saxton, damn him, run him through.' This witness was not dismissed, nor accused of incredibility, nor did he mutter.

This, then, is Mr Walmsley's method. He batters away so

remorselessly at every piece of evidence accusatory of the Yeomanry that the reader, out of sheer tedium, is inclined to submit. The crowd attacked the peaceable Yeomanry (behind the hustings, where no one but Captain Birley could see it) and all followed on:

> All the actors in that tragedy were victims. The radicals on the platform, the militants in the crowd, the peaceable in the crowd, the Yeomanry, the constables, the magistrates in their room, the captives in the New Bayley, were each and severally as much the victims of the tragic chain of circumstances as the dead special constable lying in the Bull's Head, the wounded in the infirmary, and Mrs Partington, crushed to death, lying at the bottom of the cellar steps.

If a case is constructed largely out of negations, it is logical that at the centre of it there will be, not a fact, but a hole. Mr Walmsley is well aware of this hole – who *did*, then, attack the Yeomanry? – and he would have been wisest to have left it empty; but he could not resist the urge to fill it, and it is here, at the heart of his thesis, that his special pleading becomes excessive.

There was a row, in *February*, 1819, at Sandy Brow in Stockport, where some cavalry attempted to seize a Cap of Liberty, and where the Radicals beat them off and crowed about it for months afterwards. Therefore it follows, as the night the day, that the hole can be filled by the Stockport contingent. The evidence? They were behind the hustings. That is all: a mountain of speculation labours to produce this poor, moulting mouse of uncertain evidence. No one, at the time or later, noticed what Mr Walmsley, now that 150 years of dust has settled, can now see; not even Captain Birley.

Moreover, the mouse is dressed up as a lion. First Tyas of *The Times* is pressed into service. He mentioned at Hunt's trial that, while the crowd were cheering the Yeomanry on their first arrival at the edge of the field, 'Mr Hunt desired that some persons on the waggon [hustings] might be removed, as they were neither speakers or writers, and were creating a disturbance.' To Mr Walmsley, this incident suggests 'a disruptive element in the crowd actively opposing the Huntean mode of proceeding – that of passive resistance'. Well, does it? It seems to suggest an overcrowded stage and people jostling for place. But then, continues Mr Walmsley, how to account for the sinister evidence of George Swift, himself a radical speaker:

> Hunt ordered the people to stand fast. 'If they want me,' said Mr Hunt, 'let me go – don't resist, don't rush,' – pointing to a place near him. 'If them fellows won't be quiet put them down and keep them down' ...

More evidence of a 'disruptive element'. And then there is the 'remarkable' fact that James Moorhouse, the Stockport leader who accompanied Hunt to the hustings, was nevertheless not on the hustings during the action. What was he doing? And why did Hunt huff and puff so much about all this at his trial? In fact the reasons for this are ludicrously simple: first – Miss Marlow points out this one – Moorhouse had injured his hand in the door of the barouche and retired for medical attention; second, Crown witnesses swore to his presence on the hustings when it was simple to prove that he had been absent, and in all the contentious evidence this was one point at which they could clearly be faulted and even accused of perjury.

But we are allowing ourselves to fall, headlong, into the trap which Mr Walmsley has spent half a lifetime in baiting. For of course these disputed matters do not affect, centrally, an under-standing of Peterloo, even if Mr Walmsley's liberal criticisms of Prentice, Bamford, Bruton and Read, do invite a little of his own kind of correction in reply. Marshalling his thin case in support of the brickbats, Mr Walmsley avers:

> That attack on the Yeomanry, if made, is to be considered as the 'flashpoint' from which stemmed the inevitable explosion. Anything could happen after that; and in fact did.

This is the 'heart of the matter', because 'the success or failure of the radical version of Peterloo pivoted on whether this fact of striking the first blow could be pinned on the Yeomanry or not'. But this is not the case. If a meeting of some 60,000 people is surrounded by cavalry and foot-soldiers and penetrated by hostile special constables, if Yeomanry are then sent into its midst to arrest its most charismatic orator, and if a member of the crowd then throws a brick at a yeoman (which is not proven), are the crowd then guilty of being ridden and sabred off the field?

* * *

Even by the infinitely nice legalisms of Mr Walmsley's own game, the military do not resort to instant and massive retaliation at the moment when one of their members is assaulted. What Mr Walmsley has almost succeeded in making us do is to distract our attention from the actual attack on the crowd, and the nature of that attack. Give or take some emphasis this way or that, the events that preceded this attack are as follows.

A peaceable and fairly good-humoured crowd was assembled, and Hunt began to address it. Immediately the magistrates sent for the Yeomanry to assist the civil power to arrest the speakers in the midst of the assembly. The Yeomanry – local shopkeepers, dealers, dancing-masters and the rest (several of whom were probably drunk) – rode fast towards the hustings, fanning out in disorder among the crowd as they came into it. As they reached the thickest part of the crowd the more disciplined or more humane probably only brandished their swords to make the crowd give way, but others struck out, and not only with the flats. The evidence of any brickbats, &c., being thrown at them until at least several minutes after they had reached and surrounded the hustings is excessively thin. Hunt – who until that moment had exerted himself for order and to prevent panic – was then arrested. Up to that moment the situation had still not passed beyond control, but simultaneously with that moment (Hunt disappeared as if he had been shot, said one witness) the cry went up from the Yeomanry – 'Have at their flags!' – and the Peterloo Massacre really began. Some feeble attempts were made by the crowd to defend the costly embroidered banners and Caps of Liberty which the female reformers had worked over so carefully, and which the reformers had carried so many miles to the meeting. The Yeomanry struck out right and left and the special constables, not to be deprived of their share of trophies of the field, joined in. The magistrates, seeing the Yeomanry in 'difficulties', ordered the Hussars to clear the field. On the edge of the field, some of the people, finding themselves still pursued, made a brief stand.

Mr Walmsley, who has so much to say about unidentified Stockport militants, has almost no comment to offer on this – a moment of unrestrained aggression which cannot by any special pleading be offered as self-defence. Nor is there much conflict of evidence, about this, the real 'flashpoint'. Scarlett, who led the prosecution against Hunt, remained unconvinced about any attack upon the Yeomanry until this moment, and declared in a subsequent parliamentary debate: 'Had they [the Yeomanry] stopped then no real damage would have been done, but they then began to attack.' Tyas reported:

> As soon as Hunt and Johnson had jumped from the waggon a cry was made by the cavalry, 'Have at their flags'. In consequence, they immediately dashed not only at the flags which were in the waggon, but those which were posted among the crowd, cutting most indiscriminately to the right and to the left in order to get at them. This set the people running in all directions, and it was not until this act had been committed that any brickbats were hurled at the military. From that moment the Manchester Yeomanry Cavalry lost all command of temper.

Not even Captain Birley disputed the fact of this attack on the flags. His account (through the medium of Lord Stanley) declared that, when the magistrates' warrant had been executed.

> considerable tumult prevailed, and a struggle ensued between the constables and those persons in the cart, who wished to save the caps of liberty, banners, &c. Some of those who resisted were taken into custody, and the soldiers cut with their sabres. In doing this, it was possible that some persons had been hurt, but not intentionally.

It would perhaps be legalistic to point out that the magistrates' warrant was for the arrest of Hunt and not of a Cap of Liberty. We are bereft of independent witnesses to describe the sensation of

being 'hurt, but not intentionally', since neither Tyas (who himself
had been arrested, in error) nor the Rev. Edward Stanley was
fleeing on the field. We must, perforce, supply the hiatus in Mr
Walmsley's account, by drawing upon the evidence of some of
these biased victims to describe the temper of these moments:

> William Harrison (cotton spinner): ... We were all merry in
> hopes of better times.
>
> Coroner: Were you not desired to disperse?
>
> Harrison: Only with the swords – nobody asked us to disperse –
> only trying to cut our heads off with their swords.

'The soldiers began cutting and slaying', went on Harrison, 'and
the constables began to seize the colours, and the tune was
struck up; they all knew of the combination.' Amidst such
music, few paused to distinguish between flats and sharps:

> Coroner: Did they cut at you near the hustings?
>
> Harrison: No: as I was running away three soldiers came down
> upon me one after another: there was whiz this way and whiz
> that way, backwards and forwards ... and I, as they were going
> to strike, threw myself on my face, so that, if they cut, it should
> be on my bottom.
>
> The Coroner: You act as well as speak?
>
> Harrison: Yes, I'm real Lancashire blunt. Sir: I speak the truth:
> whenever any cried out 'mercy', they said 'Damn you, what
> brought you here',

Another witness related how a special constable jumped on the
hustings, 'took up the President's chair, and beat it about those
who remained'. Some of the crowd, hemmed in on all sides by
Yeomanry, crawled under the carts which formed the platform
for the hustings. According to one witness, John Lees (who later
died) was one of these:

> Jonah Andrew (cotton spinner): I saw several constables round
> him, and beating him with truncheons severely. One of them
> picked up a staff of a banner that had been cut with a sword,
> and said, 'Damn your bloody eyes, I'll break your back'.

This 'self-defence' was pursued by Yeomanry and specials to the edges, and beyond the edges, of the field. Hunt, as he was taken to the magistrates' house, ran the gauntlet of special constables' batons. Even in the side-streets around the field the cavalry pursued the people, cutting at them and saying, 'Damn you, I'll reform you: – You'll come again, will you?'. Outside one house in Windmill Street, 'special constables came up in great triumph, before my door, calling out, *"This is Waterloo for you! This is Waterloo"* '.

Mr Walmsley is of course wrong to suppose that the sober accounts of Peterloo by Bruton and Read represent, even if unwittingly, a perpetuation of the 'radical' myth. A radical interpretation of the day, derived in part from witnesses such as those just quoted, would be far more savage than anything published since Bamford or Prentice. It would see it as a clear moment of class war. Nor were the warriors only on the side of the magistracy. If Mr Walmsley had examined the Home Office papers he would have found evidence that both before the day (among those drilling on the moors) and afterwards (among those threatening vengeance) there were indeed most unpacific 'militants' among the reformers. Bamford was – at least after Peterloo – very probably among them, although he gives himself a more sober character in his reminiscences. If the report of a spy is to be credited, he was still, three months later, venting his feelings in revolutionary rodomontade, and giving in a tavern the toast: 'May the Tree of Liberty be planted in Hell, and may the bloody Butchers of Manchester be the Fruit of it!' As late as April, 1820, there was a fierce tavern brawl in Oldham between soldiers and townsmen, when one of the latter proposed the toast: 'May the skin of every loyal man be taken off his back and made into parchment to beat the Reformers to arms!'

Undoubtedly among the huge crowd which assembled on that day there were some who felt obscurely that something large might come of it, and come suddenly to the raising of the poor and the throwing down of the rich. As one of the contingents marched in that morning they passed Robert Entwisle, an attorney and clerk to the race-course, and later a witness against Hunt: 'Thou hast got a good coat to thy back', one of the marchers shouted, 'but I shall have as good a one as thee before to-night is over.'

* * *

All this was around, before and after Peterloo. But on the day itself the vast crowd was, definitively, under Hunt's control and subjected to his egotistical but emphatically constitutionalist strategy. He had spent the previous week in Manchester, seeing some of the leaders of contingents, and ensuring that his orders for peace and discipline were understood and would be obeyed. They were obeyed, and women and children came with the men upon the field. Hence Peterloo was not only a massacre, but a peculiarly cowardly one. Miss Marlow has discovered letters of Major Dyneley, who commanded the two field-pieces which were held in readiness in the wings on the day: 'The first action of the Battle of Manchester is over', he wrote, 'and I am happy to say has ended in the complete discomfiture of the Enemy.' He had been 'very much assured to see the way in which the Volunteer Cavalry knocked the people about the during the whole time we remained on the ground; the instant they saw ten or a dozen Mobbites together, they rode at them and *leathered* them properly'.

A radical interpretation, however, would re-examine with the greatest scrupulousness those parts of the received account which exonerate from blame in these events, not only the government, but also the magistracy: or which assume that the magistracy were guilty only of panic or ill-judgment, and that once they had sent the Yeomanry upon the field, all happened fortuitously. Both Prentice and J.E. Taylor offered powerful arguments against this at the time. The official *Papers Relative to the State of the Country*, published by government in November, 1819, and offering a selection of the letters of magistrates to the Home Office, depositions, &c., should be regarded as being just as much a party statement – and should be examined as scrupulously – as any radical account. Historians have not, generally, done this: although the *Papers* were selected and published in order to prevent any parliamentary enquiry: the information (Lord Liverpool admitted privately) 'may be laid safely, and much more advantageously, by Government directly rather than through the medium of any committee'. Many of the questions asked by John Edward Taylor in his brilliant and scathing *Notes and Observations, Critical and Explanatory on the Papers Relative to the Internal State of the Country* (1820) have never found a satisfactory answer.

* * *

These questions are of the order most difficult to resolve: questions of intention – did the magistrates intend beforehand that an armed dispersal should take place? – and of complicity – did Sidmouth assent to, or know of, any such intention? Mr Walmsley himself quotes important passages from a private, justificatory account which the Rev W.R. Hay drew up for Sidmouth on October 7, 1819, and which was hitherto unpublished. In this he described the actions of the select committee of magistrates which was in almost continuous session in the days leading up to August 16:

> The Committee continued to meet, and did so on Saturday, [August] the 14th, Sunday, and Monday. Prior to the Saturday, different points had been discussed as to the propriety of stopping the Meeting and the manner of doing so. They were of opinion that Multitudes coming in columns with Flags and Marching in military array were even in the approach to the Meeting a tumultuous assembly; and it was for a little time under consideration whether each Column should not be stopped at their respective entrances into the Town, but this was given up – it was considered that the Military might then be distracted and it was wished that the Town should see what the Meeting was, when assembled, and also that those who came should be satisfied they were assembled in an unlawful manner.

'Being satisfied', the account continues, 'that in point of Law [the Meeting] if assembled as it was expected, would be an illegal Meeting, we gave notice to Lieut-Col L'Estrange ... of our wish to have the assistance of the Military on the 16th.'

This is a clear enough statement of the magistrates' intention, although it does not amount to proof. It is abundantly evident that magistrates and military had a contingency plan for dispersing the meeting; and, at the very least, it would appear that Sidmouth was informed of this plan, from a letter in the Home Office papers dated August 18, in which Sidmouth conveyed to General Sir John Byng his satisfaction in the judgment of Colonel L'Estrange, the military commander on that day: 'His Judgement has in Lord S.'s mind been evinced by his employing the Yeomanry in the Van agreeably to the Plan on which I know you intended to act'. A contingency plan, it is true, does not amount to a fully-proven intention, even when the first part of it – the assembling of the military forces – is put into effect. But there is altogether too much circumstantial evidence, as well as rumour, circulating on the Sunday and the Monday morning, to allow one to discount the possibility of such a fully-formed intention: the clearing of the field by the authorities, early on Monday morning, of all stones: the industrious preparation by the magistrates of depositions from prominent citizens that they were alarmed by the banners and military array of the crowd: the rumours such as those which reached the ears of J.E. Taylor:

> ... early in the forenoon on August 16th persons supposed to be acquainted with the intentions of the magistrates distinctly asserted that Mr Hunt would be arrested on the hustings, and the meeting dispersed. I myself was more than once told so, but could not conceive it possible ...

The intention was expressed, the contingency plan was prepared, the military forces were assembled, the rumours and more-than-rumours were circulating: and yet we are *still* invited to believe that the dispersal of the crowd was fortuitous, and that the magistrates determined to send cavalry into the midst of it to arrest the speakers because one Richard Owen, a pawnbroker, swore an affidavit that Hunt had arrived and that 'an immense mob is collected and he considers the town in danger'.

(The affrighted Richard Owen, in his alternating role as a special constable, is supposed to have signally distinguished himself on the field by capturing the black flag of the Saddleworth contingent – 'Equal Representation or Death' – the mere sight of which so many official witnesses at subsequent proceedings testified as having thrown them into consternation and alarm.)

There is a simpler explanation than Mr Walmsley's for Peterloo. There was a plan. It was put into operation. The magistrates knew, for some hours, and perhaps days, before Hunt arrived on the hustings, what they intended to do; the special constables were expecting the arrival of the Yeomanry; the Yeomanry did, on the field, very much what was expected of them, although neither as efficiently nor as decorously as the authorities might have wished: and the regulars performed a part in which their officers (like Major Dyneley) were well versed.

This case has not been established, but it seems, at the least, open to enquiry. If established, it would not necessarily exclude the authorities from any larger historical defence. The magistrates were faced with a new phenomenon of which they had no understanding. The crowd was not attending a Whitsun walk nor even a miners' gala. Its size, it discipline, its high morale, were ominous to the old order. Neither in the magistrates' room nor in the crowd did men look forward complacently to 1832 and all that; it was more natural, in 1819, when two incompatible social forces confronted each other, to remember 1789.

Some such historical defence might be offered. Mr Walmsley, however, would not wish to offer it. His zealous partisanship is, in a serious sense, worthy of the Peterloo tradition; and his book, which has turned over the ground freshly, will certainly join the enduring literature of the event. But he cannot allow a line of investigation, nor even of defence, which must also show that Hulton of Hulton (who denied that the magistrates had any prior intention of dispersing the crowd) was a liar. But Mr Walmsley, in his zeal, has provided evidence for this as well. William Hulton had some sort of stiffening about him which some of his fellow-magistrates lacked – an absence of humanitarian cant and a contempt for general opinion. He offered no maudlin apologies for Peterloo: indeed, he later recalled it as the 'proudest day' of his life, and many years afterwards he kept a Cap of Liberty, captured upon the field, in his study. A gentleman of Hulton's breed and station does not lie; he merely has so great a hauteur, so great a distance between himself and the seditious plebs, that it is a matter of utter indifference to him whether this or that is true of them or not.

* * *

Twelve years after Peterloo, and after fact upon fact had been disputed for as long, Hulton could throw off a public letter containing a manifest farrago of mis-statements about the day – two people were killed in St Peter's Field – one, a woman, who having personated the Goddess of Reason, was trampled to death in the crowd ....: On the succeeding day, an old pensioner was beaten to death with portions of his own loom, because he had expressed a loyal attachment to the King'. He was as inflexibly convinced, in 1831 as he had been in 1817, that the defence of 'this vast aegis' of our liberties required the hunting of Jacobins and the sharpening of swords. The defeat of the Tories in South Lancashire in the Reform election of 1832 led only to an adjustment of tactics. 'A few despondent individuals', Hulton of Hulton later recalled, then met in a common pot-house in Newton-le-Willows: 'It occurred to them that it was their duty to call up every friend to the monarchy and the Church to counteract the machinations of the enemies to both.' As a result of that meeting 'the foundations of the South Lancashire Conservative Association were laid ... and from that stem at Newton. Conservative associations had branched out all over Her Majesty's dominions.' It is well to remember that British conservatism has not only been made by the great, the well-endowed, the fluent. It has also had its stubborn provincial grass-roots.

From *The Times Literary Supplement* 11th December 1969

Sold Like a Sheep for £1

James Hammett was the only one of the six transported Dorchester labourers to live out his life, on his return, in his home village of Tolpuddle. He worked as a builders' labourer (perhaps a freer life than working for resentful farmers) and, taciturn even in his youth, he matured into a beery old boy, a rum ol' card.

Taciturnity in fact had taken him as far as New South Wales, since it had been his brother, John, and not himself, who had been present when the fateful union oath was taken – a fact which James kept to himself for a good many years. After all, at the time of the arrests John's wife was expecting, and, in these circumstances, it seemed to be the right thing to do to stand in for his brother.

Taciturnity was briefly broken in 1875 when the new Agricultural Labourers Union held a demonstration and presentation to the surviving martyr. After long and elevated speeches, a purse and a gold watch were presented to Mr Hammett, who looked these over with care, and then remarked: 'It appears a great deal better than what I got 41 years ago.' Then he unthawed sufficiently to make his one recorded political statement: 'We only tried to do good to one another, the same as you're doing now.' His other comment is more famous. When friends and relatives asked Grandfather Hammett why he kept so quiet about his time in New South Wales he answered (referring to his assignment as convict-labour to a settler): 'If you'd been sold like a sheep for £1 would *you* want to talk about it?'

Mr Hammett's precisions (which I glean from Joyce Marlow, not from the book under review) seem to me to settle most of the theoretical problems raised by Professor Rudé. Most of his 'protesters' were innured to being clouted across the ear-hole by Fate (or the British ruling class) for trying to 'do good to one another'; but they bitterly resented it nonetheless. To be 'sold like a sheep for £1' was a humiliation to manhood too shaming to remember. Many of them were not especially articulate practioners of political theory, although many of them were. Along these lines of enquiry neither statistical chat nor sociological lucubrations are likely get us much further.

James Hammett would have disapproved of George Rudé's book, even though both had been fellow visitants to the antipodes. For, in an episode in the unwritten history of British McCarthyism, Rudé was stripped of all academic employment, and as a consequence had to transport himself to the more liberal soil of Australia. The episode is discreditable, although certainly not to Rudé. At that time he had laid down the foundations of the very substantial work in the history of the crowd in eighteenth-century France and England – the Bastille crowd, *taxation populaire*, Gordon rioters – and he was already on his way to Wilkes. Even though he had opened up a new continent to historical explanation, no British university wanted to know. Since that time many lesser and reputably-placed younger scholars have been paddling up the creeks which his early charts first disclosed.

No doubt the Australian emigration brought many advantages both to Professor Rudé and to his hosts. But it put him at a great distance from his sources. And his more recent, voluntary expatriation to Canada has done the same. So ... what was he to do? Helpful general textbooks were one answer. The other answer seemed to lie in the project now before us. Generations of 'protesters' – Irish rebels of several kinds, Luddites, Pentridge insurgents and Chartists, Swing rioters, arsonists, and even Canadian rebels of 1837 and 1838, had preceded him on the long journey to N.S.Wales or Van Diemen's Land. It must have seemed inevitable to Rudé that he was to be their chosen chronicler, employing his fine archival craftsmanship in the records of England, Canada, Ireland and Australia, to weave a richly-figured pattern in that stark warp of transportation.

Yet the book disappoints. It is even quite bad. Rudé has never been at home in the nineteenth century, the 'Swing' riots of 1830 apart (and here he had Eric Hobsbawm as collaborator). The book, commences with some ninety pages of insecure statistical passes and gestures at criminological generalisation: the only adequate critic for these pages would be a pair of scissors. There follow sixty pages on the protesters and their offences. These summary accounts are useful only when Rudé, by good fortune rather than judgement, chances upon a useful secondary account.

At last, in part Four, we have the Australian end of the story, and here we may set the scissors aside. Rudé has accumulated, with the fine archival crafting which is his trademark, an immense amount of detail about the fates of the convicts: how often they were disciplined: when they got their tickets-of-leave: how they fared when they got their freedom. There are some remarkable examples of success and upward mobility – for example, among the Irish rebels of 1798. By contrast many Luddites, Pentridge rebels and 'Swing' rioters remained much at a level, in artisan or labouring trades. This is all helpful stuff, it is sometimes lively, and on occasion it is vintage Rudé.

But it is not good enough. What strikes one is the erratic and one-sided nature of the research. Rudé has absolute faith in the original and prior virtue of scraps of Tasmanian prison archives over all other sources. Extensive legal records, published trials, the British Radical, local, and Chartist press (which reported copiously on many of his protesters and followed their subsequent history), and local historians (who subsequently made transported men into folk heroes) – all those remain unconsulted. Rudé prefers to fall back, for biographies, upon the *Annual Register* or the Australian *D.N.B.*

Far more is known about the transported 'Jacobins' of the 1790s than is hinted at in these pages. Some unexplained 'Yorkshire radical weavers, 1821' turn up in the statistics: but Rudé never identifies these as the men transported for the 'Grange Moor' rising near Barnsley, a familiar enough event. It is of interest to know how the leaders – Addy and Comstive – went on in Van Diemen's Land, but it would have been of more interest if Rudé had put his own findings together with those in recent doctoral theses (Kajage, Donnelly, Baxter). And if these can easily be overlooked, there is surely less excuse for missing Joyce Marlow's *The Tolpuddle Martyrs* (1971), which devotes most of five chapters to the experiences of the Dorset men in Australia and which discovers certain details which correct Rudé's account.

The later the period, and the more copious the unconsulted sources, the more Rudé stumbles and fumbles. From gnomic

Tasmanian records he tries to puzzle out for what offences Luddites were transported: but plentiful accounts exist. He does not seem to know that old Thomas Bacon of the Pentridge affair was an old 'Jacobin' and a political leader of stature. He does not seem to know Gwyn William's definitive articles (and now book) on the Merthyr rising of 1831. William Ashton and 'Francis' Mirfield flit across his pages as 'industrial protesters', filling their prescribed role for 'destroying linen yarn'. But Ashton and Mirfield were leaders of a major – and fully-reported – strike of Barnsley linen-weavers; they were singled out as *political* rebels, and (by Ashton's account) they were framed; in response to memorials from their fellow-weavers they were pardoned before their sentences expired, their fares home were paid by money raised by the Yorkshire radical movement, and they both then played a leading part in the Barnsley Chartist movement. Ashton, a most articulate if somewhat opinionated man, was imprisoned for two years for his Chartist activities, while Frank Mirfield still represented Barnsley at the Chartist National Convention of 1848. Ashton, having quarrelled fiercely with O'Connor, returned to Victoria as a voluntary emigrant, and continued to send accounts of the new territory back to the Barnsley press: 'The same system prevails here as is the general rule at home – the rich get richer, whilst the poor get poorer.'

None of this in Rudé. Moving on to Chartism one's heart sinks even lower. If Rudé really wishes to know whether the Colne (Lancs) riot of 1840 in which a policeman was killed had political associations, he would do best to consult, not Tasmanian records, but the Lancashire and Chartist press: he will there discover that 'police-bashing' is not an adequate category for analysing resistance to the new police. The scissors must be brought out once more for his accounts of what he insists upon calling 'the Plug-Plot Riots' of 1842. These did not, as he once seems to propose, assume 'the complexion of a food riot'! Once again, devout attention is paid to what the transported felons *said* they had been transported for when they arrived in Tasmania. With delight Rudé italicises every 'confession' by a convict that his offence had been to riot *'for an increase of wages'*. This seems to Rudé to be a proper proletarian motive, as against any high-flying bourgeois-democratic false consciousness, such as staying on strike until the Charter was the law of the land.

Well, yes, the strikes and riots *were* about wages: they were about the Charter as well: and for some they were about the millenium. As hundreds of depositions, and scores of extensive press reports make plain. Must it always be either/or? And has it not occurred to Professor Rudé that if you are a convict facing a prison officer's interrogation in Van Diemen's Land, you select among possible responses the one most likely to meet with the approval of your interrogator? If you squared your shoulders, looked the officer in the eye, and said: 'Every valley shall be exalted, and every bleeding jumped-up mole-hill like your honour shall be laid low', then you would find yourself, with a bare back, chained to the flogging triangle. But even prison officers had heard about Political Economy and could understand that the poor wanted more wages. And even James Hammett, with his scandalously low level of Theory, was sly enough to know his way through the proper responses.

So ... But, wait, *what* does Rudé think he is doing when he describes William Ellis, the Chartist leader in the Potteries, as 'a firebrand' and 'one of the most dangerous men in the potteries'? His sources? The *Annual Register* and a historical novel published in 1962!! But all Chartists and many others believed that Ellis was framed: his conviction rested upon identification by a dubious witness who claimed to have glimpsed him, with blackened face, on the scene of arson. Ellis's own letters of indignant rebuttal were published; his fellow-prisoner, Thomas Cooper, championed him; he was the subject of a national campaign for pardon, and his name was often added to that of Frost, Williams and Jones, the leaders of the Newport rising. Ellis was a temperance advocate and an Owenite socialist (in prison after being sentenced to twenty-one years transportation he spoke, wrote Cooper, 'of the coming age of universal brotherhood, of the world-spread establishment of the great community'). Waiting in the transport off Spithead this dangerous firebrand wrote urgently for 'Burns's poems and the poetical works of Percy Bysshe Shelley'. Not a word of this in Rudé.

And what about John Frost? Of his Australian experiences,

Rudé tells us only that Frost escaped any 'dire penalties', was first
a clerk and then a schoolmaster, and then 'held teaching posts in
various parts of the island'. All very comfortable, and perhaps a
premonition of subsequent academic careers? But that fine historian, David Williams, in his biography of Frost tells another story.
A letter home was broken open in which Frost referred to Lord
John Russell with sarcasm. In consequence, Frost was sentenced, at
the age of fifty-seven, to two year's hard labour in a quarry.
[David Williams's sources in the Welsh press are far more
informative than the terse Tasmanian records.] I do not know of
the evidence which substantiates Rudé's claim that Frost, on his
return to England, 'gradually abandoned his old political beliefs'. It
is true that he gave up the pastime of marching in drenching rain
at the head of armed Chartists upon Newport, but some respite
may be allowed to a man in his seventies, and in any case
Chartism was now quiescent. Frost duly took part in a great
Chartist rally with its last leader, Ernest Jones, and to suggest that
he ever abandoned the cause of the Charter seems to me to be
calumny.

Some of these errors and omissions must have resulted from the
difficulties of conducting research from Australia or Canada. Even
so, a publishing-house as prestigious as Oxford might surely have
found a reader who would have pointed some of them out?

And George Rudé. It gives me no pleasure to write so severely
about an old colleague and mentor of mine. What has gone wrong?

The major problem is this. Rudé has become the prisoner of his
own method, and then has transported that method to the wrong
century. When he commenced to work in the eighteenth century,
all that area which has now become the history of the crowd was
simply an indistinct blur labelled as 'riot' or 'mob'. By tracing the
members of that 'mob' back into legal records or rate-books he
gave to them a brief identity: occupations, roles, faces, and
sometimes voices. He broke open the way to new questions – the
trades and their solidarities – motivations and beliefs. This chosen
method was then essential because, in that century, so little other
evidence existed, or, if it did, it could only be prised open by their
prior enquiry.

But this does not assign to this method some universal and

prior virtue. When we move into a period in which there are copious alternative records, then the method may remain as a useful control but it is folly to employ it as if it were some guarantee of objectivity and 'rigour' at the expense of the equal rigour demanded by the legal and literary records. A method which opened one century up simply shuts the next century down. Before Rudé's scrupulous investigation, the stature of obscure men and women in the eighteenth century enlarged; before the same treatment, in the nineteenth century, their stature shrinks. The protesters end up in these pages with less intelligence, self-consciousness, political conviction, and complexity of motivation than we know them, from other sources, to have had. All are reduced to the same uninformative level of entries in the schedules and ledgers of the prison authorities – records which, in some cases, were only a cover-up. This is to order historical evidence not according to the consciousness of the prisoners but according to the their administrative disposition by the authorities.

What then are left are a succession of minute details of men whose consciousness has been excluded by the very nature of the convict records. For some of these details we may be grateful: what happened to the United Men of 1798, when Thomas Bacon died. This last part of the book will be much consulted, and, ultimately, revised.

But even this final part might have prompted questions more interesting than any that are asked. Rudé shares with much dominant historiography and sociology a positivist faith in the virtues of quantities and a suspicion of 'literary' evidence which raises questions too large to enter here. But here are a couple of matters which seem to arise from his own material.

First, how did the protesters experience life in the southern hemisphere? I do not mean the sub-life of the convict settlements, the chain-gangs, the triangle: Hammett has answered that. But, once the ticket-of-leave came through, and they commenced to work at their own trades, how did they respond to the culture shock? Rudé adds many touches which lead one to suppose that they responded well: they *liked* Australia. Many accumulated land or money enough to have paid a passage home; but they stayed. A few returned to their homelands, and then went back: John

Frost's daughter, Caroline; William Ashton who, having tried America, took his family to Victoria. Five of the Tolpuddle Martyrs felt so unsettled back in England that they took off again, not to Australia, but to Canada. One suspects that many of them experienced their new life as in part a liberation, from the tight class structure and obligatory deference, the spatial closures, of the old country. And in this new environment it was not necessary for them to abandon their old protesting beliefs: perhaps William Ellis's dreams of 'universal brotherhood' became dim but they may have blended naturally into a more humdrum and practical egalitarianism. We must look once again at Rudé's sources, and also at the accounts and letters in the British and Australian press, to tease this problem out.

Second, there is the interesting question of kinship ties and familial and neighbourhood relationships. Rudé cites briefly the letters which Thomas Holden, a Lancashire weaver transported for Luddite oath-administering, sent back from Sidney to his wife and parents. He appears to have overlooked the fact that extensive extracts from these, together with details of the Holden family, were published a few years ago in the *Transactions of the Lancs & Cheshire Antiquarian Society*. These letters tells us little about political protest, and not much about New South Wales, but a great deal about the tenacious maintenance of familial ties across half the world. And, if we run through the material looking for this, evidence accumulates. Wives and children joined their transported husbands; correspondence and messages passed; Irish wives and sweethearts (Rudé tells us) would burn down haystacks in order to get free tickets as arsonists to join their lovers. Convicts, transported for the same offence from the same village or town, would pass messages and keep an eye on each other's welfare, even when illiterate and divided from each other by hundreds of miles of bush. (They also, as is the way of exiles, sometimes quarrelled violently, as did some Scottish Jacobins and as did the Welsh Chartists, Williams and Jones).

It is from material of this kind (and of course this is only one straw from a whole rick) that I derive my scepticism as to those modern theories of 'the family' which offer kinship loyalties as a middle-class innovation, and see the working people's familial relations as brutish, instrumental, casual or almost unstructured. Of course, some wives and some convicts got tired of waiting, and set up new families, perhaps bringing down a charge of bigamy to add to their archives. But such has been known to happen even in the most modernised and bourgeois of establishments. The evidence is mixed and does not allow for a firm statistical conclusion. In 1896 an old woman died near Burford (M.K. Ashby tells us in her study of Bledington) whose husband and brother had both been transported in 1831, as 'Swing' rioters, for 14 and 7 years respectively. After seven years, when neither came back, she comforted herself with the thought that 'the one must wait for the other'. 'Fifty years later they still had not come and she died in her chair looking towards the east – as she thought towards Australia.' What is one to make of that illiterate old lass, whose patience was so large, and whose knowledge of geography was so small? It is not recorded that anyone thought of presenting her with a gold watch.

From *New Society*

History and Anthropology

I must come before you at once with the frank confession that I am an impostor. In my current work, over the past ten years, in eighteenth-century English social history, it is true that I am facing problems of the recovery and understanding of popular culture and ritual which may, very generally, be described as being closer to the concerns of social anthropology than to those of economic history. I hope to explain this further. It is also true that I am increasingly attempting to put to use folklore materials. But I certainly cannot offer myself to you as one who is qualified in the discipline of anthropology, nor as a conventional scholar of folklore; my knowledge of Western anthropology is intermittent and eclectic, and of Indian anthropology and folklore it is not even rudimentary. Much of what I have to say may well appear to you to be commonplace and to require no saying.

There may, however, be something which still requires debating among historians within the Marxist tradition (East or West) who have shown overmuch reluctance, until recently, to come to terms with certain problems. I intend in my conclusion to offer, as a historian of this tradition, some points in Marxist self-criticism. But first I would speak more generally to the profession, and enter a defence of that very eclecticism to which I have pleaded guilty. In a recent exchange in the *Journal of Interdisciplinary History* (1975), Keith Thomas, the author of *Religion and the Decline of Magic* (1971), was taken to task by Hildred Geertz for exactly this sin. The implication of her critique was that Thomas had borrowed approaches from several disparate anthropological schools, whereas he should have clearly placed himself within the discipline of one or another. Without a consistent theoretical discipline such borrowings betray empiricist opportunism or merely amateurism. Witchcraft must be explained in one way or another: we may not play with several alternative categories of explanation, drawn from incompatible anthropological theories.

But in this controversy I would stand with Thomas. Anthropological studies of Witchcraft (or of other beliefs and rituals) in primitive societies, or in more advanced contemporary African societies, need not provide us with all the necessary categories of explanation for Witchcraft beliefs in Elizabethan England or in eighteenth-century India, where we may have more complex plural societies, with many levels of belief, sophistication and scepticism. Categories or 'models' derived from one context must be tested, refined, and perhaps re-formed in the course of historical investigation: we have to sit to them loosely, for the time being. In my own practice I stand closely with Thomas and with Natalie Zemon Davis;[1] for us, the anthropological impulse is chiefly felt, not in model-building, but in locating new problems, in seeing old problems in new ways, in an emphasis upon norms or value-systems and upon rituals, in attention to expressive functions of forms of riot and disturbance, and upon symbolic expressions of authority, control and hegemony. We are in common in departing sharply from positivistic or utilitarian categories of explanation, and from the penetration of these categories into an economistic tradition of Marxism. But this work remains provisional. Clearly, differences of emphasis can already be detected, which foreshadow debates within historical anthropology between functionalist, structuralist, symbolist and other ulterior assumptions. But in my view these debates can be delayed; until much more work has been done – and comparative work in several national histories – it would be premature to force them on to a conclusion.

I was led to these problems, in my own work, at the point when I completed *The Making of the English Working Class* (1963), and decided to carry my researches backwards in time, to the plebeian consciousness and forms of protest (such as food riots) of the eighteenth century. This entailed leaving the territory of the Industrial Revolution and exploring what is sometimes called a 'pre-industrial' society. It is an unsatisfactory term; for eighteenth-century Britain (as eighteenth-century India) contained a vigorous manufacturing industry, albeit mainly handicraft. But to move from the first society to the second was to move from a society with an accelerating rate of change to one which was, to a much greater extent, governed by custom. There were customary agrarian practices, customary forms of initiation to skills (apprenticeship), customary expectations as to roles (domestic and social), customary modes of work, and customary expectations and 'wants' or 'needs'.

But the consideration of custom leads on to problems which cannot be handled within the discipline of economic history. Nor can orally transmitted customary norms be handled as a sub-section of 'the history of ideas'. For some part of the evidence as to customs and their significance I found myself turning to the compilations of folklorists. Now I need not insist, in this gathering, that such evidence is sadly unsatisfactory. I was so much impressed with this fact – indeed, prejudiced – that (I confess with shame) when I wrote *The Making of the English Working Class* I had not even read John Brand's *Observations on Popular Antiquities* (1777). This foundation-study of folklore set a pattern which was followed by British folklorists throughout the nineteenth century – and by some British observers of Indian customs – and in its organization according to 'calendar customs' and customs surrounding the rites of passage, its influence may still be detected in sophisticated ethnographic studies in our two countries today.[2]

The descriptive material gathered by nineteenth-century folklorists was of value and can still be drawn upon with caution. But custom and ritual were seen, often by the paternal gentleman (or even, as in India, alien) from above and across a class gulf, and divorced from their total situation or context. Questions proposed of customs were rarely those of contemporary usage or function. Customs were, rather, seen as 'relics' of a remote and lost antiquity, like the crumbled ruins of ancient hill-forts and settlements. They were seen, sometimes, as clues to a pre-Christian, pagan, or Aryan inheritance: these broken forms survived, and the 'vulgar' people repeated them by rote, like somnambulists, with no notion as to their meaning; or perhaps, as in the derivation of rituals from fertility cults, with a subconscious, intuitive acceptance of their meaning. To this was added, under the impulse of the linguistic researches of Max Müller and others, the notion that folklore could be used as a tool for detecting the prehistoric dispersal of races and cultures. Reviewing Edward Burnet Tylor's *Researches into the Early History of Mankind, and the Development of Civilisation* (1965), Müller claimed that 'the ground-plan of a new science has been sketched out, and broken relics of the ancient folklore of the Aryan family have been picked up in the cottages of Scotland, the spinning-rooms of Germany, the bazaars of Herat, and the monasteries of Ceylon'.[3] This notion of a common Indo-European 'Aryan' inheritance led, as Romila Thapar has noted,[4] to a quite new sympathy with Indian culture on the part of European Indologists and ethnographers. But its consequences for the study of folklore were less happy. For what interested Tylor and his followers, when they considered customs, was how far these provided 'evidence bearing on the early history of mankind', and how far these customs showed that the people who observed them 'are allied by blood, or have been in contact, or have been influenced indirectly one from the other, or both from a common source ... '.[5] There followed upon this a close classificatory interest in custom and myth, akin to the classificatory interest in other nineteenth-century sciences; customs and beliefs were scrupulously examined according to their formal attributes, and then these formal properties were compared across immense gulfs of culture and of time; we move in a few pages from 'the ancient Hindus' to the Germany of Tacatitus to contemporary Greenlanders to Java and Polynesia, Mongolia and the American Indian Mandans and Choctaws.[6] The end of this road was finally reached in Sir James Frazer's *The Golden Bough* (London, 1936).

The academic disrepute into which that work fell dragged folklore studies, in British universities, under with it. In French scholarship no such eclipse of folklore took place, because it effected, in the work of Arnold van Gennep, a junction with anthropology. But in Britain anthropologists have seen folklore as an antiquarian pursuit of customary and mythic 'relics', wrested out of their context in a total culture, and then arranged and compared in improper ways.[7] And to this academic disrepute there was added the political suspicions of Marxist and radical scholars. In the early years of this century, the collection of folk song, dance, and custom in England had been a cause which enlisted the sympathies of the intellectual Left, but by the 1930s this sympathy had dispersed. The rise of Fascism led to an identification of folk studies with deeply reactionary or racist ideology. And even on less sensitive historical ground, an interest in customary behaviour tended to be the prerogative of the more conservative historians. For custom is, by its nature, conservative. Historians of the Left tended to be interested in innovative, rationalizing movements, whether Puritan sects or early trade unions, leaving it to Sir Arthur Bryant and his friends to celebrate 'Merrie England' with its maypoles, its church-ales, and its relations of paternalism and deference.

This thumb-nail sketch, which passes over too many difficult questions too easily, may go some way towards explaining why folklore is so little studied today in English [8] universities; and how I could have written *The Making of the English Working Class* without having read Brand. The vigorous revival in recent years of interest in folk song and custom has taken place outside the universities and only the preliminary evidence of any revival in academic interest can as yet be seen.[9] But in self-defence it should be said that the problems facing a British historian, in the scholarly use of folklore materials, are perhaps greater than those which are encountered in this country. Our materials are dead, inert, and corrupt whereas yours still live. Folklore, in England is largely a literary record of eighteenth and nineteenth century survivals, recorded by parsons and by genteel antiquarians regarding them across a gulf of class condescension. In the work of a contemporary Indian scholar I learn that he collected his research in two villages (one in Rajasthan, the other in UP) '1500 folk songs, 200 folk tales, 175 riddles, 800 proverbs and some charms'.[10] I turn green with envy as I write this, as would any British collector, who might consider himself lucky if in the course of one year's collecting he found *one* original folk song, as well as a few corrupt variants of songs already known.

So that what we have to do, in England, is to re-examine old, long-collected material, asking new questions of it, and seeking to recover lost customs and the beliefs which informed them. I can best illustrate the problem by turning away from the materials and the method, and addressing the kinds of questions which must be asked. These questions, when we examine a customary culture, may often be concerned less with the processes and logic of change than with the recovery of past states of consciousness and the texturing of social and domestic relationships. They are concerned less with *becoming* than with *being*. As some of the leading actors of history recede from our attention – the politicians, the thinkers, the entrepreneurs, the generals – so an immense supporting cast, whom we had supposed to be mere attendants upon this process, press themselves forward. If we are concerned only with becoming, then there are whole periods in history in which an entire sex has been neglected by historians, because women are rarely seen as prime agents in political, military or even economic life. If we are concerned with being, then the exclusion of women would reduce history to futility. We cannot understand the agrarian system of small cultivators without examining inheritance practices, dowry, and (where appropriate) the familial development cycle.[11] And these practices rest, in turn, upon the obligations and reciprocities of kinship, whose maintenance and observation will often be found to be the peculiar responsibility of the women. The 'economy' can only be understood within the context of a society textured in these kinds of ways; the 'public' life arises out of the dense determinations of the 'domestic' life.

I am especially concerned to recover evidence as to the norms and expectations in sexual and marital relations in the customary culture of eighteenth-century England – a subject about which a good deal has been written but very little is known. They are, in fact, those aspects of a society which appear to contemporaries as wholly 'natural' and matter-of-course which often leave the most imperfect historical evidence. A historian in two hundred years' time may easily recover how today's industrial citizens felt about having too little money – or about other people having too much – but he will find it more difficult to recover how we felt about money itself, as the universal mediator of social relations, because we assume this so deeply that we do not articulate it ourselves. One way to discover unspoken norms is often to examine the *un*typical episode or situation. A riot throws light upon the norms of tranquil years, and a sudden breach of deference enables us to better understand the deferential habits which have been broken. This may be true equally of public and social and of more private, domestic, conduct. M N Srinivas notes, of his own field work, that it was when disputes suddenly arose in the village that 'facts normally hidden surfaced':

> The passion which was ignited during the heat of a dispute led
> the disputants to say and do things which revealed motivations
> and relationships with the clarity with which lightning illumines,
> albeit momentarily, the surroundings on a dark night ....
> Disputes roused people's memories and led to the citing and
> examination of precedents .... Disputes ... were a rich mine of
> data which the anthropologist could not ignore.[12]

Even a highly untypical ritual may thus provide a valuable window
onto norms. I became interested some ten years ago in the ritual
'sale' of wives in England in the eighteenth and nineteenth
centuries. This practice, found among labourers, farmers and others,
cannot be taken as typical of anything. But I have found a
sufficient number of cases (some 300) and sufficient evidence to
show that the practice was universally understood among the 'lower
orders', and that the rituals were endorsed by the working
community as signifying a legitimate transfer of marriage partners.
But it remains an unusual ritual which provoked comment –
indeed, a small sensation.

The ritual had to be undergone in proper form: in a public
market-place, with advance notice, the wife led by a halter
around her neck or middle, with an auctioneer (usually the
husband), open bidding, and finally the transfer of the end of the
halter from the seller to the purchaser. My collection of cases
has been built up, partly from brief newspaper paragraphs, partly
from the records of folklore collectors. Editors, journalists and
folklorists were all in general outside spectators, looking in upon
a spectacle whose significance they attempted to read from its
formal attributes: as a 'sale'. An enlightened middle class which,
in the nineteenth century, had become vociferous in the cause of
anti-slavery was deeply embarrassed to find this barbarism in its
own midst, in the heart of 'progressive' England. A few
folklorists toyed half-heartedly with notions of pre-Christian
Anglo-Saxon survivals; one or two (and these exceptions are
always the important ones for the historian) even examined the
practice with the insight of objective observation. But in general
the practice was condemned in the sternest and most moralistic
terms.[13]

However, closer examination of the evidence has enabled the practice to be seen in a different aspect. The ritual was in fact a form of divorce, at a time when no other form of divorce was available to the people of England. In nearly every case the 'sale' took place with the wife's consent. In most cases the preceding marriage had already broken down, and it can be shown that the 'open' auction was only fictional - the wife's purchaser was pre-arranged, and in many cases was already the wife's lover.

Moreover, the husband who was selling a wife whom, emotionally, he had already 'lost', often behaved with a generosity more humane than is encountered in today's divorce courts. The affair was performed in the public eye, and he covered his shame at having lost his wife, first by the fictional ritual that it was he who was selling her, and second by some gesture of liberality or goodwill. Commonly he gave all or most of the small sun exchanged as purchase money to drink the health of the new couple at the market inn. On occasion a husband parting with his wife caused the church bells to be rung, paid for the new couple's coach-hire, or gave them a gift of food or clothes.

Thus the ritual turns out to have complexities. At first sight we appear to have a form reminiscent of negative bridewealth, or perhaps of mere chattel-purchase: the wife, with a halter around her, sold in the cattle-market, is seen as a chattel or beast. Here is the *ne plus ultra* of a dominant male order. But at second sight, when we look through the form to the actual relations expressed within it, it appears differently. The ritual (whatever its origin and manifest symbolism) has been adapted to new purposes in which it regulates an exchange of partners by mutual consent. But although we find within the ritual greater evidence of sexual equality than we had, at first, expected to find, the ritual itself remains one of feminine subordination. Wives did not, except in very exceptional circumstance, sell their husbands.

Thus the untypical may serve to give a glimpse into norms. And in the course of this research I have been afforded other insights into the ways in which marriage was regarded by the labouring people in England: that a public (and shaming) ritual of this kind was employed to legitimate divorce is, paradoxically, evidence that marriage was not lightly regarded. The meaning of the ritual can only be read when the evidence (some of it recorded by folklorists) ceases to be regarded as a fragment of folklore, a 'survival',[14] and is replaced within its total context.

But ritual of course permeates social and political, as well as domestic life. In recent years, historians have been looking in new ways at long familiar aspects of the life: at the calendar of ritual and of festivity, both in the countryside and in the corporate city;[15] at the place of sports in social life;[16] at the different rhythms of work and of leisure before and after the Industrial Revolution;[17] at the changing place of adolescents within the community;[18] at the market or bazaar when considered less as an economic nexus than as a social nexus, and as a gathering-centre for news, gossip, rumour; and at the symbolic meaning of forms of popular protest.[19] Historians in the Marxist tradition who have been influenced by the Gramscian concept of hegemony have also been looking with fresh eyes at the forms of ruling class domination and control. Very rarely in history – and then only for short intervals – does any ruling class exercise authority by direct and unmediated military or even economic force. People are born into a society whose forms and relations seem as fixed and immutable as the overarching sky. The 'commonsense' of the time is saturated with the deafening propaganda of the *status quo*; but the strongest element in this propaganda is simply the fact that what exists exists.

In examining the forms of this control in the eighteenth century I have myself increasingly been using the notion of 'theatre'. In all societies, of course, theatre is an essential component both of political control and of protest or even rebellion. The rulers act out the theatre of majesty, superstition, power, wealth, sublime justice; the poor enact their counter-theatre, occupying the stages of the streets for markets and employing the symbolism of ridicule or protest. To say that control or domination may take the form of theatre is not (I have argued) 'to say that it was immaterial, too fragile for analysis, insubstantial':

To define control in terms of cultural hegemony is not to give up attempts at analysis, but to prepare for analysis at the points at which it should be made: into the images of power and authority, the popular mentalities of subordination.[20]

In eighteenth-century England the law provides the most formidable theatre of control; and Tyburn and other public places of execution the most dramatic occasions. One may point here to a contrast between quantitative and qualitative methods in the analysis of crime, or 'violence', and its repression. Those historians who have entered this field, employing the quantitative statistical techniques appropriate to economic history, have concentrated their efforts upon counting offences, offenders, and so on. There have even been extensive labours expended upon countering the somewhat dubious quantities of 'violence' or 'disturbance'. There are very great problems here – for example, as legal categories of 'crime' change or as the efficiency of police improves. The best scholars are, of course, aware of these problems and develop techniques for taking such variables into account. But even when such problems are carefully handled, we are still left with only a very limited knowledge. For the symbolic importance of violence – whether the violence of the state and the law or the violence of protest – may have no direct correlation with quantities. A hundred people may lose their lives in a natural disaster and it will provoke no more than pity; one man may be beaten to death in a police station and it may provoke a wave of protest which transforms the politics of a nation. We need only consider the consequences of the 'massacres' at Peterloo and at Jallianwala Bag: in both cases these episodes assume, in historical perspective, the character of a victory for the victims. In both cases the ensuing wave of popular outrage, skilfully employed by the victims (in inquests, trials, enquiries, protest meetings), resulted in a consensus which inhibited the repetition of such repressive actions and which even induced some split within the ruling authorities themselves. Neither terror nor counter-terror can disclose their meaning under purely quantitative examination, for the quantities must be seen within a total context, and this includes a symbolic context which assigns different values to different kinds of violence.

Thus attention to the forms and gestures of ritual can afford a significant addition to historical knowledge. And certain forms can only be fully understood if we recover the beliefs of the customary culture. Thus Tyburn, the central place of execution in eighteenth-century London, is a supreme example of the theatre of class control, through the terror of *example*. There is no straining of metaphor in describing this as theatre: it was clearly seen to be such, at the time, and immense attention was given to the ceremony of execution and the publicity afforded to the examples.[21] Publicity in those times depended upon local resources: the crowds which witnessed the procession to the gallows, the ensuing gossip in the markets and the workshops, the sale of broadsheets with the 'last dying speeches' of the victims. As the means of centralized publicity have, in this century, enlarged, so perhaps even a small quantum of terror can produce an even greater effect: the resources of a mass circulation press, of the radio or television, magnify the event, turning up the volume-control of terror. One thinks – as an example – of the extraordinary impact upon a whole nation of the execution of two individuals: the Rosenbergs.

Since the eighteenth-century state did not have such resources, recourse was taken to forms of aggravated terror against offenders. For several centuries the punishment decreed for certain offences entailed not only execution but also the *post mortem* mutilation of the corpse. Smugglers' or highwaymen's bodies were hanged in chains near the site of their offence, until they corrupted to skeletons; pirates were left hanging at the docks; the heads of traitors were left, for many years, on spikes over gates on busy thoroughfares; and, later, the more 'rational' method was taken of granting the bodies of murderers and others to the surgeons as specimens for dissection. Against this aggravated penalty, as Peter Linebaugh has shown, the friends of the condemned rioted around the gallows.[22] But we can only understand the outrage provoked by such penalties if we understand also that the mutilation of the corpse (the refusal of 'Christian burial') was indeed an aggravated terror, since the authorities were deliberately breaching the most sensitive popular taboos. To understand the nature of these taboos – the deeply superstitious respect for the integrity of the corpse – Linebaugh has taken the evidence upon death customs of folklore collectors; and by putting this evidence to new uses he has, in turn, transformed information which was only antiquarian and inert into an active ingredient in social history.

I hope that it is not necessary to argue the case for renewed attention to folklore materials any further. It is not a matter of drawing upon this material uncritically, but of employing it selectively in the examination of questions which earlier folklorists often passed by. But when we bring social history into relation with the greatly more sophisticated discipline of anthropology, then clearly we are faced with greater theoretical difficulties. It is sometimes supposed that anthropology can offer certain findings, not about particular societies but about society in general: that basic functions or structures have been disclosed which, however sophisticated or masked these may be in modern societies, still underlie modern forms. But history is a discipline of context and of process: every meaning is a meaning-in-context, and structures change while old forms may express new functions or old functions may find expression in new forms.[23] As Marc Bloch remarked: 'To the great despair of historians, men fail to change their vocabulary every time they change their customs', and this is true also of the vocabulary of ritual forms.[24]

I will illustrate this by taking issue with one passage in the work of a historian who is, like myself, writing within the Marxist tradition. Gareth Stedman Jones, in an able study of *Outcast London*[25] in the later nineteenth century, offers a chapter entitled 'The Deformation of the Gift'. He is analysing middle class attitudes towards poverty and charity, and concepts of Weber and of Marcel Mauss come to hand. These enable 'the social meaning of charitable gift-giving' to be 'properly understood':

> In all known traditional societies, the gift has played a central status-maintaining function. From the work of sociologists and social anthropologists, it is possible to isolate three structural features which are to a greater or lesser extent inherent in the act of giving.

These are, first, the idea of sacrifice – primarily to God – or as an act of grace in the giver. Second, gifts are symbols of prestige, implying subordination in the recipient. Third, the recipient is placed under an obligation: hence the gift 'serves as method of social control'. Once these points are 'properly understood', Stedman Jones is able to offer an analysis of attitudes of poverty in London (and of the ideology of the Charity Organisation Society) in terms of 'the deformation of the gift', a deformation brought about by 'the separation of classes' – the social and geographical distance between rich and poor – which destroyed the 'original integrity of the gift relationship', with its 'elements of prestige, subordination, and obligation'.

I wish to examine this argument closely. First, there is a suggestion of some constant, primeval relationship – an 'act of giving' – which 'in all known traditional societies' has 'three structural features'. The first of these does not appear to be a structural feature at all. The notion of charity as grace, and of the holiness of the beggar, not in himself but as one whose need occasions grace in the donor, takes very different expressions within different ideological and religious contexts, even in traditional societies. It survives into modern societies in varied (for example, Catholic, Hindu or Buddhist) forms. Although Protestantism is generally resistant to this notion (and its 'deformation' or drastic limitation may be coincident with capitalist ascendancy) it can still recur, in comparatively recent times, as in Wordsworth's 'Old Cumberland Beggar' –

> While from door to door,
> This old Man creeps, the villagers in him
> Behold a record which together binds
> Past deeds and offices of charity ....

I am more ready to see the other two features in structural terms, since prestige, subordination, obligation and social control imply a coincidence between the relationships implied in the 'act of giving' and the context of particular social structures which might (despite major changes) still maintain universal features. But one must still ask why these features, and only these features, are given heuristic priority? Is it suggested that there is some deep level of structure, disclosed by anthropological findings and in the study of 'traditional' societies, which must be prior to any functions subsequently disclosed? For other features in the act of giving may easily be proposed. Thus the description offered is seen 'from above', whereas ' from below' very different, and more calculated, features may be disclosed. The beggar or the poor may wish to exact all that is possible from the rich; they know that the refusal of alms provokes guilt in the refuser, and that guilt is an excellent soil in which to sow slight suggestions of physical or magical threat. The recipient of gifts need not feel an obligation to the donor nor acknowledge his prestige, except in the necessary dues of an assumed deference and the degree of subordination ensured by charity may depend upon a calculation of advantages.

Thus even these features appear to be seen undialectically. The structure, in any relation between rich and poor, always runs in both directions, and the same relationship, when turned around and viewed in reverse, may present an alternative heuristic. But if one thinks of a definite modern context – let us say eighteenth-century England – the act of giving may suggest other features. Prestige (a reputation for 'liberality') remains eminently present: one thinks of the elaborate gifts of venison and game by the aristocratic park-keepers to the subordinate gentry and clergy. But 'gifts' by the rich to the poor have become exceedingly complex. Some gifts are already mediated by the Poor Laws, a continuing arena of conflict, of discipline, and of protest: can the wholly characteristic form of a dispute between the overseers of two adjacent parishes, each anxious to expel to the other a sick or pregnant pauper, be subsumed within any of Stedman Jones's three features? Other gifts, such as the bribery of electors, are a direct and undisguised form of purchase of influence. Gifts, such as the farmers' payments in kind to the their labourers or 'vails' to servants (that is, gifts of clothing, food, or 'tips' by visitors to the great house), are equally direct means of reducing money wages and enforcing dependence and subordination. And perhaps the most important gifts of all – charity and subsidized foods in times of dearth – are (as I must have argued elsewhere[26]) enforced directly upon the rich by the poor by a highly developed practice of riot and threat of riot, a practice which has structural features of its own. And finally there remain examples of uncalculating generosity which belong to a minority tradition of benevolent paternalism which, while it may be related to these three structural features, may not, under close examination, fall wholly within them. Thus neighbours who provide, at Christmas or at other times of feast, food and drink to their poorer fellows may have been expressing other ('structural'?) community solidarities which take us into a different field of analysis.

In short, if there is any constant – 'the gift' – we must say that it was altogether 'deformed' by the eighteenth century. Stedman Jones' account suggests a constant which breaks down, suddenly, in the London of the 1860s. Thereby his account overleaps (among other matters) the Tudor dissolution of Church charities, the Elizabethan Poor Laws, the shameless appropriation of foundations by private interests in the eighteenth century, the complex structural relation between rich and poor, evidenced by food riots, the nation-wide crisis entailed by the 1834 Poor Law, and so on. But even if he were to revise his account and make the process of deformation more protracted, my central objection would still stand. There is no such constant 'act of giving' with constant features, which may be isolated from particular social contexts: indeed the *structure* is to be found in the historical particularity of 'the *ensemble* of the social relations' and not in a particular ritual or form isolated from these.[27] In history new features arise and the structural organisation of features to the whole changes as the structure of societies change. This mode of transposing anthropological findings to history is wrong.

And yet, at the point of saying this, my criticism appears ungenerous. It is not only that I have put undue weight upon a suggestive two-page passage of this historian's work, which was never intended to carry such weight. It is also that, by introducing a synchronic model of the 'act of giving', Stedman Jones succeeds in making us see the relationship entailed in charity in the 1860s in new ways, and he provokes one also to generalized comparative thoughts as to the functions of charity in different historical contexts. Scores of histories of charities or of the Poor Laws have been written which scarcely raise the critical question of prestige, subordination and social control (or, as I prefer, class control): at their worst these represent the donors wholly in terms of their own professed intentions, self-image and ideological justifications. Stedman Jones may have offered too tidy an explanation. But by inducing this kind of reflection he has opened the way to serious analysis of a new kind. Hence my criticism must be inadequate. If we may not transpose synchronic finding in this way – as ideal types, constant functions, universal deep structures – we can rarely discover the inwardness of a particular context without having some such typology to bring to it and to argue with.

I have found myself forced to reflect upon this in my current work on 'rough music' or *charivari*.[28] Here I am examining another 'border' ritual which throws light upon norms. The rituals expose some individual who has offended against community norms to the most public forms of insult, humiliation and sometimes ostracism – riding victims upon an ass or upon a pole, burning them in effigy, performing raucous 'music' outside their cottages upon tin cans, the horns of beasts, and so on, and reciting obscene traditional rhymes. I have argued that these forms are of importance, not – as Lévi-Strauss has suggested – as universal structures but precisely because the immediate functions of the rituals change. The kinds of offender subjected to rough music are not the same, from one country to another, or from one century to the next. So that once again I have had to resist an anthropological finding that *charivari* has one constant trans-cultural function or significance.[29] Hence the importance of these rituals lies in the fact that, since they identify which kinds of (sexual, marital, public) conduct incurred outrage in the community, they also offer a signpost to that community's norms.

But, even so, I feel the need for guidance at many points from social anthropology – and for much greater expertise in the discipline than I possess. If what goes on within the forms changes, the forms still remain important; and the forms themselves deploy symbolism which derives from the ulterior cognitive system of the community. (The driving out of evil or of 'the other' by raucous noise is one of the most constant and most ancient symbolic modes.) Just as Stedman Jones needs to think about the 'act of giving', so I need to think about the act of ostracism, the expulsion of 'the other', the ways a boundary is set upon a norm. In this way, a dialogue with anthropology becomes an insistent need.

In the examples which I have given I must apologize for

drawing so exclusively upon English materials. To attempt a
translation into Indian terms would only be to expose my own
ignorance. I must leave the translation to my auditors. I have been
told that *charivari* is well-known also in Indian village life, and
that the ritual shaming of riding upon an ass may still survive in
some parts of north India. I have no doubt that the ancient
traditions of charity and of ritual mendicancy in India offer
examples of social mediations which require more delicate retrieval
and more subtle analysis than any I have offered. And of course
the kinds of sources which we must use will be different. But I
suspect that both British and Indian historians face a similar
problem in the fact that those who recorded the evidence which we
must employ often failed to penetrate to the meaning of what they
recorded. The great class distance of the British gentry when facing
the common people of their own or of other countries requires no
further comment. But it is often suggested that the brahmin
tradition also failed on many occasions to penetrate all the
meanings of the culture of the Indian poor.[30] To the British rulers
the defences of these poor were often seen as passivity or
'fatalism'. But within this fatalism there may have been hidden a
wisdom of survival: as the Chinese proverb has it, 'Do not help on
the great chariot, you will only get covered in dust', or, as they
say in north India, 'Spitting on the sky falls on one's own
mouth'.[31]

     If we need this dialogue with anthropology, there are still some
problems as to the way in which this can be conducted. The
equation comes easily to mind: just as economic history presup-
poses the discipline of economics, so social history (in its
systematic examination of norms, expectations, values) must presuppose the discipline of social anthropology. We cannot examine
rituals, customs, kinship relations, without stopping the process of
history from time to time, and subjecting the elements to a static,
synchronic structural analysis.

     Let us say that there is some truth in this equation. But it
remains a little too easy. Economics and economic history developed in close intellectual partnership. But more recently emergent
social history has been offered (or, more often, has had to solicit in
the face of some indifference) a partnership with social disciplines

which are, in some part, explicitly *anti*-historical: one thinks of the influence of Durkheim, Radcliffe-Brown, Talcott Parsons and Lévi-Strauss. Moreover, some social anthropology is also anti-economic, or, more accurately, innocent of advanced economic categories. That is, while it takes in considerations of 'material life' at the level discussed by Fernand Braudel,[32] its traditional subject-matter leaves it thin, and sometimes actively resistant, to 'economies'. But we cannot wish to see an 'advance' in systematic social history which is purchased only by turning its back upon economic history. And, finally, socio-economic history already has its own concepts and categories – and among these, and of paramount importance in the Marxist tradition, the concepts of capitalism, of ideology, and of social class – which are *historical* concepts, arising from the analysis of diachronic process, of repeated regularities of behaviour over time, and which for that reason are often resisted, and even wilfully misunderstood (as in the case of class) by the synchronic disciplines.

This is to emphasize that while a relationship must be encouraged between social anthropology and social history, this cannot be *any* kind of relationship. A third party is needed as match-maker, whose name is generally given as philosophy. If we try to bring parts of the disciplines together by setting up 'blind dates' – introducing positivist econometric history to Lévi-Straussian structuralism, or Marxist historiography to the sociology of Talcott Parsons – then we can be very sure that no consummation will ensue.

This is increasingly recognized by scholars within each discipline. But when we come to this point, we must cease to pretend to speak for our discipline as a whole, and can only speak for our own position within it. In my own case, I would have to define my relation to the Marxist tradition. I could not use certain familiar sociological concepts unless they were given, first, a new dialectical ambivalence: an 'act of giving' must be seen simultaneously as an 'act of getting', a social consensus as a class hegemony, social control (very often) as class control, and some (but not all) norms as needs. But, equally, if I wish to effect a junction not with 'social anthropology' but with a Marxist anthropology I am persuaded that I must abandon that curiously static concept, 'basis' and 'superstructure', which in a dominant Marxist tradition identifies 'basis' with economies and affirms a heuristic priority to economic needs and behaviour over norms and value-systems. We may both assert that 'social being determines social consciousness' (an assertion which still calls for scrupulous examination and qualification) while leaving open for common investigation the question as to how far it is meaningful, in any given society, to describe 'social being' independently of the norms, and primary cognitive structures, as well as material needs, around which existence is organized.

We may conclude by examining this problem a little more carefully. Historical materialism has, in general, held firmly to an underlying model of societies, which, for the purpose of analysis, may be seen as horizontally structured according to a basis and superstructure. The Marxist method has directed attention first to the mode of production and its attendant productive relations, and this is commonly interpreted as disclosing an ultimate 'economic' determinism. This model has often been employed with great subtlety by historians who have borne in mind such warnings as those of Engels in his famous letter to Bloch;[33] in recent years there has been renewed emphasis upon the reciprocal interaction of basis and superstructure, upon the 'relative autonomy' of elements of the superstructure, and of determination being only 'in the last instance' economic. And there has been some further refinement and qualification of the notion of 'determination'.

What is radically wrong, however, is the analogy, or the metaphor, we start with, and also the employment of too narrow a category, 'economic'. Marx himself did not frequently employ this analogy, although he did so once in a critically important summary of his theory, which proved to be influential.[34] But we should recall that on occasion he had recourse to quite different analogies for the historical process.

Thus in the *Grundrisse* he wrote:

In all forms of society it is a determinate production and its relations which assign every other production and its relations their rank and influence. It is a general illumination in which all other colours are plunged and which modifies their specific tonalities. It is a special ether which defines the specific gravity of everything found in it.[35]

What this emphasizes is the simultaneity of expression of characteristic productive relations in *all* systems and areas of social life rather than any notion of the primacy (more 'real') of the 'economic', with the norms and culture seen as some secondary 'reflection' of the primary. What I am calling in question is not the centrality of the mode of production (and attendant relations of power and ownership) to any materialist understanding of history. I am calling in question – and Marxists, if they wish to have an honest dialogue with anthropologists, *must* call in question – the notion that it is possible to describe a mode of production in 'economic' terms, leaving aside as secondary (less 'real') the norms, the culture, the critical concepts around which this mode of production is organized. Such an arbitrary theoretical division into an economic basis and a cultural superstructure may be made in the head, and it may look all right on paper for a while. But it is only an argument in the head. When we turn to the examination of any real society we very rapidly discover, or ought to discover, the futility of attempting to enforce such divisions. Anthropologists, including Marxist anthropologists, have long insisted upon the impossibility of describing the economy of primitive societies independently of the kinship systems according to which these are structured, and the kinship obligations and reciprocities which are as much endorsed and enforced by norms as by needs.[36] But it is equally true that in more advanced societies the same distinctions are invalid. We cannot even begin to describe feudal or capitalist society in 'economic' terms independently of the relations of power and domination, the concepts of use-right or private ownership (and attendant laws), the culturally-endorsed norms and the culturally-formed needs characteristic of the mode of production. No agrarian system could be continued for a day without complex concepts of rights of use and access and ownership: where are we to put such concepts – in a 'basis' or a 'superstructure'?[37] Where are we to put customs of inheritance – patrilinear or matriclinear, partible or impartible – which are tenaciously transmitted in non-'economic' ways and yet which profoundly influence agrarian history?[38] Where are we to put the customary rhythms of work and of leisure (or festival) of traditional societies, rhythms intrinsic to the very act of production and yet which are often ritualized, whether in Hindu or Catholic societies, by religious institutions and according to religious beliefs? There is no way in which I find it possible to describe the Puritan or Methodist work-discipline as an element of the 'superstructure' and then put work itself in a 'basis' somewhere else.

However much the notion is sophisticated, however subtly it has on many occasions been employed, the analogy of basis and superstructure is radically defective. It cannot be repaired. It has an in-built tendency to lead the mind towards reductionism or a vulgar economic determinism, by sorting out human activities and attributes and placing some (as Law, the Arts, Religion, 'Morality') in a superstructure, others (as technology, economics, the applied sciences) in a basis, and leaving yet others (as linguistics, work-discipline) to float unhappily in-between. In this form it has a tendency to move into an alliance with utilitarian and positivist thought: that is, with central positions, not of Marxist, but of bourgeois ideology. The good society can be created simply (as in Stalinist theory) by building a heavy industrial 'base'; given this, a cultural superstructure will somehow build itself. In more recent (Althusserian) form, with its emphasis upon 'relative autonomy' and 'in the last instance determination', the problems of historical and cultural materialism are not so much solved as shuffled away or evaded; since the lonely hour of the last instance never strikes, we may at one and the same time pay pious lip-service to the theory and take out a licence to ignore it in our practice.

I am of course by no means the first Marxist to have voiced these objections.[39] Indeed, the objections have now become so apparent that one wishes that more of one's fellow Marxists would attend carefully to the argument before sniffing the air for 'heresy'. A living system of historical and political thought has come to a point of crisis if its continued existence depends upon maintaining an ill-considered analogy. The question of the category of 'economics' raises other questions again. We all think that we know what we mean by the term, but historians do not need the reminder that it is a term of comparatively recent evolution. Still, in eighteenth-century England, 'oeconomy' could be used to mean the regulation and adjustment of all the affairs of a household (and, by analogy, of a state), with no particular reference only to those material and financial affairs which, today, we would designate as 'economic'. If we turn to earlier British history, or to other societies in many different stages of development, we find that 'economics', in the modern sense, is a notion for which there is no word and no exactly corresponding concept. Religious and moral imperatives remain inextricably intermeshed with economic needs. One of the offences against mankind brought about within full-grown market society, and within its ideology, has been, precisely, to define all compelling social relations as 'economic', and to replace affective bonds by the more impersonal but no less compulsive bonds of money.

It follows that 'economic' categories of explanation, which may be adequate for industrialized societies, are often less adequate for understanding earlier societies. This is not of course to argue that there can be no valid economic history of pre-industrial or pre-capitalist societies, but to remind ourselves that the expectations and motivations of the people who then lived cannot be understood in anachronistic economic terms. The same problem reappears in a more subtle form within industrial capitalism itself. When Marx contested the dominant bourgeois political economy of his time, with its underlying assumptions as to the nature of acquisitive economic man, he counterposed to these the proletariat, or exploited economic man, who was destined to become, through economic struggle, revolutionary man. But while this was not the whole of Marx's meaning, this deeply affected an economism in the theories and strategies of subsequent Marxist thinkers and Marxist parties. These too often forgot the prior offence of capitalism in defining all relations in economic terms at all. And in fact we find that antagonistic values add to a general criticism of the 'commonsense' of power. By involuntary change I mean those ulterior changes in technology, demography, and so on (Braudel's 'material life' – new crops, new trade-routes, the discovery of new reserves of gold, changes in the incidence of epidemics, new mechanical inventions) whose involuntary consequences affect the mode of production itself and perceptibly alter the balance of productive relations.

This last may still, perhaps, be seen as a change in the 'basis'. But no such involuntary changes have ever spontaneously restructured or reorganized a mode of production; they have, perhaps, brought new forces onto the scene, altered the balance of power and wealth as between different social classes: but the consequent restructuring of *relations* of power, forms of domination and of social organization, has always been the outcome of struggle. Change in material life determines the conditions of that struggle, and some of its character: but the particular outcome is determined only by the struggle itself. This is to say that historical change eventuates, not because a given 'basis' must give rise to a correspondent 'superstructure', but because changes in productive relationships are *experienced* in social and cultural life, refracted in men's ideas and their values, and argued through in their actions, their choices and their beliefs.

In my own work I have found that I can handle neither the congruities nor the contradictions of the deeper historical process without attending to the problems which anthropologists disclose. I am well aware that other historians have long reached the same conclusion, and that they have not found it necessary to justify their enlargement of history's methods and resources with this kind of theoretical disquisition. I have attempted this only because it seems to me that historians in the Marxist tradition have shown some reluctance in furthering this necessary enlargement; and it has seemed that this has arisen from an ulterior theoretical resistance, which rests upon an over-narrow notion of 'the economy' and the use of an unhappy analogy. If I have helped to identify where the difficulty lies, then my purpose has been satisfied. If not, then you must forgive me for thinking aloud.

This is a revised version of a lecture given at the Indian History Congress, Calicut, Kerala, 30th December 1976.

Notes

1   *Society and Culture in Early Modern France* (Stanford, California, 1975).
2   Brand's *Observations* may best be consulted in subsequent editions (1813, 1849, &c.), edited and enlarged by Sir Henry Ellis. The term 'folklore' did not come into use until 1846, when it was employed by Williams John Thoms. For its subsequent history, see Richard M Dorson, *The British Folklorists & History* (London, 1968).
3   Max Müller, 'On Manners and Customs', in *Chips from a German Workshop*, ii (London, 1867), 260.
4   *The Past and Prejudice* (New Delhi, 1975), pp. 8–10.
5   Tylor, *op.cit.* p. 273. Tylor preferred the term 'ethnologist' to folklorist.
6   Max Müller, *op.cit.* ii, 265–70. Müller, however, was severely critical of loose and unscholarly attempts to offer analogies between Indian and European myth and custom: see his 'Folklore', a censorious review of W K Kelly, *Curiosities of Indo-European Tradition and Folklore* (London, 1863), in Müller, *op.cit.* ii, 197–207. Instead of facile comparisons (he argues) the myths and tales of each continent should be traced backwards to their original source in Aryan antiquity, and then 'let us see how the same conception and the same myths have gradually expanded and become diversified under the bright sky of India and in the forests of Germany'.
7   The conventional British academic case against folklore is restated (anonymously) in 'The Study of Folklore', *Times Literary Supplement*, 16 September 1969.
8   I say 'English' rather than British, since Celtic and national traditions have (as might be expected) received greater favour in the universities of Scotland, Wales and Ireland. One might mention the work of the School of Scottish Studies, Edinburgh University, and the influence in several universities in Wales of the folk-life studies pioneered by Dr Iorwerth Peate.
9   The pioneering work of G C Homans, *English Villagers of the Thirteenth Century* (New York, 1941) had no successor for several decades. More recently, Centre for Folk-Life Studies has been established at the University of Leeds. The signs of reviving interest can be seen in Charles Phythian Adams, *Local History and Folklore* (Standing Conference for Local History, 26 Bedford Square, London WC1, 1975).

10 Shab Lal Srivastava, *Folk Culture and Oral Tradition* (New Delhi, 1974), p. 8.

11 See, *inter alia*, Jack Goody, 'The Evolution of the Family', in Peter Laslett and Richard Wall, ed, *Household and Family in Past Time* (Cambridge, 1972); Goody, 'Inheritance, Property and Women: Some Comparative Considerations', in Jack Goody, Joan Thirsk and E P Thompson, ed, *Family and Inheritance* (Cambridge, 1976); Lutz Berkner, 'The Stem Family and the Developmental Cycle of the Peasant household', *The American Historical Review*, 1972; S J Tambiah, 'Dowry and Bridewealth and the Property Rights of Women in South Asia', in Jack Goody and S J Tambiah, *Bridewealth and Dowry* (Cambridge, 1973).

12 *The Remembered Village* (Delhi, 1976), p. 42.

13 For an interesting late example of such condemnation, see *Hostages to India, or The Life Story of the Anglo-Indian Race* (Calcutta, 1936), pp. 78–9.

14 In fact the full ritual of the public wife-sale probably was not any kind of survival, but was developed in the eighteenth century.

15 C Phythian Adams, 'Ceremony and the Citizen: the Communal Year at Coventry, 1450–1550', in Peter Clark and Paul Slack, ed, *Crisis and Order in English Towns*, 1500–1700 (London, 1972).

16 Robert W Malcolmson, *Popular Recreations in English Society, 1700–1850* (Cambridge, 1973). See also the suggestive article by Gerald M Sider, 'Christmas Mumming and the New Year in Outport Newfoundland', *Past and Present*, May 1976.

17 Keith Thomas, 'Work and Leisure in Pre-Industrial Societies', *Past and Present*, December 1964; C Hill, The Uses of Sabbatarianism', in *Society and Puritanism in Pre-Revolutionary England* (London, 1964); E P Thompson, 'Time, Work-Discipline and Industrial Capitalism', *Past and Present*, December 1967; Douglas A Reid, 'The Decline of Saint Monday', *Past and Present*, May 1976; Herbert Gutman, *Work, Culture and Society in Industrializing America* (New York, 1976).

18 Keith Thomas, *Rule and Misrule in the Schools of Early Modern England* (University of Reading, 1976).

19 See, for example, Michelle Perrot, *Les ouvriers en grève* (Paris, 1974); Williams M Reddy, 'The Textile Trade and the Language of the Crowd at Rouen, 1752–1871', *Past and Present*, February 1977.

20 E P Thompson, 'Patrician Society, Plebeian Culture', *Journal of Social History* (USA), Summer 1974.

21 See Douglas Hay, 'Property, Authority and the Criminal Law', in

Douglas Hay, Peter Linebaugh and E P Thompson, ed, *Albion's Fatal Tree* (London, 1975).

22 'The Tyburn Riot against the Surgeons', in *ibid*. pp. 65–117.

23 See Keith Thomas, 'History and Anthropology', *Past and Present* no. 24, 1963; E P Thompson, 'Anthropology and the Discipline of Historical Context', *Midland History* (Birmingham University), i, no. 3, Spring 1972.

24 *The Historian's Craft* (Manchester, 1954), p. 35.

25 Oxford, 1971.

26 E P Thompson, 'The Moral Economy of the English Crowd in the Eighteenth Century,' *Past and Present*, February 1971.

27 See Marx's Sixth Thesis on Feuerbach.

28 E P Thompson, '"Rough Music"': Le Charivari anglais', *Annales: Économies, Sociétés, Civilisations*, Mars-Avril 1972.

29 See C Lévi-Strauss, *Mythologiques. I. Le Cru et le Cuit* (Paris, 1964).

30 See M N Srinivas's self-critical comments on the limitations of 'a high caste view of village society', *The Remembered Village*, pp. 197–8 *et passim*.

31 S K Srivastava, *op.cit.*, p. 279.

32 *Capitalism and Material Life*, 1400–1800 (London, 1973).

33 Engels to J Bloch, 21 September 1890; to Mehring, 14 July 1893: *Marx-Engels Selected Correspondence* (London, 1936), pp. 475–7, 510–13.

34 In the introduction to the *Critique of Political Economy*.

35 For a slightly different translation, see Karl Marx, *Grundrisse* (Penguin edition, 1973), pp. 106–7.

36 See, for example, Maurice Godelier, *Perspectives in Marxist Anthropology* (Cambridge, 1977); Jack Goody, *Production and Reproduction* (Cambridge, 1976).

37 This point is argued further in E P Thompson, *Whigs and Hunters* (London, 1975), pp. 258–69.

38 See Goody, Thirsk and Thompson, ed, *Family and Inheritance*.

39 Raymond Williams has for many years been pressing similar objections: see his very lucid treatment of the problems of basis/superstructure and of determination in *Marxism and Literature* (Oxford, 1977). My own objections have been further expressed in 'The Peculiarities of the English', *Socialist Register*, 1965 (Merlin Press, London, 1965), and 'An Open Letter to Leszek Kolakowski', *Socialist Register*, 1973.

Left Review

The original *Left Review* was in three 'volumes', the monthly
numbers of which ran from October, 1934, to May, 1938. Cass's
'new impression' (by photolithography), which was published
three years ago, has been conveniently divided into eight
volumes of some 300 pages each. At £48 the set, this is £6 a
volume – a safe enough price, one would have thought (at 1968
costs), to be covered by the purchase of a few score sets by
libraries. The economics of the case can be left aside: though
there is an irony in a review which was kept going by a
fighting-fund of its own readers – and whose editors and
contributors were unpaid – becoming a commercial property in
this way. However, the purchaser can surely expect some
editorial effort from the publishers? Apart from the caption on
the front page of each volume 'English Little Magazines No. 3:
edited by B.C. Bloomfield '– there is no evidence of editorial
attention of any kind. There is no editorial introduction. There is
not even an index to the contributors.

This presents difficulties to the reviewer in the 1970s. It will
present greater difficulties to the scholar in the 1990s. An important
area of obscurity is in the editorial conduct of the review. *Left Review*
was founded, late in 1934, by the novelist and critic Montagu Slater,
Amabel Williams-Ellis and Tom Wintringham. (In May, 1938, a brief
retrospective article associated with these three the names of Ralph
Fox and Edgell Rickword.) Sole editorship was taken over in January,
1936, by Rickword (himself a veteran of the *Calendar of Modern
Letters*), and he continued in office until July, 1937, when Randall
Swingler succeeded him. Swingler remained as editor until the review
was, abruptly and inexplicably, closed in May, 1938. A new and more
ambitious monthly review was promised as successor: but no such
review appeared, unless (eventually) the more populist *Our Time*
comes to mind.

So much is at least partially clear. Other matters are not. There were several references along the way to the reorganisation and extension of the editorial board; but the actual names of the board were never published. Ralph Fox chaired a contributors conference in April, 1935, and claimed a circulation of 3,000, but for the next three years there is no information. There were clearly some slight shifts in editorial influence. Mrs Williams-Ellis, whose main contribution appears to have been the organisation of competitions which encouraged some interesting 'worker writers', was less evident after the first year. Greybeards among us will remember that Tom Wintringham took part in the Spanish Civil War (writing *English Captain)*, was suspected of (feminine)Trotskyist contamination, broke with the Communist Party over its initial attitude to the war, advocated the preparation in Britain of guerrilla warfare and helped to found the Common Wealth Party. The Spanish War severed other contributors from the review more abruptly: Ralph Fox being only one of seven or eight mortal casualties.

Left Review was a communist literary journal, though it operated not as the internal organ of a sect but as a national review, in the presence of a national public, drawing upon many non-communists among its contributors. The point must be clearly made because two erroneous stereotypes are sometimes encountered. According to one, *Left Review* was an arena where contributors vented their callow leftist juvenilia before arriving, by various paths, at reputable anti-communist maturity. According to the other, *Left Review* was a communist fox in the lamb's clothing of the Popular Front, luring the innocent liberals into its literary lair.

With the whole run together it is possible to see the falsity of both stereotypes. For the second, nearly all the editors were well known as communists (Wintringham had been one of the British communist leaders tried in 1925), and there was never any attempt at the least woolly disguise. Non-communists contributed – one notices the good-humoured grimaces of Eric Gill and of Herbert Read – because they wished to do so, and because they respected the communist editors enough to wish to argue in the same pages.

An examination of the first stereotype brings more interesting results. One is impressed, less by the number of the now

reputable and orthodox who committed youthful indiscretions in
these pages (there are of course some of these), but by the solid
majority of contributors who evinced – and, in some cases, still
evince – a lifetime of commitment to the left: and who, while
some of them may have broken at this point or that any ties
they had with the Communist Party, never signalled that their
revolutionary god had failed. This is true of the editors: and
among contributors one notes A.L. Lloyd, Douglas Garman, Alick
West, J.D. Bernal, Jack Lindsay, Hugh MacDiarmid, James
Boswell, Allen Hutt, Alan Bush, A.L. Morton, F.D. Klingender,
T.A. Jackson, Thomas Hodgkin, Dona Torr, Nancy Cunard and
Thomas Russell. The settled tenacity with which some of this
group maintained a commitment, over thirty or forty years, to a
defined political and intellectual position recalls the tenacity of
some eighteenth-century dissenters. Nor is this true only of those
very close to the communist intellectual orbit. It is true of other
writers, who defined themselves at other points on the left: in
the second number (November, 1934) Storm Jameson wrote a
stinging open letter 'To a Labour Party Official', from her
standpoint as a constituency worker, whose drift could be
endorsed by thousands (and perhaps still by its author?) today.

There were also birds of passage, of course. These were not to
be distinguished from their companions by the brilliance of their
plumage, the originality of their flight; neither Cecil Day Lewis nor
Stephen Spender contributed any of their more substantial poems to
the review, and their lucubrations on the artist and society are
among the contributions one more gladly skips. Nor were they
wooed to stay and nest. The regular contributors fixed them, rather,
with the eye of the Teacher, now patronizing, now reproving.
Spender's (unimpressive) *Forward from Liberalism* illustrated 'that
the fact that the author has not intellectually come very far forward
from Liberalism is not due to any insincerity, but only to
insufficient thinking, lack of familiarity with the basic works of
Marxism', Day Lewis, wrote another reviewer, 'is still far from an
understanding of Marxism'.

How far, then, did a proper understanding of Marxism vitalise
the contributions of the editors and their collaborators? *Left Review*
did have vitality, pace, and style; successive editors handled their

materials with competence: the bold cartoons and drawings of Boswell. Fitton, Holland and others emphasized hard moral definitions; stories and reportage (James Hanley, Ralph Bates, George Garrett) were sometimes too 'messagey' but are generally well-observed and economically written: there is a broadening internationalism – the reader was introduced, perhaps for the first time, to Mayakovsky, Brecht, Malraux.

All this is much, and may come in the future to seem more, when readers are less oppressed by historical hindsight: when they are more ready to perceive the enlargement of sympathies and the originality of themes (as compared with any literary movement of the 1920s) and less sensitive to the blight laid upon this promise by the encroachment of doctrinal Stalinism within the review.

Even so, *Left Review* was weakened by a certain staccato style, which never paused long enough to lay down intellectual or creative foundations for the left. Few contributions were as long as 3,000 words: hence more substantial work was drained off elsewhere – perhaps to *New Writing*, or *Modern Quarterly* or the *Fact* pamphlets, or to Unity Theatre productions. The most original communist critic of the 1930s, Christopher Caudwell, never contributed in his lifetime: any one of the *Studies in a Dying Culture* would have been too long.

Moreover the review, like radical and socialist periodicals before and after it, was continually under two heavy, unrelenting, and related pressures; the pressure of immediate, urgent political responsibility, and the pressure upon the editors of a loyal, enthusiastic readership (upon whom its circulation and finances rested), eager to offer imperious and contradictory advice. 'We don't want so much of this belly-aching psychology', growled one contributor (a seaman) at the first *Left Review* conference. *Left Review* should become 'a kind of working-class *Tit-bits* after the style of *New Masses*', demanded another. 'Simplification and again simplification', demanded a third. There is a 'lack of position, direction, purpose', complained the *Daily Worker*. No wonder there was a note of desperation in Montagu Slater's reply to such critics. One of the functions of *Left Review*, he wrote:

is to begin to catch up the leeway of forty years' stoppage of
Marxist theory in England. There has been a good deal of talk
at *Left Review* conferences and elsewhere about the uselessness
of intellectuals (a slogan less fitted to revolutionary thought than
to fascist lack of thinking). What *Left Review* should say to
intellectuals is: Intellect is what we want more than most
things! To the intelligentsia: Be intelligent!

Slater, Rickword, Swingler consistently maintained this sense of
intellectual function. The pressure upon them, according to folklore,
was not only that of that section of their readership who had only
the most limited utilitarian notion of a review: it came also from
the apparatus of the party at King Street, which judged the
usefulness of the review only as an organising medium.

But the pressures were within themselves also. As the menace
of European fascism grew taller (and as Stalinism hardened within
the international communist movement) there is a sense of growing
doctrinal inhibition in the review. Douglas Garman, a former editor
of the *Calendar of Modern Letters*, was still writing in early
numbers (for example, in a review of Eliot's *After Strange Gods*)
as if there were an argument to conduct, sharply, with precision, in
the face of a public. In later numbers commination against
bourgeois decadence sufficed. When, midway through the review's
life, Herbert Read came forward (reviewing T.A. Jackson's *Dialectics*) to suggest, without the least rancour, that Marxist anthropology and social psychology were in need of development, the
argument was simply closed by Jackson: 'Nothing has been
brought to light in either field which in the least shakes either
Marx's fundamental premises or his basic conclusions.' Towards
the end of the review's history, the appearance of L.C. Knights's
truly seminal *Drama and Society in the Age of Jonson* was met, in
a review of sustained hostility, by Alick West: 'A doubt of the
relevance of Marxist analysis, not merely to literature, pervades the
book.' Knights's courteous and open reply to West, in which he
attempted to continue a discussion, dropped into silence.

The silence, perhaps, of paranoia – he who is not for me ....
A psychological deformation which, with a great deal less
justification, is very evident in some sections of the intellectual

left to this day, and which, more than anything else, prevents them from either developing their ideas or communicating what ideas they have to an uncommitted public. What is interesting is that the founders of *Left Review*, in 1934–35, very rarely used this tone. Both Slater and Wintringham wrote with a well-informed muscular middlebrow fluency, while Ralph Fox avoided doctrinal cant absolutely and could on occasion (as in two essays, one on monarchy, the other on a single day's issue of the *Daily Express*) write with a lyrical, highly modulated polemic – feinting, dancing, jabbing – reminiscent of Hazlitt. Fox was surely, like other editors and contributors, a 'premature revisionist', who would have understood instantly and made common cause with Wazyk and Kolakowski in 1956. Indeed, one can see the battle-lines being drawn as early as October and November, 1935. Francis Klingender let loose a severe, abstraction-laden doctrinal reproof against Slater, which, taking off from differing judgments of the merit of Tsapline's sculpture, escalated into a general theory of Marxist art criticism:

> The Marxian critic must convince [the abstract artist] that only the class struggle pervading every sphere of our existence, only the aim of the working class to establish a new social order can enable him to find vital content for art to-day.

This (and much more) brought the light of polemic to Fox's eyes. In a furious assault ('Abyssinian Methods') he unloaded upon Klingender his pent-up fury at the whole doctrinal emaciation of language and of sensibility:

> Mr. Klingender is sure that the best way to 'help' Tsapline is to tell him he is a misguided bourgeois with a very, very naughty tendency towards carving molluscs and fishes. I am sure the best way to help Mr. Klingender would be to deprive him of pen and ink for the rest of his life .... Where in all this conception is dialectic? In this horrible jumble of rigid moral and sociological conceptions, where is the idea of inner development, where the real connection between form and content?

It was Fox's last article for the *Review*: just over a year later he was killed in action on the Cordoba front.

These 'severe pseudo-Marxists', Slater commented in the same controversy, 'renounce life like puritans'. But, in the end, puritanism closed in. The reason is not to be attributed as the pseudo-Trotskyist explanation now so prevalent and so fashionable would have it – solely to the evil genius of Stalinism. It lay in the actual evil of the times. It was not unrelated to that generous death at Cordoba, and to so many other deaths, in Spain, in Germany, in Italy – round the world. 'From China to Brazil', the *Review* editorialised in August, 1936, 'men are being oppressed, tortured and killed for their opinions with a ferocity and on a wider scale than the world ever knew, even at the worst times of religious persecution.' In the final year of the review the sense of the imminence of war, of the urgency of the times, was all-pervasive: the contributors were like men gesticulating on a raft which is being carried towards the rapids.

In such a context the function of the review simply as an organiser of intellectual opinion for short-term political urgencies inevitably engrossed all other functions. That kind of political (or human) responsibility was a sufficient cause of creative and intellectual inhibition, even if it had not been seconded by a doctrinal sclerosis. Looking back across thirty-odd years it is natural that one should ask of *Left Review*: what lasting additions did it make to the cultural sum, or, in a more limited view, to the sum of the socialist intellectual tradition? No doubt the editors of the contemporary *New Left Review* would – if they acknowledged any kinship at all – shake their élitist heads and answer, 'very little'.

But, after the first year, one doubts whether editors or contributors expected to be judged according to such a function. They looked, not back down a tradition, but across the sea to Germany and Spain, and forward to the next World War. Increasingly they saw themselves as activists, mobilising a sector of public opinion. If this mobilisation could be shown to have been effective enough to have contributed, at this point or that, to the ultimate defeat of fascism, they would probably have found *Left Review* to have fulfilled its function. The weight of this political urgency was so great that it meant, for some of them, the death or the suspension of their own creative identity. 'To recognise a communal need', wrote Randall Swingler, 'is to be liable at once to a claim which it will be desperately hard and perhaps dangerous to answer.' (It is notable that editorship of the review seems to have entailed, for both Rickword and Swingler, a creative intermission.) As for the revolutionary socialist tradition, they were, increasingly, less concerned to affirm it than to preserve the human conditions within which it could in the end be once again affirmed.

Times Literary Supplement, 19th February 1971, reviewing *Left Review*, October 1934–May 1938 (8 volumes). Cass.

Edgell Rickword

I have never known Edgell Rickword well. But we have had
friends in common over the years, and have trudged on together –
a few files apart – in the same disorderly contingent of 'the Left'.
Sometimes we have exchanged a few words.

I saw him most often, I suppose, in a pub near the offices of
Our Time in Southampton Street. I would call in, on leave from
the army (1942–43), in search of my particular friends, Arnold
Rattenbury and (later) Randall Swingler. I doubt whether Edgell
often saw me. I was a nineteen-year-old in uniform, like half of the
rest of the world, and (on closer acquaintance) an exceedingly
callow youth, full of anti-fascist bluster and instant political
solutions to every cosmic question. Edgell would be talking to one
of the review's contributors, or he would be squinting with intense
concentration into the very bottom of his beer glass – a habit of
abstraction which offered a defence against the importunities of
youth.

After the war I was three years older by biology and some eight
or nine years less callow. There was a choppy year or two – 1946?
1947? – which I cannot now reconstruct accurately from memory,
when I was around Southampton Street once more, before I took
off for the North and drifted beyond its view. There was some
snarling row going on within the cultural appendices of the
Communist Party. In retrospect it can be seen that the shadows of
the Cold War were closing in, the radical 'populist' euphoria of
1944 was collapsing, and certain administrators at 'King Street'
were rehearsing for parts as local Zhdanovs.

Jack Lindsay was unmasked as some kind of revisionist heretic.
He had fallen on the 1844 MSS, was high on alienation and
reification (which he insisted upon rendering as 'thingification'),
and he had put Marx and Freud together in the bed of a single
book. This book or another was (as I recall) 'withdrawn' as

'incorrect', and Lindsay was denounced at an enlarged 'aggregate' of the Writers' Group. I remember the immense shaggy head of the anthropologist V. Gordon Childe, just in front of me, shaking in fury at the general scene of dogmatism. Lindsay tells me that I was one of the only ones to rise to his defence, but that – and all else – has slipped my mind.

That time produced one of the sharpest mental frosts I can remember on the Left. Vitalities shrivelled up and books lost their leaves. (It was at about this time that the Party blocked the publication of Hamish Henderson's translation of Gramsci's prison letters – it had been discovered [we were told] that Gramsci was guilty of some nameless 'deviation'). *Our Time* was to come to an end as a casualty of the same state of mind. Its circulation was falling – as was that of nearly all cultural reviews in the aftermath of war, when the immense railway bookstall sales plummeted – and the Marxist theoreticians at King Street decided that this must of course be because of its 'incorrect line'. Emile Burns was superimposed upon its structure, and King Street descended on Southampton Street, rather as Laputa descended upon a refractory province, 'letting the Island drop directly upon their Heads, which makes a universal Destruction both of Houses and Men'. Palace revolutions were engendered, and the Party solicited the aid of 'youth', who, as we know, always have correct and uncomplicated views. There was some strategy of replacing the flagging old guard of Rickword and Swingler with a whole 'team' or collective of 'youth', and, for a month or so, I was nominated to this team.

I attended a disgraceful meeting, at which Emile Burns scolded Rickword and Swingler for their political, cultural, publishing and financial sins and omissions. (I should add that the Party neither owned the publishing firm, nor had set up the review.) Scolded in this way, these two immensely more wise, more deeply-political, and more cultured men – men who were heroes to me, and to whom I looked for guidance – sat passively, winced, and suffered without making a defence. They agreed that the falling circulation figures convicted them. It was a shameful episode and I shared in the shame, for, however 'youthful' I was, I had allowed myself to be made use of as part of the team of uncultured yobbos and musclemen under the command of the elderly Burns. But I was sad and puzzled also that my heroes had not allowed me to fight on their side.

They had at once lost all their customary confidence, wit and vitality when placed in the formal posture of receiving criticism from one of the Party's senior officers. I felt – and I still feel today – that Edgell Rickword received some brutally insensitive treatment, at more than one time, from officials of the Party to which he has remained so loyal; that the cultural consequences of this kind of *dirigisme* were very seriously destructive; and that Edgell has been over-reticent about these episodes, from which writers and socialists may still have something to learn.

I am sorry that my reconstruction of these events is so imprecise. I may do better one day. My theoretical conclusions, which may overleap the facts and which are influenced by much subsequent discussion with Randall Swingler and others, are rather more clear. First, there was not only a formal structure but also a psychological structure among Communist intellectuals from the mid-1930s to the late-1940s which left us all lacking in self-confidence when confronted by the intrusion of 'the Party'. The political issues of those years were so critical as to make all literary or cultural concerns appears as somehow subordinate. The practical initiatives of the Party and of its membership were so ardent, so fraught with significance, and sometimes so heroic (in successive numbers of *Left Review* in 1937, Edgell Rickword, as editor, had to pay tribute to Ralph Fox, John Cornford, Christopher Caudwell and Charles Donnelly – all of whom had met their deaths in Spain), that this imputed a peculiar merit to the Party's leaders and officials: the heroism and significance of the times invested a certain charisma on them.

I doubt whether, in Edgell's case, the classic self-abnegation of bourgeois guilt and self-mistrust in the face of 'proletarian' truth had much part to play. He had, he has, too strong a sense of cultural realities to fall for that. But by the 1940s the stream of 'apostates' was so full that all of us were apt to recoil, wilfully and unthinkingly, from the brink of any heresy for fear of toppling into the flood. And we had become habituated to the formal rituals of 'criticism and self-criticism' – in origin an admirable democratic process, but one which had become perverted into a ritual in which the criticism came always from the Party's senior spokesmen on cultural matters (Garman, Burns, Dr John Lewis) and the self-criticism was intoned by congregated intellectuals in response.

There was, indeed, a certain obliteration of the intellect inseparable from the Party's rehearsed collective forms; wit, independence, vitality, humour, were somehow displaced from the agenda in the interests of an earnest and self-righteous sense of 'political responsibility'. The comrades, chatting outside the door, or, later, in the pub, were always more various, more observant, and more intelligent than when they had gone inside to pray. I don't say this as an 'anti-Communist' jibe. It is just the same today in the Labour party and the Marxist sects, perhaps in institutions of most kinds. But it was very much the case in the international Communist movement, whose forms and ideology were cloned everywhere, in those years.

What I am saying is that this small and shameful episode, when Emile Burns bullied Rickword and Swingler, and when they – the founders of the review and creators of a certain cultural moment – responded with vexed silence, can be understood only with a whole set of forms and also a mind-set within the international Communist movement of that time. It was a little shadow-play reflecting those more grotesque plays of self-accusation enacted in the Soviet Union and Eastern Europe in those years. Its outcome was characteristically destructive. Rickword and Swingler were evicted from *Our Time* (they probably resigned with a sense of relief) and the review, after a year or so of opportunist tacking, collapsed. With its collapse a decade of aggressive cultural vitality on the Left came to an end.

My second conclusion, or observation, is this. Long before '1956' there were centres of 'premature revisionism' among Communist intellectuals and others, who resisted the didactic methods of the Party's officers, the wooden economism of its policies, and the correct pabulum offered as 'Marxism'. This incipient heresy was unfocussed, lacking in articulation, was expressed as often as not in jokes and resistances, and we identified our enemy far too loosely as 'King Street' – a bullying and bumbling bureaucracy rather than (as it was) a highly-articulated Stalinist clerisy. Like it or not, Edgell Rickword was close to one of the sources of this revisionist resistance.

He may not wish me to say so. He may even argue that this is a case of misrecognition. But I and my friends among the dwindling numbers of the Communist intellectual 'youth' recognized him in that way. It was not only – although this was always important – that in every line that he wrote there was a more measured cultural response, a wider resonance, than in the abbreviated class taxonomies which passed for Marxist criticism, even at times in such fertile minds as those of Caudwell and Fox. It was also, and particularly, a matter of the 'Englishness' of Edgell Rickword.

This is a difficult question to discuss, for two reasons. First, it is paradoxical, since this 'national' emphasis is not evident in *Left Review* when it was under his editorial conduct: indeed, it is the internationalism of that moment – and the sense of European crisis – which first strikes the reader. (With *Our Time*, during the war years, preoccupation with national democratic traditions is more evident). Second, it is exactly this emphasis upon national cultural experience which a contemporary generation of Marxist intellectuals in England (but not in Scotland or Wales) most distrust and deride in their forerunners. Are we not told, and on every side, that British intellectuality became submerged, until some moment in the 1960s, in a suffocating provincialism, and that the British Left was a vector of the same insularity and chauvinism?

So that it is precisely within the context of 'premature revisionism' – the struggle for vitality and for actuality against the *déraciné* uniformity and abstracted internationalist *lingua franca* of the Stalinist zenith – that the significance of the return to national cultural resources must be understood. Fuller analysis would require the painful attention to the denaturalized rhetoric of such texts as the Third International's *Inprecorr* or the British CP's *World News and Views*. The Communist mind of the decade 1936–46 was not, as is supposed by some today, corrupted by the gross epistemological errors of Frederick Engels but by row upon row of *Selected Lenins* and *Collected Stalins*, by absurdly utopian fairy-tales about the Soviet Union, by sloppy Russophilia, and by the mediocre productions of ideologues of the International whose mental strategies and vocabularies were designed to evade actualities. *The Short History of the C.P.S.U.(B)*, which was the fundamental 'education' text of Communists from Stalingrad to Cardiff and from Calcutta to Marseilles, is a document of the very first historical importance – a gigantic historical fabrication for the induction of idealist and military mental habits.

It was against *that* which Edgell Rickword, Randall Swingler, Montagu Slater and their friends were fighting – against those habits of idealism, falsetto utopianism, and the consequent evacuation of actuality. Others will be writing in these pages about Edgell Rickword's poetry, his criticism, and his editorial influence. These were, no doubt, his major contribution, his mode of insertion into his times. I wish to add a tribute to work which he may himself have regarded as more marginal – his influence as a *historian*.

When Christopher Hill, Margaret James and Edgell Rickword published, in 1940, *The English Revolution, 1640*, this initiated a major reconstitution of seventeenth-century historiography. It was also a major step towards the apprehension of actual and complex cultural evidence as opposed to preconceived class taxonomies. It is difficult to explain today, thirty-eight years later, the piquancy of the title of Rickword's own essay: 'Milton: the revolutionary intellectual'. It proposed not only a revaluation of Milton (perhaps the germ of Hill's recent study), but also a revaluation of the notion of a 'revolutionary intellectual' which could not be so tidily composed within Bolshevik categories as some had come to suppose.

This essay has not been forgotten. What has been forgotten by most contemporaries is the remarkable *Handbook of Freedom*, prepared by Rickword and Lindsay, first published in 1939 and re-issued in the Workers' Library in 1941 as *Spokesmen for Liberty*. This extraordinarily rich compendium of primary materials was selected from twelve centuries of 'English Democracy'. It is impressive for its length of reach (one hundred pages, or one quarter of the book, precedes the year 1600); the diversity and catholicity of the sources drawn upon, bringing, with a sense of surprised recognition, unlikely voices into a common discourse; the generosity of the editorial minds which called such diverse values into evidence; and the implicit intellectual command not only of

these various sources but also of the wider historical process out of
which these voices arose.

I think that the *Handbook of Freedom* was among the two or
three books which I managed to keep around with me in the army.
Certainly I know that others did so. When I left for the North,
after the choppy year or two in which *Our Time* entered its
terminal stage, I took, the book with me; I used it in adult classes
and in political meetings; it led me to new sources, and thence to
researches and work of my own. In retrospect I have sometimes
reflected upon the reading that went into that book, reading which
must have gone on during the extreme emergencies of the late
1930s. If we look at *Left Review* under Rickword's editorship, we
see an alert and informed internationalist concern. But it must be
that at the same time he was renewing his confidence in human
resources by returning, through his reading, to a more local
tradition of democratic assertion and organization. In recovering
this particular English tradition – voices which were passionate but
never 'correct', spokesmen who made affirmations but who never
descended to 'concrete formulations' – Rickword and Lindsay made
these energies available at a time when they were needed once
again.

The 'English Democracy' which they presented was a particular
historical record of struggle and of practices. As Rickword wrote in
his Introduction:

> Experience, too, bitter experience, has weaned us from over-
> much enthusiasm for freedom in the abstract, for the freedom
> which is the climax of the politician's oratory. We have always
> been concerned with freedom in some specific form, of associa-
> tion, or from arbitrary imprisonment, and such rights have
> proved essential tactical positions when it comes to defending or
> extending the material conditions which really measure the
> degree to which a society is effectively democratic.

Notice the stubborn avoidance of jargon, and the use of 'we', with
its confident assertion of the continuities of an alternative tradition.
Notice also how the critic's eye for the resonance of a word is
turned to historical analysis:

It will be noticed how the word 'common' and its derivatives, now so strangely altered in drawing-room usage, appear and re-appear like a theme throughout the centuries. It was for the once vast common lands that the peasants took up arms; it was as the 'true commons' that they spoke of themselves when they assembled, and it was the aspiration of men not corrupted by petty proprietorship 'that all things should be in common'.

This insight, and the critical and editorial work which supported it over the years, gave to some of us a notion of Communism with a new complexity and also concretion. I am arguing that Edgell Rickword was an architect of the conjunction between an internationalist socialist theory and a vigorous national historical practice. Between 1930 and 1950 a similar conjunction was being made in many places and in many minds: one might think of Hugh MacDiarmid in Scotland, D.D. Kosambi in India, Tibor Dery in Hungary, even of Gramsci. In contemporary fashion the 'insularity' of this national tradition may be seen only as a matter for regret. I have been arguing on the other side: I see this 'premature revisionism', this resistance to the abstracted idealist modes of internationalist Marxist dogmatism in the era of Stalin, and this turn towards complex cultural actualities, as a liberating moment – very certainly liberating for the critic and the historian, but ultimately liberating for 'theory' itself. I say 'ultimately', for, in the first place, the moment appeared as a flight *from* a theory which had become brutalized and dogmatic, and a return to the direct appropriation of the text of the poem and of the historical record. But the mind which returned was not an innocent mind: it was theoretically-informed. How matters have gone on since, and how they go on now, is another argument, and one which is not yet closed.

A contribution to a symposium reported in *Poetry Nation Review*, Supplement xxviii, Vol. 6 No. 1, 1979

Country and City

The British 'new left' was among the first of this international family. It began in the mid-fifties as a strongly political movement, taking hostile views of both orthodox social democracy and communism, and since 1960 it has gone through many mutations. The founding influences – such men as Claude Bourdet, Lelio Basso, Wright Mills, Isaac Deutscher, the voices of communist dissent – gave way successively to other influences such as those of Sartre, Marcuse, Fanon, R D Laing, to the rediscovery of Lukacs and of Gramsci, and thence to a highly sophisticated European Marxist tradition. But if we are to understand Raymond Williams – and his remarkable and stubborn consistency – we have to return to the early moment.

The British new left is supposed to have arisen on the tripod of three experiences: the communist crisis of 1956: the Campaign for Nuclear Disarmament, which enlisted onto the margins of British political life a new generation of activists: and the far-reaching cultural criticism of contemporary society identified with the names of Richard Hoggart and Raymond Williams. The 'tripod' explanation is much too tidy, but the influence of Hoggart and Williams was of undoubted importance, and of the two, Williams was the more important theoretician.

What is remarkable is that Williams remains an influence, outlasting changes in fashion. He has never allowed faddists-campus Guevarists, for example – to ruffle his socialist composure. He has argued quietly and rationally, endorsing what is worthwhile in recent movements: the resistance to imperialism and racism, the necessary transformation of academic institutions and routines.

His work can be accused of insularity: certainly it has grown from avowedly national cultural traditions. *Culture and Society* (1958) owed something to an old dialogue with F R Leavis, surveying and drawing conclusions from a long native tradition of moralism from Burke and Cobbett to D H Lawrence and Orwell. His best novel, *Border Country* (1960), is partly autobiographical and explores the conflict of values between a railwayman from the Welsh border and his son who enters a wider intellectual universe. *The Long Revolution* (1961) offered both a critique of Marxist cultural theory and an interpretation of the history and sociology of British writing, publishing, journalism: it concluded with a statement of the political positions of the (then) British new left. In 1967–68 when this movement had fragmented, he brought some elements back together and edited the *May Day Manifesto*, one of the most concrete works of political analysis to come from the British left.

I emphasise these works over his more specialised criticism of drama and the novel because I wish to emphasise Williams's importance as a political theorist. This emphasis explains also the unusual and unassimilated nature of his position in England. For English intellectual life has a powerful tendency to assimilate the radical and the nonconformist. The island's institutions, its modes, its inhibitions against the vulgarity of plain speaking, its close intellectual cousinship, its traffic in favours and privileges – all combine to produce a ritual of assimilation and accommodation. Dissent appears less as discord than as one more sound to be orchestrated in a sceptical, world-weary consensus.

To remain unassimilated is Raymond Williams's special achievement. No one has been able to orchestrate him, and it is apparent, after the last twenty years, that no one ever will. He remains at Cambridge a plebeian rock sticking out above the fashionable rightist or leftist tides, a doggedly democratic, anti-utilitarian, revolutionary socialist. In the 1950s he was unfashionable in maintaining an open but critical dialogue with Marxism: he was never a communist, and was perhaps close to some of the independent radical positions of *The Monthly Review*. In the 1970s he has been overtaken by a fashionable and sometimes scholastic Marxism that derives not from his own work but from Paris or Milan. He has taken from the Marxist tradition a complex and flexible sense of capital as a process, but whatever else Marxism offers, as philosophy or doctrine, he is ready to question.

A stubborn indifference to the reputable world is evident in the

form of the *The Country and the City*, which considers changing
attitudes toward rural and urban society, mainly in England. It
ignores – and for this it has been disliked by some – the sacred
academic unities of period, subject, and tone. Williams discusses
the tradition of the country-house poem, with acute attention to the
poems themselves; and then moves abruptly to social history, to a
chapter of analysis of mortgages, entail, rack-renting, marketing, in
which the contradictory findings of experts are worked into his
own synthesis. He discusses the images of anomie and alienation
clustering around the city, and then shifts without apology to an
account of trade unionism, town planning, local government.

This book is angrier, more impatient of academic evasion, more
plain-spoken than some of Williams's earlier works. There are
moments when he considers several centuries of polite culture, of
its retrospective celebration of paternalist or 'organic' country
values, then exposes this culture to the scrutiny of a field
labourer's experience and sensibility – makes an abrupt gesture of
dismissal and turns to musing on other matters.

The musing is that of a scholarly mind. But the book is not
a conventional work of scholarship, and whoever attempts to read
it in this way will end up only in disagreements and irritation. It
is the work of a moralist, wearing a literary habit. (This is why
it cannot be assimilated to the dominant mode of Marxist
thought today, which as the Althusserians are busily telling us,
consigns moralism with humanism to the most treacherous
regions of bourgeois false consciousness.) *The Country and the
City* belongs to a line which includes Burke and Cobbett,
Thoreau and Emerson, *Culture and Anarchy* and *Unto This Last*,
the essays of William Morris, D H Lawrence, and Orwell.
Williams's mind moves among whatever evidence seems relevant,
regards 'history' and 'literature' as aspects of man's experience,
refuses to permit questions of knowledge and questions of value
and political choice to be segregated in specialist enclosures. This
is, of course, thinking of the most serious kind. But it also goes
without saying that thought of this kind is of interest only if the
thinker has an interesting mind.

This Williams has: but his style bears some scars from his long
struggle to resist assimilation. He is rarely a crisp writer and he

can be a portentous one. He can imply depths which he does not always disclose; he is over-fond of the words 'decisive,' 'in the end,' 'fundamental,' and yet it is not always clear what has, in the end, been fundamentally decided, since we return, as we began, to 'complexities.' He is sometimes a little deaf to other voices, too determined to stand aside on his own.

The book begins powerfully and with conviction. The 'country,' the 'city' – there are few stronger sources of imagery than the opposition between these: sometimes formulated as 'nature' against 'culture,' as purity against corruption, as 'organic' against artificial society, sometimes as 'rural idiocy' or escapism against enlightenment or against the city seen as the arena for every decisive social conflict.

And in few countries has the country/city opposition entered more pervasively into central literary traditions. In Britain the world's first industrial revolution was preceded by a capitalist agrarian revolution. For generations, for centuries, money made in trade or in the city was invested in land. It was invested, at the same time, in status; and with landed status went identification with a certain group of supposedly rural values – the values of settlement, of paternal authority and care, of a bountiful and beautiful mode of agrarian production, and lesser values of hunting, horsemanship, attachment to country crafts. Around and within this repeated movement of wealth back to the countryseat there grew up a celebration of retrospective values – indeed, an entire way of feeling – whose supreme term of approval was 'old.' Good Old England!

As Williams shows, this structure of feeling was supported always by illusion. It was the newly rich and settled who were most anxious to be seen to have the status of settlement. Ben Jonson's idealised countryseat, Penshurst, 'rear'd with no man's ruine, no mans grone,' was in fact a manor which had been lost to its owners by execution and attainder fifty years before the poem was written, and had come into the possession of its new owners through court favour. Here we have lands seized from the Church; there we have the fruits of court faction; here again of successful commercial speculation. But it is not only that the 'old' settlements and seats have such ruthless origins; the illusion of old and simple country virtues can be sustained only by concealing the fact that the rural gentry are pursuing the same aggressive capitalist modes of exploitation – mediated by mortgages, advantageous marriage-settlements, rack-renting, or enclosure – in their normal agrarian relations.

The illusion, however, was so powerful that those writers who criticised the inhumanity of these practices did so only by clinging the more closely to rural fantasies. It was always the vulgar 'new' men who were coming into the country and disturbing 'good old' customary agrarian ways. From this there grew up an entire cultural myth, in which approved values always were seen as existing not here and now, but as vanishing into a recent past:

> Thus a humane instinct was separated from society: it became temporarily absent, or as the good old people succeeded by the bad new people – themselves succeeding themselves. We have heard this sad song for many centuries now: a seductive song, turning protest into retrospect, until we die of time.

For the humane retrospective compassion of Goldsmith's 'Deserted Village' this is just. But the myth, Williams argues, extended itself, by way of subtle transitions, to an artificial moral view, from which industrial capitalist society could itself be criticised. As the city came to be seen as corrupt, exploitive, atomised, so the country was seen as whatever was not-city – and hence pre-capitalist or not-capitalist. At this stage the rural myth becomes a main source for 'the perpetual retrospect to an "organic" or "natural" society':

> But it is also a main source for that last protecting illusion in the crisis of our own time: that it is not capitalism which is injuring us, but the more isolable, more evident system of urban industrialism.

To sustain this important argument it is right and necessary that the author should move simultaneously into political, cultural, and economic evidence. This he does, and with success. I found his evidence most convincing here when he was attending most closely to texts – notably in his discussions of Dickens and Hardy – and also in some of his very generalised, sinewy passages of historical argument. His social history is the history of a moralist with a profound sense of the process of capitalism.

At points where I would argue with him the history has not yet been adequately written. Thus Williams is right to question the myth that the enclosure movement of the eighteenth century displaced at a blow an 'organic' pre-capitalist community. The unenclosed open-field village at that time showed often only the husk of communal forms, while the grain within had long been eaten away by capitalist relations. But he overstates the case: and this may be because our historiography still fails to give an adequate account of the breaking of copy-hold and customary tenures, and the effective demise of the 'yeoman,' in the century before the maximum enclosure took place. The previous contests between the customary users of the land and the new market-exploiters had been very sharp. Although the enclosure of the commons was only the last episode of this struggle, the petty use-rights which were part of the subsistence economy of the poor and of the small men were still valued very highly. They were seen as the last resource of an 'independence,' and as such they became a symbol and entered into rural myth.

But the repeated contests over commons were not mythical. Nor was the feeling of a copy-hold farmer who faced the loss of generations of tenure merely nostalgic: he was giving up something valuable to him here and now, albeit based on inherited right. The defence of threatened rights or usages is not necessarily retrospective in any nostalgic sense. Most radical criticism of society, and especially of capitalist society with its repeated rationalisations, starts from such a sense of being threatened. The Luddites of 1811 were defending craft skills and the Clydeside engineers of 1917 or of 1971 were defending established craft positions.

What was wrong with this 'myth' of rural life was that it became softened, prettified, protracted, and then taken over by city-dwellers as a major point from which to criticise 'industrialism.' Thus it became a substitute for the utopian courage of imagining what a true community, in an industrial city might be – indeed of imaging how far community may have already been attained. England and the United States have different modes: we have different woods to go back to. But Williams would see the idealising of country life as a continuous cultural haemorrhage, a loss of rebellious blood, draining away now to Walden, now to Afghanistan, now to Cornwall, now to Mexico, the emigrants from cities solving nothing in their own countries, but kidding themselves that they had somehow opted out of contamination by a social system of which they are themselves the cultural artifacts. In a sombre late chapter he reminds us that the idyllic labourers, the Corins and Mertillas upon whom the myth was long sustained, are now the poor of Nigeria, Bolivia, Pakistan.

It is not of course the actual emigrations to the country that concern Williams but the intellectual or spiritual emigration from our own internal cultural complexities. His target here is a certain view of an old 'organic' society which did central service in the thought of F R Leavis, and which, at its worst, could turn every contemporary problem into a lament for the loss of older ways of social life, older language, older sensibility.

Regrettably the argument, which broadens and becomes more complex as it proceeds, appears to break up at the end. The compressed critical judgements become more abrupt, less supported by texts. This makes me uneasy. I have no objection to a critic writing as a moralist. Those who do object must discard not only Williams but also Trilling, Orwell, Lucien Goldmann, Edmund Wilson – indeed any writer who strays beyond the fences of the safely academic. But the literary judgments must carry critical conviction, and in these final chapters they are too compressed to do so.

There are other difficulties, Williams defines the capitalist process so inclusively that it becomes difficult to know if there is any cultural phenomenon of the past four hundred years which could not be found relevant to his theme. Capitalism, he argues,

is the mode of production, which is the basic process of what we know as the history of country and city. Its abstracted economic drives, its fundamental priorities in social relations, its criteria of growth and of profit and loss, have over several centuries altered our country and created our kinds of city. In its final forms of imperialism it has altered our world. Seeing the history in this way, I am then of course convinced that resistance to capitalism is the decisive form of the necessary human defence.

To this, and most of all to the final sentence, I assent. But then everything in four centuries of literature must relate in some way to this. Capitalism, like sin, is ever present; and if field labourers may escape the moralist's lash, since they are always in the last analysis the exploited, every other class, and its culture, becomes in some way contaminated by its covert or overt association with sin.

We need reminding of this truth: it takes us a little way. But only a little. For we live in society just as we live in our flesh. And it is within a more precise view of society that discriminations of value must usually begin. For if capitalism is the basic economic process of four centuries of history, there has been evidence throughout (and this is the challenge which socialist theory makes) of *human* processes that are alternatives to capitalism. We have to go on to ask: what form could a human protest take against an ongoing, all-triumphant economic process unless as 'retrospect'? And it is exactly this defence – of use values against money values, of affections and loyalties against the marketing of values, of idealised old community against new competition – that we find in some of the most interesting works of English literature. Williams, for example, could have looked more scrupulously than he does at the values at stake in that central Leavisite text, George Sturt's *Wheelwright's Shop.*

But the major omission in a book with this theme, is any central treatment of Wordsworth. There are perceptive pages on how Wordsworth saw the city. For the rest, we have little more than a comment upon 'The Old Cumberland Beggar,' a comment based on a selective reading, with which I am in disagreement and which does not come to terms with the central concern of the poem: its radical assault upon utilitarian attitudes.

Williams offers his reading of the poem as an index of the inauguration of a 'decisive phase' of country writing. But other, and no less decisive, issues have been overlooked. Williams has not examined Wordsworth's transposed Godwinism, his Jacobin-

ism of the primary affections and loyalties, situated (it is true) in
an idealised rural scene, which is strongly felt in the poetry of
1796–1806, and which institutes a far more decisive break with
the paternalist sensibility than anything to be found in Crabbe.
Even if some of the themes have been flogged to death, it is
still impossible to examine that profound and contradictory
complex of attitudes we find in Wordsworth without some
attention to Rousseau, the idea of Nature, Jacobinism versus
Godwinism.

This perhaps could not have been attempted in a book of this
sweeping scale. For after decades of Wordsworth scholarship, many
issues remain unclear. It is necessary to go back to the notebooks
and drafts of *The Prelude*: to observe how paternalist attitudes
excluded from 'The Ruined Cottage' were later stealthily restored
as the poem was revised for *The Excursion*. Without examining
such evidence one cannot understand how a certain tradition of
'nature' poetry could be a resource of defences against capitalist
Utilitarianism – defences far more intransigent than Williams
suggests.

I find two other major difficulties in the book's conclusion, but
these lie in the intractable nature of the problems being dealt with.
The first is posed by Williams himself. If resistance to capitalism
is 'the decisive form of the necessary human defence,' and if this
is properly seen as relevant to literary value, then to what social
ideals (as opposed to rural, 'organic,' and nostalgic ones) may this
resistance rally?

The difficulty, for this very political moralist, is, exactly,
political. Williams was never a Stalinist, nor was he ever much
attracted by orthodox Trotskyism. What he finds discouraging in
the dominant Marxist traditions is their sanctified catch-phrases
about 'rural idiocy'; their ambiguous assent to the 'progressive,'
rationalising character of capitalism; the strategic priority they
attribute to the role of an urban proletariat, all combining to reject
those emphases upon 'natural' process to which (with whatever
qualifications) Williams evidently remains stubbornly committed.
Thus Williams is on the side of use values as opposed to market
values, and he shares with his own labouring grandparents a
sympathy for certain traditional modes of human growth and

experience as opposed to the arbitrary rationalisations of administrators. But the loudest Marxist voices describe exactly these
preferences and sympathises as sentimentalism about 'rural idiocy';
while both capitalist and communist apologists are committed to
the arbitrary rationalisations of industrial bureaucracy.

Thus both orthodox communism and orthodox social democracy
shared, twenty-five years ago, the same intellectual priorities as
capitalist thought itself – a contempt for rural backwardness (which
could only too easily justify imperialist exploitation) and a practical
acceptance of the division and opposition between town and
country, manual and mental labour. Such arguments were used to
justify Stalin's 'victory' over the kulaks, which Williams sees as
'one of the most terrible phases in the whole history of rural
society.'

But to recognise this, twenty or thirty years ago, was to
recognise also that there was no social force to which one's
aspirations could be attached. It was 'to be pressed back toward the
extreme subjectivism and fatalism which then, and for a generation,
dominated our thought.' The deadlock, he suggests, has been
breaking up in practice, as, following the Chinese example,
revolutionary agrarian movements have, in the 'undeveloped' world,
enforced change upon the cities: and, ultimately, have challenged
the 'developed' world itself. But the deadlock remains within the
culture of the developed world – and not least within the minds of
an urban Marxist intelligentsia – which remains assured of its own
priorities. One objective of this book is to help break this deadlock.

Which leaves us with a final difficulty – not overlooked by
Williams, but the most critical of all. For we are trapped, as he has
shown, within certain structures of feeling: the prevailing rationalising urban mode on the one hand, the evasive, retrospective rural
mode on the other. And you can't *argue* people into a new
structure of feeling. What is needed, at the end of this book, is not
an argument but a poem or a novel: *Border Country* rewritten from
the author's new standpoint.

Perhaps an English canvass would be too narrow for this. The
evidence for a new structure of feeling is unlikely to be found in a
island whose peasantry is a memory and whose beautiful countryside is regarded in an urban consciousness as a park land to be

maintained by farmers but to be conserved for urban aesthetic consumption.

Williams tries to redress the picture by inserting a late discursive chapter surveying writing from the former colonial world. But the survey is too compressed. All the major novels of agrarian life in this century come from outside the British Isles. And even in the densely urbanised United States there are traditions of writing which might have enabled Williams to define more exactly the changed structure of feeling for which he is in search. One thinks of the first book of Thomas McGrath's *Letter to an Imaginary Friend* [1] that record of the growth of a twentieth-century poet's mind, a *Prelude* in which the mountain shepherd (or Frost's New England variant of the Cumberland 'statesman') is displaced by the combine harvester and the conflicts of Wobbly organisation in North Dakota. This is a landscape, whether urban or rural (and McGrath's imagery serves to break down conventional dichotomies and to emphasise unitary experiences both of exploitation and of resistance) under 'the continual wind of money, that blows the birds through the clocks.' At the end of this book, McGrath returns to Dakota from the city, with a retrospect seen in a way which Williams perhaps might approve. 'It is not *my* past that I mourn – *that* I can never lose'.

> – No, but the past of this place and the place itself and what was: the Possible Future that never arrived ...

For the past, and especially the rural past, needn't always be seen retrospectively, in a lament over old and dying modes which, when examined scrupulously, were never real. It may also be seen as a vast reserve of unrealised, or only partially achieved, possibilities – a past that gives us glimpses of other possibilities of human nature, other ways of behaving (even 'organic' ones). There are passages of Wordsworth which can too easily be faulted by contrasting them with the reports on Cumberland of the Poor Law Commissioners. For these passages could also be read as the evocation of 'the future that never arrived,' which offered just enough evidence, in a rite of neighbourhood, in a traditional skill, to furnish fuel for a poet's imagination.

I don't think Williams would disagree. Nor would he disagree that his themes must be pursued far beyond his own national exploration. For if his material is largely national, the moral inquiry which informs his book is not. It remains part of that stubborn, uncompromising clarification of socialist thought which historians will come to see as more important and more lasting in influence than better advertised products of the international new left. There is something in the unruffled stamina of this man which suggests a major thinker. The very awkwardness of his style is that of a mind which must always find its own way. The idiom is too English to fall easily into international discourse; but I believe that in time it will.

From the *New York Review of Books*, reviewing *The Country and the City* by Raymond Williams. Oxford University Press.

Note
1   Swallow Press, 1970.

George Sturt

One of my English teachers at school was strongly influenced by F.R. Leavis and he introduced his pupils to this book. That will have been (for me) around 1939. For George Sturt (1863–1927), writing under the name 'George Bourne,' was warmly approved of by Leavis, and several of his books – notably *Change in the Village* (1912) and *The Wheelwright's Shop* (1923) – were commended in the Leavisite canon, not only for their lucid and economical English but also as exemplars of 'the organic community.'

For example in *Culture and Environment* (1933), Leavis and Denys Thompson wrote:

> Sturt's villagers expressed their human nature, they satisfied their human needs, in terms of the natural environment; and the things they made – cottages, barns, ricks, and waggons – together with their relations with one another constituted a human environment, and a subtlety of adjustment and adaptation ...

This was contrasted with the mechanical organisation of modern industrial society, in which work is 'meaningless' to most workers, 'merely something they have to do in order to earn a livelihood' and to gain some leisure; and hence the leisure, exploited by all the resources of commercial society, is meaningless also. Raymond Williams in *Culture and Society* (1958), while praising the 'original and valuable' observation in Sturt's books, contested the uses to which the Leavisites put his work as 'myth,' 'a late version of medievalism, with its attachments to an 'adjusted' feudal society .... If there is one thing certain about 'the organic community,' it is that it has always gone.' However this argument (which still continues in new forms) is resolved, *The Wheelwright's Shop* continues on in its independent life.

But it is worth remembering that we owe the recognition of the book as a classic to literary critics rather than to social historians, and historians should be grateful to literary critics for their percipience. This accords well with Sturt's own inclination. He became owner and manager of a wheelwright's shop, not by choice but through force of circumstance. He always saw himself as a writer, and this is abundantly clear in his journals.[1] Also, at the time of his initiation into the wheelwright's trade, in the years 1884–90 upon the recollection of which much of this book is based, he saw himself as a revolutionary socialist. Sturt does not tell us this, although there is a reference to 'my Ruskinian absurdities.'

In the early 1950s, while researching a book on William Morris, I was surprised to come across a number of articles by George Sturt in the journal of the Socialist League, *Commonweal*. These commence with a letter (5 February 1887) deploring the attacks which *Justice* and *Commonweal* made upon each other: a protest on behalf of 'we Socialists in small towns or villages, who, from our isolated position, feel especially the need of unity and good-feeling.' They conclude with a brief note on 18 January 1890. In between is a series of articles of no particular distinction, several of which give the impression of being literary exercises. If one looks for any closely observed passages on labour or on country life one will be disappointed. The more successful pieces are polemics with the comfortable anti-socialist lampoons of the time. The Gatling gun gets a roasting: 'Think of it, you Christians, and invest your money! For every dead nigger will help to swell your dividends!' (12 May 1888). But the impression left is most un-Sturt-like: of a theoretic socialism, which had little engagement or traffic with experience. In a long letter (20 April 1889) he referred to Ruskin ('to whom I owe it that I am a Socialist') but also declared himself an Anarchist, with strong sympathy for Communism. It is not clear why he discontinued his contributions – or perhaps the editor of *Commonweal* no longer accepted them? His last article was on 21 December 1889, recommending in an overblown and patronising manner the work of the Ruskin Reading Guild: this is not a theme likely to commend itself to the excitable anarchists who were taking over the Socialist League.

Much of the rest of Sturt's life can be read in the *Journals*, or inferred from them. He once claimed, in a letter to Arnold Bennett, that the journal is 'the best book I shall ever write.' It is not. When he commenced it he was heavily under the influence of Thoreau and, to a lesser degree, Emerson and Whitman. It is curious that little direct influence of William Morris can be detected: in 1892 he deplored the contemporary 'fantastic reversions to old methods' and attempts to revive 'traditions dead and gone,' and instanced Morris's Kelmscott Press. But Sturt was not at that time consciously reflecting on traditional skills. The character of the early *Journals* is self-consciously and sometimes pretentiously 'literary,' and it would be possible for an inattentive reader to hurry through the early years unaware that the author was in the throes of apprenticing himself to a highly skilled trade. There is one sentence, in November 1890, it is true, which suggests the germ of *The Wheelwright's Shop*:

> It has come to my mind, that an account, however scrappy, of my relations with the men at work for me would somewhen be interesting, – even perhaps of some value.[2]

But the book, when it came thirty-odd years later is never scrappy, and the entry suggests that Sturt was at that time less interested in the work and transmitted skills than in his managerial functions and 'the misery of being a Socialist employer of labour.'[3] His early *Journals* are largely made up of studious exercises in the description of weather, light, and landscape, notes on his reading, and pseudo-philosophical reflections upon such topics as Art, Duty and Self-Realisation.

The wheelwright's business is sensed, off-stage, as a distraction from his literary vocation. Minor disputes with his workers about time-keeping and so on caused him excessive irritation. Customers were worse:

> If I could carry on business without customers, I think I shouldn't *hate* it (though I might get deadly sick of it). A low meanminded lot, always looking to take advantage of you.[4]

As early as January 1891 he was trying to sell the business.

What began to change was not the workshop but George Sturt. There are gaps in his *Journals* for most of 1893 and all of 1894. They resume in 1895 with a major new character, Frederick Grover, whose recollections filled up much of the *Journals* until Grover's death in September 1905. Grover (or 'Bettesworth') was an old villager whom Sturt employed as gardener and handyman at his cottage near Farnham; he was full of conversation about country lore, traditions and skills. He was Sturt's tutor, teaching him to observe more closely and also to write in a new way. Among the fruits of this new influence were *The Bettesworth Book* (1901), *Memoirs of a Surrey Labourer* (1907), *Change in the Village* (1912) and *Lucy Bettesworth* (1913). It is not too much to say that Grover took Sturt out of his self-preoccupied literary mannerisms and taught him to listen and to watch the world around him.

For Sturt became an excellent listener and observer, as this book testifies. Increasingly his *Journals* carry entries like this one (October 1908):

> My uncle last week gave me the following names for the different parts of a flail:
>
> 1. Handstaff.
>
> 2. Start (a metal knob or button in the end of the handstaff).
>
> 3. Capping (a piece of bent wood fastened over the capping (*start?*) apparently with a slot in it to receive the thong on to the start).
>
> 4. Middle-band (the leather thong uniting the two staves).
>
> 5. Swingle (Pronounced with a soft g. This is the other staff).

He was concerned to record in exact detail tools, their operation, and the materials operated on. This took him into dimensions of 'epistemology' which the academic mind, now as then, rarely enters or even allows for. It is the formation of knowledge, not from theory, but from practice and practical transmission, from the ground up. The skilled workman is taught by his materials, and their resources and qualities enter through his hand and thence to his mind. The artefact takes it form from the functions it must perform, the 'dish' of a wheel from the movement of the horses, the ruts in the tracks, the weight of the average load. These are not finely calculated on paper, they are learned through practice.

Sturt, as he records this, is always aware of the wider implications for the less practical reader. The skills must have emerged with the invention of the wheel, in pre-historic times; indeed, some must have preceded this. Sturt plays sometimes with the notion of the memory of 'the race' and of the wandering 'tribes' who first brought their skills to England. (His *Journals*, at the time when he was writing this book, have many reflections on the Group Life and the Group Understanding.) But at a time when academic hubris has never been higher, it is of great value to have this whole mode of transmission and of learning – which applied in all trades, including the skills of domestic homework, and which still applies in many today – recorded with such observation and truth. One learns from Sturt of the multiplicity of skills which must be acquired by a 'tradesman' in any craft, skills often assumed or passed over unseen in the single word, 'apprenticeship'; as one also learns of the many skills that must be combined to make a single artefact, such as a farm waggon: felling and carrying timber, seasoning, the work of sawyer, the work of the foreman or manager in selecting timber of the right kind and grain, the work of the wheelwright with his many skills, and then the skills of the blacksmith.

There has been, in heavy theoretical fields, much discussion about 'at the point of production,' a point defined in theory but not in observation. It is, then, refreshing to find Sturt at the end of his life, insisting upon the closest attention to 'the Moment of Production, when the Craftsman is actually getting his effects – this Moment which has been at the heart of Village life or of all the labour of Peasants ...' – a moment (Sturt implies) neglected or misunderstood by most academic minds:

At the very moment of change, when the effort actually comes off and has its effect – this keeps the 'peasant' more or less satisfied, but 'superior' people never experience that satisfaction.

The moment of effectiveness, when skill is changing the raw
material into the desired product is always worth 'realising.'
It is momentous every time ....[5]

There is something heroic about the writing of this book. As Sturt
indicates in his Preface, he was paralysed by a stroke in 1916, and
despite some recovery successive lesser strokes followed. Yet the
next ten years were productive, and, with much help from his
unmarried sisters, Mary and Susan, he persisted with his work with
much fortitude. He was confined in the main to his bed or to a
chair, his powers of speech were impaired, but until his final year
he could still write legibly. There is an entry in his *Journals* that
suggests that the major themes of this book were assembled in his
mind by 30 January 1919.[6] He must have commenced the book in
that year, and despite two more strokes in 1920, he was writing the
last note to the book on 12 May 1921. Over a year later he found
a publisher in the Cambridge University Press, but his constant
helper, Mary, had then died.

It is a superb and necessary contribution to cultural theory,
social history and (in its upside-down way) epistemology. It was
Sturt who made the best comment on his own lucid style: 'all I am
conscious of is the effort to get very close home to a subject, to be
very truthful in dealing with it, even to the faintest cadence.'[7] This
commended the book to sensitive critics, and it should still
commend it today. One should also note the elegaiac mood in
which many passages are written. This may come in part from
Sturt's sense of loss at the passing of ancient trades and customs.
And it also comes from Sturt's recognition of the passing of his
own health and strength. The book, after all, records in the main
his experiences in his twenties. And many passages – for example,
when he recalls opening up the workshop at six o'clock on a cold
winter morning, or his visits to the woods to inspect and measure
timber – reveal both the pleasure and the pain of recalling lost
youth. As he was confined by paralysis he seems to have been able
to rehearse past activities with the greatest veracity. What might
seem to be 'things' recalled the makers of those things and the
environment: 'the repairs to "rollers" are singularly pleasant to
remember, so suggestive are they of summer and country roads'.

When the time came for repairs,

> You felt as if you were on a dusty road then. For road-dust lay in the wheel-track which the roller so closely followed; hot summer road-dust rose in clouds from the horse hoofs and smothered the roller. No doubt there was sometimes mud, yet that was not what you thought of when you saw the roller, or at any rate what I remember now.

So writing *The Wheelwright's Shop* was a resource which enabled Sturt to endure his disabilities and equally his disabilities enabled him to find the patience to retrace all those activities of his youth. Cultural theorists may have been wrong to make an 'organic community' out of all this: testimony from other sources of evidence is less reassuring. But they are wholly right to see this as a work of classical distinction, whose testimony must weigh heavily in the scales of judgement.

Foreword to re-issue of *The Wheelwright's Shop* (Cambridge, 1992).

Notes

1. His *Journals* continued from 1890 until the year of his death, 1927, and they have been edited in two volumes by E.D. Mackerness, and published by Cambridge University Press, 1967.
2. Ibid., I, p. 62.
3. Ibid., I, p. 127.
4. Ibid., I, pp. 98–9.
5. Ibid., II, pp. 879–80, November 1926.
6. II, p. 816.
7. Ibid., II, p. 868.

The Grid of Inheritance

The essays in this volume have told us a great deal about the sociological texture of given communities and about existent relationships within them, as exemplified by their inheritance practices. We have perhaps learned less about process over time, since intentions in inheritance systems, as in other matters, often eventuate in conclusions very different from those intended. If we anatomize inheritance systems in a condition of stasis, it is possible for the mind to assent to a fallacy which, in our waking hours, we know very well to be untrue – that what is being inherited remains a historical constant: 'property', 'ownership', or, more simply, 'the land' – land which, after all, did pass on from generation to generation, which is still there for us to walk over, which may even carry today much the same kind of crops or timber or stock as three hundred years ago.

Of course we know that this constancy is illusory. In land what is being transmitted through inheritance systems is very often not so much property in the land as property in the usufruct, or a place within a complex gradation of coincident use-rights. It is the tenure – and sometimes functions and roles attached to the tenure – which is being transmitted. Perhaps a little light may be thrown backwards upon what was being transmitted by considering aspects of the decomposition of certain kinds of tenure in England in the eighteenth century.

It is difficult to estimate the proportion of landholdings governed by copyhold or by other forms of customary tenure in the years from the Restoration to the mid eighteenth century – the period which is generally accepted as the classic period for the accelerated decline of the 'yeoman'. We should remember that there are two different totals to be counted: the acres and the farmers. It is not difficult to find, in the early eighteenth century, manors in which the average size of customary holdings was small, so that the acreage of freehold or of land subject to non-customary economic rental greatly exceeded the acreage in copyhold, but in which the total number of customary farmers exceeded the number of freeholders or of tenants-at-will. The point is important, since the economic historian may find that the clues to expanding agrarian process lie in the 'free' sector, while the social historian may find that the psychological horizons and expectations of the majority of the farming community lie still within the customary sector.[1]

Without attempting any quantitative assessment it will be sufficient, for this comment, to emphasise that the survival of customary tenure into the eighteenth century was very considerable: in very many private manors: in Church and collegiate lands: in Crown lands, forest areas, etc.[2] It is also my impression that there was, from the 1720s onwards, some revival of careful court-keeping, and considerable activity in the field of customary law. This had nothing to do with some unlocated 'reaction' or with antiquarian sentiment. Customs of manors were scrutinized in new ways by stewards and by lawyers, whose employers saw property in new and more marketable ways. Where custom inhibited rack-renting, 'fringe' use-rights – timber, mineral-rights, stone, peat and turves – might assume even greater importance for the manorial lord anxious to improve his revenue. In general agricultural improvement and the enlargement of the market economy meant that customary use-rights had a more valuable cash equivalent than before, if only they could be prised loose from their sociological and tenurial context.

Despite the consolidation at law of rights of copyhold in the late fourteenth and fifteenth centuries, these were not of course absolute. If copyhold could be sold, mortgaged, bequeathed in any direction (although not according to the custom of all manors), it could still be forfeited for felony and for waste: and it was on occasion so forfeited.[3] Tenures unsecured by a will or by a clear lineage of heritable descent, according to the custom of the manor, could fall back into the hands of the lord. Where tenancies for lives were predominant, as in some parts of western England, the eighteenth century may have seen greater insecurity of tenure. Such tenures were copyhold (in the sense that they were held by copy of the court roll) but they remained tenancies-at-will and subject to arbitrary fines at the entry of new lives.[4] Perhaps such insecure tenures were increasing.[5] Where fines were truly arbitrary this could effectively enforce insecurity of tenure: thus at Whiston and Caines (Worcs.) it was reported in 1825 that 'the customary tenants have been copyholders of inheritance until within these hundred years ... But for many years past the tenants have been constrained to fine at the lord's pleasure; and some to let their inheritance be granted over their heads, for want of ability to pay such great fines as were required of them, or to try their rights with the lords.'[6] In other Worcestershire manors there is an evident tension between 'custom' in the sense of practices and expectations, and custom as enforceable in terms of law. At Hartlebury the custom is 'to grant one life in possession, and three in reversion, and to alter and change at the will of the lord; when three lives are dropt the lord may grant the estate to whom he pleases; though the tenants claim the first offer'.[7]

But in general customary tenures in the eighteenth century appear to have been falling away through a process of attrition rather than through any frontal assault from landowners and the law. (Since many substantial landowners themselves had an interest in copyhold, through purchase or inheritance, the form of tenure was by no means coterminous with the interests of the yeoman or husbandman). If the lord or his steward could see an advantage in bringing the land back into hand, either to set it out again in an economic leasehold or in anticipation of enclosure, they had opportunities to hasten on the process. Fines on entry or on surrenders could be forced up, based upon the improved rather than upon the customary rents, and these could hasten a copyholder's career towards indebtedness. The well-situated copyholder could claim equal security of tenure with the freeholder. But he could of course claim no *greater* security. Both were equally subject to those vagaries of economic or familial situation which could lead them to mortgage their lands and to heap debts upon the heads of their sons. And, when we discuss inheritance systems, we should not forget that one of their important functions in some peasant and petty tenurial societies was precisely to ensure security down the generations for the landlord's or moneylender's interest upon the farmer's debt.

Customary tenure is seen, very often, in its legal status only, as defined as case-law. But custom always had a sociological dimension also, and one recognized at law in the reservation 'according to the custom of the manor'. This can perhaps be seen most clearly in the in-between world of Church and collegiate tenures. Such tenures did not have the security of copyhold, nor can they be regarded as tenancies-at-will. The definition is not one at law but in customary usage. The historian of the finances of St John's College, Cambridge, comments (on the seventeenth and early eighteenth centuries):

> For some reason the College over a long period appears to have acted on the assumption that it was precluded from varying the rents of its estates. It is not possible to discover an entirely satisfying ground for this assumption. So far as is known it rests on no legal basis ...[8]

But he goes on to show that successive Bursars found ways of overcoming their inhibitions from the first quarter of the eighteenth century; and the increase in revenue came first of all from fines.[9]

The reason for this situation lies less in law than in a certain balance of social relations. From 1576 ('Sir Thomas Smith's Act' of 18 Elizabeth) Church and college tenures were normally limited to three lives and 21 years, with renewals expected every seventh year. Undoubtedly Church tenures, as well as royal and manorial over-rights in forest areas, had been deeply shaken in the Interregnum. After the Restoration, the Church scrutinized all tenures and raised substantial fines upon those which were confirmed. These tenants, and their children, no doubt felt that they had paid for the security of a copyhold. Their tenure had (it was argued) 'by long Custom become Hereditary, purchased almost as dear as Freeholds, from the Confidence reposed in their Landlords of Renewals on customary Terms'.[10] But the security of tenure was never endorsed at law. Church and college tenures remained as 'beneficial' lease, in which the right of renewal at a 'reasonable' fine was assumed but not prescribed.

That fines became less 'reasonable' after 1720 was a consequence of the Whig ascendancy, and the greed of the Whig bishops.[11] The raising of fines of course encountered resistance: a steward will report (as one reported to St John's from Windlesham, Surrey, in 1726) 'the Homage insisted that my demands were very extraordinary'.[12] On such a matter the homage could usually be overruled. But to overrule or alienate a homage was not quite as simple a matter as it may appear to our eyes – eyes which have long been habituated to seeing property-rights overruling functions and needs. These were the farmers, large and small, on the spot, and a distant corporate manorial owner found it necessary to work in some cooperation with them.[13] The steward of College or Church might encounter, on some matter of antagonistic interest, a conspiracy of silence among the tenants. In 1687 an informant wrote to the Bursar of St John's about one estate:

> I cannot learn what life is in it, I am told by some 'tis an old woman in Suffolke and by others that two old women have their lives in it. They possibly may be dead, and the thing conceal'd ...[14]

The Bursar was at a loss to obtain true information about matters in other manors. When he sought to secure the help of the incumbent of the College's living at Ipsden, asking him to enquire into matters at Northstoke (Oxon) in 1683, the vicar was thrown into a paroxysm of alarm. There would be 'suspition and great jealousies' if he was known to report to the College: his 'affections to the College' already made him suspect. As to one enquiry:

> This is thing of so tender a nature that if there be given any shadow of suspicion I am unserviceable for ever, for it is the maxim of the country people to be very silent to these ... and it is in all virtue among them, to be vindificative [sic] where their Interest is affected ...

Even to set this down in writing made the poor gentleman sweat: 'I desire to hear that my letter cometh safely to your hand, I shall be in paine till I am assured thereof ...'[15]

A rich bishopric, like Winchester, was better equipped with a bureaucracy of stewards, woodwards, etc., to deal with such problems. St John's (and no doubt other colleges) got round the problem in the eighteenth century by leasing whole manors to prosperous laymen.

But in the seventeenth century the beneficial lease still involved non-economic mutualities, and even some paternal responsibilities. In 1610 Joan Lingard, a widow of over seventy, was petitioning the Master of St John's on a delicate matter. Her tenure (described as a copyhold) was by virtue of her widow's 'free bench' in the right of her first husband. But in the interval of twenty years since this husband's decease she had married twice more and had been left twice more a widow. Her second and third husbands continued the tenancy of the land, but in her widow's right. She had no issue by her first husband, and now wished to surrender her copyhold to her eldest son, by her second husband: her son had convenanted to reserve for her use a tenement 'together with other helpes towardes my maintenance during my life ...'[16] Tenure is here being sought as descending through the widow's right: presumably this was contrary to the custom of the manor, and for this reason the permission of the Master and Fellows was solicited.

In the case of beneficial leases, renewal of tenure was not of right, but it appears to have been difficult to refuse. We still understand only imperfectly the tenacity and force of local custom. In a lease for three lives or 21 years surrenders must be made and fines paid for the renewal of years or lives with regularity. If the renewal was left over for more than seven years, the fine was raised in proportion. The balance between custom and courtesy here is illustrated by a letter to the College in 1630 from an old student of St John's, soliciting charity for a poor widow, his own kinswoman. She was the relict of a tenant whose lease was within four years of expiry, and she doubted whether the College would renew because of the tardy application. 'Peradventure', her kinsman wrote, 'you may thinke that hir husband and his son, both now with God, had noe purpose to be suitors to your Colledge in renewing theire lease in regard they detracted and let their lease weare out almost to the stumps.' But (he explained) her husband had had a lingering illness, had left debts, and six small children; while the son – a seventh child – had enjoyed only one year's tenure, during which time he had settled his father's debts, and then himself died, leaving a widow and three children in his turn. The widow so circumstanced could clearly not pay the high fine due at a point so close to the expiry of the lease. The charity of the Master and Fellows was invoked, in the name of 'the vowes and prayers of widdowes and fatherles children'.[17]

In theory beneficial leases could be allowed to run out, unrenewed, and the Church or collegiate owner could bring all back into its own hands, in order to lease the land out once again at its 'improved' or market value. This did happen on occasion, where only a few tenants were involved.[18] But it entailed an immediate loss of revenue – the existing lives and leases must be run through, and meanwhile there would be no revenue from fines.[19] This required an active, exploitive owner, or a rich one with several manors in hand. It also required an expansionist agriculture in which suitable new tenants, with capital on hand, were available. Moreover, where rights in usufruct extended over common lands – and this included upon fields held in severalty but over which lammas grazing rights existed, etc. – the tenants, if they briefed a good lawyer, could prevent the manorial owner from entering into his land until the last lease had fallen in. For the 'inheritance' which we have here is that of communal use-rights, governed by the custom of the manor, and secured at law. When the College determined to regain possession of one manor in 1700, it was advised that this could not take place until the death of the last survivor – 'namely the lives then in being and the last widdowe ...' Serjeant Wright of the Temple added: 'The Tenants must now spit on their hands and live as long as they can, and the estates will be good to them to the end of the last life and widdow's estate ...'[20] Only then could the College accomplish its proposed rationalization, reletting the land at economic leases for 21 years.

By the early eighteenth century we have the sense that there was a deepening (albeit submerged and confused) conflict as to the very nature of landed property, a widening gap between definitions at law and in local custom – and by custom I do not mean only what the custumal may say but the denser reality of social practice. In Berkshire and in Hampshire in the 1720s, conflict over turves, grazing, timber-rights and over the raids by deer upon the farmers' corn, contributed to episodes of armed disturbance.[21] But my point, in this comment, is only to emphasize that it is not helpful to discuss inheritance systems unless we keep always in mind what it is that is being inherited. If we refer vaguely to 'land' then at once anachronistic images spring to mind of the patrimonial farm, with its ancient olives or its well-drained pastures, laboriously-built sheepfolds or spreading oaks. But in many of the farming systems under consideration inheritance of tenure was not so much the passage of land from one generation to the next (although certain closes and tenements might so pass) as the inheritance of use-rights over land (sometimes inherited only as security upon debt), some of which rights might be held in severalty, much of which was subject to at least some communal and manorial control and regulation.

There is a distinction here in social psychology. The farmer, confronted with a dozen scattered strips in different lands, and with prescribed stints in the commons, did not (one supposes) feel fiercely that he *owned* this land, that it was *his*. What he inherited was a place within the hierarchy of use-rights; the right to send his beasts, with a follower, down the lane-sides, to tether his horse in the sykes or on the baulks, the right to unloose his stock for lammas grazing, or for the cottager the right to glean and to get away with some timber-foraging and casual grazing. All this made up into a delicate agrarian equilibrium. It depended not only upon the inherited right but also upon the inherited grid of customs and controls within which that right was exercised. This customary grid was as intrinsic to inheritance as the grid of banking and of the stock exchange is to the inheritance of money. Indeed one could say that the beneficiary inherited both his right *and* the grid within which it was effectual: hence he must inherit a certain kind of social or communal psychology of ownership: the property not of his family but of his-family-within-the-commune.

Thus alongside the 'Cartesian' logic of differing inheritance systems we must place the complementary logic of differing agrarian practices and tenures: and then assess the impact of the logic of the market, of capitalist agrarian practices. For what my scattered illustrations of the operation of some tenurial system shows, at the point of decomposition, is (1) the reification of use-right and its divorce from the actuality of use. An old woman whose death may be concealed is a property, albeit of uncertain value. Stints, abandoned messuages and tenements to which common rights are attached, the reversion of lives, may be bought and sold, independent of the user, just as dove-cots or pig-styes may be bought and sold for the burgage-rights attached to them. (2) The grid itself which validates the exercise of these rights is becoming increasingly insecure. The reification of the rights of some may mean in practice the limitation of the rights of the rest of the community. In extreme cases the manorial owner may be able to extinguish the grid without recourse to enclosure, although if his customary tenants know their law and have the stomach and purses to take recourse to it, the grid will survive as long as the last surviving customary tenant or his widow. As the grid becomes threatened, the small man (the copyholder or the freeholder with common rights appurtenant) must calculate his advantages. Enclosure may bring absolute freehold heritable rights, as well as the extinction of some petty customary claims over their land by the poor. But it may also threaten the equilibrium of crop and stock, in which the old grid carried many advantages. Some of these advantages were those sanctioned in practice in the village, although they could not be sustained at law.[22] (3) There is some evidence of the breaking-apart in the seventeenth and early eighteenth centuries of the agrarian inheritance system (conceived of as a body of rules enshrined in case-law) and the received customary traditions and practices of the village.

This breaking-apart lay along the lines of socio-economic cleavage, between the greater and the lesser rights of usage. Kerridge has identified the advance of capitalist process with greater security of tenure:

> To assert that capitalism throve on unjust expropriations is a monstrous and malicious slander. Security of property and tenure answered capitalism's first and most heartfelt need. Where insecurity reigned, it was because of the absence, not of the advent or presence of capitalism.[23]

No doubt, for tenures and rights of substance, the judgement is true. But to the degree that substantial usages were defined and secured, the insubstantial usages were disallowed. Kerridge (and many others) step bravely into a self-fulfilling argument, whose premises are entailed in its conclusions. Those usages which the law subsequently endorsed and secured as rights (such as heritable copyhold) are seen as genuine and lawful usages, those usages which the law subsequently disallowed are seen as pretended rights or illicit intrusions upon the rights of others. And yet it was the law itself which allowed one and disallowed the other; for it was the law which served as a superb instrument for enforcing the reification of right and for tearing down the remnants of the threadbare communal grid. At the outset of the seventeenth century the judgement in Gateward's Case both confirmed the customary rights of copyholders and disallowed those of vaguer categories – 'inhabitants', 'residents': if the latter were to be allowed their claims upon use-rights, then 'no improvements can be made in any wastes'.[24] But still in many areas indefinite rights of 'inhabitants' prevailed until demographic pressure or the realities of local power resulted in their extinguishment or their tighter regulation by by-law. In many forest areas – among them Windsor, the New Forest, the Forest of Dean – large and ill-defined rights were claimed throughout the eighteenth century, and they appear to have been effectively exercised.[25] How far this situation obtained depended upon factors peculiar to each region and each manor.[26] But where the appeal was made to law the decisions moved in one direction: that of reification and limitation.

Copyhold itself, as an alienable property with a cashable monetary equivalent, had been very widely secured by the sixteenth century, partly because many men of substantial property and interest had a stake in this kind of tenure themselves. During the eighteenth century it became of more evident advantage to such men to bring into their own hands messuages which would carry at enclosure, substantial common-right values. But as the indefinite rights of the poor were excluded, so what may be called the fringe-benefits of the communal grid were extinguished. In a Chancery decision of 1741 an indefinite claim by 'occupants' to enjoy the right of turbary was disallowed in the tradition of 'Gateward's Case': the claim was found to be 'a very great absurdity, for an occupant, who is no more than a tenant at will, can never have a right to take away the soil of the lord'.[27] Similar judgements extended over other fringe rights. In 1788 the claim of 'poor, necessitous and indigend householders' in Whaddon (Bucks.) to take dead wood in the local coppice was disallowed since 'there is no limitation ... the description of poor householder is too vague and uncertain ...'[28] The famous decision against gleaning in the same year did not of course extinguish (unless here and there) the *practice* of gleaning. What it did was to extinguish the claim of the villagers to glean *as of right*, even though that right may be seen clearly defined in dozens of early manorial by-laws.[29] Hence, at a stroke of the pen, a most ancient use-right was decreed to be uncashable at law – might one use such an ugly concept as *un*reified?

This law evolved from a Baconian and not a Cartesian mind. It is a law which resisted (as Blackstone proclaimed with proud chauvinism)[30] the influence of Justinian and of the revival of Roman law in general. Its precedents were piecemeal: it evolved with empirical caution. But behind this empirical evolution one may detect the no-less-Cartesian logic of capitalist evolution. Coke's decision in 'Gateward's Case' rested less upon legal than upon economic logic – 'no improvements can be made in any wastes'. The judges sought to reduce use-rights to an equivalent in things or in money, and hence to bring them within the universal currency of capitalist definitions of ownership. Property must be made palpable, loosed for the market from its uses and from its social situation, made capable of being hedged and fenced, of being owned quite independently of any grid of custom or of mutuality. As between substantial rights, and even as between the greater and the lesser of such rights, the law was impartial: it was tender of property of whatever degree. What it abhorred was an indefinite sociological praxis, a *coincidence* of several use-rights, unreified usages. And this English law, following upon the heels of the Pilgrim Fathers and of the John Company, attempted to reify and translate into terms of palpable property ownership the customs and usages of whole peoples which had inherited communal grids of a totally different character.

The consequences in these cases were far-reaching. The bearing

upon the problem of inheritance in England was more subtle. Any
system of impartible inheritance in an agrarian system which has
ceased to expand must be subject to a delicate demographic equilibrium. The fringe-benefits of the grid are not things distinct from the
transmitted tenurial rights. Some laxness in the definition of rights of
grazing, gleaning, firing, etc., can help to support the sons who do not
inherit tenures, stock and implements. With these benefits extinguished, the excess population may be reduced to a landless proletariat or ejected like lemmings from the community. One need not
propose a simple typological model of a 'swapping' equilibrium, one
son inheriting, one daughter married to a tenant or freeholder, half a
son or daughter remaining to be provided for. It is rather that we have
to take the total context together; the inheritance customs, the
actuality of what was being inherited, the character of the economy,
the manorial by-laws or field regulations, the poor law. If in the
fifteenth and sixteenth centuries younger children sometimes inherited
beasts or implements (but no land) we must assume that they
expected access to land somehow. If (as I suppose) in the same
centuries communal agrarian regulation became tighter, excluding
those without land from certain unacknowledged but practised grazing rights, then to the same degree what the occupier inherited
became better, what the younger child had left to him became worse.
The yeoman is advantaged: it is less easy for his brother to make do
as a husbandman or a craftsman with a few sheep and a cow on the
common. What matters then becomes the inheritance of capital, for
both land and stints on the common may still be rented.

In certain areas, such as forests, the fringe-benefits may be so large
as to afford a livelihood of sorts for many younger brothers, and even
immigrants. This will also be so in areas where a scanty agrarian
income may be supplemented by developing domestic industries and
crafts. Such areas, one might suppose, favoured practices of partible
inheritance – practices which cannot be deduced from the registration
of tenures in the court-roll. The successor who enters upon the tenure
may be seen (from the evidence of the will) to be acting as trustee for
the widow [31] or, as trustee for the children whose portions are to be
divided 'share and share alike'.[32] Forms may grow up whereby the
lives in being [33] or reversionary [34] entered in the court-roll are
fictitious. The actual practices of inheritance, as evidenced by wills,

may be completely at odds with the recited customs of the manor; and even where custom specifically enforced the impartibility of a tenure, devices could be arranged to circumvent custom.[35]

In Windsor Forest in the early years of the eighteenth century there is a little evidence of such practices of partible inheritance.[36] Percy Hatch, a yeoman of Winkfield, with about 70 acres (mostly in freehold) sought in 1727 to benefit his four sons and a married daughter.[37]

In this (p. 344) the oldest son is clearly advantaged, although the other sons receive some money in compensation. The second son, who is charged with his sister's dowry, is also advantaged, but as

	House	Land	Furniture	Money
1st Son	Messuage & Farmhouse, 'Sumertons'	27½ acres & 4 doles of land in common fields	Furnace Clothes- press Biggest spit Malt mill	–
2nd Son	Messuage & Farmhoue, 'Berkshire House'	c. 14 acres	–	£30 [a]
3rd Son	–	11 acres	–	£20
4th Son	–	11 acres	Is executor and has residue of estate	
Daughter	–	–	Best chest of drawers	[a]

[a] The daughter was married to a substantial famer. The second son was charged to pay £60 to her husband. This presumably was her dowry, but it is not clear whether this debt was her settlement in part or in full.

between the second, third and fourth there is clearly some notional sense of equality. Eleven acres of poor land might seem inadequate for a livelihood: but Winkfield, an extensive parish in the heart of the forest, enjoyed large grazing rights, for sheep as well as cattle,[38] substantial (if contested) rights of turbary, access to timber, as well as brick-kilns (perhaps this explains the furnace?) and a little forest industry. There were several branches of the Hatch family in the parish, the eldest of which 'time out of mind has had an handsome estate and good interest therein ...'[39] We do not know the degree of kinship of Percy Hatch to this older branch: but some degree of kinship was likely to have added a supportive social context to the younger son's struggle for a livelihood – and we know from other evidence that Winkfield parishioners defended their community's rights with the greatest vigour.[40]

Much of this rests on inference. But it may add a little flesh to the bone of the conjecture that it was in such a context, where the grid of communal inheritance was strong and where fringe-rights were indefinite and extensive, that a yeoman could risk the practice of partible inheritance without condemning his children to poverty. Below a certain minimum further partition would be ridiculous: husbandmen (in the evidence of one local study) were unlikely to divide their land.[41] But in the normal course of succession portions would not only be divided but also, through marriage, death, legacies from childless kin, be thrown together: Percy Hatch evidently held two distinct farms, one of which ('Sumerton') he left intact to his oldest son, from the other of which ('Berkshire House') he took out portions of land for his third and fourth.

If we learn more about the regions where such 'egalitarian' practices were prevalent, these may throw light upon the relationship of inheritance customs to industrialisation.[42] But in fielden, arable regions, in which little extension of land-use was possible, such 'share and share alike' practices would have led to economic suicide: tenure must pass as one parcel along with buildings, implements and stock. But this certainly faced the yeoman with a dilemma. Kiernan doubts whether a love of private property can be seen as a constant in 'human nature', and one may agree. But a desire to secure the expectations of one's children – to try to throw forward some grid which will support them – has at least had a long run in social history. It is here that Spufford's findings are important, for they seem to emphasize that the 'yeoman' were seeking to transmit down the generations not only 'land' (particular tenures) but also a social status to *all* their children. The nobility and gentry devised with care their own grid of transmission through entail and marriage settlement. Such a grid was not available to the yeoman. The merchants and professions might throw forward a grid of money. The small farmer could hope to do a little in this way himself, by bequeathing legacies as a charge upon his estate. In such cases, the moment of death was for the small man a moment of great familial financial risk. M.K. Ashby, examining the village of Bledington – a village with slight manorial presence and with a large number of freeholders – keeps a careful eye on the farmers' wills. She observes two points of change. In the early seventeenth century the wills of farmers and of widows indicate still 'a world of wide family connections and affections, a valuation of persons and also of objects, goods: charitable bequests are frequent'. But the movable property given away is in small amounts. 'After 1675 the family recognised is the immediate group of parents and children, charity is absent and money is prominent, and in larger amounts.' The second change is in accentuation of the first: by the early eighteenth century farmers 'are leaving their estates burdened by very large monetary legacies, to be paid by those who inherit the land ... The pattern they adopt ... is that of the owner of large estates in which, e.g. the head of the family provides for widow, daughter and younger sons out of the receipts of a landed estate.'[43] But the outpayments to be made by their heir sometimes appear as unrealistic. Mortgages must be taken up or debts incurred to meet the legacies. Possibly it is exactly in this inheritance practice that we may see the death-warrant of the yeomanry as a class? They were seeking to project forward a grid of legacies upon which the children who did not inherit land or its tenure could yet be maintained at yeoman status. In doing so they were withdrawing capital which could have been dunging their own land. Not all of this need leave the village: some would pass, by way of a daughter's portion, to another farm: some younger brothers might rent land and stints or settle to local crafts. But it would seem that the practice of laying legacies upon the heir (a practice with some analogies to the French 'recall') could equally have been a way of diverting capital from the countryside to the town.

The attempt to impose large portions – perhaps approaching to some notional 'share and share alike' – upon the heir led him not only into debt but into a different kind of debt from the neighbour- hood borrowing often found in the traditional village. This neighbour- hood petty indebtedness was itself a sort of 'swapping' which often had a social as well as economic dimension: loans were exchanged among kin, neighbours, sometimes as part of a reciprocity of services. The new mortgages carried the small man into a wider and more ruthless money market quite outside his own expertise. An alert manorial owner who wished to bring tenures back into his own hands could take advantage of the same situation by granting and foreclos- ing mortgages upon his own copyholds: by such means the St Johns of Dogmersfield managed in the years after the South Sea Bubble to lose a village and turn much of it into a deer-park.[44] In this case some of the tenants seem to have resorted to arson, to the shooting of cattle and the felling of trees. But so far as one can see they were victims not of forced dispossession but of 'fair' economic process, of good lawyers, and of the debt incurred by the Bubble.

The old communal grid had been eaten away by law and by money long before enclosure: eighteenth-century enclosure regis- tered the end rather than the climax of that process. The tenures which we have been discussing can be seen also as roles, functions, access to use-rights, governed by communal rules and expectations as well as by customary law. They are part of one impartible bundle, a dense socio-economic nexus. The attempt to define these by law was in itself an abstraction from that nexus. For a practice to be offensive to the community or to the homage does not provide any compelling reason at law or in cash for the practice not to continue. But opinion can be more effective than we suppose: in some parts of Ireland in the eighteenth and early nineteenth centuries there was no reason at law why a landlord might not expel his tenants and lease more advantageously to new ones. The only trouble was that the steward might be shot and the new tenants' cabins be burned down. In Hampshire in 1711 they were more polite. When Bishop Trelawny's assertive, rationalizing steward, Dr Heron, showed excessive zeal and rapacity in seizing herriots upon the death of a tenant, he was exposed by the bereaved son to public rebuke in front of his officers and strangers. This cost the steward no more than some loss of face; he should have taken it as a danger signal, an inhibition upon his action. When he failed to do so, the tenants and other episcopal officers closed against him and commenced an agitation which forced the bishop to replace his steward.[45]

Small victories like this, in defence of customary practice, were won here and there. But the campaign itself was always lost. (The bishop's next steward attained much the same ends, with a little more diplomacy and a little more care in favouring his subordinate officials.) For to the impartible bundle of communal practice capitalism introduces its own kind of partible inheritance. Uses are divorced from the user, properties from the exercise of functions. But once you break the bundle up into parts what becomes inherited is not a communal equilibrium but the properties of particular men and of particular social groups. Le Roy Ladurie speaks of the equal division by value of tenures as 'egalitarian'; and if we mean by this nothing more than equal division then the term need not be disputed. But he proposes to take the thought further: 'spreading progressively through the rural world this current of egalitarianism will ... finally submerge all the hierarchies of ordered society'.[46] But we have here proposed that in some parts of England the egalitarian desire of the yeoman to advantage as far as possible equally all of his children ended up, through a surfeit of mortgages, in submerging not the hierarchies of ordered societies but the yeomanry as a class. We should perhaps recall some lines of William Blake:

Is this thy soft Family Love
Thy cruel Patriarchal pride
Planting thy Family alone,
Destroying all the World beside.

And Blake adds to this a suggestion of the same logic through which the yeomen fell:

And he who make his law a curse
By his own law shall surely die.

For it had been these same copyholders, anxious to maintain their
status within the rural hierarchy, who had taken an active part in
the previous two centuries in breaking the communal bundle apart,
in drawing up more stringent by-laws which advantaged the
landholder and disadvantaged those without tenures, in limiting the
fringe benefits of the grid, in setting use-rights to market.[47] In their
anxiety as a social class to plant their own family alone they
prepared the means of their own destruction.

Perhaps another characteristic of traditional tenurial society
was lost. Free bench or widow's estate, as it pertained in many
manor into the eighteenth century, did allow for a considerable
feminine presence. Female tenure, either as free bench or in the
woman's own right, does not of course prove that the agrarian
and other attendant functions were always performed by the
tenants: a subtenant could be put in, or the farm could be left
under the control of male kin. But we would be making a hasty
judgement if we assumed that most feminine tenures were only
fictionally so. This was certainly not true at the top of society,
which saw the formidable presence of such women as Sarah,
duchess of Marlborough, or of Ruperta Howe, the ranger of
Alice Holt Forest. And we must all have encountered evidence
which suggests that women of the yeoman class acquitted
themselves, at the head of farming households, with equal vigour.
In the early eighteenth century a steward of St John's was
engaged in a protracted and inconclusive negotiation with one
infuriating tenant, whose evasions always left her in possession
of all the points at issue: 'I had rather' (he wrote) 'have
business with three men than one woman.'[48]

The customary grid did allow for a female presence, although
usually – but not necessarily – on condition of either widowhood
or spinsterhood. There was an eye – an in the eighteenth century
a continuing eye – upon the continuity of the familial tenure
through the male line. Free bench was often conditional upon no
remarriage, and also upon chaste living – a prohibition which
arose less from Puritanism than from jealousy of the influence of

new children, or of the waste to the estate which might be committed by the stepfather. Where the widow did not lose her tenure upon remarriage there is sometimes a suggestion that the lord, his steward, or the homage had some kind of paternal responsibilities for overwatching the children's right. In 1635 a clergyman petitioned St Johns' on behalf of the children of William Haddlesen. In this case, the father had willed his lease to the children, who were not yet of age; and Haddlesen's widow 'hath married verry unluckely, so that if the Colledge stand not the children's friend to lett it to some in trust for their use (for the mother is not to be trusted) the children are like to be undunne ...'[49] (One wonders whether it was cases of remarriage of this kind which would have been the particular occasion of rough music in England and charivari in France?)

Manors had different customs to make allowance for frailty or to deal with unusual circumstances. The 'jocular' customs of Enborne (Berks.) and of Kilmersdon (Somerset) – and probably of other places – were not as ridiculous as they may seem. In Enborne if the woman 'commits incontinency she forfeits her Widow's estate' –

Yet, after this, if she comes into the next Court held for the Manor, riding backward upon a Black Ram, with his Tail in her hand, and says the Words following, the Steward is bound by the Custom to re-admit her to her Free Bench:

Here I am,
Riding upon a Black Ram,
Like a Whore as I am;
And for my Crincum Crancum,
Have lost my Bincum Bancum;
And for my Tail's game
Am brought to this Worldly Shame,

Therefore good Mr Steward let me have my Lands again.

At Kilmesdon the recitative required was more brief, and the offender need only ride astride the ram:

For mine Arse's Fault I take this Pain,
Therefore, my Lord, give me my Land again.[50]

In other customs more rational controls or adjustments are established.[51]

One trouble with the customs of manors rehearsed between 1660 and 1800 is that we know rather little about the relation of custom to practice. And this is, mainly, because we have not bothered to find out. The Webbs noted in 1908 that there was no comprehensive study of the Lord's Court in the period 1689–1835 [52] and the position remains much the same today. (Recent advances in agrarian history have inevitably been addressed more to the improving and market-orientated sectors of the economy than to the customary.) In the case of customs of the manor governing inheritance, these came into force only when the tenant died intestate and without effecting a previous surrender: and it was usual to allow a death-bed surrender, in the presence of two customary tenants, bequeathing the tenure to an heir. Hence practice and recited customs of inheritance may long have parted company. But there is a further difficulty of a different kind. Customs formally presented at a survey (for example, upon the entry of a new lord) may have recited only a small portion of the uncodified but accepted customary practices of a manor. The uncodified portion could have remained in the custody of the memories of the steward and of the homage, with reference to the case-law built up in the court rolls. Only when we find a strong body of copyholders whose customs have become insecure in the face of an invasive or absent lord do we find an attempt to codify this case-law in all its dense social particularity.[53]

Probably the practice of widow's estate or free bench is least confused by these difficulties. Since the widow normally entered upon her free bench without any fine, this constituted a bonus of years to the existent tenure. Unless the husband had some distinct reason for making an alternative arrangement, he was likely to leave the free bench to run according to the custom of the manor: and even the briefest eighteenth-century recitals of customs normally take care to establish what the custom on this important point was. Thus custom here is some indication as to practice.

Perhaps custom within the manor may even have influenced practice outside the customary sector? The customs of Waltham St Lawrence (Berks.), rehearsed in 1735, afford to the widow full free bench during widowhood and chaste living. If she remarries or lives unchaste, she is to have one-third of the rental value of the tenure – that is, a reversion to an earlier notion of dower.[54] But if she had had issue *before* marriage, then she had neither free bench nor moiety.[55] Waltham St Lawrence lies within the same hundred as Warfield, and it is interesting to find that a yeoman of Warfield, in 1721, willed eight acres of *freehold* to his widow for life, on condition that the timber was not to be wasted nor the land ploughed: if she broke these conditions 'my will is that she shall thenceforth have out of the same no more than her Dower or Thirds'.[56] At nearby Binfield in Windsor Forest in the same year another yeoman left all lands and tenements to his wife 'during her natural life if she keep her selfe a widow but if she should happen to be married again ... then only to have and enjoy the Thirds thereof ...'[57] For some forest farmers, custom and practice in free bench appear to have run a parallel course.

Customs varied between one region and the next and, within each region, from one manor to another. I can offer only an impression, based on limited research into two or three districts. It would seem that by the eighteenth-century free bench was one of the most secure and universal of customs, applicable both to copyholds of inheritance and tenures for lives; distinctions between customary and common law terms or between tenures of customary or demesne lands had generally lapsed, and free bench generally signified continuance in the whole tenure, not in a moiety of its profits. The customs collected in Watkins' *Treatise on Copyholds* (1825 edn) offer no systematic sample, being such as came to the editor's hand or were sent in by correspondents. Custom is often reported in imprecise terms – 'the widow has her free bench', the manor 'gives no dower'. But for what the collection is worth it reports the status of widows in some sixty manors in terms which suggest that the customs were still operative or had at least survived into the eighteenth century.[58] Of these some forty show free bench, either for life or during widowhood; ten show no 'dower'; ten show dower of one-third moiety, and one of one-half.

The manors with free bench are drawn from fifteen counties (with Worcestershire greatly over-represented). The manors with no 'dower' or moieties only are drawn from six counties: in these Norfolk is over-represented, while in Middlesex and Surrey it is probable that the custom of free bench was weak where the practice of the alternative form of security – the jointure or joint-tenancy of husband and wife – was strong.[59]

Where free bench was assured the main distinction between manors turned on the question of its continuance or discontinuance upon remarriage. At Mayfield (Sussex) the ancient distinction between bond-land and assert-land tenure survived: 'yard-land widow, to hold during widowhood, Assert-widow during life,'[60] At Littlecot (Wilts.) the widow has full widow's estate and may marry again without the loss of her tenure, but if she was a *second* wife she 'can have but her widowhood'.[61] At Stoke Prior (Worcs.) the widow enjoys 'the moiety' of the lands 'and to receive only the rent of the heir if they can agree' – any difference to be referred to the homage.[62] At Balsall (Warws.) free bench was granted to the widow if a first wife, but only one-third moiety of rents and profits if she was the second or third.[63] At Farnham, a manor with a strong homage, jealous of its privileges, the customs were rehearsed in 1707 with great vigour and detail and it is fair to assume that they were correspondent to practice and that we have in them some codification of the precedents that had come before the court. In these a surrender by the husband (even to the use of his will) bars the wife's dower: such a provision was essential if the land was to be alienable. But the husband could, by surrender in the court or surrender to the use of his will, reserve his wife's life: that is, afford her free bench in precedence to the next reversion. If he were to surrender without making any such condition then his widow 'shall neither have tearmes of Life or Widow's estate; but if he die without Surrender she shall have her Widow's estate if she live sole and Chastly'.[64] And, by an additional provision, 'if she comes to the next court after her husband's death and pays half a fine, she becomes tenant for life, and may marry again without forfeiting her estate'.[65]

These divergent customs record different solutions offered to adjust the same insoluble problems. On the one hand there is an attempt to afford security to the widow, and perhaps to her underage children. On the other hand if copyhold was to be truly alienable then no absolute security could be afforded. Moreover where tenure was expected to descend to the children, remarriage presented a threat to the line of inheritance. This also called for nice adjustments, sometimes recorded in the customs. Once again the Farnham customs of 1707 reveal a complex codification and sociological government. Where a tenant had a daughter by one wife, and a son and daughter by a second, the daughter by the second marriage had precedence over the daughter by the first, even if the son (her brother) had predeceased the tenant and never been admitted to the tenure ('yet shall his sister by his mother inherit the land ... as heire to her brother ... notwithstanding her elder sister by the first woman ...')[66] It is difficult to address Cartesian logic to this solution. It looks very much like a piece of case-law, decided by the court and then added to the custumal. What appears to be emphasized here is the transmission of the tenure with the least domestic friction: presumably the first daughter will already be likely to have left the farm, the second wife (now widowed) is likely to remain in residence with her daughter: she seems the most 'natural' heir.

In any case we are not looking at any sort of sexually egalitarian customs. No 'jocular' custom has yet come to light in which a fornicating old widower had to submit himself to the pain of riding into court on a goat. But we do have an accepted area of feminine presence, and this may have been an effective and creative one, and one felt, at any given time, palpably in the customary village.[67] Kerridge, who sometimes appears to hold a conspiratorial theory of tenure, in which the customary tenants are seen as constantly seeking for new ways to exploit their lords, has doubts as to the morality of the practice of free bench: it was 'open to abuse in a loose and disreputable manner, as when an aged and ailing customer took a young wife merely in order that she or a third party might enjoy the holding during her expected widowhood'.[68] No doubt on occasion this happened:[69] but as a general comment on the value or functions of free bench the judgement is flippant. It is even possible that habituation to this active feminine presence in areas of strong customary and yeoman occupancy served to modify sexual roles and inheritance customs more generally, even outside the customary sector.[70] Where I have compared the wills of Berkshire yeomen and tradesmen with the customs in Berkshire parishes in the 1720s and 1730s I have noted no evidence in the former of any bias against female kin,[71] and, on occasion, a little bias the other way.[72] When in 1721 the Rev. Thomas Power, the curate of Easthampstead (Berks.) sought to persuade his recalcitrant wife to sign over some messuages to him by hanging her by a leg from the window and threatening to cut the rope, so far from meeting with the applause of the neighbourhood he was subjected by some local gallants to some very rough music and to a mock execution.[73] But this no doubt is another example of 'loose and disreputable' practice.

Freehold could of course also be transmitted to women: and it was so transmitted, to widows, to sisters, to daughters and to grand-daughters. But if we accept that between 1660 and 1760 there was a severe decline in the numbers of yeomen, both free and copy, it may follow that there will also have been an equivalent decline in the effective female agrarian presence. Where lands came out of customary tenure, and were leased out again at will, they would be leased to men. A tenancy-at-will carried no widow's estate: at the most it would be allowed as a favour. Security of the customary grid was lost; and if the yeoman was only at a further point in his secular decline, the yeowoman had been served notice to quit.

As a final point I wish to return to the difference between the inheritance of a family, and inheritance of security, status, power, by a social group, caste, or class. The first depends generally upon the second. We have the particular inheritance practices of families, and the grid of law, custom, expectation, upon which these practices operate. And these grids differ greatly between social groups. What is happening is the devising of rules and practices by which particular social groups project forwards provisions and (as they hope) guarantees of security for their children. Cooper has examined the grid of the great. The moneyed class had a different grid, although it meshed in closely with that of the land. But the eighteenth century had also a third, complementary, grid for the propertied classes: that of interest, preferment to office, purchase of commissions, reversions to sinecures, placings within the Church and so on. In this grid of nepotism and interest, possession was not all: one must also supplement possession with continuing interest and the right kind of political connections. One must both have (or find for one's child) an office and maintain the influence to exploit that office to the full. The parent might attend to the first: his child must see to the second.

Throughout the eighteenth century the grid of interest and preferment remained as a bundle of that kind. Along this grid the lesser gentry sought to secure the future of their families. The papers of the great patrons show the incessant activity of petitioners on behalf of their kin, in the attempt to secure the whole structure of the Church and State as a kind of Trust for their own class. Middle-class reformers, rallying under the banner of the 'career open to talent', at the same time sought to secure the future status of their own children upon a grid of educational qualification and professional exclusiveness. Moreover, this reminds us that a privileged group could – and still can – secure its own grid while trying to tear down the grid of another. In the twentieth century the see-saw of social-democratic and conservative politics has often turned on such rivalries. But in the eighteenth and nineteenth centuries similar contests were fought which will be overlooked if we only take into account post-mortem inheritance. Sabean appears, momentarily, to have allowed this oversight to enter when he cites the case of a poor village in the Sologne and concludes from its evidence that 'in the absence of property there is little tendency to develop extended kin ties'.[74] Of course if there is an absence of land and of movable property then neither of these can be transmitted through inheritance: nor are the poor in any position to 'arrange for good marriages'. So that Sabean's generalization may hold good for a poor peasant economy. But even for the landless rural labourer, and certainly for an urban proletariat, the critical point of familial transmission has not been *post mortem* but at the point of giving the children a 'start in life'. If we wish to examine inheritance and the family in the eighteenth century among urban craftsmen, we have to look, not at wills, but at apprenticeship regulations, apprenticeship premiums, and at trades in which a strong family tradition was preserved by offering a preference to

sons or kin and by limiting apprentices.[75] Even among the rural
poor (one suspects) the business of placing a son on a good farm,
a daughter in service at the great house, occupied much effort and
anxiety, and was part of the effort of transmitting to the next
generation a 'respectable' status, on the right side of the poor law.
And in the early nineteenth century, by clipping away at apprenticeship, by repealing the Statute of Artificers, the rulers of
England were threatening the inheritance system of the skilled
workmen; while in 1834, by striking at all out-relief, they
threatened the only grid of ultimate security known to the poor.

Of course, no guarantee has ever secured to the individual
family immunity from the accidents of mutability. Remarkable as
are certain continuities among aristocracy and gentry, there are
many more cases of the downward turn of fortune's wheel. As
Raymond Williams has recently argued, the very literary values of
landed estate and settlement are often those espoused by the
newly-rich anxious to pretend to the values of settlement. Penshurst, the subject of Ben Jonson's classic country house poem,
raised by 'no man's ruin, no man's grone', was in fact a manor
which had lapsed by execution and attainder some fifty years
before Jonson wrote.[76] For other poets the family and its fortune
are taken as an illustration of mutability:

And what if my descendants lose the flower
Through natural declension of the soul,
Through too much business with the passing hour,
Through too much play, or marriage with a fool?
May this laborious stair and this stark tower
Become a roofless ruin that the owl
May build in the cracked masonry and cry
Her desolation to the desolate sky.

For Yeats no forethought could hold back the cyclical mutability of
things;

The Primum Mobile that fashioned us
Has made the very owls in circles move ...

Yeats underestimated certain continuities, and notably the remarkable longevity of certain corporate landowners – those wise old owls, Merton College and St John's College, Cambridge, have flown directly to us from the twelfth or thirteenth centuries. But common observation (or a brief consultation of any genealogical authority) confirms this thought: as Yorkshire people have it, from clogs to clogs in three generations. What this may conceal is that independent of the rise and fall of families, the inheritance-grids themselves have often proved to be extremely effective as a vehicle of another kind of corporate inheritance – the means by which a social group has extended its historical tenure of status and of privilege. We are busy with it still today, as accountants and lawyers devise new trusts, new hedges against inflation, setting up investment trusts with one leg upon each of the four corners of the capitalist world. But we should be on our guard. We commence by examining the inheritance systems of particular families: but, over time, family fortunes rise and fall; what is inherited is property itself, the claim on the resources of a future society; and the beneficiary may be, not any descendant of that particular family, but the historical descendant of the social class to which that family once belonged.

From *Family and Inheritance*, edited by Goody, Thirsk and Thompson. (Cambridge 1976), the report of a *Past and Present* Conference. These comments which arose in the course of the conference are based upon work, some of which is yet to be published: for the forest areas of Berkshire and eastern Hampshire, *Whigs and Hunters* (London, 1975) and for some other aspects of eighteenth-century customs, 'Common Right and Enclosure' in *Customs in Common*. In any case, many points are proposed here as questions, requiring further research, rather than as conclusions. My thanks are due to Jeanette Neeson and to editors and contributors to this volume for reading this comment in manuscript and for sending me valuable criticisms, some of which raised questions too complex to answer in the context of this study.

Notes

1. Since much copyhold land was itself sub-let on economic leases, it may well be true that by the eighteenth-century leasehold at rack-rent

'had largely displaced all other tenancies': Eric Kerridge, *Agrarian Problems in the Sixteenth Century and After* (London, 1969), p. 46. But the number of occupying customary tenants remained substantial and they should not be allowed to be lost to view.

2. Here I will use the term 'customary tenure' in a general (and sociological) rather than precise (and legal) definition. Copyhold need not be held according to the custom of the manor, while beneficial leases were not, at law, customary tenures although Church and collegiate manors were in fact often subject to customary practices. See Kerridge, ch. 2 for a lucid discrimination between forms of tenure, which (however) affords priority to legal definitions over customary practice.

3. Thus the Court Baron of Uphaven (Wilts.), 20 October 1742; Rinaldo Monk's copyhold cottage forfeited to the lord, he having been convicted of felony and transported: P.R.O. T.S. 19.3. Forfeiture for waste (often compounded by a fine) is more common.

4. In a copyhold of inheritance even a fine uncertain must be 'reasonable' – a definition which was set by common law at around two years' improved rental. But a copyhold at the will of the lord limited fines to no such legal rationality: R.B. Fisher, *A Practical Treatise on Copyhold Tenure* (London, 1794), pp. 81–2, 90. Six or seven years' improved rental might be charged in such cases, 'the only alternative left to the tenant is to pay the fine, or let the estate fall in'.

5. R.B. Fisher who was Steward of Magdalen College claimed to be writing from practical knowledge of manorial usages in many parts of the country: Coke had been writing only of 'pure and genuine copyholds' but 'at this time of day there is a sort of bastard species ... a copyhold tenure'. i.e. copyhold for lives, which was to be found 'in a multiplicity of manors within the kingdom'. How far this 'bastard species' was of recent creation, how far it indicated a degeneration of 'pure' copyhold could only be established by many local studies: *ibid.*, pp. iv, 14–15, 90.

6. Charles Watkins, *A Treatise on Copyholds* (4th edn, 1825), ii, pp. 549–550. It is difficult to set a date upon the customs which Watkins' editor assembled for the 100 pages of Appendix III to the 4th edition. Some customs cited date from the seventeenth century or earlier: but others, including most of the Worcestershire customs, appear to have been sent in by a correspondent in the attempt to describe contemporary or very recent practice.

7. *Ibid.*, ii, p. 553. At Tebberton the custom as presented in 1649 was 'that the lord hath always used to grant the copyholds for three lives

in possession, and three in reversion', the fines being arbitrary; but Watkins' correspondent notes that 'of late years the lord hath only granted for two lives in possession and two in reversion, which is no invasion of the ancient custom, as grants are entirely at the lord's pleasure'. A comment on the case of Broadwas perhaps generalizes the experience of insecurity in a number of Worcestershire manors: 'these servile tenures are inconsistent with the present times; and occasion ill-will to the lords, and uneasiness to many honest men': *ibid.*, ii, pp. 546, 564. It is interesting to note that the only instance of wrongful treatment towards copyholders which Kerridge, after his very extensive searches, is able to confirm as at least 'an allegation which found some support' concerns tenants of the Dean and Chapter of Worcester Cathedral forced, in the early seventeenth century, to take leases for years in place of copyholds of inheritance: Kerridge, *op. cit.*, p. 83.

8. H.F. Howard, *An Account of the Finances of St. John's College, Cambridge*, 1511–1926 (Cambridge, 1935), p. 47.

9. See also R.F. Scott, *Notes from the Records of St. John's College, Cambridge* (St John's, Cambridge), Second Series, 1899–1906, no. xiv, who estimates that the usual fine for surrenders and renewals in the seventeenth century was one year's gross or extended rent: this was raised over the course of the eighteenth century to 1¼, 1½ and thence to two years. See also W.S. Powell in *Eagle* (St John's College), xx, no. 115, March 1898. By the nineteenth century the fine was generally 2.6 of the gross letting value: St John's College, Cambridge, calendar of archives, drawer 100 (70): Statement of Senior Bursar at Audit for 1893. I am indebted to the Master and Fellows of St John's for permission to consult their calendar and archives, and to the Librarian and Archivist for assistance.

10. Anon., *Reasons for a Law to oblige Spiritual Persons and Bodies Politick to Renew their Leases for Customary and Reasonable Fines* (London, n.d., c. 1736).

11. Or so it is argued in *Whigs and Hunters* (London, 1975), Chapter 4, *passim*. The Church appears to have introduced new tables for the assessment of fines, computed according to the interest on the capital investment, the age of the life in being, the number of years lapsed since the last renewal, etc., at some time between 1715 and 1720. The rules demanded 1½ years' extended rental value for renewal of twenty-one year leases, and so in proportion for more or fewer years out: and, in leases for lives, two years' value be insisted on for one life out, and where two are void in proportion, or (preferably) conversion of a lease for three lives to a twenty-

one-years' lease. These tables, known as 'Sir Isaac Newton's Tables', created great resentment among tenants: they raised fines, replaced personal and flexible negotiations by a uniform rationalized standard, and above all disallowed the tenants' claim to have established themselves by long precedent in tenures which in effect were customary, heritable and subject (like copyholds) to a fine certain. See St John's College calendar, drawer 109 (38), 'Rules agreed to by the Church of Canterbury at your Audit 1720, according to Sir I. Newton's Tables, thus allowing your Tenants 9 per cent which they think favour sufficient': also. C. Trimnell to W. Wake, 4 July 1720, Christ Church College Library, Oxford. Arch. Wake Epist, XXI. For the case of the tenants (some of whom were substantial landholders), *Reasons for a Law, cit. supra* note 10; 'Everard Fleetwood' (Samuel Burroughs). *An Enquiry into the Customary-Estates and Tenant-Rights of those who hold Lands of Church and other Foundations* (London, 1731). For the case of Church and Colleges, see *inter alia*, Anon., *Tables for Renewing and Purchasing of Cathedral Churches and Colleges* (London, 1731).

12. John Aldridge, 27 October 1726, St John's College calendar, drawer 109 (185). For other complaints at the raising of fines, all in 1725, see *ibid.* drawer 109 (80), (84), (92), (99).

13. This was acknowledged by the Colleges' own defenders. Thus *Tables for Renewing, supra*, p. 55, agreed that leases 'of a considerable term of years', and reasonably renewable, were beneficial to both parties 'because Men of Letters and Bodies Corporate cannot so well manage their Estates as Laymen or a single Person may do, if they kept them in their own Hands, or let them out at Rack-Rent', especially where such properties were at a distance. In such circumstance a good tenant might be given favour much as if he were acting as the College's Steward: thus Mr John Baber was entered as tenant of the manor of Broomhall (at Sunninghill, Berks.) in 1719: he was long in possession, and when there was an extensive fall of timber in the manor in 1766 it was resolved that 'if the sale of the timber answers our expectations [we intend] to make him a present of fifty guineas for the care that has been taken of it'. The sale exceeded expectations and Baber's gift was increased to £100: St John's College archives. 'Old Dividend and Fine Book', p. 66; Conclusion Book, I, pp. 176, 178.

14. Howard, *Finances of St. John's College*, pp. 71–2.

15. Rev. T. Longland to Senior Bursar, 27 November 1683, St John's College calendar, drawer 86 (62).

16. Joan Lingard (a tenant at Staveley) to Master, *ibid.*, drawer 94 (25).

The College held certain properties through gift or purchase in which regular copyhold (rather than beneficial leases) pertained.

17. Robert Pain to Master, 26 October 1630, *ibid.*, drawer 94 (52). The tenant in question held land in Paxton Magna (Hunts.).

18. George Davies, 3 July 1725, *ibid.*, drawer 109 (96), concerning a few tenants at Marfleet (Yorks.): 'I am of opinion it will be better for the College that they do not renew but take the estates, as they fall, into their own hands.'

19. The College did not finally decide to end the system of beneficial leases until 1851. The Fellows endured a loss of revenue from fines in the 1850s, but benefited considerably from the improved income from economic rentals after the mid 1860s: 'Statement of the Senior Bursar at Audit for 1893', *ibid.*, drawer 100 (70).

20. John Blackburne to Charles Head, 27 August 1700, *ibid.*, drawer 94 (284). This manor had come to the College as a gift from the Duchess of Somerset: Howard, *Finances of St. John's College*, pp. 98–9.

21. See my *Whigs and Hunters, passim*.

22. Thus it was said that the signatories to a petition against the enclosure of the common fields at Hooknorton in 1773 were made up from 'the smaller' proprietors 'who have now an opportunity of committing trespasses on their neighbour's property with their sheep, which in so large a field cannot be altogether prevented': R. Bignall, 10 January 1773. Bodleian Library, MS Oxford,. Archd. Papers, Berks. b.5.

23. Kerridge, *Agrarian Problems*, p. 93.

24. 6 Co. Rep. 59/b. As Lord Eversley pointed out we should be careful not to confuse a legal decision of general significance with the general adoption of it in practice: 'so long ... as a common remained open and unenclosed, the decision in Gateward's case did not practically affect the position of the inhabitants ... (who) continued to exercise the customary user of turbary, estovers, or pasture'. Lord Eversley, *Commons, Forests and Footpaths* (London, revised edn, 1910), pp. 10–12.

25. For a not exceptional example see the customs claimed in the manor of Warfield in Windsor Forest during a survey of 1735: all 'tenants and inhabitants' have common pasture in all commons and wastes for all kinds of beasts 'as well without stint of number, as also without restraint of any season or time of year'. Rights were also claimed to dig loam and sand (and to cut heath, fern and furzes 'without any leave, lycence or molestation'). Only the part of the claim inserted within brackets was objected to by the steward as an

innovation on the old books of survey: Berkshire Rec. Off. D/EN M 73/1. For practice in the forest generally, see *Whigs and Hunters*, pp. 32, 239–40.

26. In the poor soils of Windsor Forest (within the Blackheath Country) and of the New Forest the family farmer came into his own, 'largely in subsistence husbandry on land that working and gentlemen farmers considered unfit for their purposes': E. Kerridge, *The Farmers of Old England* (London, 1973), p. 81. In the case of the Forest of Dean the Free Miners were very fortunate that their ancient usages were *not* challenged at law in the eighteenth century since they would almost certainly have been disallowed in the spirit of Gateward's Case: see Lord Eversley, *op. cit.*, pp. 178–9.

27. Dean and Chapter of Ely v. Warren, 2 Atk. 189–90.

28. Selby v. Robinson, 2 T.R. 759.

29. It is true that this right was controlled and regulated (like all other common rights) and often limited to particular categories of persons – the very young, the old, the decrepit, etc.: see W.O. Ault, *Open-Field Farming in Medieval England* (London, 1972), pp. 29–32. Ault appears to take Blackstone to task for accepting gleaning as a right of 'the poor' by 'the common law and custom of England' (*Commentaries*, 1772, iii, p. 212). But it would not have disturbed Blackstone to know that there is no reference to such right in thirteenth-century by-laws, 'nor is there a single mention of the poor as gleaners'. Custom did not rest on suppositious origin but established itself in common law by four criteria: antiquity, continuance, certainty and reason – and 'customs are to be construed according to vulgar apprehension, because customs grow generally, and are bred and brought up amongst the Lay-gents': S.C. (S. Carter), *Lex Custumaria: or a Treatise of Copy-hold Estates* (London, 1701), pp. 27–9. By such criteria gleaning by the poor was of greater antiquity, and of equal continuity, certainty and rationality as most customary tenures.

30. Blackstone, *op. cit.*, i, section 1.

31. The form can be seen in the manor of Barrington-in-Thriplow: Benjamin Wedd is admitted (11 November 1756) according to the use of the will of his deceased father-in-law: he is charged by this will to pay an annuity of £60 to his mother-in-law: St John's College calendar, drawer 99 (214). Such practices were of course very widespread.

32. The form may be seen in the will of William Cooke of East Hendred (Berks.), probat. 7 September 1728, who left two sons and two daughters. After small monetary legacies, the residue of his

estate was left to his brothers Thomas and Edmund Cooke, in trust to divide amongst all and every of his children 'share and share alike'. The lives of his brothers 'are in the copy of court roll by which I hold my copyhold', but the brothers are bound to surrender all rents and profits to the above used, and to distribute it among the children 'share and share alike': Bodleian Library, MS Wills Berks. 20, p. 48.

33. This form was especially used in copyholds for lives, as two or three lives in being, others in reversion: one or more of the lives in being were inserted as trustees for the actual tenants, as security that the tenure should pass on to his heirs: on occasion the actual tenant, who paid for the entry fines, was not even entered in the court roll: see R.B. Fisher, *op. cit.*, pp. 15–16.

34. The form may be seen in the will of Timothy Lyford of Drayton (Berks.), probat. 5 December 1724: 'whereas my daughter Elizabeth Cowdrey is the first reversion named in my copyhold estate in Sutton Cortney my will is that the said copyhold estate be surrendered into the hands of the Lord of the manor pursuant to a certain obligation to me entered into for that purpose with intent that my daughter Jane the wife of John Chear may be admitted tenant thereof for her own life and such other lives as she can agree for': Bodleian Library, MS Will Berks. 19, p. 239.

35. As in Knaresborough, where 'it was possible ... for a man with more than one son to make provision for the younger sons by transferring the title of part of his land to them during his lifetime, receiving back a life interest': *A History of Harrogate and Knaresborough*, ed. Bernard Jennings (Huddersfield, 1970), pp. 80, 178–9.

36. When I say 'a little evidence' I mean that a little evidence has come to my hand while working on other matters. There may (or may not) be much evidence. The impressions offered in these pages are not intended as a substitute for the systematic research which I have not undertaken.

37. Bodleian Library, MS Wills Berks. 19, pp. 338–9.

38. Percy Hatch's daughter was married to William Lyford. This could have been the same William Lyford who was presented at the Windsor Forest Swanimote court in 1717 for staffherding sheep in the forest: P.R.O. L.R. 3.3 'Staffherding' (accompanying the sheep in the forest with a herdsman) was an offence since it frightened the deer and secured the best grazing for the sheep: left to their own unaided competition the deer enforced their own priorities.

39. Reverend Will Waterson, Memorandum Book, I, the Ranelagh School, Bracknell, Berks.

40. See *Whigs and Hunters*, Part I, *passim*: Winkfield was the epicentre of 'Blacking' in the forest in the 1720s.

41. See J.A. Johnston, 'The Probate Inventories and Wills of a Worcestershire Parish, 1676–1775', *Midland History*, i, 1 (Spring 1971), pp. 20–33. The author finds that the husbandmen all 'showed an inclination to preserve their estates intact, all leaving their land to their eldest sons': they also 'favoured their male relations outside the immediate family'. No other social group showed such rigidity of custom, nor a stress on primogeniture: of 87 landowners, 36 willed their land intact to a single heir, the remaining 51 left their land to 122 new owners. The parish in question (Powick) is only two miles from Worcester: rich land with opportunities for dairy farming, fruit growing and some horse-breeding. Possibly this could be another kind of regimen in which partible inheritance was viable?

42. Bernard Jennings informs me that in the very extensive manor of Wakefield practices of partible inheritance were continued analogous to those in Knaresborough (*supra*, note 35). His researches, with the cooperation of extra-mural classes, have demonstrated a coincidence between this practice and the density of looms in different districts of the West Riding: i.e. where the holding was too small to provide a livelihood this became an incentive for the development of domestic industry (spinning and weaving), in the first place as a supplementary income. One looks forward to the publication of these findings.

43. M.K. Ashby, *The Changing English Village: a History of Bledington* (Kineton, 1974), pp. 162–4, 194–5.

44. See *Whigs and Hunters*, pp. 106–8.

45. *Ibid.*, pp. 125–33, and 'Articles against Heron' and Heron's responses, Hants. Rec. Off. Heron's reply complains that 'at Waltham Court, without any Previous notice, the Son of the Widow was brought into the Room where wee dined (with some Clergymen & Strangers of Mr. Kerby's Acquaintance all unknown to mee) to Challenge mee publickly for this unjust Seizure'. This confrontation was engineered by Kerby, the Woodward, and Heron's rival.

46. See above p. 50.

47. I hope to substantiate these generalizations in 'Common Right and Enclosure', *Customs in Common*.

48. St John's College, Cambridge, calendar, drawer 109 (16). But Mrs Allen who had outlived two husbands and had repudiated the debts of both – 'a very sharp self interested woman' – may be untypical and may offer evidence on Le Roy Ladurie's side of the question: since she turns out to have been a 'saucy Frenchwoman'; and 'an

unaccountable Frenchwoman, and regards no body': *ibid.*, 109 (7), (13), (14).

49. Reverend Richard Perrot to College, petitioning on behalf of a customary tenant at Marfleet (Yorks.), 2 February 1635, *ibid.*, drawer 94 (289). The Manor Court at Farnham also took unusual care to overwatch the interest of orphans. 'It is a principall poynt in the Court of this Mannor and to be remembered' that if a tenant left an orphan under age 'then the next in kind and farthiest from the Land shall have the tuition and Guardianship of such an heir untill he come to the age of 14 years', when he may chose his own tenant to farm. The guardian shall pay his ward's charges and education, and account to him for the rest. But if the appropriate person as guardian 'be insufficient by defect of Nature or otherwise', then the court, with the consent of the homage, could appoint a guardian. By 'next of kind and farthiest from the land' I understand the closest kin who is at the same time not in the direct line of customary inheritance: e.g. an uncle or aunt on the mother's side: Farnham Custom Roll, 1707, Dean and Chapter archives, Winchester Cathedral Library. Compare the custom at nearby Woking: 'If any copyholder die, his heir being within age, the custody of the body and the land of such heir shall be committed by the lord to the next of kindred of the heir to whom the land cannot descend, he being a fit person ...': Watkins, *op. cit.*, ii. p. 559.

50. Josiah Beckwith's edition of Thomas Blount's *Fragmenta Antiquitatis; or Antient Tenures of Land, and Jocular Customs of Some Manors* (York, 1784) pp. 265–6. A similar custom is claimed to have existed in Tor (Devon).

51. At Balsall (Warwks.) the customs presented in 1657 included the provision: 'If any female heir, being in possession of any copyhold, for lack of grace should happen to commit fornication or be begotten with child, she was not to forfeit her estate, but she must come into the lord's court' and pay a fine of five shillings: if a widow committed fornication or adultery 'she is to forfeit her estate for her life, until she agree with the lord by fine to be restored': Watkins, *op, cit.*, ii, p. 576. It is doubtful whether such customs were effective in the eighteenth century, unless in unusual circumstances; however, in 1809 Lord Ellenborough, C.J. upheld judgement for the plaintiff, thus ousting from her tenure a widow (a tenant of Lord Lonsdale in Westmorland) who had breached the custom of tenure during 'her chaste viduity' by having a child: but a witness could cite only one other case in that manor in the previous sixty years (in 1753) and in that case the widow had died before the case

came to an issue: William Askew v. Agnes Askew, 10 East. 520.

52. S. & B. Webb, *The Manor and the Borough* (London, 1908), p. 11.

53. An excellent example of this is to be found in the Farnham Customs of 1707. Here we have a strong body of customers prospering through hopfarming, claiming the security of socage tenure, but suffering from the insecurity of being a Church manor (the Bishop of Winchester). The homage recited its customs with unusual detail and precision because of continuing disputes with successive Bishops and their officers: 'every new Lord brings in a new procurator who for private gains Racketh the Custom and oftentimes breaketh it ...' Mrs Elfrida Manning of the Farnham Museum Society has recently discovered an almost identical Farnham Custumal of the 1670s.

54. Dower in common law was defined as a moiety and the custom that the wife shall have the whole as free bench is contrary to the maxim of common law: but the custom of each manor remained good and overrode common law: S. Carter, *op.cit.*, p. 34. Thus a textbook of 1701. By the 1790s the terms free bench and dower were often being used indiscriminately, although they differed: 'Free bench is a widow's estate in such lands as the husband died seized of, and not of such lands as he was seized of during the coverture, whereas dower is the estate of the widow in all lands, the husband was seized of during the coverture': R.B. Fisher, *op. cit.*, p. 26, citing 2 Atk. 525.

55. Survey and customs of Waltham St Lawrence, November 1735, Berks. Rec. Off. D/EN M 82/A/1.

56. Will of Richard Simmons, probat. 21 April 1721, Bodleian Library, MS Wills Berks. 19, p. 100.

57. Will of Thomas Punter, probat. 21 April 1721, *ibid.*, p. 97. But forest customs varied from parish to parish: in the neighbouring parish of Winkfield it seems that the widow could remarry and her husband enjoy her estate in her right during her life, subject to stringent provisions against waste: Rev. Will Waterson, Memorandum Book, pp. 362, 365 Ranelagh School, Bracknell, Berks.

58. I have subtracted from this 'sample' some customs which evidently dated back to the early years of the seventeenth century or before, but others may well have been obsolete.

59. Watkins, *op. cit.*, ii., pp. 477–576. The North and the North Midlands are scarcely represented in this collection.

60. *Ibid.*, ii, pp. 501–2.

61. *Ibid.*, ii, p. 498.

62. *Ibid.*, ii, pp. 552–3.

63. *Ibid.*, ii, p. 575.

64. Farnham Custom Roll, 1707., Winchester Cathedral Library.

65. This last provision is cited by Watkins, *op. cit.*, i, p. 552 and indicates a slight modification and clarification over the 1707 Customs.

66. Farnham Custom Roll, 1707, *loc. cit.*

67. The effect of free bench in strengthening a feminine presence in the village in late medieval society is discussed by Rodney Hilton, *The English Peasantry in the Later Middle Ages* (London, 1975), ch. vi, esp, pp. 98–101. Many of his comments may remain apposite to districts in the eighteenth century which maintained traditions of yeoman customary occupancy: for an example of strong feminine tenure, see Matthew Imber, *The Case, or an Abstract of the Custom of the Manor of Mardon in the Parish of Hursley* (London, 1707): in this Hampshire manor, whose customs were borough English, more than 20 per cent (11 out of 52) of the copyholders were women.

68. Kerridge, *op. cit.*, p. 83.

69. By the custom of Berkeley (Glos.) 'marriage *in extremis* gives no free bench': Watkins, *op. cit.*, ii, p. 479.

70. In the parish of Winkfield the Earl of Ranelagh founded a charity school for forty poor children. The Reverend Will Waterson, Rector of Winkfield, was also Master of the school for more than thirty years. He took in the daughters as well as the sons of the parish 'poor', but noted: 'Its much to be wish'd that the Girles were restrain'd from learning any thing that is not requisite in an ordinary servant, and that they were imploy'd in Spinning and makeing their own and the Boys cloths ... Fine work ... serves only to puff them up with pride and vanity, and to make them slight and overlook such places as they ought chiefly to be qualified for.' But Waterson, writing towards the end of his life, had perhaps become disillusioned and defensive in the face of accusations that the 'charity schools are nurseries of Rebellion, and disqualify poor children for such country business ... as they are most wanted for'. For boys also (he noted) 'the plow must find them employment, or they'll do nothing': but he appears to have conscientiously afforded to the children of both sexes elementary instruction in literacy and numeracy: Waterson MS, Reading Ref. Lib. BOR/D: the passages cited were perhaps written in the early 1740s.

71. Among wills of yeomen and husbandmen in Berkshire at this time one frequently finds evidence of attention to the interests of female heirs. Thus Robert Dee of Winkfield, yeoman (probat. 10 April 1730), left two parcels of land, one of 16½ acres, the other of 2½ acres: the larger parcel was willed to his grandson, together with

house and furniture, the smaller to his grand-daughter: but (in compensation) the grandson was to receive also £100, the grand-daughter £200. Among freeholders, tradesmen, etc., there is some evidence of egalitarian inheritance customs: thus Joseph Collier (probat. 12 July 1737), a Reading yeoman who owned some tenements and mills: all left to his brother in trust to sell and distribute 'share and share alike' among his six children (four daughters – all married – and two sons); Mary Maynard (probat. 20 May 1736) the widow of a Reading waggoner – a business which she had continued – the estate to be valued and to be distributed 'share and share alike' among six children (three of each sex) as each attained the age of 21: the two oldest children (one son, one daughter) to act as executors, but the daughter to lapse her function if she marries: Bodleian Library, MS Wills Berks. 20, p. 117; 21, p. 113, p. 72 verso.

72. Thus the will of William Towsey, yeoman, of Letcombe Regis, probat. 22 August 1722, leaving to his daughter Ann Hawks £50 'to her own seperate use and disposicon wholy exempt from the Power or intermedling of her husband Thomas Hawks notwithstanding the Coverture between him and my said daughter': *ibid.*, 19, pp. 150–1.

73. See *Whigs and Hunters*, pp. 71–2. If, as I suppose, Mrs Power was born Ann Ticknor, then she hold more than 80 acres as well as barns, orchards, cottages, etc., in the forest, in jointure with her sister: the jointure explains why the land could not fall to the Reverend Power in consequence of his avaricious coverture. (Yeomen were perfectly capable of using the devices of jointures and of trusts to safeguard their daughters' rights). It is reassuring to note that Mrs Power endured the hazards of her marriage and died 'without doing any Act to affect' her property: Abstract of Aaron Maynard's title to four closes in Wokingham, Berks. Rec. Off. D/ER E 12.

74. Above p. 98.

75. For a study of artisan occupational inheritance see William H. Sewell, Jr, 'Social Change and the Rise of Working-Class Politics in Nineteenth-Century Marseilles', *Past and Present*, 65, November 1974.

76. Raymond Williams, *The Country and the City* (London, 1973), pp. 40–1.

Happy Families

Lawrence Stone offers us a history of the family in England between 1500 and 1800, a history of social attitudes towards the family and marriage, and of domestic and sexual behaviour. The aspect of this history which most interests him is that of the evolution of affective relationships: familial and sexual norms, expectations, roles, and the feelings which informed these.

This history commences with the Open Lineage Family of the 16th century and carries us through to the Closed Domesticated Nuclear Family of the 18th century, which is itself the precursor of the Modern Family. But this has not been a simple unilinear evolution, since it was interrupted, in the 17th century, by the Restricted Patriarchal Family characteristic of Puritanism. As the nuclear family closed itself off from the wider society and shed its diffused supportive network of kinship, so the internal bonding became more tight. But the 18th century did not bring us to the threshold of liberated modernity, because the 19th century was an era of reversal, and Victorianism saw a return to patriarchal norms and sexual repression. Stone hints that there may be some cyclical oscillation between permissiveness and repression: we can expect the northern ice-cap to expand at any time now. But this is not central to his general argument, which turns away from any monocausal explanation and emphasises, instead, the complexity of the interaction of many variables.

Nevertheless, through all these complexities one very substantial change has been steadily making its way: the rise of Affective Individualism. This is, Stone argues, 'one of the most significant transformations that has ever taken place, not only in the most intimate aspects of human life, but also in the nature of social organisation.'

This notion is not original, but Stone is the first to isolate its familial and sexual consequences in English history in this way,

and to submit these to sustained interrogation. Affective individualism should not be confused with affection. True, the point where
we commence, with the Open Lineage Family, is seen as one
without warm affective domestic bonding. Procreation perpetuates
the 'line' and the line is supported by the network of cousinships
and kin. The tightly-swaddled infant is fostered out with a
wet-nurse; returning home, he or she is entrusted to servants, and
then departs once more, before reaching the teens, to serve (or be
educated) in the household of others, perhaps kin. Demography
suggests that if the child did not die, it was probable that father or
mother might. In all these circumstances parents and children saw
little of each other, and their feelings remained cold and distant.

But it should not be supposed that warm emotions, denied
familial expressions, suffused a wider society of neighbours and
associates. These swaddled and fostered demi-orphans, their wills
broken by beating, entered adulthood with 'primary responses to
others ... at best a calculating indifference and at worst a mixture
of suspicion and hostility, tyranny and submission, alienation and
rage.' The analysis is derived in the main from the upper levels of
society, but for somewhat abrupt reasons Stone is ready to
generalise it to 16th century society as a whole. The Elizabethan
village receives a sad testimonial , as 'a place filled with malice
and hatred, its only unifying bond being the occasional episode of
mass hysteria' directed against the local witch. Emotion, displaced
from personal relations, surged into religious enthusiasms (mainly
hatred of religionists of other persuasions), or found expression in a
high general level of violence.

But, in the Puritanical society of 17th century England or New
England, the evidence of stronger affective bonding need not be
found in any growth in sentiment or love. The invigilation of a
child's psyche or plain old-fashioned punishment could be the expression of a new kind of concern and caring. It is only in the 18th
century, and then at first only among the urban bourgeoisie and the
gentry, that strong affective bonding found unambiguous expression
in sentiment and permissiveness towards children, and in less inhibited sexuality. Interrupted by the 19th century reversal, we are today
the beneficiaries of the full fruition – and thence extension to other
subordinate social classes – of that 18th century breakthrough.

One must write 'beneficiaries' and 'breakthrough' because, despite disclaimers of any normative intent, Stone cannot prevent 'the modern family' from becoming the hero of his book. This hero has even managed to find its way onto the dustjacket: the modern family is 'liberal rather than patriarchal in the distribution of power; bonded by affection between spouses rather than economic interests; deeply concerned with and attached to children; and frank in its expression of sexuality.'

This is certainly a yes-type definition. The prospective purchaser is supposed to squeal excitedly: 'Darling, look, the history of us!' Instantly The Modern Family is visualised, tanned and beautiful, gazing into each others' companionable eyes, caring and sharing like the Co-op, and always climaxing together. Who among us will dare to vote publicly against any of these virtues of modernity? Against these, how pitiful or reactionary appear those ancient virtues of honour, or chastity, or good housewifery, or filial obedience!

This definition of modernity is very close to that offered by 'modernization theory,' a pseudo-knowledge which has prestige on a few American campuses. Stone rejects this theory, because his Modern Family originated in the upper bourgeoisie (the professional and mercantile middle classes and the gentry) and only thence diffused itself to lesser mortals, whereas the standard Modern Family of M Theory arises from 'the market' and 'industrialization.' In Edward Shorter's recent historical imposture, *The Making of the Modern Family*, the MF is the product of the liberated sexuality of the lads and lasses set free by the industrial revolution, and thence it works its way *up*wards to the benighted bourgeoisie. Stone's view is paternalist and Shorter's view is populist; we may make our choice according to temperament, since neither view is supported by any relevant evidence.

Both Stone and Shorter agree, however, as to what was not modern: specifically, the families of the poor peasantry or of the labourers at any time before 1800, at which time, in Stone's view, the Sunday School began to convert some respectable workers to familial virtues and affections. (How the Sunday Schools inculcated frank sexuality is left unexplained). Before 1800 these families were not sharing and caring or companionate or sexually frank or fulfilled. Marriage was formed from motives of economic interest, children were bred by the parents with a view to their subsequent exploitation (or to provide a pension fund for the parents) and there was no trace of affection in the marital relationship. It is difficult to document this kind of negative, so that at this point Stone several times falls back upon Shorter's French reserves. Thus: 'a late 18th century doctor, writing about the Auvergne, which is admittedly notorious for its backwardness, was shocked to find that "people do not feel that true happiness consists of kindness to those about you, who will always respond in like manner."'

One would not like to think that any of the English were ever as backward as that. However, Stone is reasonably confident that the labouring poor were much given to infanticide, child-battering and wife-beating. When not beating them, the husbands treated their wives 'as domestic slaves.' One reason why the spouses did not love one another was that they were illiterate. 'Anthropological studies of the many societies in which sentiment is unknown' (no such studies are cited) support the view that love is a product of learned cultural expectations. But by 1600 or 1800 the English peasantry and working people had not had any chance to learn about love, because learning requires literacy. They did not learn to love each other because they couldn't read novels, and they couldn't have a companionate marriage because, until both husband and wife could read the newspapers, they could have little 'in common to talk about.'

It should by now be apparent that Lawrence Stone has written a very odd book. Since the author is a formidable scholar, this book will undoubtedly acquire, in some quarters, an awesome reputation as a work of formidable authority and learning. But it is not. It is a curious, hit-or-miss affair. Some parts – those dealing with the upper classes, about which Stone knows a great deal – are of great interest. Other parts – such as the chapter on plebeian sexual behaviour – should be pulped.

How did this come about? Some part of the trouble Stone brings upon himself by over-confidence. He likes to present himself as a sturdy, no-nonsense Anglo-Saxon thinker, indeed as a bit of a bully. As he lays about him on all sides with his stout quarter-staff of common-sense, effeminate and alien theories fall away to right and left nursing their cracked ribs.

This is usually good fun, because Stone is an unaffected and serious man, intent upon stirring up an argument about significant issues. He doesn't mind chancing his arm in the process. He is ready to slap down on the page sentences so brash or inept as to make other scholars blench: 'there were certainly plenty of cheerful and affectionate Wives of Bath in real life as well as in the works of Shakespeare.' Where other historians might spend weeks in covering up their own sensitive areas of ignorance, Stone shouts 'Don't know!' and walks blithely into them, whistling and swinging his good ashplant.

Such sensitive areas, in this book, include much of 18th century intellectual and social life, and nearly all of the experience of the lower classes. Unless I have misread him, Stone appears to think that assizes were held four times a year; that the Dissenters had become 'conformist Unitarians' by 1720; that there was no radical feminist movement between the time of Mary Wollstonecraft and the 20th century (and that Hannah Moore was a feminist); that the system of sinecures in church and state for the sons of the rich did not come under attack until after 1850; and that in 'the early 19th century' parents in Bethnal Green succeeded in hiring out their children for labour for sums (15s 8d and 25s 6d a week) well in excess of the wages of skilled artisans.

Maybe the last results from an error in transcription (Stone's source gives 1s 8d and 2s 6d, in the 1860s), and maybe the transcription was a Freudian slip, since it makes the parents seem more avaricious and mercenary (part of Stone's argument). Many slips add up to a mist, and that is what Stone likes fighting in. That way he can pulverize the features of an opponent before we can even see them. It is never clear whether Stone doesn't know, doesn't *want* to know, or doesn't want *us* to know. On one occasion (let me cite the page, which is 646) he clearly identifies 'capitalism' with the factory system, and the 'spread of a market economy' with 'industrialization.' Now Stone knows very well that these entities are not identical and are not historically coincident, and that none of the important originators of thought in his chosen area, the rise of affective individualism, supposed that they were: I am thinking of Marx, Weber and

Tawney. It is, however, convenient for Stone to create this definitional mist, since it enables him to ambush and beat into pulp at one go several antagonists who have never even been introduced to the reader: in this case, several contemporary descendants of marxist and Weberian theory.

But in this book he has allowed the mist to spread too far. Some demographic evidence apart, he relies for his central evidence upon a great quantity of literary material – many volumes (mostly published) of diaries, correspondence, and memories of the aristocracy, gentry and professional bourgeoisie. One hazards that in ploughing through all this material he has employed, among other things, a careful subject-index, and has entered each reference to adultery; anal sex; contraception; courtship; kinship networks; kissing in public; masturbation; midwives; toilet training; wives (beaten); wives (deserted); wives (murdered); and so on. In this way much interesting and much curious information is assembled. In addition, in some of the most arresting passages of the book, Stone runs through individual case-studies, where the documentation is unusually good. It does not make very lovely reading: some of the sexual studies (Boswell's utterly self-centred sensuality) might be a medical record of male excretion. Indeed, as in other studies drawn from this kind of material, women appear more defeated and exploited, more as the defenceless subjects of history than they ever allowed themselves to be.

The difficulty with Stone's method is that the research is very rarely finely-enough aimed. There is something about most things, but nothing very decisive about any. He is too easily content with the random evidence which has fallen out of the diaries onto his cards. But on a hundred subjects, from obstetrics to domestic architecture, some finely-aimed research into different kinds of sources could have given a quite different authority to his findings. His few pages on marriage law are perfunctory; case-law is scarcely consulted; the church courts make only a brief appearance. His evidence on that critically important arrangement, the marriage settlement, is largely based on a 25-year-old article by Habbakuk: an adequate article for some purposes, but not for the purposes of the historian of the family.

Thus there are problems of method and interpretation, even

when we consider those social groups which left copious literary evidence about their marriages and affairs. How is Stone to write the history of the family among those groups – small farmers, shopkeepers, artisans, the labouring poor – who were either illiterate or left little written record? Demographic evidence apart (and Stone is able to draw upon statistics for prenuptial pregnancy, and so on, to be found in Shorter's and Laslett's work), what else is there to go on?

There are several answers on offer. Quantifiers argue (naturally) that only quantities are real. Or it may be argued that it is impossible (or premature) to write a history of the family which extends to all classes – that until something more than demographic generalities are available, the historian would do best to belt up. Lawrence Stone would regard that evasion as despicable cowardice. So he opts for the most unlikely answer of all: since the lower orders left no literary record of their interior and familial emotional life, this is evidence that they had none.

His huge self-confidence makes all worse. When dealing with the common people, Stone assumes that whatever he does not happen to know is either unimportant or unknowable. Opportunities for research – as into dowry and inheritance practices among small farmers – are passed by. His accounts of popular customs (spousals, bundling, wife-sales) are skewed, and misunderstandings are compounded by mistranscribed dates and the misreading of his own sources. Page after page about the labouring poor or plebeian sex are beyond repair: if one took them out with scissors, one would be left with a better book.

There must be some ulterior theoretical explanation for this disaster: and indeed there is. It arises from the prior assumption that there can be such a thing as a history of *the* family. In this first error all the subsequent errors are entailed. If this history is defined as one of affect or attitude, then it must be located somewhere; a history of feeling must be a history of someone's feeling; what better locus than the garrulous and literary upper middle class? All that lies outside *that* history then becomes null, a darkness: a darkness which may only be enlightened according to Stone's Law of 'stratified diffusion' or 'seeping down' from the middle class to the plebs. At last, in our own time, light has broken over the whole social landscape: we have The Modern Family.

I am fully persuaded of the importance of historical attention to familial and sexual relations. But there cannot be any such historical entity as *the* family. For familial relations are inextricably part and parcel of every other kind of relation and occupation: that is, they are components of a whole way of life. And the way of life of Stone's 'leading sector,' the upper bourgeoisie, has been so remote from those of the majority of the English people as to leave no room for one single history of attitude or affective relations.

Stone's hypotheses (as to the great outer darkness) are that the affective familial life of the common people was either null, or competitive and hostile (thus, the poor resented their own children as competitors for food); and that their motives were either animalistic or 'economic' in the meanest and most calculating way: they married wives and begat children in order to exploit them. These hypotheses reproduce, with comical accuracy, the ideology and sensibility of 18th century upper class paternalists, prior to the Wordsworthian challenge. That is, Stone has fallen into the traps laid by his own gentry sources, with their incapacity to accept the authenticity of the experience of those to whom 'words are but under-agents of their souls.' These are traps which have a special succulence for browsing academics, for whom it seems self-evident that the professional classes are the 'leading sector' – as well as by far the most sensitive people – and that both wisdom and sensibility must 'seep downward' from them through the channels of literacy and education.

I won't attempt now an agenda for an alternative history of 'the family' of 'the common people.' But a great deal *can* be found out about that history, certainly in the 18th and 19th centuries, by patient and logical attention to many kinds of source. A first principle of this inquiry must be that we cannot put 'affect' or feeling here, and economics or 'interest' there. Very obviously, certain kinds of emotional and familial and sexual expression – such as courtly love or writing diaries or keeping actresses as mistresses – presuppose leisure and resources which belong only to the upper class. Stone tends to offer this as if the emotional life has somehow become liberated from 'economics,' and has at the same time become more real and more deeply-felt. This is nonsense: leisure allows for the cultivation of some kinds of sentiment, but economic necessities have only been masked or distanced, and Boswell's narcissistic sexual exploits depend upon the ulterior exploitation of the Scottish poor. The genteel sensibility is, in that sense, a product of surplus value; and the genteel family is as much a consequence of 'economic' process as is the harsh contest for a marginal existence (the men at risk at sea, the women carrying peats home on their backs) of the Highland crofters.

But the Highland crofters' family was not the same as the Cornish tinners' nor as the Yorkshire weavers'. And to understand these families, and to detect the signs and gestures which disclose their interior emotional life, we must attend very closely indeed to 'economics' – or to that daily occupation (farming, fishing, weaving, begging) which gives us their way of living: a way of living which was not merely a way of surviving but also a way of relating and of valuing. Some of the best historical work now being done on the family – Hans Medick, of Gottingen, outlines it in a recent issue of *Social History* from Hull – arises, exactly, out of the closest examination of the whole way of life of German cottage industry.

I am not criticizing Stone on the grounds that 'marriage' and 'the family' indicate unchanging universals of relationship and feeling (or of 'human nature') – that, at bottom, the 18th century poor felt just like us. They did not, and Stone is right to hold resolutely to a historical perspective; as our ancestors knew, manners makyth man, and woman also. It is true that whole cultures seem to swing between the repressive and the relaxed, and in addressing such problems, and refusing the mono-causal explanations beloved by 'psycho-historians,' Stone has advanced knowledge.

But he sadly misunderstands the differential social and occupational determinants upon sexual relations; how, for the majority throughout history, familial relations have been intermeshed with the structures of work. Feeling may be *more*, rather than less, tender or intense *because* relations are 'economic' and critical to mutual survival. Anthropologists may know of societies without 'sentiment' but they do not often show us societies without norms or value-systems. That people did not feel and relate like us does not mean that they did not feel at all nor relate in ways which to them were imbued with the profoundest meaning.

The history of the 'lower sort of people' between 1500 and 1800 discloses many different familial modes: some may seem to us to be rough, lacking in any foresight, picaresque: others may seem to be cold and bound to elemental needs. But the point of history is not to see their occasions through the mist of our feelings, nor to measure them against the Modern Us. It is first of all to understand the past: to reconstruct those forgotten norms, decode the obsolete rituals, and detect the hidden gestures. Because peasant marriages were arranged out of circumstance and necessity, it does not mean that many families did not learn a profound mutual dependence, a habit of love. Why should Stone assume (for example) that when men marry older women it is evidence of marriage for the sake of interest or economic advantage, whereas when men marry younger women it is proof of a shift towards marriage founded upon affection? That is a culture-bound assumption, an expectation learned within our own immature but sexually overstimulated time.

I am persuaded that we are different, as parents or as lovers, from those in the past; but I am not persuaded that we are so much better, more companionate, more caring, than our forefathers and mothers. It may depend, somewhat, upon class and occupation, then and now. As a quantitative certainty we – all of us – have more leisure to examine our own feelings than all except a small elite used to have; but it is less certain that, in those days, hearts broke less painfully or lifted with less joy than they do now. It annoys me that both Professor Stone and Professor Shorter leave their readers to feel so complacent about their own modernity. It annoys me even more that both should indict the poor, on so little evidence, of indifference to their children and of callous complicity in their high rate of mortality. Much the same is said, in some quarters, about the Indian poor today. No doubt the Modern Family would do better, since it would never allow itself to become so poor nor to have so many children. But if the lower orders had not formed some kind of affective bonding and familial loyalty, we, their descendants, might never have made our gracious descent.

I suppose that Lawrence Stone wished to stir this kind of argument up. He is an excellent historical provocateur. He is also a good photographer, and the best illustrations in the book are from his own photos of monumental tombs. The notes are at the end of the book, which, in a work of this weight, is a disgrace for which both publisher and author must share responsibility. There are some 1,300 notes, but, as a conscientious reviewer, I have had to scrabble through to the back to find them some 2,000 times. Perhaps this made me cross.

From *New Society*, vol. 41 no. 779, 8th September 1977 reviewing Lawrence Stone's. *The Family, Sex and Marriage in England, 1500–1800*, New York, Harper & Row 1977.

Herbert Gutman

Here is a rich book – a dozen essays, of uneven quality, some hitherto unpublished, some published in inaccessible places, which, taken together, offer a conspectus of Herbert Gutman's energetic genius. Yet the volume would seem shapeless and sprawling – now labour struggles in the Gilded Age, now coal miners on the prairie, now the post-emancipation efforts of black communities to found and support their own schools – if it were not for the introductory study by the book's editor, Ira Berlin.

This seventy-page essay is outstanding, a model of what such a study ought to be but almost never is. This is far more than a conventional tribute paid to a friend and fellow scholar. Berlin has read with care all of Gutman's published and much of his unpublished work; he places it in its context, evaluates it, provides necessary intellectual biography, assesses, commends, praises, and on occasion criticises. In doing this with such clarity and honesty, Berlin has not only given unity and focus to this collection, he has also written a major study in recent intellectual history.

He has, furthermore, given a more analytical account of Gutman's historiographical 'project' – of the direction and parameters of his work – than anything given to us by Gutman himself. This may be considered by the sophisticated upthrusting generation to be disgraceful, and to be yet one more illustration of the theoretical immaturity of the historical profession of yesteryear. If Gutman was a major historian – as so many of his contemporaries insist – where are the conceptual breakthroughs? If these are 'essays on the American Working Class,' where is the essay that defines the nature of 'class'? If his work was about 'power' and 'culture,' where are these two concepts ratified and defined?

Confronted by the rigorous inquisition of today's aspirant theorists, Gutman does not come out of it too well. He started publishing late. He did not plan his *oeuvre* as a real historian – let us say

Foucault – would do: one mighty general study after another, the results already known (and arriving from some ulterior theoretical area) in advance of the research, and the research performed by obedient assistants in order to illustrate the theses. Gutman muddled into arguments, which grew into articles too long to be published, went into bottom drawers, were dug out and rewritten, grew even longer, and in some cases had to be rescued and shaped by editors or publisher. (He was fortunate to find in Pantheon a publisher both strongly supportive and intellectually adventurous.) So far from knowing always where he was going – what his conclusions would or ought to be – he suffered from prolonged writing blocks and depressions. Writing was never easy for him and sometimes his early drafts buried the reader in a reiteration of examples. If he wished to demonstrate a contested point conclusively, he would do this, not by elegant formulations but by emptying a whole sack of confirmatory evidence upon the reader's head.

Gutman could not meet with my notional critic's approval. Yet, viewed from another aspect, Gutman was one of the most critically alert historians of our time. His blocks and depressions, his rewritings and polemics, were, exactly, testimony to this critical engagement with the past – reformulating old historical problems and proposing new ones, questioning received texts and their stereotypes, experimenting with novel methodologies, reading widely in adjacent disciplines (ethnography, demography, sociology) in search of new ways of decoding slave cultural inheritances or artisan work customs.

If musicians or artists are 'born' before they are trained, then it may not be unreasonable to suppose that there is such a thing as a historical sense, a sense with which Herb Gutman was endowed in superabundance. I do not know in what part of the cranium phrenologists place the 'historical imagination' or with which faculties it is associated, but one could not be in Herb's company for half an hour without being astounded at his restless and inquisitive historical consciousness, his superb capacity for empathy with the 'anonymous' workers of the past to whom he gave back voices and identities. Add to this a craftsman's appetite for the archives and a trained skill in interrogating the text, and one is some way towards itemising his qualities.

I think of his working life as being spent in a kind of *wrestling*, and this collection exemplifies this stance. His favoured mode was dialogue. He situated himself between the evidence and the received historiography and made them interrogate each other. He tried out his ideas (and read aloud his latest finds) in a ceaseless dialogue with friends, colleagues, graduates, and with his wife and fellow historian, Judy. His prose flowed most readily when he was engaged in polemic, and several of the studies in this collection had their origin in this kind of engagement: his polemic against stereotyped views of general working-class assent to the values of the Gilded Age, his polemic against models of the 'breakdown' of immigrant cultures and traditions.

If this is not theoretically informed history, then I do not know what that can be. The interventions were always in sensitive and significant areas. There is the tumultuous (and sometimes hilarious) polemic against Fogel and Engerman's *Time on the Cross*, published as *Slavery and the Numbers Game* (and some part republished here), and first appearing in the *Journal of Negro History* in 1975. What is difficult to remember now is the ecstatic terms in which *Time on the Cross* had been received on almost all sides, at a time when 'cliometrics' was carrying all before it. The critique of *Time on the Cross* was a decisive check to the excessive claims of the quantifiers and to their uncritical reception.

Gutman himself was in no way hostile to sophisticated techniques of counting, as several studies in the book demonstrate. But he showed that no elaboration of statistical techniques could displace the need for historical logic – the asking of intelligent and appropriate questions – nor could the computer somehow sanitise the evidence and provide a positivist guarantee against the infiltration of ideological assumptions. He was acutely aware of the way in which the ideological premises of the present put down roots in the form of falsified histories, in a self-fulfilling procedure by which one feeds the others.

The Black Family in Slavery and Freedom found its source in precisely such a polemic, in this case against Daniel P. Moynihan's report on the racial crisis in American cities, in which much is set down as caused by the 'deterioration of the Negro family,' which in its turn is given a historical explanation in the 'deep-seated structural distortions in the life of the Negro American,' created by slavery and segregation. This gave to Gutman a thesis against which his research proposed antitheses. 'To argue, as I am doing,' he wrote to me, 'that blacks – even as slaves – "made their own history" ... is to quarrel with 3/4ths of a century of terrible scholarship mired in class and race bias.' It also led him to his own countertheses. In the book (he explained) 'slavery is described as an adaptive experience, and ... the blacks are viewed as a special instance of a working-class population.'

Yet even when Gutman arrived at theses, these were not carefully crafted and given dogmatic finality. In this book one can certainly find definitions of culture, class and class formation, and the rest. But these appear seriatim, in the course of argument and critique, rather than as System. They are not, in my view, the worse for that; indeed, when theory is presented as critique, it acquires definition and clarity. But what leaves some readers dissatisfied is that Gutman offers every finding as provisional, every definition as imperfect and awaiting refinement, every conclusion as open-ended and under the profession's review. Even here, in *Power & Culture*, there are several places where he reviews and revises his own earlier work, or accepts, with frankness and generosity – perhaps, in his interview with Mike Merrill, accepts too easily? – the criticisms of others.

This was a quality in him that was admired by his fellow historians. His open, strenuously argumentative, self-critical style, his way of proposing new questions and agendas, made for stimulating seminars and for memorable interventions at conferences. There was nothing smooth or self-defensive about this style. Its vigorous interrogatives had a way of leaping over barriers of language and of culture. My wife, Dorothy, and I visited several history departments in Chinese universities in 1985, a year or so after a group of American scholars, which included Herb, had been through. The impression he had made was profound, and at every place they were scheming to get him back. He had conveyed, not so much a method – perhaps they have enough methods and too many answers? – but an anti-method: stop looking for answers and start looking for the right questions.

When I speak of 'antimethod' I do not mean lack of
theoretical concern or of consistency. I mean, rather, resistance to
conceptual closures and to the reification of findings into
systems. Perhaps provisionality and open-endedness was itself his
method? Nowhere is this more clearly presented than in the
interview (for the Radical Historians Organization, MARHO)
undertaken by Mike Merrill and included in this volume.

The interview form can be a lazy one. But Merrill is a gifted
interviewer, an able historian, and he prepares his interviews with
comprehensive reading and with a careful selection of points of
pressure. The passage where Merrill is trying to clarify Gutman's
allegiances and his relation to Marxist historiography deserves to
be quoted at length:

Q: How does the new labour history answer the question, 'Why
has there been no mass socialist movement in the United
States?'

Gutman: I don't think that is a well-put historical question. We
need to put aside notions that workers' movements have
developed properly elsewhere and in the United States they
developed improperly. We need to put aside the English model,
the French model, and the Cuban model, and then ask a set of
very, very tough questions about what American workers
actually thought and did – and why ....

Q: Based on your work for before 1900 and on [David]
Montgomery's for the period after 1900, can you make judgments about whether or not workers' movements in these
periods were adequate to the historical tasks they faced if they
were to achieve their political goals?

Gutman: I don't think that way as a historian. What does it
mean to talk about historical tasks that workers faced? We are
letting in through the back door a notion of fixed and
predetermined historical development. We are measuring the
American worker (or the French worker of the Polish worker)
against an ideal type. That is the Whig fallacy of history once
again.

Q: It is not just the Whig fallacy. Some would call it the Marxist fallacy.

Gutman: Yes, there is a Marxist variant of the Whig fallacy. It comes from an essentialist view of workers or the working-class, one that emphasizes a predetermined pattern of historical development.

Q: But some would argue that such a notion is central to classical Marxism.

Gutman: And it contains within it dangerous notions of vanguard leadership and vanguard parties ....

Q: But vanguard parties are not central to the vision of classical Marxism, the Marxism of Marx. What is central is some notion of historical progress and some direction to history. What is left of Marxism, in your view, when you have stripped away this aspect?

Gutman: What is left when you clear away the determinist and teleological elements is good questions that direct your attention to critical ways of looking at ongoing historical processes ....

This does not seem to me to be evasive. Gutman's refusal to be tied in with any 'notion of fixed and predetermined historical development' is a defence of the discipline of history. The historian's object is, in part, to 'understand' history – that is, to answer relevant questions that are appropriate to the evidence. To this Gutman adds less manifest functions:

The central value of historical understanding is that it transforms historical givens into historical contingencies. It enables us to see the structures in which we live and the inequality people experience as only one among many other possible experiences. By doing that, you free people for creative and critical (or radical) thought.

The argument is that historical understanding liberates the mind from the fatalism that both ignorance and an inert capitulation to determinism bring: 'Once you surrender the fixed older forms of

historical explanation and process, the future becomes open. It
then becomes even more important to analyse and examine the
history of those structures and ideologies that shape our lives.'

But neither the 'goals' of history nor history's 'meaning' are
inscribed within 'history' itself. These are premises imported by
the historical observer – and legitimately imported if the contra-
band is not concealed. The premises of Gutman are those of
democratic socialism, revealed on page after page in his interest
in working-class self-activity and in mutuality. To this one might
add a respect for the 'anonymous' individual and her/his experience. Nothing drove him more swiftly to polemic than the
contemptuous dismissal of the experiences of 'ordinary' working
people, whether it came from modernisers or Marxists or
quantifiers or intellectual elitists. He expected to find that any
individual would turn out to be extraordinary.

I notice that some commentators assume that Gutman's style
of history, and its reception, belong in some way to the radical
1960s as one of the fashions of that time. This suggests an
activity more ephemeral and less solidly constructed than is
revealed in this volume. There is *something* in it, but only if we
see the 1960s as more contradictory than the stereotypes propose.
For one thing, some of the 'New Left' intelligentsia did not
want to know about working-class history at all. At the end of
that decade Herb wrote to Dorothy and me about a talk he gave
to the Socialist Scholars Conference:

> It was a disaster – to put it mildly. The young radicals would
> have none of this kind of 'history.' The responses were wild,
> not mild, and some were very angry because I had obfuscated
> the criminal character of our entire history by talking about
> work habits, culture, etc. There is a very real need for such
> persons to believe that this has always been a culture dominated
> by the industrial-military complex. Their alienation from the
> present drives them to reject the past in its entirety. The
> American past is the unredeeming saga of a mixture of
> corporate exploitation, all-pervasive racism, and a compliant and
> corrupted working-class and radical movement. It is almost as if
> Mayor Daley and the Chicago police landed at Plymouth Rock

and as if agents for General Motors dumped the tea in Boston Harbor.

This makes it clear that Gutman was not some ephemeral radical culture hero. At the same time, he was a stanch and active supporter of the civil rights movement and the opposition to the Viet Nam war, and he admired many of the initiatives of SDS. His letter to us continued: 'I have a group of really fine graduate students [at Rochester] .... The young American 'new left' is not the monolith that popularizers have made of it. Among these dedicated young people are a number deeply committed to serious social history and torn between that commitment and an equally strong desire to alter this society.'

What made Herb growl was the limitless capacity of the intelligentsia to write off working-class initiatives within elaborately theorized systems – structures or determinisms – from whose compulsions only they, the intelligentsia, are supposed to be exempt. What made him growl even louder was when intellectuals theorised such compulsions in radical or Marxist rhetoric, offering conservative or defeatist ideology in fancy leftist dress. (This is in fact one leading form that reaction takes today on many campuses – sometimes in the fancy dress of Marxism or of 'critical theory' – whose strategy is to show that all, except a small number of initiated theorists, are unfree.) It concerned him that such defeatism (and fear of all 'populism') blocked the channels of communications between the campus and the general public.

Americans' loss of historical memory is the theme of the final chapter. He was concerned, as the poet Thomas McGrath has been concerned (although expressed in different terms), that, in the eastern United States, 'history no longer functions, has been forgotten, has been 'paved over.' In the East man begins every day for himself.' In Gutman's words there was a 'vast distance' separating 'working historians and other American intellectuals – and, indeed, ordinary Americans of all kinds.' In his last few years Gutman did more and more, through summer schools with trade unionists, through the American Social History Project (a project that continues), and through efforts at some popular synthesis of the 'new' history, to open the clogged channels of communication.

But he did not overlook the fact that some of the loss of historical memory was self-willed and owed as much to the self-suppression of an alienated and privileged 'left' as to the ideologically motivated amnesia of the 'right.'

If I have not entered into a close discussion of several of the themes in this book, that is because it would have taken me beyond my competence. But there is one matter within my competence where I must dissent from Ira Berlin's excellent introduction. Rather too often throughout it there is reference to the 'Thompsonian' influence upon Gutman. One would not suppose, from this account, that the influence was very much two-way, and should more properly be called a dialogue. When I was first invited by Herb for several weeks to Buffalo in 1966 I did not go there as an instructor. On the contrary, from my first arrival at the airport I was immersed in debate, and was subjected to an intense course of instruction in American labour historiography. Our dialogue soon took in many others, on both sides of the Atlantic, so that it would be possible to chart, not a Thompsonian influence, but an Anglo-American impulse in social history. Nor is there any warrant for identifying this as 'Thompsonian culturalism' – 'culturalism' is a term that Herb and I always refused, a spurious term invented by systematizers whose business it is to rigidify differences and to set up specious boundaries between approaches that are perfectly compatible. Gutman never proposed that there was only One True Method of history – indeed, one of my strongest recollections is of the generosity and enthusiasm with which he would commend the work of scholars whose approach might differ from his own.

I should add that *Power & Culture* includes an excellent checklist of Herbert Gutman's published writings, prepared by Andrew Gyory. It is an important and necessary book, but not one to read at a single sitting. The essays should be savoured one at a time. And pondered.

From *Dissent*, fall 1988, reviewing *Power and Culture: Essays on the American Working Class*, by Herbert G. Gutman, edited by Ira Berlin,. New York: Pantheon, 1987. 452 pp. $29.95.

Which Britons?

King Henry: Methinks I could not die anywhere so contented as
in the king's company, – his cause being just, and his quarrel
honorable.
Michael Williams: That's more than we know.

Since I am going to argue with some parts of this book, let me say
at once that it is a significant study and well deserves the praise
with which it has been received. Linda Colley writes with clarity
and grace – and how much is won by these uncommon virtues!
She also has a capacity for historical generalisation which puts her
into the front rank among her contemporaries. She has also been
well served, in most respects, by her publishers, Yale University
Press, who have allowed her a multitude of illustrations – perhaps
one to every five or six pages of text. These are evocative and
well-selected, even though some require a magnifying glass to
understand (but why not?). Professor Colley has an alias as
Director of the Lewis Walpole Library at Yale, and she has clearly
put time there to good use. Some of the illustrations are
extraordinarily good, such as Romney's 'Eton leaving portrait' of
the young Charles Grey, and very many will be new to most
readers. The one respect in which the publisher fails is in putting
the notes at the end of the book instead of at the foot of the page.
This is to wreck a historical work, but I will not argue that
familiar case over again. The directors of a prestigious academic
press should be ashamed.

Britons is an interpretive essay and not a chronological study.
Colley has an enviable command of the secondary sources published in the past fifteen years, although her recourse to primary
evidence is less fluent. Her thesis is that it was in the 18th century
that English, Welsh and Scots became a British nation, and that a
shared Protestantism facilitated this and gave to this junction an

identity. This in turn was enforced by a century and more of wars and confrontations with the French 'Other', a Catholic Other which was also a prime competitor in trade and empire. The rivalry with France and, to a lesser degree, with another Catholic power, Spain, consolidated the British nation and pointed out the Jacobite and then the 'Jacobin' oppositions as treasonable.

War was the formative and binding British experience of the 18th century (her thesis continues) and this had unplanned and unintended consequences, or what Pasternak once called 'the consequences of consequences'. For the men, service in the armed forces educated them not only in patriotism but also in citizenship – they returned after the Napoleonic Wars to demand political rights. Although the culture of loyalism in the same period was profoundly anti-feminist, yet the widespread participation of women in patriotic activities and in support of the armed forces provided them with education in self-organisation and with a new sense of public space. At the apex of this loyal new nation of Britons was the monarchy, and George III's long reign culminating in his 'apotheosis' as the king was celebrated with more and more elaborate ceremony. In a few suggestive asides Colley hints that today, in the absence of an enemy Other and with the decline of Protestantism, the British nation may be about to fall apart.

It is a persuasive argument which hangs together well. But some parts of it are presented too confidently, and I am sure that Colley would prefer to be challenged rather than receiving facile assent. In any interpretive essay the author tends to select evidence which confirms the interpretation and to neglect whatever is inconvenient. I am sure that I have been guilty of this sometimes myself. In this case there is no micrometer which will measure degrees of patriotism or loyalism. Colley is able to make convincing soundings here and there. Her general thesis about Protestantism will scarcely be challenged, and she can confirm it with reference to the Gordon Riots (1780), sparked off in large part by crowd hostility to the relief of disabilities on Catholics; this disposition continued to be evidenced by the volume of petitions against Catholic Emancipation in 1829. However, in using 'Protestantism' as a blanket term she has little to say about the fact that that extraordinary hybrid creature, the Church of England, balanced itself between two opponents, the Catholics and the Dissenters (who also were subject to limitations on their civic rights). The ensuing divisions were more significant than her somewhat complacent account of Protestantism suggests.

The difficulty of interpretive selectivity may be illustrated with reference to two other recent books which deal with the British people – or some British people – in the same period. One, by a Conservative peer and sound historical scholar, Ian Gilmour, is entitled *Riot, Risings and Revolution: Governance and Violence in 18th Century England*. This chronicles and analyses the repeated confrontation between a turbulent crowd and the authorities which punctuated the entire century. Another is the striking work by a North American Marxist, Peter Linebaugh, *The London Hanged*, which examines 'from below' the short life experience of many of those and ended up on the Tyburn gallows; quite a few of these had served in the armed forces or at sea in defending and extending the British empire. Taking these books with Colley's, each of them might be describing different 'Britons'. This also indicates some of the evidence which Linda Colley hurries past with averted eyes.

Despite her high intelligence and liberal disposition she has written a 'top down' history, flattering to a conservative self-image of Britons. One is often impelled to ask: *which* Britons? How far has she written a thesis on the making of the British ruling class, and how far is she entitled to incorporate the common people into the same thesis? The first thesis is undoubtedly true, and she shows it to be so. As to how far the common people participated in this new loyal British consensus, I remain sceptical. As Michael Williams said, when King Hal wandered incognito among his troops on the eve of the battle of Agincourt, 'That's more than we know.'

I have been trying for much of my life to find out, but I remain an agnostic. The answer probably varied according to persons and places, times and contexts. The disposition of the majority of Britons was probably ambivalent. Colley makes her argument easier by laying great stress upon the papers of the Volunteers, those part-time civil defence forces which were raised

to meet a French invasion, in 1797–1800 and again in 1803–08.
Inevitably such evidence will tend to confirm a loyalist thesis.
But in doing so she passes by the considerable archive of
'Home Office Papers' – that is, the extensive correspondence
between anxious magistrates and the Home Office. This tells a
very different story, of popular disaffection and class alienation,
especially between 1797 and 1803, years of severe food shortage
and soaring prices, of discontent against taxes (which extended to
the middling orders), of mutiny in the navy, insurrection in
Ireland, and war weariness which may have compelled government to accept the brief Peace of Amiens. This evidence has
been drawn upon extensively in two books by Roger Wells,
Wretched Faces and *Insurrection*. If one were to discount all this
testimony, one would have to conclude that the British ruling
class was made up of paranoiacs and fools, which it was not.

The evidence of Volunteers is not as unequivocal as might be
supposed. Those who volunteered were exempted from service as
regulars. They might serve only in their immediate vicinity and
choose preferred (non-military) roles such as waggoners or
drovers. Colley makes much of their numbers, but does not tell
us much about what they did. Most of the yeomanry/cavalry
were sub-gentry or their clients and tenants, and one of the
things that many of them did was to join or form fox hunts,
where they could ride about in a manly way and signal their
loyalism by calling the unfortunate creature whom they pursued
'Charlie', after the radical and pro-peace Whig leader, Charles
James Fox. (To this day English fox-hunters call the fox
'Charlie', although few know why.)

They also, as Colley acknowledges, dressed up in uniform,
rode around in macho postures, and were sometimes employed
against crowds who were rioting against the high price of bread;
one anonymous letter writer remarked that 'we dont care a Dam
for them fellows that Call Themselves Gentlemen Soldiers But in
our opinion they Look moore like Monkeys Riding on bears ....'
Nor need their loyalty be always assumed. We know that some
reformers joined the Volunteers in order to get hold of arms. In
1801 sensationally seditious anonymous letters were circulating in
a corner of Somerset:

Then raise yr drooping spirits up
Nor starve by Pitt's decree
Fix up the sacred Guillotine
Proclaim – French liberty!

The authorities, by comparing handwriting, identified the suspected author of these letters as a sergeant in the Volunteers. (This does not mean that we must take those sentiments at their face value, for in an old popular tradition, which I have called 'counter-theatre', the discontented chose the vocabulary – Jacobite or Jacobin – most likely to alarm the authorities).

William Cobbett, himself a former regular soldier who had not yet crossed to the side of the reformers, utterly despised the Volunteers. In 1804 he described the Manchester Volunteers as 'a parcel of empty coxcombs of manufacturers, whom the imbecility of government had dressed up in swords and red coats.' No doubt if the French had invaded some of them might have given a better account of themselves. But the French did not, so the valour and loyalty of the Volunteers must remain a hypothesis. One must recall that the most triumphant engagement of their direct successors took place after the wars, and was *against* Britons, when these solicitor's clerks, dancing masters and wine-merchants in fancy dress rode down the Lancashire working people of both sexes who were demonstrating for political reform in the 'battle' of 'Peterloo'.

My examples are more biased than are Colley's. There is no way of telling how many shared the views of Jonathan Panther, a London coachmaker, who was indicted for seditious libel in August 1803, for saying 'it is a war of the rich men against the most sober, Honest and Industrious part of the people of this nation, who have always been the principal support of the rich ... ' We have nothing like the remarkable testimonies of liberated slaves now presented by Ira Berlin and his colleagues in *Free at Last* (New Press). If we should treat with respect Colley's informed hunch (for it is not much more) as to British loyalism, then I may be allowed to offer my own different hunch. I think that there was a marked change in popular responses between the first and second French Wars. In the first there was widespread disaffection, of the Jonathan Panther kind, and even some sympathy with the French. In the second war – the truly 'Napoleonic War' – there was a powerful surge towards a national patriotic and anti-Gallican consensus. Undoubtedly this was stimulated from above, but it met with a strong response as French invasion forces threatened the British coast, and it came to a climax in the famous naval victory of Trafalgar.

At any time between 1803 and about 1810 the Colley thesis is probably right. There was a political element in this change also. These years were the very nadir of any British 'Jacobin' enthusiasm. The earnest follower of Tom Paine's *Rights of Man* was utterly turned off France by French betrayal of revolutionary principles – by the elevation of Napoleon as First Consul and then as Emperor, by the re-establishment of hierarchy and of slavery, by French aggression and aggrandisement in Europe. Most of those middle-class reformers, as well as working-class Painites who had been disaffected in the first French war became ardent anti-Gallicans in the second. Wordsworth, who was surveilled as a suspected Jacobin in 1797, was drilling with the Grassmere Volunteers in 1803. John Thelwall, the leading reformer of the 1790s, was writing an ode on the death of Admiral Nelson in 1805.

All this made a difference. Such persons were the potential leaders of an alternative Britain. People can swing swiftly between poles when their leaders shift. But even loud patriotism must be inspected carefully for its nuances, its authenticity and also its ego-trips. Whole cart-loads of patriotic ballads came off the presses in those years. Most of them were songs that one suspects were never sung, such as one in praise of the Royal Manchester Volunteers to the tune of 'Our Cannon Balls, and Bumshells':

You'll have a Band of Music Boys,
Your Loyal Hearts to cheer,
A dashing sword, Yourself to guard,
Roast Beef, and British beer;
Your head adorned with Ribbon Blue,
And in each Arm, – a wench;
And all the work you have to do,
Will be to beat the French.

Chorus
In the Manchester Volunteers,
Haste, Britons, Haste to go,
Along with Captain Delhoste,
To fight the Gallic foe.

(Perhaps the Volunteers were somewhat encumbered in their military duties by the wenches on their arms, which may be why the 'dashing sword' was reserved for wielding against the unarmed handloom weavers and cotton spinners on the field of Peterloo). There were also merry ballads which were anti-Gallican *tout court*. Thus one, called 'Jolly Jack of Dover', is supposed to be spoken by a ferryman who brought emigrants across from Calais:

I brought o'er a Milliner, who said her name was Nancy.
She said she had some fringes that wou'ld arouse my fancy;
But I said avast there, my dear, I am not so eager,
Nor so tir'd of English meat to long for your soup meagre.

Chorus
O! no, the Devil a bit with jolly Jack of Dover,
None of your murd'ring Frenchmen to England shall come over.

As with all texts in popular culture, then as now, it is not easy to decide whether such provided texts reveal the thoughts of their readers. But the reader or the viewer today at least must choose to buy the rubbish or to turn on the knob, whereas bundles of these masterpieces were, like Hannah More's *Cheap Repository Tracts*, bought in bulk by the gentry and their ladies to be sent down to the servants' quarters or distributed to the poor. Colley at one point high-mindedly rebukes unnamed historians for 'confusing patriotism with simple conservatism, or smothering it with damning and dismissive references to chauvinism and jingoism.' The point is valid, but she would be more persuasive if she allowed her readers to learn that some Volunteer patriotism *was* humbug and that chauvinism and jingoism were among its components. She insists that patriotism 'requires flexible, sensitive and above all, imaginative reconstruction.' Yes, but if such ballads as I have quoted –

and they were numerous – did not represent chauvinistic humbug, then, dammit, what does? And can a sensitive and imaginative reconstruction succeed which holds its hand over this kind of inconvenient evidence?

This is not to reject Colley's theses but to seek to qualify them. If they are 100% correct then my old study, *The Making of the English Working Class*, must be wrong. For I argued there, and elsewhere, that a significant part of the British experience in these years was the formation of the structures, oppositions and contradictory cultures of 'class'. 'Class' was perhaps overworked in the 1960s and 1970s and it has become merely boring. It is a concept long past its sell-by date. Colley appears to share the prevalent view and evades any full discussion of the alienation, in the 18th century, between patricians and plebs, and in the early 19th century between aristocracy, the middle class and the emergent working class. But I am not ready to capitulate. I cannot find one univocal nation of 'Britons'. I am not convinced as to the 'apotheosis' of George III; I find in the sources some examples of conciliated crowds shouting 'God Save the King', but this is a ritualised concession to loyalism and it rarely focussed upon the royal person. (By contrast disloyalty could focus sensationally on the person of George IV in the Queen Caroline agitation). I consider that Colley much overstates – and thereby weakens – her case by asserting that 'training in arms under the auspices of the state ... was the most common collective working-class experience in the late eighteenth and early nineteenth centuries' and more common than the 'experience of work'. (I wonder if it was even more common than being a supplicant for the Poor law?) And I consider that the common people were not always as stupid as she appears to suppose: at one point she remarks approvingly of the cult of monarchy under George III 'it was more securely at one with the politics of unreason and emotionalism.' As Americans may remember.

This leads into another quarrel which I must deal with more briefly. There is a Whiggish tone to some of Colley's argument 'the gradual but relentless shift of opinion' – which sometimes suggests that all came about in a determined way, and without sharp conflict or purposive agency. I will take as an example her treatment of feminism in the 1790s. Colley says that the revelations about her private life after her death in 1797 'savagely limited [Wollstonecraft's] influence.' That is about all that we hear of the feminist impulse of the 1790s: it was 'savagely limited' by an unfortunate contingency. It is perfectly true that William Godwin's posthumous *Memoir* of Wollstonecraft was tactless and sadly inopportune. But what savagely limited and indeed defeated the cause of the *Rights of Woman* was the unprecedentedly strident and brutal attack upon them, from such quarters as the *Anti-Jacobin*, and the loyalist equation of Wollstonecraft and feminism with promiscuity and potential treason:

> Fierce passion's slave, she veer'd with every gust,
> Love, Rights and Wrongs, Philosophy, and Lust.

The sheer volume and universality of this anti-Jacobinism (the British precursor of McCarthyism) is scarcely glimpsed in *Britons* and yet it was the inseparable obverse of loyalism. It can be seen, for example, in a House of Lords debate in 1798 on a divorce bill. Lord Auckland said that such a bill 'was better adapted to the proceedings before the municipality of Paris.

A loud cry of 'Hear, hear!' from the Bishop of Rochester and others.

The Bishop of Durham concurred:

> The French rulers, while they despaired of making any impression on us by force of arms, attempted a more subtle and alarming warfare, by endeavouring ... to taint and undermine the morals of our ingenuous youth. They sent amongst us a number of female dancers, who, by the allurement of the most indecent attitudes, succeeded but too effectually in loosening and corrupting the moral feelings of the people.

And so on. There are mountains of such humbug, which contributed not only to halting but to reversing the feminist impulse. We often think of Dr Bowdler, who gained fame by 'bowdlerising' Shakespeare's plays, as a 'Victorian' figure, but he belongs – as do many features of that repression which we have come to think of as 'Victorianism' – to the anti-Jacobin repression of the 1800s.

All this did not just happen, in a Whiggish way. It was made to happen, by some men and women and against others. I am unimpressed by the argument, heard often today and even supported by some feminists, that Hannah More, the well-supported anti-Jacobin and anti-feminist polemicist, was in fact enlarging feminine space and expectations by becoming such a public figure (Linda Colley makes some portentous concessions to this view and adds that More was the 'first British woman ever to make a fortune with her pen, and this fact alone should warn us against seeing her simply as a conservative figure.' With equal or more force one might say the same of Margaret Thatcher, the first British woman to become prime minister. But if More and Thatcher were not conservatives what are we to call them?)

On the other hand, there were some women and some men who stood up against the avalanche of state-sponsored anti-Jacobinism. And reformers, like royalists, could have their own ceremonies. Thus in the parliamentary elections of 1802 advanced reformers were elected in some constituencies with a wide franchise. Windham, the War Minister and close ally of Pitt, was defeated in Norwich. And in Nottingham, where a reformer was elected, an over-excited magistrate sent to the Home Secretary a sensational account. The reformer had secured election with the support of a 'lawless mob', and the ensuing triumphal procession 'was done in a style unlike any thing ever before exhibited in this Country':

> The Goddess of Reason attended by four & twenty Virgins dress'd or rather half dress'd in white in the French fashion, followed by the Tree of Liberty and the tricolour'd Flag; a Band of Music playing the Tune of 'Millions be free' and the Multitude singing the words ...

In other accounts the Goddess of Reason was naked, although she was probably wearing a flesh-coloured garment. No wonder that a committee of the House of Commons solemnly declared the election to be invalid.

My point is not only that the evidence is difficult to read but that it is always evidence of *conflict*, of competing agencies, with the outcome undecided, and not of determined Whiggish evolution. Hannah More had the goodwill of the whole state and of much of the ruling-class to propel her to fame and fortune, whereas the Nottingham Goddess of Reason was bound to be found, on enquiry, to be invalid. But that is no reason for historians to follow suit.

Perhaps we could compromise by saying that the truth lies somewhere between my view and Colley's? I am certainly not proposing that there was an almost-revolution in Britain in the 1790s. In my view – as I've said before – the only time when that was a historical possibility was during the crisis leading up to the Reform Act of 1832, when the rulers were divided and when great sections of the middle and working classes were making common cause. I concur strongly with a note of Colley's in which she says that to discuss the strains of the 1790s 'primarily in terms of the potential for revolution is unhelpful.' But it still remains necessary to take the full message of those strains to qualify the theses of *Britons*.

What all this is about may only be a matter of emphasis. Most of my points would be acknowledged by Colley, and indeed find some mention (if only marginally) in her carefully-qualified argument. She may fairly respond that historians have written enough about riots and popular radicalism, and that her purpose is to mark out firmly the boundaries of national consensus within which all that took place. She does this superbly well, with controlled judgements and with abundant information. Her stimulating book will be, and deserves to be, influential. Instead of trying for some mid-way compromise, we might say that *both* views might be true. Not only were the British sometimes highly loyalist and sometimes decidedly not so, but also Colley's argument about the making of one British nation need not contradict arguments about the 'Two Nations' of class. After all, English, Scottish and Welsh reformers and Chartists managed to work together, and the most prominent British Chartist leader, Feargus O'Connor, was an Irishman. There are times when the patriot must also be a revolutionary. And on that note I am willing to welcome this book and to call out 'Pax!'

From *Dissent*, Summer 1993, reviewing Linda Colley's *Britons* (1992).

Commitment in Poetry

I distrust the term 'commitment' because it can slide only too easily into usages which defeat its apparent intention. In the first stage, commitment appears as an attitude appropriate in a poet, without further relational definition: that is, it finds its definition in terms of the poet's own sensibility or ego-state – one poet has Fancy, another has Self-concentration, and another has Commitment. In the second stage, 'commitment' must be followed by 'in' or 'to': the commitment is a disposition of concern in the poet, but what the poet is committed *to* lies ready-made, over there, outside the poet awaiting appropriation. The poem does not create the commitment, it simply endorses causes which are already known and which have been disclosed without any poet's exercise.

I will not delay to argue with this slide in usage: in the first stage it has a romantic, in the second stage a utilitarian pedigree. Taken together, these leave the poet free to choose causes like hats, whether from history's attic or form the radical boutiques of today. In either case the hats should be scrutinised, since their selection may well be the index to ulterior commitments of a profounder kind. The advanced 'radical' who continually chooses to wear military or Maoist forage caps may perhaps be signalling a commitment to self-display, an itch for violence and verbal *outrance*, at odds with his professedly rational or democratic commitments. What the 'royalist' may be signalling when he tries on the hat of Maurras can be disclosed only by the informed scrutiny of which John Silkin's essay is exemplary. Historical hats (Like the Nazi insignia worn by last year's deluded NF youngsters) may look splendid, provocative and bizarre, but they ought to receive this kind of scrupulous examination within history's own terms.

Yet this does not always settle the matter. Poets are often pitifully bad as political judges, and they have a habit of getting lost in mazes of misrecognition. Sometimes we need to attend more carefully to the chooser and his values, less to the article chosen. Cairns Craig in his thoughtful essay can easily assume that Yeats was 'deeply reactionary' in his politics. I think otherwise, although I couldn't hope to defend my view in a short comment. This is, in some part, because I find an unusual disjunction in Yeats between the opinions he tried on and the values which impelled his choice. As William Morris remarked, after that fracas in the Socialist Clubroom at Kelmscott House, 'I rang my chairman's bell because you were not being understood.' Very certainly Yeats had a genius for selecting for himself exhibitionist reactionary hats. He courted misunderstanding.

And yet I can't see any way in which compassion must be defined as a reactionary quality, and the kind of self-critical compassion evidenced in 'Meditations in Time of Civil War' or in 'Nineteen Hundred and Nineteen' is a quality – and a *political* quality – with which some part of today's intellectual Left is not richly endowed:

> We had fed the heart on fantasies,
> The heart's grown brutal from the fare;
> More substance in our enmities
> Than in our love ...

Perhaps one day some honey-bees will tremulously return to the empty house of socialist aspiration which Stalinism and bureaucratic social-democracy have vacated. If they do not, then I can see few affirmative prospects. For attempts on the intellectual Right to invoke (on *their* side!) a historical 'England' are either callow or whimsical. For if that older 'organic society' in which classes were an unquestioned 'order of nature' is not an England which social historians can find, the attempt is certainly far advanced to put us all into an organic order today. And it is 'capital' – now insecure and supra-national, but still with an imperative inertia – which is daily dismantling that historic England over our heads: inexorably destroying old landscapes, old buildings, old cultural modes, old institutions, and striving to compact us conveniently into a modernised and managed circuit of conditioned need and consonant supply. It is money which seeks to make over society as its organ. And the *real* Right (not the Right of party hats and churchgoing homiletics) has long been negotiating points of privilege within this circuit. They have long been into business studies, iconoclasm, conspicuous sexual consumption, Auberon Waugh, rationalisation, pseudo-classlessness and swinging airports. When they are not in Washington they are packing a weekend bag for Brussels. Or for Frankfurt, where the multi-national signs welcome visitors with Customs, Duty Free Goods, Taxis, and Sexshop, whose sign (for the illiterate) is a pair of legs and boobs. That is what the Right is into now, and I have no doubt that it gives Davie and Sisson pain. What does the real Right care about their 'various Englands'?

Meanwhile the old values (for very few new ones have been discovered in the last decades) dither around at sixes and sevens in search of social referents. Above their heads the old unreconstructed political rhetoric booms on. The Right (just back from Brussels) claims national this and that, or history, or (just back from Frankfurt) the family. The Left (fighting bitterly over the texts of 1844, 1848, 1917) claims modernity, progress, innovation. The values get bored with all this, and look out for a quiet place to realign themselves. We must watch and see what they do.

II

One place in which they might realign themselves is poetry. Perhaps we should reverse the customary question, and ask, not about poetry's commitment to ... whatever it may be, but about the commitment of people to poetry.

I don't mean the problem of the loss of a mass audience for poetry, of the 'good attendance once' at Galway Races. I mean the marginality of poetry among other intellectual activities: have the functions commonly attributed to poetry in the past, of signalling shifts in sensibility, of stating and organising values, of enhancing our perception within the primary terms of communication, *and of disclosing and defining commitments* – have these functions been displaced, driven into a margin, taken over by some surrogate? Or has the place from which some of the profoundest commitments of the past have arisen simply been left vacant? Left or Right, what contemporary poet and which poems – unless as a marginal solace – are we to be committed to? In emergency, in crises of choice, or in the longer reaches of endurance, which images and forms assist us to define our human loyalties?

It is an unfair question. Perhaps commitment of that kind, to poets or to poetry, has always been rare, and has generally been to poets of a prior generation. And if we have no contemporary poets who can command that commitment, then that is no-one's fault. But there might be 'reasons' for it, worth examination. Perhaps, here or there, are persons who might, in a more conducive climate, have been the poets or moralists of the past decades, whose talents are buried instead in sociology or historical research? And the paucity of relevant poetic statements adjacent to public and social life – the kind of statement which might enable people to envisage political action as the carrier of significant value – may be a very substantial part of our problem. By 'our problem' I do not mean a problem exclusive to poets, critics and visiting historians, but the general problem of a society void of aspirations, directionless. If we had better poetry we might have less bad sociology and less empty and mendacious politics. People with cleansed perception would no longer tolerate these offences against language and these trivialisations of values.

III

Thus, when the argument is reversed, it appears in this form. Poetry in our time has failed to state relevant values, or to disclose and define social commitments: thinkers, artists, and moralists have failed also. Hence much of social and public life appears void of value unless as a habit of rhetoric. Poets can't be committed *to* any actual politics because these are devoid of any value stubborn or palpable enough to bear the weight of poetic commitment. They are left to espouse *unreal* politics (whether 'royalist' or 'revolutionary') which entail few consequences, which enmesh them in no enduring obligations or loyalties, and hence which should be seen as attitudes or poses rather than as commitments. They are acting out parts to each other in a psychodrama on the margins of society, some in Guevara caps, others in splendid affairs with plumes.

I state it thus to clarify argument and to emphasise the reciprocity implicit in a profounder notion of commitment. The poem may indicate and define values which disclose political commitments, and those who are politically active may hold stubbornly to this commitment because they are, in their turn, committed to the poem and to its values. Nothing of this kind goes on now, of course. Nor do I suppose that the complex historical processes of value-formation can really be tidied up inside this paradigm. This may be how some fish swim, but the fish do not control the currents or the tides.

The sea itself, the crippling pressure of waters, the flux of tides, is taken as given: and, taken thus, it is easy to pass, as I have done, to generalities: 'politics', 'poetry', 'values', as if these were unproblematic and constant universals. But this has been no universal sea. We have been passing in the last decades through a particular historical experience and a unique disturbance of values. And when we look at the whole seascape, we may find that our problem remains, in the deepest and most generous sense, a political one after all: a problem, not of 'politics' and 'poetry', 'public' and 'personal', but a particular problem of total disturbance in a particular moment of historical transition.

I made my own diagnosis of the genesis of the problem in an essay of 1959, 'Outside the Whale', in which I argued that the crisis of poetry could be understood only in relation to the spiritual withdrawal consequent upon disenchantment with Communism, as well as the numbing inertia of the Cold War. I could not hope to review that argument here, nor to update it by twenty years. If I did so, I would wish to assent to much of Cairns Craig's searching view of the 'English' predicament. But his critique, which falls squarely upon a nostalgic 'Right', must surely be complemented by a critique, no less unforgiving, of a déraciné 'Left'? For if not only the utilitarian and positivist Left but also (as I have argued in 'The Poverty of Theory') the Marxist-structuralist Left have reduced politics to the negotiation or confrontation of 'scientifically' determinable interests, then the very notion of politics as the disclosure and choice of values becomes suspect and repugnant ('romanticism', 'utopianism', 'humanism', 'moralism'): at the most, value-formation becomes a subordinate and determined exercise, the appropriate sour spoonful of 'de-mystification' of moralistic ideology, the appropriate cough in confirmation of what 'science' has disclosed. No poetry with any dignity would leave its personal corner to enter the service of that philistinism. And no poets have.

Well, we may not agree on that. We might come closer to an agreement if we looked at ourselves against the background of a comparable historical moment of profound disenchantment and disturbance of values. I am, as is Cairns Craig, preoccupied with the 1790s. I have walked up and down in that decade for years. Everything in those years was shifting or was premonitory of the shifts that were to come.

Rhetoric and values were coming apart, new values were in formation. Humane permissive paternalism collapsed into hysteric anti-Jacobinism (the last years of Burke) or invigilatory Evangelicalism (the Clapham Saints, Hannah More); in a few exceptional cases (Major Cartwright) it broke through to a more active democratic persuasion. In an astonishing cartwheel, Cobbett turned over from patriotic anti-Jacobinism to anti-Establishment populism, ultra-democracy in the garb of traditionalism. And what of the 'Left'? Side by side, sometimes inhabiting common movements (opposition to the French Wars and to the Two Acts) we find patrician Whiggish élitism, self-satisfied benevolism, illuminism, courageous sexual innovation, archaic republicanism, blunt populism, emergent bourgeois utilitarianism, mystic millenarianism. Cohabitants of that 'Left' are committed to antagonistic strategies and ends, appeal to alternative values, and are already meditating decisions which (by 1800 or 1810) have plainly set them upon opposing trajectories:

That righteous cause (such power hath freedom) bound,
For one hostility, in friendly league,
Ethereal natures and the worst of slaves;
Was served by rival advocates that came
From regions opposite as heaven and hell.
One courage seemed to animate them all ...

What was happening *in*side the 'Right' and 'Left' was often of more significance than the manifest antagonism between the two.

We cannot read off the character of persons from a recital of their *opinions*: the advanced Godwinian iconoclast of 1797, John Stoddart (Hazlitt's brother-in-law) was on his way to becoming (twenty years later) 'Dr. Slop', the prosecutor-in-chief of plebeian free-thinkers and seditionists. It is easy enough to itemise what people were *against*: the Godwinians, who were so very progressive, were against the family, the law, Gothic institutions, gratitude, love of parents for children or children for parents, the ignorance of the populace, the inconstancy of the French, the injudicious agitations of popular reform societies. This left them with rather little to be *for*, apart from Reason and Benevolence, for which it was not easy to find a local habitation and a name outside of their own heads. For some, radicalism was a youthful ego-trip which took them rapidly to the maturity of the Right. Perhaps that is what that unsatisfactory work *The Borderers* is about? For others, disenchantment in the utopian expectations aroused by the French Revolution led on to prolonged historical and philosophical reflection, and to self-examination, in the search for secure affirmatives.

We know how important were poetry and criticism in this whole exploration and re-organisation of values. And some of the sharpest confrontations were *within* the 'Left': Blake polemicised against mechanical materialism and benevolism, Wordsworth (while still a republican) polemicised against the ghost of Godwin, Coleridge at 30 (or at 35 or 45) polemicised against Coleridge at 25: all polemicised against utilitarianism.

I am suggesting, in what can only be shorthand, that our own times may be something like this. 'Left' and' Right' have lost their stability of meaning in similar ways. The pressure of disenchantment has led to cartwheeling commitments. Friends and enemies cohabit in the same movements. It is easier to know what other people (and perhaps ourselves?) are against than what we are for. And we have a similar advanced intellectual radicalism of *opinion* which is displaced from any real or serious social commitments (indeed, which makes a merit of this displacement) and whose affirmatives are problematic or have yet to be disclosed.

If this is so, then there is very certainly the most serious work for poets to do. Historical experience, in that period and in our own, has made the old kinds of political commitments irrelevant.

To rebuild those commitments, both programmes and people must be sorted out, and the values which these stand on – the affirmatives even more than the negatives – must be fully disclosed. I do not argue that in all periods and places poetry must be the path-finder for intellectual culture. I am only arguing that we are in such a period now.

IV

If there were such poetry, what would it be doing, what would it say? The question is ridiculous: if one knew, in prose, there would be no need for poets. And in any case the poets, like those of the 1790s, would say many, and opposing, and idiosyncratic, things.

I would suspect only that a poetry which recreated the values of a 'Left' might prove to be uncomfortable to most of us who think ourselves to be on the Left, and exceedingly distasteful to some part of that intellectual Left which is so stridently competitive in its pursuit of advanced and 'revolutionary' causes.

But the poets would not create the politics. What they might do would be to disclose the values lurking beneath the abstract constructions, indicate the consonancy of clusters of value, and the incompatibility of one cluster with another. Then people would have to make their choice. An exercise of this kind might bring light but very little sweetness. It might turn out that the Left is inhabited by values at furious enmity with each other, and that people would get on better if they rearranged themselves in new parties and looked for different names: ego-freaks here, aggros there, and *communitas* somewhere else.

For the Left in the last fifteen years has been becoming a very odd place. I am not as worried as most intellectuals seem to be about the 'conservatism' of traditional trade unionism and Labourism ('cooperative', 'subordinate', 'reformist', &c &c): a bloody-minded defensiveness against the management of money seems to me a humane, if not an adequate, response. I am more worried by the intellectuals, or by some of them. I can't assume, as Jon Silkin seems to do, that intellectual violence and élitism are only to be found on the Right. Might not his vigilance and anxiety be extended also to the Left? No doubt Malcolm Bradbury's *The*

History Man is a vicious counter-revolutionary lampoon, but it was
near enough to the mark to worry me, just as Ben Johnson's
wittier lampoon of Tribulation Wholesome ought to have worried
(and no doubt did) Puritans of that day. There are some on the
'Left' who flirt with conceits of violence and aggression in a way
which suggests a disorder of the imagination, a mere bravura of
opinions. I have watched the eyes of a young woman, whom I
know to be gentle and sensitive, glitter with excitement at the
Manson murders: acts which she supposed to have some 'revolutionary' significance. I have argued more than once with comfortable middle-class persons, who would regard joining the Labour
Party (or the Communist Party or any other on offer) as an offence
to their high principles, but who have tried to persuade me that
Baader-Meinhof and Red Brigades are engaging in a justified
struggle against the repressive violence of the State. Within the
vocabulary of this kind of 'Left' there are many 'dainty terms for
fratricide' –

> Terms which we trundle smoothly o'er our tongues
> Like mere abstractions, empty sounds to which
> We join no feeling and attach no form!
> As if the soldier died without a wound ...

The other thing is that an intellectual generation which has made it
through educational selection really has developed a colossal
contempt for those who have not. And I find this also in a section
of the intellectual Left, with its élitism, its distrust for experience
and practice, its accent on youth and repute and fashion, its silence
about people who are old or monogamous or ugly or unfortunate in
uninteresting ways.

Of course, this is not all the Left, nor all of the intellectuals.
But it suggests to me that odd separations are going on. And,
oddly again, some of the values of 'tradition' and of 'England'
(and Scotland and Wales) are coming across and regrouping at
another corner of the Left. Some of us found ourselves, at the
end of 1978, somewhat to our own surprise, defending passion-
ately the integrity of the jury system (one of our oldest
institutions) against not only conservative judges and police but a

Labour Attorney-General, and in the face of an astonished audience of advanced intellectuals and Marxist-structuralists who saw us as entrapped within the ideological mystifications of bourgeois liberalism. Where was the 'various England' of the right then? And where was the Left?

Of course the Left does not belong to me. Maybe it *should* belong to revolutionary aggro. But if the message of the Left is to be *bang! bang!* then I wish they would get themselves poets to imagine this, to join feeling and attach form to the bangs, so that these become a full-blooded aggressive commitment to banging and not the cap-pistol of opinion. Or if the Left is to be traded into the keeping of structuralist scientists for whom the very notion of experience is anathema ('empiricism'), then let them get poets who can imagine *that*. The rest of us can then creep out and invent for ourselves another name.

Somewhere (if poets did their work) another cluster of values would be defining themselves. These might be a little quieter, less invigilatory and dominative, less strident and more compassionate, than those recently to be noted on the Left. They might (as William Morris did) demand less of structures and institutions and more of our own creative resources. The imagination would explore into the dark ahead of us once more instead of lagging a few paces behind opinion. As the earth gets colder under the winter of money, who knows? A few traditional values out of 'various England' might join this cluster to keep warm. I would not repudiate them. It would be heartless to drive them back into 'history'.

Perhaps all this work of disclosing and defining the values on which our commitments are based is being done in poetry already and I have failed to keep up. Or perhaps it is being done and we haven't yet heard: who, in the 1790s, knew of William Blake? All that I am arguing is that our sense of political reality, in any generous historical sense, has become lost within faded rhetoric and threatening abstractions, and that poetry, most of all, is what we now need. And this must be poetry more ambitious, more confident of its historical rights among other intellectual disciplines, than any that is commonly presented to us today.

The Poetry Magazine, *Stand*, invited me to comment on a debate on this theme.

Powers and Names

(With apologies to Szuma Chien)

You have the power to name:
Naming gives power over all.
But who will name the power to name?
Asked the oracle.

Speech

Like a silkworm on a mulberry leaf
The unmannerly earth
Gnawed at the edge of the sky and bit out mountains.

Gorged with matter it dropped by the edge of the ocean,
Cocooned in unconsciousness and grass,
An existence unknown to itself,
Waiting to be spun by nimble tongues into languages.

Let us conciliate the powers by giving them names.
Let us swallow the worm.
Let us tame the world by taking it into ourselves.

Art

The dragons and the lions are furious.
They would like to eat us.
If we model their rage in clay
Will we drive terror away?

Naming the Gods

Ten suns flared in the sky.
They scorched the crops and hatched out of the clay
Fire-breathing demons. The great archer Yi
Chose from his pouch
Nine arrows flighted with a shaman's charm
And slew one sun with each, and ever after we
Named Yi as deity.

But Heaven's pillars cracked
And water gushed out of the broken arch,
Washing the corpses to the sea. So Nüwa raised
A paste of melted rocks
To patch the gashes in the sky, and from a giant turtle
She hewed its legs to prop Heaven back in place.
The goddess Nüwa be praised!

Then water must be educated
And led in levels to the fields. Yu the Great
Accomplished this in thirteen years of toil.
A winged dragon aided him
And once he changed himself into a bear
To scratch a passage through an obstinate hill.
We named Yu god of the soil

And Chi is son hereditary
Owner of all under Heaven, he and his family
In perpetuity. From that ancestral power
Sprouted the state:
Armies invented slavery: astronomy
Led the stars captive through the calendar:
Taxes invented the poor.

The Scholars

In scarcely a millennium
Spring diminished into autumn.
Was the world worse
In the time of incessant wars
Between the city states
Or were there benefits
For the autonomy of thought
In the competition of courts?

Congestion on the roads
As the scholars and their schools
Imagined luminous codes –
Ideologues and pedants,
An orator with an umbrella,
A sophist astride a mule,
A hermit in sandals of straw –
Pestered for audience,
Oppressed the courts of kings
And persecuted princes,
Urging them to restore
Obedience to Heaven's law.

When Confucius was lecturing
Lord Ling, the Duke of Vei,
Enforcing Heaven's rules
On the virtues of benevolence,
The Duke allowed his eyes
To leave his tutor and follow
Some wild geese in the sky.
At this indiscipline
Confucius took offence
And gathering up his school
Went off in a huff to Chen.

Says the Grand Historian:
It was a great mistake
To tutor power, for when
The law at last was learned
From legalist or mystic
By the Emperor of Chin
He ordered the imperial rule
Of benevolence to begin:
He buried the scholars alive
And the *Book of Songs* was burned.

O that Confucius
Had learned to keep his cool,
And had lingered to watch the geese
With the duke and his fool!

The First Emperor

In the 26th year of his reign the King of Chin
Assembled his counsellors.

In the desert of his nature little winds of boredom
Stirred eddies of dust. His throat was dry
And malice constricted his voice like that of a jackal.
Dust stirred in his slitted eyes. He said:
'I have conquered six states, I have captured or killed their
    kings.
Whoever opposed me has been enslaved.
All between the four seas has fallen under my rule.
I have defined the laws, making known what is forbidden,
And discovering (to the surprise of some) 600 degrees of sin
Hitherto nameless and now made manifest to all.
I have closed up the gaps in the Great Wall and garrisoned it
    from end to end.
What is there left for me to be omnipotent in?'

The counsellors bowed and puffed their sleeves:
The first minister, the marshall, the grand censor,
The executioner and the eunuchs of the royal commission.
They said: 'O thou ineffable Vocative!
Great Staightener, Almighty Regulator of All!
How couldst thou be more egregious than thou already art?
Thou has brought letters level, made measures match,
And thou hast brought cash and morals into uniformity.
Men and women must now walk on different sides of the street,
Thanks to thy wisdom. Thou showest no favour no way.
Adulterers (if they are poor) may be boiled in cauldrons.
Officials abusing thy ordinances are always castrated.
Indeed, thy benevolence
Blesses the beasts in the fields, who press to the court,
Bleating to be thy meat. The water buffalo
Bellows thy name; the bees bring thee wax; the fish
Wish only to be thy dish; the rice crowds into the carts
And offers itself as tax ... ' Et cetera.

The King of Chin was gratified,
He ordered that their speeches be engraved upon stone
At the gateways to his 36 provinces.

Then he ascended a throne of alabaster
And, hiding his regal presence within veils,
Announced that Empire had commenced:

'Hereby I augurate a new age.
Lo, let us begin by renaming all names.
Since I have swallowed six kings I now assume plurality.
It is ordered that henceforth we shall be us,
Becoming Our First Exalted Sovereign Emperor.
Whatever we want will be known as Heaven's decree.
Our laws will be named edicts.
We hereby rename the poor our loyal black-headed people.
When we are satisfied all their wants are met.
When we eat the nation has been fed.

When we shit All have shat.
On, and since our brilliance will strike mortals blind,
Henceforth our imperial self will give audience only through
    screens
And we shall never be seen.'

The counsellors bowed and trembled for their balls.
They ordered to be engraved in stone on Mount Tai:
'The Sovereign Emperor made decrees and edicts which all his
    subjects heeded;
Great and manifest, his virtue is handed down to ages yet to
    come, to be followed without change.

The sage Emperor who has pacified all under Heaven is tireless
    in his rule;
He rises early and makes marginalia on his officials' reports;
He sets a standard of proper bearings and signs for all things;
The black-headed people are reformed; he surpasses the ancients
    and has never known error.
Oh gosh! he is so bright that he graciously saves our eyes by
    hiding behind screens.
His omnipotence knows no end, and his orders will be obeyed
    through eternity.'

The Emperor was pleased.
He sacrificed six white horses to the power of water,
Drowning them slowly. A picul of rice and a pig
Were ordered to be sent to every village in the land.
It was found (alas!) that demand exceeded supply,
But the intention (at least) was distributed to the poor,
Who raised their worn and empty hands
And blessed the Emperor.

Then he decreed that he had become immortal.
And was transmogrified. But was visited by doubt.
He sent boatloads of children out to find the fairy isles
Far in the mist eastern oceans where the immortals live.
They did not return. Perhaps they were stopped by whales?

He sent out alchemists to visit the barbarians,
In search of magic fungi and cunning elixirs.
But they were thwarted by demons ...

Behind his screens the Emperor raged and aged.
He issued an edict condemning time:
'Whereas learning has confused our loyal B.H.P.,
We abolish all histories which do not mention our name.
Let only despotic sciences be preserved:
Geometry, census, the computation of tax,
Econometrics, caryatics, castrametation, casuistics,
Cacodoxy, calculus, calibration, nefandous necromantics,
Decapitation, doctrinarianism and the division of parts.
Let the arts be banned,
And the *Book of Songs* be burned and the *Book of Music*.
Whoever recalls the past shall be cut in half
And whoever fails to report these crimes shall be burned with
    brands.'
The counsellors clapped their hands.

The Emperor retired into 200 palaces
Whose walls hung with the fungi of sycophancy.
The marsh creatures of lust clung around him.
He fed on sharks' fins and the pads of camels,
Tangerines, lychees and fantasies.
The white faces of treachery
Whispered around him and ministered to his lechery.

A eunuch hissed a signal of suspected treason.
The Emperor called in the scholars for a course of self-criticism.
They hastened to the court to incriminate each other.
Chuckling like a jackal he caused in the sands to be opened
A vault lit with dark lanterns
And stocked with the confiscated texts of Confucius.
460 sages were sent underground
To sound off in ghostly seminar through the ages.

Each day the Emperor rose and weighed his official reports.
He shifted half a picul of scrolls from his left to his right:
Ah, momentous imauguration of the dynasty of bumf!
According to auguries or according to the weather
He marked in the margins those he decreed to be dead.
On his capital errands
The palace eunuchs spurred with their imperial wands
In an incessant circulation of dread.

When he had first ascended to the throne of Chin
He had ordered work to begin on a bloody great tomb.
Now 700,000 castrati, convicts and slaves
Were impressed to Mount Li
To magnify his gigantic mausoleum
Which (however) the Emperor did not intend to go dead in,
Preferring to be an Eternal, whom water cannot wet,
Who rides on the clouds, impervious to fire,
And coeval with evil ...

Changed name again. Became pure spirit.
We became It:
And, to fox the evil eye, it became invisible.
It flitted in secret
In screened arcades between Its 270 palaces.
Places of ecstacy, what with golden orioles
Shouting in the flowering cherries and the lakes stocked
With exotic goldfish. Everywhere bells and drums
Exhorted the Eternal to come,
As did the countless beauties attendant on its every will
With which the pavilions and secret chambers were stacked.
Sheathed in green gauze
They back-combed their hair into pyramids like orchids
And languished for Its cock
(It having decreed that each must bear It a son
Or else ...)
But were visited only by flaccid concupiscence
Since It could no longer fuck.

The Eternal flitted from palace to palace and moped.
It raged and aged.
It pawed and groped.
It wittered and moaned.
It decreed death
On any who disclosed where It was or where It might even be.
It issued an edict that It had ceased to exist
Except as despotic Essence.

You must imagine it now as pure vacancy
Here is Its Name:

***

300 astrologers
Were abjured to conjure beneficent omens from the stars.
It ordered the spiritual purification of poetry:
The elimination of dentals, the utter ending of gutterals.
Musicians were ordered to oil their strings.
Ululation of sibilants and labials
As vowels howled in the shrouded corridors
And the pavilions wailed of immortality ...

And in the 37th year of ascending to the throne of Chin
Eleven years on from assuming the name of We
And two years from the annunciation of spirituality
A stranger thrust into the censor's hand a disc of jade
On which was written *The Primal Dragon Will Die!*
And vanished in smoke ....
In terror it fled.

It consulted oracles. It gave it out
That It had gone to inspect the empire's extremities.
For fear of lurking assassins
It sent forward convicts to fell the forests ahead.
Archers with crossbows marched in the vanguard
With orders to shoot all whales.

It remained invisible within a covered litter
Carried by slaves. It decreed the pains of hell
Upon any who mentioned death.
And at Pingtai

In the 7th month of the 38th year
It died.
But, being invisible, who could tell?

The first minister, Li Szu, thought the moment inauspicious.
He wasn't sure the old despot would stay dead.
Besides, he had designs on immortality himself,
By raising his creature, Hu-hai, to succeed as emperor
In place of the Crown Prince who had stayed in the capital.

Li Szu, Hu-hai, and the chosen eunuchs kept mum.

And so It continued on Its imperial progress
On the chariot roads in a swaying litter.
The B.H.P. abased themselves before It.
The eunuchs humbly entered the screens bearing dishes
(Which they scoffed with relish within), ushering out
Flourishing fresh imperial decrees (drawn up by Li Szu).
Ah, then It was truly Idea
Disincarnate, aseptic apotheosis of Power,
Which issued an edict condemning Its own son and heir
(Who stood in the way of Hu-hai) and the Lord High Marshall
(Whom Li Szu disliked). Who both duly died
Of the death-sting of the invisible Eternal
Who at length began to stink to high heaven.
The stench caused gossip. To cover the matter
A cartload of salted fish was hitched to Its litter.

And in this manner the bizarre procession
Re-entered Hsienyang, capital of the empire,
Where the Prince and Marshall's heads grinned on the gates.

First came the outriders scouring for rice
Convicts with axes
Alchemists wishing for fungi
Augurers fishing for auguries
Archers warily watching for whales
The black imperial banners
Trumpeters, drummers
Then:
10,000 horsemen, 1000 charioteers
A myriad foot-soldiers sweating in full armour
Hu-hai, Li Szu, and the ministers of rank
The concubines swaying in palanquins
Eunuchs in rich insignia
Then:
The huge unfurled imperial dragon
The dead Eternal stinking in Its Litter
And a cartload of salted fish.
A few explanations followed
Followed by exemplary executions.

After which It was borne
To the yawning mausoleum beneath Mount Li.
Laid in a coffin of copper
In a vault over which the constellations turned
And the floor was the world over which It had ruled
With the rivers and oceans sketched in mercury.
All the imperial palaces wee modelled in jade:
Miraculous artifice guarded by gins and traps!
Oh, and those of the Eternal's ladies who had fallen down in
     their function
Of bearing It heirs (viz. male) (i.e. nearly all)
Were given the honour of going in gorgeous weeds
Into the vault to tend Its ghostly needs
and rub unguent on the offal.

In an afterthought
It was ordered to close the inner and outer gates
Upon the artificers and labourers
Who were also immured in that foetid space
So that they wouldn't betray the secrets of the place.

The Grand Historian erred
In neglecting to record where the fish were interred.

Rebellion

Suction of terror's swirling hysteria
Drew inwards all that could move on wheels or legs
In an acceleration of dread:
The livestock (including maidens).
Conscripts to close the tomb. Droves of geese.
Carts of millet. Pigs. What difference did
It make to be marked as dead

Or only as listed to die? 900 villagers
Were trudging west when the roads were barred by floods.
They were under orders to garrison the Wall,
Led by a farmer's son,
Chen Sheng who said: 'Since it has been decreed
That if we are late for duty the offence is capital,
What is the point of it all?'

Strange lights showed in the temples.
The foxes howled in prophecy:
'Heaven's mandate is withdrawn from Chin Shih Huang.'
A fisherman
Found in the belly of a carp a silken cloth
Marked in vermilion lettering:
'Chen Sheng will be the king.'

He killed the guards
And named himself as Magnifier of Chu.

The eastern provinces rose up against the west.
Villagers with their hoes
Cut down the governors, the collectors of tax,
And pillaged the palaces. In a ferocious harvest
They levelled and laid waste

All visible evidence of the Omnipotence
Who still lingered on as awe, an assertion of function
Unfulfilled, a need for Defence against the Huns.
It hissed in Its tomb
And advertised Its post as a vacancy
And from Its insatiate appetites began
The dynasty named as Han.

The Villagers

It had been the Emperor's whim
To have his armies buried with him,
But when the exchequer was destitute
He graciously stopped the soldiers' pay
And permitted them to substitute
Their persons precisely modelled in clay.

For an eternity the cows
Grazed round the tomb. No one could tell
Where under earth the warriors lay
Until in the time of immortal Mao
Labour brigaders sinking a well
Came on the mighty garrison
Still standing guard.

As for the bones
Of the Emperor, the generations
Living beneath the ancestral mound
Have let two millennia pass:
It was best to leave It underground
And mow the last inch of grass.

The Warriors of Hsienyang

Clay-imaged warriors drilling in the sand
Stand ready to be inspected by war.
The kneeling archer has a lethal eye:
The deft fingers of the charioteer
Contain his mischievous horses as they shy.
The sergeant bullshits to belie his fear.
The browned-off soldiers waiting for commands
Are ready to fight but disinclined to die.

Rank upon rank their graven images
Stare through us into distant places.
We are their visions, like mirages
Which shimmer in the mirror of their faces.
Their scouts inspect us vacantly and say
That we are vapours plagiarising clay.

History Lessons

Neanderthal and Peking man
Barely survived the glacial age,
Neglecting to make a collective plan.

Accurate measurement of the brain
Reveals a capacity for speech.
This may be counted as a gain

And proves what Comrade Stalin said:
Tools manufactured humankind:
Necessity enlarged the head
And matter reflected itself as mind.

Art plays a contradictory role.
Scapulimancy was a trick
Used as a means of social control.

Magic's arcane languages
Cowed the masses within the caves
And established the shaman's privilege.

Astrologers served the ruling class
And sought in the stars a class reflection:
Society caught a religious infection
And primitive communism passed.

History marching through its phases
Found in the Emperor of Chin
A monarch to modernise its basis.

The superstructure united the nation
Determining a progressive mode
Of hydraulic civilisation.

However many the Emperor slew
The scientific historian
(While taking note of contradiction)
Affirms that productive forces grew.

The Rectification of Names

Heaven's mandate swarmed the land like locusts:
Taxation's inquisition racked the rocks and holes
Extracting the confession of their surplus.
The peasants hacked at famine with their hoes
And stirred the dirt to flower:
A hundred million hoes held up the vault of power.

Or was it propped up by the arch of awe
Whose proper name is self-expropriation?
If so, materialism turns a somersault:
We are the subjects of our own negation
And exploitation's basis floats
On the cold surface of our confiscated thought.

Modes of production like electric grids
Transmit us as their errands to their ends:
From matter's terminals to spirit's terminus
The circuits run as strict as continence,
Their only business to enforce
Relations of production into intercourse.

Necessity determinates our paths
Into preordinates in history's casette:
We utter into print-out, ruled by roles,
And ranked like terracotta warriors. Yet
How could necessity dictate
That immane mausoleum, that predatory state,

Unless the programmer was high on mescalin?
Some manic ego in the mask of destiny
Dreams on the highest stair of ritual,
Hallucinating those despotic dynasties
Which know no longer what they are,
Forgetful of their origins in that exotic air.

Who tutored time in power's paradigms?
Did the Eternal on the stairs of Chin
Hallucinate our century's malignancies
And programme on our skies a swarm of acronyms?
It seems the aim of modern man
Is to fulfil the Emperor's two-millennial plan.

O starry Superalpha, terminal Amen!
Thou great First Cause, egregious Omega!
Our eunuchs and our censors clap their hands:
From day to day the unwearied media
Their great Original proclaim
And hallelujah their hosannahs to Thy Name.

O great totalitarian archetype
In whose ancestral influence we fall,
Who levelled all to uniformity and left
Humanity bisected by a Wall:
Know that all progress tends
To modernise Thy Means and end Thy Awful Ends.

The whale-oil gutters in the lamps below.
The vault is sealed. The women fear to stir
Their shadows which are threatening themselves.
Each sings and suffers with her sisters,
Ending as she began
In awe and incense and the categories of man.

Abstraction dreams of destiny again.
The mind is sealed with absolutist nouns
Which steal our names and alienate our powers:
The Emperor hisses in his funeral mound.
It's time the oppressed arose
And cut down categories with their hoes.

From the green earth's imagined holocaust
Arise ye starveling images and blow
Our servile minds out of their algorithms
And blow the fuse of history's teleo:
Arise and repossess
The surplus value of your swindled consciousness!

Plato thought nature plagiarises spirit:
Being determines consciousness determined Marx:
But in the contradictions of the Way
The human dialectic osculates and arcs
And quarrels to insert
Some transient motive in the motiveless inert.

By getting right the proper names of things
Confucius said that order would commence,
And Taoism taught all would be kind
If they forgot about 'benevolence':
Cut down the props, the skies above
Will still hold up upon the menial rites of love

Whose needs are the material habitus
From which the goddesses and dragons came,
Whose archers will shoot down the nuclear fire,
Whose nameless pillars are imagination's flames,
Whose arcane oracles proclaim
The rectification of the human name.

A Charm against Evil

Throw the forbidden places open.
Let the dragons and the lions play.
Let us swallow the worm of power
And the name pass away.

London Review of Books 23rd January 1986

This was written in China in 1980. It is intended not to describe China,
but to convey the bewilderment Western historical mind when first
encountering that great country.

Agenda for Radical History

I feel like an impostor here, because for six years now my trade has been submerged in peace activity, and I have to explain to you the position I speak from now. It's been six years, not just of doing this or that every now and then for peace, but, with the exception of two short spells of teaching in this country, total, full-time activity. In five years I've addressed more than five hundred meetings, attended endless committees, visited as an emissary of the peace movement nineteen or twenty different countries. I've had in my own house a weight of correspondence which has buried any possibility of work. Much of it has been fascinating papers, letters dropping out of different parts of the world. A very curious rebirth of internationalism is taking place in a very curious way, not coming through the normal structures of political parties or institutions. Partly by accident a few names got thrown up a few years ago and became widely known – of which mine was one. People found out the address, and the letters come to me.

Some letters have to be attended to very urgently. They may come from the other side; they may come from Hungarian independents or persecuted Soviet peaceniks; they may come from the United States peace movement; they may come from Canada or Australia or wherever. And this has meant that I really have evacuated perforce my trade as a historian for a long time.

I don't even have a valid ticket to the British Library or the Public Record Office. As I passed the New York Public Library this morning, I felt a knife inside me – the sense of how long it was since I had been able to work among the bounty that is there. I am at least five years behind in my reading, including the reading of the work of close friends, colleagues and former students. I'm trying to return, but there is no guarantee of certainty. This is not a position one can easily walk out of. I have to tell you that when I was attempting to get on this year with *Customs in Common*, – I suddenly had to turn aside and to try and master all the weird acronymic vocabulary and technology of the Strategic Defence Initiative, and to edit and (in part) write a book on *Star Wars*.

But this has also involved exchanges between East and West of a very interesting and perhaps potentially very important kind. I'm not recommending others to follow my course. Although one way to liberate me, if you want to do so, is for more hands to be engaging in this international work. I know some of you will be doing this. But I hope all those hands will not start writing letters to me!

I'm not apologizing. When in our country, as in yours, professional groups started forming their own anti-nuclear organisations, historians had a bit of a problem because, unless they were post-Hiroshima, there really wasn't very much history that historians could actually contribute (they thought) to the anti-nuclear movement. But at length someone came up with the right banner for Historians against Nuclear Weapons: 'Historians Demand a Continuing Supply of History.' And they're right. Because under the criticism of this shadow of nuclear war, all talk of history and culture becomes empty. Even in this city, one of the densest population centres in the world, which is now to become a home base for a nuclear armed pirate Armada, the colleges and the faculties here have to consider their position. I'm therefore not in any mood to offer advice to future historians.

If, or as, I return to my trade, my preoccupations are rather personal: William Morris said to Burne-Jones when he was my age, 'the best way of lengthening out the rest of our days now old chap, is to finish off our old things.' And perhaps there is a sense in which three of us on this platform are doing that and needn't apologize for it. We are completing and enlarging work which was commenced in some cases forty or more years ago. A certain breakthrough in British radical history, associated particularly at that point with the Marxist tradition, took place some 45 years ago. (I'm sorry to use military imagery.) We are still exploiting the terrain that was opened up with that breakthrough. For me in 1940 as a school student it came through the work of Christopher Hill: his first brief study of 1640. I sat down at the age of 16 to write for the sixth form history society a paper on the Marxist interpretation of history and the English civil war, leafing through Christopher's work, and Bernstein, and Petagorsky, and Winstanley's pamphlets and such Leveller tracts as I could get, and some Marx, Engels and Plekhanov. And there followed upon this other breakthroughs: one thinks of Eric's magnificent essay on 'The Tramping Artisan.' The rest of us followed through that gap.

My own 'old things', most of which are half or more than half written, include the studies of 18th century social history, custom, practice, and popular culture, which I call *Customs in Common*, some of which has already been published; my half-written book on William Blake; my work on the Romantics in England in the 1790s – young Wordsworth, young Coleridge, and the assertion and defeat of the cause of women's rights; and I also have a book I hope to do on an odd corner of the Balkans in World War II.

If and when I return, will it be with a different eye? I think it may. I have to say honestly, without any sense of particular criticism, or of any large theoretical statement, that I'm less and less interested in Marxism as a Theoretical System. I'm neither pro- nor anti- so much as bored with some of the argument that goes on. I find some of the argument a distraction from the historical problems, an impediment to completing my work. Perry Anderson and I had an argument – or rather I had an argument with Althusser some ten years ago, and Perry, in a generous and constructive way, commented on this argument in his *Arguments in English Marxism*. I've been asked why didn't I reply to Perry? I feel no need to reply to Perry. I think he had many important and interesting things to say. I think we'd call it a draw. And I bequeath it to you to continue that argument, if it needs to be continued.

I will just say there were two terrible things which Perry did: he defended Walpole, and he showed insufficient respect for Jonathan Swift. Those two points I might like to argue some time, particularly because I regard *Gulliver's Travels* as the most savage indictment of the reasons of power that has ever been written. It still has a vitality of an extraordinary kind. And if, for political reasons, we try to devalue that, then somehow our categories are too limited.

There is a political problem here of a very straightforward kind.

I find it difficult to say what my relationship to the Marxist tradition is, because, in Mrs. Thatcher's Britain, the popular press puts down *any* form of radicalism as 'Marxist'. If I can give one illustration: four or five years ago I was with my daughter and we stopped the car and went for a walk in an Oxfordshire wood. And we had our dog with us, who'd seen a pheasant. Fortunately we got the dog back on the lead when the gamekeeper came along with a gun. He said this wood was owned, not by a Lord now, but by some huge banking or investment institution, and we were trespassing and so on and so forth. As a deferential Englishman I was about to retreat. Unfortunately my daughter turned out to be a freeborn Englishwoman. She started to give him quite a lot of sass about civil rights and the law of trespass. Whereupon the gamekeeper said, 'What are you then, *Marxists*?' In a situation like that, no-one is going to deny they're a Marxist.

I feel happier with the term 'historical materialism'. And also with the sense that ideas and values are situated in a material context, and material needs are situated in a context of norms and expectations, and one turns around this many-sided societal object of investigation. From one aspect it is a mode of production, from another a way of life. Marxism has given us a universal vocabulary, although there are some surprises that are going to come to us. A friend of mine was in the Soviet Union last year. After a historical seminar in which he was discussing questions of class struggle and class relations, he was taken aside quietly – not by 'dissidents', but by members of the Soviet historical profession, who told him, 'serious scientists no longer use the concept of class in the Soviet Union.' In so far as an opening between East and West comes, we may find that the teeth of the children have been so much set on edge by the sour doctrinaire ideology of the Stalinist past that the discourse becomes very difficult.

I think the provisional categories of Marxism to which Perry has referred – those of class, ideology, and mode of production, are difficult but still creative concepts. But, in particular, the historical notion of the dialectic between social being and social conscious-ness – although it is a dialectical interrelationship which I would sometimes wish to invert – is extraordinarily powerful and important. Yet I find also in the tradition pressures towards

reductionism, affording priority to 'economy' over 'culture'; and a
radical confusion introduced by the chance metaphor of 'base and
superstructure'. I find a lot in the Marxist tradition – there are
many Marxisms now – marked by what is ultimately a capitalist
definition of human need, even though it was a revolutionary
upside-downing of that definition. This definition of need, in
economic material terms, tends to enforce a hierarchy of causation
which affords insufficient priority to other needs: the needs of
identity, the needs of gender identity, the need for respect and
status among working people themselves. I do indeed agree with
all the speakers here upon the need to try and see history as a
whole cloth, as an objective record of causally interrelated activities, while agreeing also with Perry that the concept of cause is
extraordinarily difficult, toward which we always attain to only
approximate understanding.

I think the renewed emphasis upon power and power relations,
especially in history, is right. Some studies of 'culture' forget the
controlling context of power. And yet so many of the great
problems of the 20th century, something that has called itself
'Marxism' has had so little helpful to say about. The tenacities of
nationalism; the whole problem of Nazism; the problem of
Stalinism; of the Chinese cultural revolution; of the Cold War
today, which in my view is not acting out a conflict between
modes of production or economies but is acting out a conflict from
an outworn ideological script which threatens indeed to be terminal
to all modes of production alike. I think we've had an insufficient
vocabulary for examining the structure of power relations through
symbolism, from the awe of empire or monarchy to the awe today
of nuclear weapons. Our concern increasingly must be with finding
the 'rationality' of social unreason. That is not throwing up one's
hands and saying 'anything can happen in history' – but, rather,
finding the 'reasons' of social unreason. To give an example
among the few articles I've had time to read recently the one
which fascinated me most of all, completely outside my field, was
an article in *Past & Present* (May 1985) by Inga Clendinnen on
'The Cost of Courage in Aztec Society'.

And where, again, from the materialist vocabulary do agency,
initiatives, ideas, and even love come from? This is why I'm so

concerned with Blake and Blake's quarrel with the Deists and the Godwinian utilitarians. His political sympathies were with so many of their positions; and yet in the end he said there must be an affirmation, 'Thou Shalt Love.' Where does the affirmative, 'Thou Shalt Love', come from? This argument with necessitarianism continues Milton's old argument with predestinarianism and prefigures today's argument with determinisms and structuralisms – which themselves are ideologically-inflected products of a defeated and disillusioned age. If we can de-structure the Cold War, then a new age of ideas may be coming, as in the 1790s or the 1640s.

I have nothing else to say except that our radical impulses are really hemmed in in many ways. We've said little about this, but we all know it. I don't know exactly how things are in the States, but, in the last ten years in Britain I feel very much a closing-down of the situation. A lack of originality. A playing safe. A job situation which is so difficult that one senses a loss of vitality, a cramping of the radical initiative. And this comes partly from straight political ideological pressures.

This symposium may seem rather like an Anglo-Marxist invasion of Manhattan. I remember that there was a *Collége Des Hautes Etudes*, which had the generous welcome of the New School during World War II; I wonder whether we are the forerunners of a British college in exile in refuge from Mrs. Thatcher?

I don't want to tell anyone how to write history. They must find out in their own way. Those of us on the platform are as much subject to our own time's formation and determinations as any others. If our work is continued by others, it will be continued differently. What's radical in it demands some relations between the academy and active experience, whether in the forms of adult education or the kind of work which MARHO and the *Radical History Review* do here in Manhatten; and some distrust of easy assimilation by the lost society, an awareness of the institutional and ideological determinations of the societies in which we work, which are founded upon unreason, or on the reasons of power and the reasons of money.

Wollstonecraft in the 1790s said 'mind has no sex'. I know that some contemporary feminists want to revise that position, because the mind is situated very much within a gender context. But I think we want to remember Wollstonecraft's astonishing courage in saying exactly that in the 1790s. When she said 'mind has no sex', she both demanded entry into the whole world of the mind for her gender, and she also refused any privilege for her gender. If I can use an analogy, radical history should not ask for any privilege of any kind. Radical history demands the most exacting standards of the historical discipline. Radical history must be good history. It must be as good as history can be.

The New School for Social Research, learning that all the contributors would be in New York at the same time, invited Eric Hobsbawm, Christopher Hill, Perry Anderson and myself to take part in a public discussion, on 20 October 1985. This is my contribution. My thanks are due to the New School and to Margaret C. Jacob who initiated the dialogue. The other contributions will be found in *Radical History Review*, no. 36, 1986.